This collection brings together thirteen new essays by some of the most respected contemporary scholars of Schopenhauer's aesthetics from a wide spectrum of philosophical perspectives. The dynamics of the empirical will and Will as a thing-in-itself in the interplay of Schopenhauer's metaphysics and philosophy of fine art has important implications for the freedom, salvation, and tragic suffering of the artist, the representation of Platonic Ideas in art, and the role of artistic inspiration, emotion, and aesthetic pleasure in the beautiful and sublime. These essays examine the unique theory Schopenhauer developed to explain the life and work of the artist, and the influence his aesthetic philosophy has had on subsequent artistic traditions in such diverse areas as music, painting, poetry, literature, and architecture. The authors present Schopenhauer's thought as a vital and enduring contribution to aesthetic theory, and to the idealist vision that continues to guide Romantic and neo-Romantic art.

CAMBRIDGE STUDIES IN PHILOSOPHY AND THE ARTS

Series editors
SALIM KEMAL *and* IVAN GASKELL

Schopenhauer, philosophy, and the arts

CAMBRIDGE STUDIES IN PHILOSOPHY AND THE ARTS

Series editors

SALIM KEMAL *and* IVAN GASKELL

Cambridge Studies in Philosophy and the Arts is a forum for examining issues common to philosophy and critical disciplines that deal with the history of art, literature, film, music, and drama. In order to inform and advance both critical practice and philosophical approaches, the series analyses the aims, procedures, language and results of inquiry in the critical fields, and examines philosophical theories by reference to the needs of arts disciplines. This interaction of ideas and findings, and the ensuing discussion, brings into focus new perspectives and expands the terms in which the debate is conducted.

Schopenhauer, philosophy, and the arts

Edited by

DALE JACQUETTE

The Pennsylvania State University

Published by the Press Syndicate of the University of Cambridge
The Pitt Building, Trumpington Street, Cambridge CB2 1RP
40 West 20th Street, New York, NY 10011–4211, USA
10 Stamford Road, Oakleigh, Melbourne 3166, Australia

First published 1996

Printed in Great Britain at the University Press, Cambridge

A catalogue record for this book is available from the British Library

Library of Congress cataloguing in publication data

Schopenhauer, philosophy, and the arts / edited by Dale Jacquette.
      p.   cm. – (Cambridge studies in philosophy and the arts)
            Includes bibliographical references and index.
                  ISBN 0 521 47388 8 (hardback)
1. Schopenhauer, Arthur, 1788–1860 – Aesthetics. 2. Aesthetics,
   German – 19th century. I. Jacquette, Dale. II. Series.
                  B3149.A4S37 1996
            111'.85'092 – dc20   95–7248 CIP

ISBN 0 521 47388 8 hardback

C E

For Mabel Sass,
who knew suffering and loved beauty

In the aesthetic method of consideration we found *two inseparable constituent parts*: namely knowledge of the object not as individual thing, but as Platonic *Idea*, in other words, as persistent form of this whole species of things; and the self-consciousness of the knower, not as individual, but as *pure, will-less subject of knowledge*.

Schopenhauer, *The World as Will and Representation*, I.2 §38

Contents

ix

Contents

Contributors

JOHN E. ATWELL
Temple University

T. J. DIFFEY
University of Sussex at Brighton

SHEHIRA DOSS-DAVEZAC
Indiana University

LAWRENCE FERRARA
New York University

CHERYL FOSTER
University of Rhode Island

LYDIA GOEHR
Wesleyan University

PAUL GUYER
University of Pennsylvania

DALE JACQUETTE
The Pennsylvania State University

CHRISTOPHER JANAWAY
University of London

LUCIAN KRUKOWSKI
Washington University in St. Louis

NATHAN ROTENSTREICH
Israel Academy of Sciences and Humanities

MITCHELL SCHWARZER
University of Illinois at Chicago

JULIAN YOUNG
University of Auckland

Editor's acknowledgments

I am grateful to the authors for their superb work, and for their patience and good faith during the early stages of this project. I would like to thank series editors Salim Kemal and Ivan Gaskell for their invitation to offer the collection to Cambridge Studies in Philosophy and the Arts, David E. Cartwright for encouragement and advice, and Hilary Gaskin, Philosophy Editor at Cambridge, for guiding the book to completion. Nathan Rotenstreich, and John E. Atwell, after distinguished careers in philosophy, passed away tragically and unexpectedly while this volume was in preparation. I had previously received their contributions, which I am pleased to include in their memory.

Abbreviations

WWR 1,2	*The World as Will and Representation*, 2 vols. E. F. J. Payne, trans. (New York: Dover Publications, 1966)
FFR	*The Fourfold Root of the Principle of Sufficient Reason*, E. F. J. Payne, trans. (LaSalle: Open Court Publishing Co., 1974)
PP 1,2	*Parerga amd Paralipomena*, 2 vols. E. F. J. Payne, trans. (Oxford: Clarendon Press, 1974)
HN 1,2,3,4	*Arthur Schopenhauer: Manuscript Remains in Four Volumes*, trans. E. F. J. Payne [*handschriftliche Nachlaß*] (Oxford: Berg, 1988)

Schopenhauer's metaphysics of appearance and Will in the philosophy of art

DALE JACQUETTE

INTRODUCTION

The essays collected in this volume are previously unpublished writings by some of the most respected contemporary scholars of Arthur Schopenhauer's philosophy and the history and philosophy of art. The idea of the collection is to highlight three aspects of Schopenhauer's aesthetics: his metaphysics and psychology of artistic creativity, his theory of the appreciation of beauty and the sublime, and his influence on the development of the philosophy and practice of the fine arts.

I hope that while engaging the specialist the book will also serve as a friendly introduction for those who have not yet looked into Schopenhauer's pages, and for whom no prior knowledge of Schopenhauer is assumed. The reader will find here a stimulating selection of detailed, comprehensive, but highly accessible studies in Schopenhauer's aesthetics, in the history and theory of art from Plato to major thinkers of the eighteenth, nineteenth and early twentieth centuries, and in the evolution of idealism, symbolism, and romanticism in music, literature, painting, and architecture.

Schopenhauer's impact on such diverse thinkers as Nietzsche, Freud, and Wittgenstein is widely recognized, and his insights into the metaphysics of the human condition have been touchstones for generations of philosophers, social-psychological theorists, and others in search of a personal philosophy. The idealism set forth in Schopenhauer's system serves as a counterpoise to the post-Kantianism of Fichte, Schelling, and Hegel, against whom Schopenhauer reinterprets Kant's critical idealism as its self-proclaimed only legitimate heir.[1] But Schopenhauer's thought also influenced a surprising number of musicians, writers, and artists, including

Richard Wagner, Thomas Hardy, Emile Zola, Edgar Allan Poe, Joseph Conrad, Eugene Delacroix, Thomas Mann, Marcel Proust, and William Butler Yeats.

In his monumental treatise, *The World as Will and Representation*, Schopenhauer offers a simply conceived but powerful metaphysical distinction between the world as it appears to mind in *idea*, and as it exists outside of thought behind the world of appearance as *Will*. The theory is presented with remarkable élan and conviction, interwoven with a marvelously eclectic learning that combines the teachings of Plato, Immanuel Kant, J. Wolfgang Goethe, the Upanishads, and other sources, into an extraordinary grand synthesis. The exposition is enlivened with sharp criticism and bitterly sardonic polemics, and served up in an elegant aphoristic prose that takes the best English and French writing as its literary model in preference to the breathless, often deliberately enigmatic *geisteswissenschaftlichen* philosophical paradigms of nineteenth-century German idealism.[2]

The essays to follow are arranged under these headings: "The work of art: Schopenhauer on the nature of artistic creation," "The experience of beauty: Schopenhauer's theory of aesthetic encounter," and "Schopenhauer's enduring influence on the arts: idealism and romanticism." Parts I and II examine Schopenhauer's thesis of the subject-object symbiosis as it relates to his analysis of creative artistry and art appreciation within the framework of his ontology of appearance and Will. Part III explores Schopenhauer's impact on the history of the fine arts, and the influence of his aesthetics on a formidable array of philosophers, artists, and art critics. To better understand the problems our authors address, we must begin with an account of Schopenhauer's metaphysics as background to the principal themes of his philosophy of art.

APPEARANCE AND WILL

The world for Schopenhauer has two aspects. One side is shown to us, the other kept hidden. The fundamental metaphysical distinction of Schopenhauer's system divides the world as Will from the world as idea or representation (*Wille* and *Vorstellung*). Schopenhauer invokes the Vedic myth of the veil of Maya that conceals reality from mortal eyes as an emblem of the distinction between the world as it appears to the mind and as it is in itself.

The world we experience in sensation as the object of empirical science is a mere fabric of appearance. The world in reality, as it is independently of how it subjectively appears to mind or as it would exist even if there were no minds, is referred to by Schopenhauer as the *thing-in-itself* (*Ding an sich*). Schopenhauer adapts the distinction between appearance and thing-in-itself from Kant's transcendental philosophy. The thing-in-itself is the world as it is intrinsically or in itself, apart from its apprehension by thought. Kant claims that the thing-in-itself is strictly unknowable, since it exists without the mind. Schopenhauer, however, speaks metaphorically of the thing-in-itself as Will, by which he means monstrous blind urging, unindividuated force or power, or endless undirected striving. To explain why Schopenhauer interprets thing-in-itself as Will, and his thesis that we can look beyond the world of appearance to discover the world as Will, we must consider his proposal for overcoming the impenetrability of Kant's thing-in-itself.[3]

By its very nature, Kant's *Ding an sich* is descriptively unknowable. Knowledge of the world is necessarily limited to the phenomena of appearance in the mind's conception. Kant, in the section of the *Critique* on "The Refutation of Idealism" (the so-called B-edition deduction or B-deduction), claims nevertheless to prove the existence of the thing-in-itself. Kant argues that the thing-in-itself must exist, since otherwise it would not be possible to experience consciousness as determined in time. There must be something external to mind, a reality that transcends the flow of consciousness, by reference to which the events of consciousness can be fixed. Whatever determines the times of conscious occurrences will be like the signs posted along a river to mark our place, that cannot show distance if they are drifting with us in the boat. The reference point for the occurrence of thought must be something other than thought, a thing unto itself, if thought is to be determined in time. Yet as a bare existence claim, Kant's proof tells us nothing about what the thing-in-itself is like. We do not know, and cannot even intelligibly imagine, whether the thing-in-itself is one or many, nor whether it resembles or fails to resemble the world of appearance. To know the thing-in-itself would be to place it under what Kant calls the pure forms of intuition or categories of understanding, whereas the thing-in-itself by definition stands entirely outside the mind's conceptual apparatus.[4]

Schopenhauer accepts a modified version of Kant's distinction between the world as appearance and as thing-in-itself. He agrees

3

with Kant that in the ordinary sense the thing-in-itself is unknowable. But unlike Kant he acknowledges two nonrepresentational modes of access to the insight that the world beyond appearance, the Kantian *Ding an sich*, is Will. It is in the phenomenology of the individual empirical will that we experience in everyday wanting and desiring, and particularly in the frustration of our wants and desires, that we acquire some inkling of the world as Will. We can gain an understanding of the world without the mind through ascetic (and moral) suffering and self-denial, or by aesthetic contemplation, because suffering and aesthetic contemplation in suppressing individual willing reveal nonrepresentational aspects of the world as it is in reality. Schopenhauer admits that we cannot strictly *know* even this about the thing-in-itself. But we can characterize Will metaphorically in terms borrowed from our experience of the world as idea. Thus, Schopenhauer thinks that we can speak with a hefty grain of salt about the world as Will, and of Will as pure blind urging or striving, energy or activity, or what the Greeks called *eros*. This for Schopenhauer is the unchanging metaphysical substance of the world. Schopenhauer insists that we cannot thematize Will representationally by offering a discursive scientific account of its properties. The world as Will is beyond description, outside of Kant's categories of space, time, and causation, and of quantity, quality, relation, and modality. We cannot know what the world is in reality, because we cannot know anything concrete about Will. But in unscientific nondiscursive ways we can at least come to recognize that the world in reality is Will.[5]

The world as Will does not literally cause the world as it appears to thought, because causation strictly speaking obtains only within the world as idea. The world as Will is rather the underlying *transcendental ground* of the world as idea. Schopenhauer claims:

the objective world, the world as representation, is not the only side of the world, but merely its external side, so to speak ... the world has an entirely different side which is its innermost being, its kernel, the thing-in-itself. This we shall consider in the following book, calling it "[W]ill" after the most immediate of its objectifications.   (*WWR* 1, 30–31)

In *WWR* 2, Chapter XVIII, "On the Possibility of Knowing the Thing-in-Itself," 191, Schopenhauer declares: "In 1836, under the title *Über den Willen in der Natur* (second edition, 1854), I already published the really essential supplement to this book, which contains the most characteristic and important step of my philosophy, namely the transition from the phenomenon to the thing-in-itself, given up by Kant as impossible." The difference, which in Schopenhauer's view constitutes his principal innovation over Kant's critical philosophy, is that whereas Kant claims that the thing-in-itself is necessarily unknowable, Schopenhauer holds that we can at least nonrepresentationally arrive at an understanding of the world as Will.

First, Schopenhauer grants Kant's point that representational knowledge is limited only to phenomena in things as they appear:

> on the path of *objective knowledge*, thus starting from the *representation*, we shall never get beyond the representation, i.e., the phenomenon. We shall therefore remain at the outside of things; we shall never be able to penetrate into their inner nature, and investigate what they are in themselves, in other words, what they may be by themselves. So far I agree with Kant.
>
> (*WWR* 2, 195)

He admits that we experience only an ephemeral world of accidental appearance individuated by the mind's innate categories and concepts under the fourfold root of the principle of sufficient reason, the principle that a true nontranscendental explanation or sufficient reason exists for every aspect of the world as idea.[6]

But Schopenhauer sees his main contribution to philosophy as going beyond Kant's prohibition on knowledge of transcendental reality. This is accomplished in two ways, by specifying another sense of nonrepresentational knowledge of the thing-in-itself, and by identifying a field of application in which nonrepresentational "knowledge" can function, from which standpoint the mind can gather nonrepresentational knowledge about the nature of the real transcendental world.

> I have stressed that other truth that we are not merely the *knowing subject*, but that *we ourselves* are also among those realities or entities we require to know, that *we ourselves are the thing-in-itself*. Consequently, a way *from within* stands open to us to that real inner nature of things to which we cannot penetrate *from without*. It is, so to speak, a subterranean passage, a secret alliance, which, as if by treachery, places us all at once in the fortress that could not be taken by attack from without. (*WWR* 2, 195)

The city of forbidden knowledge of the world as Will is entered by the Trojan horse of individual willing. We can lift the veil of Maya to gain nonrepresentational knowledge of the real transcendental world through empirical experience of desire or wanting in what Schopenhauer calls the will to life.

I admit this [the limitation of perception to phenomena excluding the thing-in-itself] of everything, but not of the knowledge everyone has of his own *willing*. This is neither a perception (for all perception is spatial), nor is it empty; on the contrary, it is more real than any other knowledge.

(WWR 2, 196)

Kant despairs of knowing the thing-in-itself. But Schopenhauer thinks that anyone in principle has direct access to reality through willing. The experience of individual will to life nonrepresentationally reveals the hidden nature of the transcendental world. Schopenhauer distinguishes between Will as thing-in-itself and individual will, but maintains that willing is the most immediate objectification of reality as Will.

Therefore in this sense I teach that the inner nature of every thing is [W]*ill*, and I call the [W]ill the thing-in-itself. In this way, Kant's doctrine of the inability to know the thing-in-itself is modified to the extent that the thing-in-itself is merely not absolutely and completely knowable; that nevertheless by far the most immediate of its phenomena, distinguished *toto genere* from all the rest by this immediateness, is its representative for us. Accordingly we have to refer the whole world of phenomena to that one in which the thing-in-itself is manifested under the lightest of all veils, and still remains phenomenon only in so far as my intellect, the only thing capable of knowledge, still always remains distinguished from me as the one who wills, and does not cast off the knowledge-form of *time*, even with *inner* perception.

(WWR 2, 197–198)

This is already saying a great deal more about the thing-in-itself than Kant permits. Schopenhauer regards his continuation of the Kantian program as an important philosophical discovery precisely because he has allowed himself to draw a fine distinction between knowledge in the narrow sense, by which he admits that the *Ding an sich* is representationally unknowable, and nonrepresentational knowledge that is not acquired by ordinary cognition, but by direct phenomenological acquaintance with willing as the most direct manifestation of reality in the world of appearance.

The problem of trying to communicate what cannot be said now emerges for Schopenhauer. The experience of willing discloses the nature of reality as whatever immediately objectifies desire, striving, urging. Schopenhauer's claim that Will is unknowable does not contradict his efforts to use an ideational term ("Will") to put some flesh on Kantian transcendental bones. Schopenhauer does not say that willing as we experience it is literally thing-in-itself. It is rather that, by calling thing-in-itself Will, for want of a better word, Schopenhauer tries to express in nondiscursive metaphorical language something that is only nonrepresentationally revealed, in something like a mystical experience.

AESTHETIC GENIUS: SUFFERING AND SALVATION

The two noncognitive channels through which Schopenhauer contends we can learn about the world as Will are ascetic (and moral) suffering and aesthetic contemplation. Saintly self-denial and the overwhelming experience of beauty and the sublime offer the ascetic and aesthetic genius a momentary nonrepresentational encounter with the thing-in-itself. Our concern is primarily with Schopenhauer's views on aesthetic contemplation, but his discussion of saintly suffering provides a useful introduction and point of departure.

Why are suffering and aesthetic contemplation able to offer a glimpse of reality, of the world as Will? Suffering is nonrepresentational, according to Schopenhauer, in the sense that it does not depict the phenomenal world. When we suffer pain or frustrations of desire, the experience of suffering by itself, unlike perception, is not a representation of the phenomenal world. To suffer is therefore to experience nonrepresentational reality as intimately as possible within the confines of empirical psychology. What individual suffering reveals about reality is that it is a force necessarily at odds with itself, in essential self-conflict. If this were not so, reality could not move the world from within through its restless activity, but would be at peace. What ascetic experiences reveal in breaking-down subjective consciousness of the distinction between subject and object is something Schopenhauer, if he is to use language at all for the representationally unknowable, chooses to call Will. For Schopenhauer, Will objectifies itself most nakedly as individual suffering, because it is in these experiences that willing encounters the harshness of an uncontrollable personally unaccommodating reality. The suffering of will in the world of appearance is also the basis for Schopenhauer's much-misunderstood romantic moral pessimism, which he regards as a consequence of the most profound truth of metaphysics, that there can be no harmony of individual wills in a world that manifests Will as reality in essential self-conflict.

Any acute suffering may reveal to the sufferer the world as Will. Ecstasy and other emotions of like intensity do not have the same effect, because they necessarily involve the will's attachment to

7

objects of desire. Schopenhauer believes that individual willing is more often an obstacle to attaining insight into the thing-in-itself, because the will persists in seeking objects in the phenomenal world (alleviation of pain, victory over an adversary) that may temporarily satisfy its frustrated desires. The best route through suffering to an understanding of the world as Will for Schopenhauer is therefore more specifically suffering induced through deliberate efforts at suppressing the will. This involves the disciplined self-denial of asceticism, leading by degrees from deprivation of the will's longing for such bodily necessities as food, water, companionship, and sleep, to the experience of a mystical loss of individuality and dissolution of the subject-object distinction. If desire intrudes, the spell is broken, and individual will is no longer effectively suppressed, disengaging the ascetic's nonrepresentational access to the world as Will.

With important differences, much the same is true of aesthetic contemplation. "Aesthetic experience is like suffering in that it involves a brief but pregnant suppression of the individual will. " What Schopenhauer means by this is that in contemplating nature or art, the aesthetic genius stands so enraptured in an encounter with beauty or the sublime that there occurs something like a mystical union of the subject with the object in a dissolving of the subject-object distinction. The desires of individual will are overruled by absorption in the moment of aesthetic appreciation, and genius thereby passively receives the Platonic Ideas instantiated as perceptible grades of the Will's objectification in the world as idea.

Schopenhauer distinguishes between Platonic Idea (*Idee*) and idea or representation (*Vorstellung*), just as he distinguishes between Will as thing-in-itself and individual will. Platonic Ideas are the archetypal forms of nature, whereas ideas or representations are their superficial appearances. Schopenhauer holds that the Ideas are acquired by sensory experience of ideas. But since they are imprinted on genius during episodes of will-suppressed perceptions of ideas, something more is needed to make sense impressions into abstract Platonic Ideas. Genius also requires imagination, according to Schopenhauer, by which it generalizes perceived natural forms into typified abstract Ideas. The philosophical and aesthetic genius for Schopenhauer does not merely report on the Platonic Ideas received from nature in moments of will-suppressed aesthetic contemplation, but completes and perfects the forms in imagination, and then finds ways to represent them in philosophy and art. The genius finishes what nature attempts but fails to achieve because of the inevitable conflict of forms in the world as idea resulting from the essential self-conflict of the world as Will. Genius is a collaboration between the passive reception of Platonic Ideas and the active role of imagination in completing and perfecting the forms nature reveals.

> the knowledge of genius would be restricted to the ideas of objects actually present to his own person, and would be dependent on the concatenation of circumstances that brought them to him, did not imagination extend his horizon far beyond the reality of his personal experience ... the man of genius requires imagination, in order to see in things not what nature has actually formed, but what she endeavoured to form, yet did not bring about, because of the conflict of her forms with one another ...   (*WWR* 1, 186)

In its efforts to grasp and communicate the Ideas received from its experience of nature, genius also suffers more acutely than ordinary persons. Like the prisoner released from Plato's cave, the philosophical or aesthetic genius, having caught sight of the forms of reality, is compelled to share nonrepresentational knowledge with those still left behind in darkness.[7] To undertake such a thankless labor is to be condemned to inevitable misunderstanding by those who have not experienced the revelation. It is also to incur additional suffering in acquiring specialized skills and applying every energy of mind and body to harness nondiscursive representational media for the expression of nonrepresentational concepts. Schopenhauer explains:

> genius is the ability to leave entirely out of sight our own interest, our willing, and our aims, and consequently to discard entirely our own personality for a time, in order to remain *pure knowing subject*, the clear eye of the world ...   (*WWR* 1, 186–187)

> the *punctum saliens* of every beautiful work, every great and profound thought, is an entirely objective perception. But such a perception is absolutely conditioned by a complete silencing of the will which leaves the person as pure subject of knowing. The aptitude for the prevalence of this state is simply genius.   (*WWR* 2, 370)

> the most excellent works of any art, the noblest productions of genius, must eternally remain sealed books to the dull majority of men, and are inaccessible to them. They are separated from them by a wide gulf, just as the society of princes is inaccessible to the common people ... [The *Idea*] is never known by the individual as such, but only by him who has raised himself above all willing and all individuality to the pure subject of knowing. Thus it is attainable only by the man of genius, and by him who, mostly with the assistance of works of genius, has raised his power of pure knowledge, and is now in the frame of mind of the genius.   (*WWR* 1, 234)

It is this connection, understanding suffering and aesthetic contemplation as an opaque nonrepresentational window on Will as thing-in-itself, that Schopenhauer regards as his greatest triumph. He sees it as a direct continuation of Kant's critical idealism that takes the next vital step forward by nondiscursively presenting privileged knowledge of natural forms and the thing-in-itself as Will. To have determined that the world in reality is Will, representationally unknowable in itself, but discernible in individual willing, is to have far outstripped Kant's colorless concept of the *Ding an sich*. Schopenhauer restricts knowledge in the ordinary sense to the world of appearance, but admits nonrepresentational ascetic and aesthetic insight into the supersensible world as Will.[8]

These two kinds of experience moreover offer the only hope of salvation from the inevitable sufferings of individual will. As beings of empirical psychology, Schopenhauer maintains, we are never fully at peace, except insofar as we can suppress individual willing. Salvation, dimly perceived in its true terms by popular religions, requires ascetic self-denial or loss of individuality in aesthetic contemplation. It is in these epiphanal moments that the self paradoxically is most free from itself, from the mental perturbations by which individual will as the direct phenomenological objectification of Will is otherwise tormented. To live is to will, and hence to suffer, and no one more so for Schopenhauer than the aesthetic genius. The artist suffers extraordinarily, according to Schopenhauer, because genius experiences the greatest frustrations of creative activity in its compulsion to represent nonrepresentational knowledge.

If the purpose of art were merely to escape from the strivings of individual will, the aesthetic genius could simply bury itself in phenomena, in the world as idea. This is what most of humanity does, disregarding the thing-in-itself or world outside the mind and thinking only of the evanescent world of appearance. Schopenhauer remarks this aesthetic mediocrity sometimes with a pitying sigh, sometimes with a contemptuous sneer. He believes that genius can never be satisfied with such a vulgar solution having once grasped the fundamental distinction between reality and appearance, the world as Will and idea. Schopenhauer considers immersion in and exclusive concern with phenomena naive and intellectually demeaning, an attitude fit only for humans who have barely risen above the condition of animals. He concludes it is the mark of greater intellect to devalue phenomena and embrace the hard truth of the inescapable turmoil of the world as Will.[9]

The artist finds release from suffering only in aesthetic contemplation, and this Schopenhauer sees as its primary importance. Schopenhauer maintains that for those few capable of moments of authentic aesthetic experience there is a transport lifting them beyond the individual sufferings of desire, want, and conflict of will. Aesthetic contemplation induces a silencing of the individual will, without which the intellect cannot be receptive to the Platonic forms embodied in nature and art. This ability Schopenhauer insists is reserved for a gifted minority. To stand enthralled before a magnificent artwork or natural scene is at least briefly to lose oneself, and to enter a state of relative will-less admiration of form, in which the slightest taint of desire or striving disqualifies the experience as truly aesthetic.

The artist, then, is first and foremost a knower, someone with a distinctive albeit nonrepresentational imagination-enhanced knowledge of Platonic Ideas acquired by sensory experience of the world as idea. The mastery of technical skills whereby Ideas are expressed for the satisfaction of genius and the enlightenment of others is secondary for Schopenhauer. It is the possession and imaginative extension of the knowledge of Ideas that makes someone an aesthetic genius, without which the most accomplished artist is a mere craftsperson. Schopenhauer observes:

Thus the *work of art* so greatly facilitates the apprehension of the Ideas in which aesthetic enjoyment consists; and this is due not merely to the fact that art presents things more clearly and characteristically by emphasising the essential and eliminating the inessential, but just as much to the fact that the absolute silence of the will, required for the purely objective apprehension of the nature of things, is attained with the greatest certainty.

(*WWR* 2, 370)

The silencing of will in aesthetic contemplation of beauty or the sublime is unavailable to the common lot of mankind. Schopenhauer maintains that aesthetic genius is as remote from ordinary persons as the society of princes. The genius, as Schopenhauer likes to say, does not let willing get the upper hand, but generally puts knowing above willing. But if suffering occurs through willing, and if aesthetic genius puts knowing above willing, why does genius suffer at all, let alone more so than the average mortal?

The reason is that genius by definition is engaged in a vocation of higher order in which will is enlisted in the service of knowledge. The aesthetic genius is involved in a noble effort doomed to the frustration and disappointment of imperfect attainment in the

11

attempt to represent nonrepresentational reality. This is the ultimate ground of the special suffering of genius. Yet it is another distinguishing mark of genius, related to the compensations of ascetic saintliness, to be endowed with distinterested aesthetic contemplation as a temporary respite from the punishing strife of individual willing. Thus, Schopenhauer finds that those who because of their sensitive natures must undergo the most exquisite sufferings of will mercifully are also those who alone are best equipped to find momentary salvation in aesthetic transcendence.

SCHOPENHAUER'S IDEALIST PHILOSOPHY OF ART

Whether Schopenhauer's metaphysics of Will as thing-in-itself is brilliant or delirious, the distinction between the world as Will and as idea or representation supports an idealist aesthetic theory that is unique in the history of philosophy. Schopenhauer's aesthetics is well worth studying for two reasons, even if we do not accept his metaphysics of Will and idea, or his heterodox interpretation of Platonic Ideas.

Friedrich Nietzsche, in his (1874) essay "Schopenhauer as Educator," in *Untimely Meditations*, states as one of the most valuable lessons of Schopenhauer's aesthetics: "It is the fundamental idea of *culture*, insofar as it sets for each one of us but one task: *to promote the production of the philosopher, the artist and the saint within us and without us and thereby to work at the perfecting of nature*. For, as nature needs the philosopher, so does it need the artist, for the achievement of a metaphysical goal, that of its own self-enlightenment ..."[10] Nietzsche, who professes to doing philosophy with a hammer,[11] once again hits the nail squarely on the head. In this compact passage he epitomizes all the essential concepts of Schopenhauer's idealist philosophy of art.[12]

Schopenhauer's philosophy provides the framework for a peculiar set of problems about the nature of art and artistic creativity. How are we to understand the conspicuous suffering of many great artists? What is the relation between knowledge and desire in art? Why does artistic creativity alienate the most gifted artists from everyday life, and occasion the personal misunderstandings of which many artists complain? Why does the contemplation of great art seem to offer sanctuary from the cares of the world beyond mere escapism? What role does imagination play in the artistic depiction of idealized natural form?

Schopenhauer bids us regard the artist of genius not merely as a craftworker making decorative objects to amuse or entertain, but as an existential hero – and victim – engaged in terrible struggles of passion and will in arriving at privileged knowledge and bringing artistic creations to the world. The picture seems appropriate to many artistic talents, and certainly to those outstanding suffering artists Schopenhauer would include as worthy of the name genius: Michelangelo, Beethoven, Dostoyevsky, Van Gogh, and others. Schopenhauer encourages us to see art as the outcome of a deep conflict and frustration of the will in the emergence of the artist's personality in what are often emotionally painful efforts of self-expression, and to expect a deeper philosophical explanation of genius than we find in the circumstantial psychological biographies of great artists. Second, in part for the reasons just mentioned, Schopenhauer's aesthetics historically exerted an enormous influence on a large and diverse number of thinkers and artists. If we are to understand their œuvre in the context of subsequent developments in idealism, symbolism, and romanticism down to the present day, then we must consider the impact of Schopenhauer's metaphysics and aesthetics on later scions of philosophers, artists, and art critics.

With the distinction between the world as Will and idea as its metaphysical foundation, Schopenhauer's theory can be seen as an elaboration of these basic themes: (1) The role of will-suppressed aesthetic contemplation versus purposive expression in artworks of genius; (2) The distinction between lower and higher grades of objectivity of Will in distinct artforms; (3) Music as the direct expression of Will, and the Socratic thesis of the imitation of nature at second remove from reality (Will as thing-in-itself) for all other artforms; (4) The distinction between the beautiful and the sublime (Schopenhauer's rethinking of Kant's analysis); (5) Criteria of evaluation for distinguishing good or successful from bad or unsuccessful art (in the intelligible expression of form and the antipathy of aesthetic genius and the charming).

Art in the world as Will and as idea

The artist's experience as a conduit between the world as Will and as idea poses special problems, both for the artist and for Schopenhauer's aesthetics. The most straightforward explanation of Schopenhauer's concept of the relation in which art stands to the world as Will and idea is that art imaginatively expresses the

Platonic Ideas in nature by which the world as Will is manifested in the world as idea.

Art is an expression of Will in Schopenhauer's metaphysics. Artworks belong to the phenomenal world of appearance or world as idea, and everything in the world as idea according to Schopenhauer objectifies Will. The artist must manage a delicate balancing act between surrendering individual will so as to receive the Platonic Ideas in experience, to convert them imaginatively into abstract Ideas, and to try to express them as intelligible forms in artworks by means of complex willful coordinations of deliberate actions. Schopenhauer is aware of the tension in the artist's conflicting need for disassociation from and engagement of will, each in the right amount and at the appropriate stage of the creative process. He remarks on the challenges of artistic genius in *Parerga and Paralipomena*:

By virtue of his objectivity, the genius with *reflectiveness* perceives all that others do not see. This gives him as a poet the ability to describe nature so clearly, palpably, and vividly, or as a painter, to portray it. On the other hand, with the *execution* of the work, where the purpose is to communicate and present what is known, the *will* can, and indeed must, again be active, just because there exists a *purpose*. (*PP* 2, 418–419)

Schopenhauer identifies three separate stages in the creative aesthetic process: sensory reception of Platonic Ideas instantiated in the world of nature; completion or perfection of the Ideas by imaginative abstraction; and nondiscursive representational expression as intelligible form in an artistic medium. The individual will is switched off involuntarily by the aesthetic genius only for the first and possibly the second part of these operations when the Platonic Ideas are unconsciously received and abstracted by imagination. This Schopenhauer thinks is the most important part of the activity, because it is at this stage that the artist receives inspiration for the work of genius. The Idea and its imaginative completion or perfection as an abstract concept is primary; its expression secondary. The purpose of aesthetic genius is fulfilled for Schopenhauer when the first or second stage is reached. The expression of abstracted nonrepresentational Ideas in the concrete representational form of public art is a dispensable afterthought that does not add much if anything to what is of real value when genius arrives at the nonrepresentational knowledge of reality.

Arguably, however, and as many artists report about their own methods and how they conceive of their endeavors, it is the third stage that is in many ways the most crucial to creative work. It is in

14

the process of making something concrete that the ideas (or Ideas) that are eventually to be expressed in the finished artwork begin to take shape opportunistically through chance and refinements of unanticipated suggestions inherent in the materials, while beforehand the end-project is often provisional and ill-defined. This is realistically when the artist in Schopenhauer's language attempts to sort out the Ideas accumulated in disinterested exposure to the world as idea, and progresses gradually during the activity of producing an art object toward their definition and abstraction.

Schopenhauer can acknowledge these facts and make the following reply. To begin, Schopenhauer is trying to describe the artist's nondiscursive expression of nonrepresentational knowledge. From this standpoint, it is perfectly understandable that the artist need not always or even typically be able to articulate the Ideas she or he is attempting to concretize in art. The nondiscursive mode of aesthetic expression of nonrepresentational knowledge might even lead Schopenhauer to disregard entirely whatever an artist has to say about the psychological occurrences that accompany the making of art. It is a commonplace to which Schopenhauer can also ascribe that artists are often the least reliable authorities to explain their own artistic practices. Schopenhauer might further clarify his position by saying that he is trying to describe the activity of aesthetic genius of the highest ideal order. The most accomplished artists of the greatest genius might then fit his three-stage model exactly, while, admittedly, lesser artists still possessed of lesser genius, the majority in fact, or all artists in practice rather than theory, might need to refine their grasp and abstraction of Ideas by actually working with art instruments and materials in a preliminary way before the finished concept dawns. The aesthetic genius can passively receive and subconsciously abstract a Platonic Idea in an aesthetic reverie or while working at an art, experiencing the changing shape of clay turning on a wheel, or musical passages tried out experimentally on a keyboard, or arrangements of pigment on canvas. The grasping and clarification of Ideas can evolve along with the making of something that is at first unexpected, as an idea takes shape as the artist works, and even without the artist's deliberate intent.

Music and nature as direct expressions of Will

The best known conclusion of Schopenhauer's aesthetic theory, familiar to many who know little else about his philosophy, is that music, like the natural world and unlike any other artform, is the direct expression of Will. Schopenhauer in this way makes music an exception to the Socratic criticism of art as an imitation at two removes from reality, an imitation of the world of appearance, which is itself an imitation of the eternal Forms or Ideas. Painting, poetry, sculpture, architecture, and the like, are all separated from reality in just this way. But good music, the only music Schopenhauer finds worthy of consideration, is entirely on a par with the world of nature as the immediate representation of the thing-in-itself, the world as Will.

As our world is nothing but the phenomenon or appearance of the Ideas in plurality through entrance into the *principium individuationis* (the form of knowledge possible to the individual as such), music, since it passes over the Ideas, is also quite independent of the phenomenal world, positively ignores it, and, to a certain extent, could still exist even if there were no world at all, which cannot be said of the other arts. Thus music is as *immediate* an objectification and copy of the whole [W]*ill* as the world itself is, indeed as the Ideas are, the multiplied phenomenon of which constitutes the world of individual things. Therefore music is by no means like the other arts, namely a copy of the Ideas, but a *copy of the [W]ill itself*, the objectivity of which are the Ideas. For this reason the effect of music is so very much more powerful and penetrating than is that of the other arts, for these others speak only of the shadow, but music of the essence. (*WWR* 1, 257)

The reason Schopenhauer gives for distinguishing between the noniterative imitation of (good) music and the iterative imitation of all other arts raises several interesting problems. Schopenhauer says that music has nothing to do with the phenomenal world, "positively ignores it," "passes over the Ideas," and, most remarkably, unlike the other arts, "could still exist even if there were no world at all."

To begin, we must note Schopenhauer's normative loading of the term "music" to refer more specifically to nonprogrammatic music that does not attempt to imitate the sounds of nature. Schopenhauer speaks only of music that meets his evaluative standard for good music by virtue of not being iteratively imitative. Thus, we have something like the following chain of inferences in Schopenhauer's theory: music is good music; good music is noniteratively imitative; noniterative imitation is the direct or immediate expression of reality, the thing-in-itself or world as Will; hence, music is the direct or immediate expression of Will.

When Schopenhauer speaks of art, he almost always means the highest and most accomplished artwork of genius. It is as though for

16

Schopenhauer so-called artworks that do not fit his definition or measure up to his aesthetic standards simply do not count as art and are not to be mentioned in the same breath as recognized master-pieces. There is a danger here. For although it is incumbent on aesthetic philosophy to define the concept of art and to establish normative guidelines for the evaluation of artworks, the combination of these features in a normative definition that distinguishes (good) art from nonart threatens to trivialize the resulting theory both as definition and as basis for judgment. Art by definition, then, according to the theory's particular bias, is necessarily good, and the concept of bad or unworthy art has no application. An approach of this sort potentially deprives the definition of significance, because what might cast doubts on the theory's evaluative pronouncements of good art, artworks that are intuitively deemed good but pronounced bad by the theory, are excluded by the theory as not genuine instances of art. To make art good by definition is to make the distinction between good and bad art meaningless, an implication that seems especially problematic in Schopenhauer's aesthetics of music.

An even greater difficulty looms for Schopenhauer's doctrine, when in his effort to distinguish music from other arts he says that music passes over the Ideas of the phenomenal world. This seems ineluctably to contradict the central proposition of Schopenhauer's theory that aesthetic genius creates art by passively receiving Platonic Ideas, extending them through imagination into abstract concepts, and then representing them in a concrete medium. If the description applies to (good) music, then, since for Schopenhauer the Platonic Ideas are imprinted on aesthetic genius in moments of will-suppressed perception of the phenomenal world, music like the other arts similarly has to do with the phenomenal world's Ideas. If the description does not apply, then Schopenhauer's theory of aesthetic genius and artistic creativity is refuted out of his own mouth by the counterexample he unwittingly provides. The problem is not resolved by acknowledging an exception, however embarrassing it might be for Schopenhauer's aesthetics. If music does not involve ideas or Ideas but is the direct expression of Will, then we have yet to understand the composer's role, and how it is that the composer of noniteratively imitative music has direct access to Will.

This is related to another puzzle. Schopenhauer states that, unlike the other arts, music would exist ("to a certain extent") even if there were no phenomenal world. If music is the direct noniterative imitation of Will, then some version of this extravagant claim must be true. At one level, it is perhaps easy enough to see what Schopenhauer is trying to say. Music is more abstract than the plastic and literary arts; it is more like mathematics. We might regard Schopenhauer as a kind of modern Pythagorean in characterizing music as independent of the phenomenal world. The difficulties entailed by such a position are at once apparent. Take away the world as idea and there are no artists, composers, performance musicians, instruments, sound vibrations, or listeners. If music exists independently of the world of experience, it can only be because music in essence is a set of abstract relationships to be instantiated in any number of different ways. The trouble is, first, that such relationships could also be nonmusically instantiated. This indeed is another implication of Pythagoreanism. But then the real nature of music as an artform eludes Schopenhauer's theory. Nor does the thesis adequately distinguish music by virtue of its abstractness alone from modern abstract and minimalist plastic art. Second, it follows that Schopenhauer as a result has not explained the relation between musical aesthetic genius, the existence of music as an artform, and musical compositions as artistic expressions of genius. Ideas are involved only in the other arts, where they derive from phenomenal contact with the world as idea and are abstracted by imagination. By hypothesis, Platonic Ideas play no essential part in the existence of music, even though music on this conception is essentially a set of abstract relations.

Higher and lower artforms

With music at one end of the fine arts spectrum, Schopenhauer distinguishes all other media as exhibiting lesser degrees of what he calls objectivity of Will. Music, as we have seen, exhibits the highest grade of the Will's objectivity, in the sense that music is independent of Idea and of the world as idea – its objectification is immediate, with no impurity of phenomenal mediation.

Opposite, and farthest away from music on the scale of the Will's objectivity in art, Schopenhauer places architecture. He offers two reasons for this separation in the relative degrees of objectification of music and architecture. Architecture unlike music is rarely if ever undertaken purely as a fine art, or as art for art's sake, and is therefore almost invariably related to purpose and satisfaction of desire. But even insofar as architecture is pursued as a fine art, Schopenhauer describes its germane Ideas as inherently among the lowest grades of the Will's objectivity. These include gravity, rigidity, hardness, and the like, with their opposites, which Schopenhauer regards as comparatively will-bound because of their obvious connection with crude material properties. Thus, Schopenhauer renounces Goethe's image of architecture as frozen music (*WWR* 2, 453–454). He writes:

Now if we consider *architecture* merely as a fine art and apart from its provision for useful purposes, in which it serves the will and not pure knowledge, and thus is no longer art in our sense, we can assign it no purpose other than that of bringing to clearer perceptiveness some of those Ideas that are the lowest grades of the [W]ill's objectivity. Such Ideas are gravity, cohesion, rigidity, hardness, those universal qualities of stone, those first, simplest, and dullest visibilities of the [W]ill, the fundamental bass-notes of nature; and along with these, light, which is in many respects their opposite. Even at this low stage of the [W]ill's objectivity, we see its inner nature revealing itself in discord; for, properly speaking, the conflict between gravity and rigidity is the sole aesthetic material of architecture; its problem is to make this conflict appear with perfect distinctness in many different ways.   (*WWR* 1, 214)

The difficulty of creating beautiful architecture that serves the mundane ends of will at the same time as it expresses the objectification of Will through its appropriate Ideas defines the unique challenge of architecture as the "lowest" fine art for Schopenhauer.

Unlike the works of the other fine arts, those of architecture are very rarely executed for purely aesthetic purposes. On the contrary, they are subordinated to other, practical ends that are foreign to art itself. Thus the great merit of the architect consists in his achieving and attaining purely aesthetic ends, in spite of their subordination to other ends foreign to them.

(*WWR* 1, 217)

Between music at the high end and architecture at the low, Schopenhauer arranges the remaining fine arts according to the relation of each to its degree of objectification of Will. The complete hierarchy is relatively easy to provide, interpolating poetry, literature, painting, and sculpture according to hints already offered. Sculpture is naturally closer to architecture than to music, painting falls between sculpture and poetry and literature, with poetry between music and literature. The hierarchy from higher to lower artforms in rough outline looks like this:

Architecture→Sculpture→Painting→Literature→Poetry→Music
(Degrees of Objectification of Will: Low→High)

Schopenhauer makes special provision for more particular arts. He locates landscape gardening between architecture and sculpture, and divides up the category of painting more finely, so that landscape painting is placed above historical painting, and these in turn above still-lifes. Similarly with respect to epic and lyric poetry, dance, opera, and orchestral music, fountain or hydraulic and other sculpture, and the like. The hierarchy supports Schopenhauer's theory of art as the objectification of Will by offering a classification of lower to higher artforms according to a certain conception of their respective grades of objectification of Will.

The beautiful and the sublime

Schopenhauer revisits the "Analytic of the Beautiful" and "Analytic of the Sublime" in Kant's *Critique of Judgement*, recommending a different basis for the distinction and an alternative account of its significance in terms of his metaphysics of the world as Will and idea.[13] The beautiful and the sublime are distinguished in non-Kantian ways by Schopenhauer as implications of the essential beauty of Idea, and the attitude of will toward itself as idea and toward the world as Will in the aesthetics of the sublime.

By beauty, Schopenhauer means nothing other than the natural form of Platonic Ideas. Ideas are beautiful by definition. Thus, Schopenhauer speaks without qualification of: "... Ideas, in which beauty, in the objective sense, consists" (*WWR* 1, 200). And later, in his Appendix, "Criticism of the Kantian Philosophy," he mentions: "... a pure perception free from reflection and from will, like that of the beautiful, the deepest comprehension of the true essence of things, in other words, of their Platonic Ideas" (*WWR* 1, 451). Clarity of expression of the Ideas is the aesthetic goal and basis for judgment of beauty. Thereby, Schopenhauer in a single stroke cuts the Gordian knot that had perplexed young Socrates in Plato's dialogue the *Parmenides*, about whether or not there are Forms or Ideas of "ugly" and disgusting things, such as hair, mud and dirt.[14] Schopenhauer excludes such possibilities by fiat on the basis of his understanding of what is implied by the concept of a Platonic Idea and of beauty, and holds that if there are such Ideas they are necessarily beautiful as natural forms, and appear loathsome if at all only in nonaesthetic relation to willing.[15]

The sublime by contrast is defined by the attitudes and emotional responses of individual will toward the world as idea. Like Kant, Schopenhauer distinguishes between two categories of the sublime, the dynamical and mathematical. The dynamical sublime is experienced through imaginative contact with great and sometimes terrifying natural forces. The mathematical sublime is the product of awe in contemplation of great distances in space and time, such as produced by an appreciation of the vast immensity of the night sky, or regression of geologic time.[16]

The impression of the sublime can arise in quite a different way by our imagining a mere magnitude in space and time, whose immensity reduces the individual to nought. By retaining Kant's terms and his correct division, we can call the first kind the dynamically sublime, although we differ from him entirely in the explanation of the inner nature of that impression, and can concede no share in this either to moral reflections or to hypostases from scholastic philosophy. (*WWR* 1, 205)

Included in the dynamical sublime are the usual textbook examples from Longinus to Edmund Burke and Kant. For Schopenhauer, great storms at sea, rushing cataracts down steep gorges, and the like, are all potentially life-threatening natural occurrences in which the individual will finds exhilaration at the thought of its survival in hostile circumstances in which its relative insignificance in size and power are personally experienced.[17] Whereas beauty appears without effort in the clear reception of natural form, the sublime additionally requires a feeling of satisfaction that results only through the struggle and victory of will.[18]

what distinguishes the feeling of the sublime from that of the beautiful is that, with the beautiful, pure knowledge has gained the upper hand without a struggle, since the beauty of the object, in other words, that quality of it which facilitates knowledge of its Idea, has removed from consciousness, without resistance and hence imperceptibly, the will and knowledge of relations that slavishly serve this will ... The feeling of the sublime is distinguished from that of the beautiful only by the addition, namely the exaltation beyond the known hostile relation of the contemplated object to the will in general. Thus there result several degrees of the sublime, in fact transitions from the beautiful to the sublime, according as this addition is strong, clamorous, urgent, and near, or only feeble, remote, and merely suggested. (*WWR* 1, 202)

Schopenhauer, in company with most other aesthetic theorists, acknowledges different degrees of the dynamical sublime, depending on the intensity of the perceived threat posed by violent natural events to the individual will, or the effort of imagination required to come to terms with the magnitude of forces. Schopenhauer's detailed description of the most impressive experience of the sublime is worth recounting at length as much for its romantic poetry as for the philosophical observations it contains:

the impression [of the sublime] becomes even stronger, when we have before our eyes the struggle of the agitated forces of nature on a large scale, when in these surroundings the roaring of a falling stream deprives us of the possibility of hearing our own voices. Or when we are abroad in the storm of tempestuous seas; mountainous waves rise and fall, are dashed violently against steep cliffs, and shoot their spray high into the air. The storm howls, the sea roars, the lightning flashes from black clouds, and thunder-claps drown the noise of storm and sea. Then in the unmoved beholder of this scene the twofold nature of his consciousness reaches the highest distinct-ness. Simultaneously, he feels himself as individual, as the feeble phenom-enon of will, which the slightest touch of these forces can annihilate, helpless against powerful nature, dependent, abandoned to chance, a vanishing nothing in face of stupendous forces; and he also feels himself as the eternal, serene subject of knowing, who as the condition of every object is the supporter of this whole world, the fearful struggle of nature being only his mental picture of representation; he himself is free from, and foreign to, all willing and all needs, in the quiet comprehension of the Ideas. This is the full impression of the sublime. Here it is caused by the sight of a power beyond all comparison superior to the individual, and threatening him with annihilation.   (*WWR* 1, 204–205)

It is clearly the dynamical rather than mathematical sublime that most impresses Schopenhauer. The theory of the sublime in its relation to the will is also accordingly quite different in Schopenhauer than in Kant. For Kant, the mathematical sublime, as seen for example in the starry heavens, suggests to imagination the infinite, which in turn leads by subtle turns of contemplation to the concept of God.[19] Schopenhauer's atheism will have none of this, and he rightly observes that despite adopting Kant's distinction between the dynamical and mathematical sublime, his theory of the sublime, making reference to the struggles and sufferings of will, is unlike Kant's. Schopenhauer elevates the dynamical over the mathematical sublime. It is in such encoun-ters with the untamed forces of nature that the individual will intimately confronts its limitations, and senses something like the raw energy of the world as Will, while glorying in the superiority of its perception and knowledge over the world as appearance, alone on the precipice with the haunting strains of a Wagnerian opera thundering in the distance.[20]

Criteria for good art

Schopenhauer says surprisingly little about the criteria by which good or successful artworks are to be distinguished from their opposites. Part of the explanation for his reticence undoubtedly has to do with the fact that he has already built so much that is normative or evaluative into the definition of art that for him the concept of art already excludes what other theorists might regard as bad or unsuccessful. Objects, however pleasing, that do not meet the requirement of expressing the will-suppressed reception of Platonic Ideas do not count as genuine artworks for Schopenhauer.

The main basis for art criticism in Schopenhauer's theory is the confusion of or failure to clearly and distinctly represent Ideas, and the antipathy of aesthetic experience and the charming. Ideas for Schopenhauer are necessarily beautiful, so that the artist need only exhibit them plainly and with bold definition, as in the best classical art, for their intrinsic beauty to appear. An artwork moreover as we have seen is supposed to enable the appreciator to enter into a will-suppressed state of contemplation similar to that in which the work of aesthetic genius is inspired. There is to be a temporary loss of self or individuality in experiencing good or successful art. The primary obstacle to a lofty experience of this kind occurs when an art object charms the viewer with representations that stir the will through appetite or desire. Of this defect, Schopenhauer identifies two paramount sources, in artworks that arouse hunger or sexual response. In a passage exceptional for singling out specific genres in art history for objection on these grounds, Schopenhauer writes:

I find in the province of art only two species of the charming, and both are unworthy of it. The one species, a very low one, is found in the still-life painting of the Dutch, when they err by depicting edible objects. By their deceptive appearance these necessarily excite the appetite, and this is just a stimulation of the will which puts an end to any aesthetic contemplation of the object ... In historical painting and in sculpture the charming consists in nude figures, the position, semi-drapery, and whole treatment of which are calculated to excite lustful feelings in the beholder. Purely aesthetic contemplation is at once abolished, and the purpose of art thus defeated. This mistake is wholly in keeping with what was just censured when speaking of the Dutch. In the case of all beauty and complete nakedness of form, the ancients are almost always free from this fault, since the artist himself created them with a purely objective spirit filled with ideal beauty, not in the spirit of subjective, base sensuality. The charming, therefore, is everywhere to be avoided in art. (*WWR* 1, 207–208)

The difficulty is that many Dutch still-life masters are so adept at realistically representing delicious items especially of prepared foods that the will is unavoidably summoned to desire, thus adulterating the purely aesthetic objective contemplation of art.

Schopenhauer distinguishes between permissible still-life renderings of fruit and flowers from aesthetically unacceptable portrayals of gourmet table delicacies. "Painted fruit ... is admissible," he writes, "for it exhibits itself as a further development of the flower, and as a beautiful product of nature through form and colour, without our being positively forced to think of its edibility." But he adds: "... unfortunately we often find, depicted with deceptive naturalness, prepared and served-up dishes, oysters, herrings, crabs, bread and butter, beer, wine, and so on, all of which is wholly objectionable" (*WWR* 1, 208).

It is the base direction of desire that troubles Schopenhauer in still-lifes of food and historical paintings of nudes. What is to be avoided is not merely the ripples of will that disturb the calm of purely aesthetic contemplation, but the stirrings of will toward eating and sex. The latter source of carnal charm led Nietzsche in *The Genealogy of Morals* to speculate that Schopenhauer's theory of art and the Will-idea dichotomy may have arisen from an ascetic attitude to resist the sexual impulse. Nietzsche says: "... one is tempted to ask if [Schopenhauer's] fundamental conception of Will and Idea, the thought that there can only exist freedom from the 'will' by means of 'idea,' did not originate in a generalization from this sexual experience."[21] Parenthetically, and in the spirit of apology, Nietzsche adds the reminder that Schopenhauer was just twenty-six years old when he arrived at the central principles of his idealist philosophy, and that his thought may therefore partake of "what is peculiar to that special period of his life," in particular, we may suppose, struggles with sexual desire. "[Schopenhauer] says of [aesthetic contemplation]," Nietzsche claims in another passage, "that it simply counteracts sexual interest, like lupulin and camphor; he [Schopenhauer] never gets tired of glorifying this escape from the 'Life-Will' as the great advantage and utility of the aesthetic state."[22]

Schopenhauer extends his criticism of the charming in still-life and historical painting to misguided efforts to incorporate realistic imitations of the phenomenal world as idea in music. Painting and music are placed in widely separate categories by Schopenhauer because of his thesis that music like the natural world itself and unlike any other artform is the direct expression of Will. But there is a link between his remarks about Dutch still-lifes of edibles and voluptuous historical paintings of nudes with cannon shots and marching timpani in military program music, which many critics agree in finding objectionable as a miscalculated effort to charm by imitation. Schopenhauer argues:

> the analogy discovered by the composer between these two [a composition and perceptive expression] must have come from the immediate knowledge of the inner nature of the world unknown to reason; it cannot be an imitation brought about with conscious intention by means of concepts, otherwise the music does not express the inner nature of the will itself, but merely imitates its phenomenon inadequately. All really imitative music does this; for example, *The Seasons* by Haydn, also many passages of his *Creation*, where phenomena of the world of perception are directly imitated; also in all battle pieces. All this is to be entirely rejected. (*WWR* 1, 263–264)

Schopenhauer's Socratic criticism is implied by the proposition that music is the direct objectification of Will. The composer true to the artform is therefore obligated to express Will immediately, without imitating other natural representations of Will at a further remove, such as oboes trilling bird songs or violins imitating the sound of water cascading over stones. The proper role for music is to express Will directly, not iteratively by (artistic) representations of (natural) representations of Will.

Yet there is an obvious incongruity in Schopenhauer's rejection of Dutch still-lifes of comestibles and historical paintings of nudes. With equal justification and on his own aesthetic principles Schopenhauer might have drawn the opposite conclusion, that these artworks on the contrary are among the aesthetically most praiseworthy and highly recommended objects of contemplation for the person of true aesthetic genius. The appeal to motivation of individual will through appetite and desire in such artworks tempts aesthetic genius to respond with purely disinterested observation under the most trying circumstances. Genius is a matter of degree, as Schopenhauer suggests when he writes: ". . . the objectivity of knowledge, and above all of knowledge of perception, has innumerable degrees, depending on the energy of the intellect and its separation from the will. The highest degree is *genius* . . ." (*WWR* 2, 291) It seems appropriate therefore to distinguish between those aesthetes who on Schopenhauer's assumptions are better able to transcend individuality and experience purely objective perception in the presence of more and more provocative objects. The real test of aesthetic genius by Schopenhauer's account in that case should surely be the ability to restrain desire and preserve a purely objective contemplation in the face of the greatest temptations, including the most savory photo-realistic depictions of foods and nudes.[23]

THE ESSAYS

The concept of aesthetic genius and the sufferings and salvation unique to artists are the topics of papers by Christopher Janaway, Lucian Krukowski, and John E. Atwell. These three essays form a natural progression in discussing the metaphysical, psychological, and redemptive aspects of Schopenhauer's portrait of the artist.

Janaway focuses on the historical question of the extent to which Schopenhauer was influenced by Plato's theory of Ideas. What is strange about Schopenhauer's adaptation of Plato's metaphysics is his claim that Platonic Ideas are perceivable. Schopenhauer holds that Ideas are available to sensation rather than abstract, received by aesthetic genius in moments of will-suppressed objectivity, and abstracted only thereafter in imagination. Many commentators have failed to recognize Plato's theory in this part of Schopenhauer's system. Yet Schopenhauer repeatedly insists that this is the correct account of Ideas as Plato intends it. By following the thread of Schopenhauer's references to Plato from the early manuscripts through several editions of the major writings, Janaway makes a convincing case for the importance of this eccentric interpretation of Platonic Ideas in Schopenhauer's aesthetic philosophy.

Krukowski sees in Schopenhauer's account of genius an historic attempt to make the creative artistic process a subject for aesthetic theory. Schopenhauer's treatment of the suffering and madness of great artists constitutes a ground-breaking effort to describe the social and psychological characteristics of the artistic personality. The madness and social malaise experienced by artistic genius is understandable from a psychological reading of Schopenhauer's aesthetics. It arises because of frustrations endemic in the need to reconcile essentially opposed elements in creative artistic activity. Here the connection between Schopenhauer and Freud is instructive. There are interesting analogies between Schopenhauer's metaphysical concept of Will and Freud's psychological concept of libido, and between Schopenhauer's concept of salvation through oblivion in the silencing of the individual will and Freud's concept of the deathwish. Krukowski charts Freud's avowed debt to Schopenhauer's philosophy in the field of psychological explanations of the relation between neurosis and creativity, and explores the parallelism linking Schopenhauer's opposition of aesthetic experience and individual will with Freud's theory of art as an imaginative substitute for forbidden desires.

Atwell surveys Schopenhauer's doctrine of aesthetic experience as a way of attaining existential liberation from the sufferings of individual will. Schopenhauer's interests in Asian philosophy, and particularly in the teachings of Buddhism and Hinduism, are reflected in his aesthetic mysticism. Atwell relates Schopenhauer's notion of *aufheben* (exalting) to the paradoxes of the self's liberation from self, and from the will-dominated way of knowing. The comparison of the genius and the saint, and the role of pity in the aesthetics of tragedy as an artform particularly suited to Schopenhauer's concept of aesthetic salvation, are explicated as cardinal themes of Schopenhauer's philosophy.

The essays by Paul Guyer, Cheryl Foster, Nathan Rotenstreich, and Julian Young concern Schopenhauer's theory of the aesthetic appreciation of beauty and the sublime. Guyer raises the intriguing problem of the relative importance of cognitivism and emotivism in Schopenhauer's aesthetics. Schopenhauer is usually interpreted as offering a cognitive theory of aesthetic value, according to which the important element of aesthetic experience is arriving at non-representational knowledge of Platonic Ideas. But Schopenhauer also speaks of emotive aspects of aesthetic experience, and in this he touches base with empiricist aesthetic theories that gauge aesthetic value in terms of the pleasure an artwork affords. Some of Schopenhauer's claims about the ability of aesthetic experience to quiet desire and wanting, and so to provide salvation from the strife of individual will, suggest that art is no more than a nonpharmaceutical pain-killer. Guyer places Schopenhauer's philosophy of art in the context of cognitivist traditions in German aesthetics, distinguishes between positive and negative pleasure, and between active and passive components in the artist's creative process. He discusses music as an apparent anomaly for Schopenhauer, as the highest artform with the greatest degree of objectification of Will, but with no special propensity to alleviate pain. Guyer resolves these difficulties by interpreting the Dionysian emotivism of Schopenhauer's aesthetics as more important than, though presupposing, its Apollonian cognitivism. He avoids naive emotivism by attributing to Schopenhauer a complex affirmative account of aesthetic pleasure, not merely as a negative anaesthetic, but as a positively exalting experience.

Foster, by contrast, emphasizes the cognitive bent of Schopenhauer's aesthetics. She regards the primary lesson of Schopenhauer's philosophy as the knowledge acquired through aesthetic contemplation of our engagement with the natural world, and she discovers in this the basis for a Schopenhauerian challenge to contemporary institutional theories of art. Foster also downplays the importance of Schopenhauer's metaphysics to his aesthetics, and calls attention to the fact that for Schopenhauer the inspiration of genius in the passive objective perception of Platonic Ideas is a gift of nature. The will's attachment to life is epitomized by Schopenhauer's frequent references to the beauty of the plant world, an interest he shares with Goethe. Schopenhauer is equally fond of organic metaphors that stress the commonality of social and biological manifestations of Will through the vigor of naturalistic fine art. Ultimately, for Foster, Schopenhauer values aesthetic experience as yielding recognition of the earthly predicament of individual human wills related to the world as Will.

Rotenstreich perceives Schopenhauer's aesthetics as deriving from Kant's thesis that interest vitiates judgments of taste. There is in both thinkers, beginning with Kant, the idea that association with personal and social concerns is an impurity in aesthetic judgment. This is a view reminiscent of Kant's objection to any empirical element of self-interest as contaminating the rationalist metaphysics of morals. As a corollary, Rotenstreich is impressed with Kant's and Schopenhauer's concept of the finality and self-containment of the artwork, in asserting its value as independent of its reference to other things. Kant, unlike Schopenhauer, in his concept of genius as a rule-exempt aptitude for giving rules, does not investigate the metaphysics of creativity as a philosophical problem, but treats the production of art more or less as a given pre-established datum for aesthetic reflection. Schopenhauer's revisionary Kantian aesthetic theory, Rotenstreich argues, must be understood as achieving a unique synthesis of psychological reflection in aesthetic judgment with an idealist ontology of beauty.

In setting forth points of agreement and disagreement between Schopenhauer and the early and later Martin Heidegger on the relation of art and will, Young finds in the early Heidegger an ontic conception of the differences among things as stemming from the standpoint of the perceiver's will and purposive preoccupations.

28

This yields a Schopenhauerian anticipation of Heidegger's key notions of ready-to-handedness and human being-in-the-world. Young explains Heidegger's turn from the early to the later philosophy as a recognition of the need to alter his system to make room for something like Schopenhauer's account of salvation through aesthetic experience. Heidegger defines being-in-the-world by reference to time, and to social circumstances in particular. What Heidegger, expanding on Schopenhauer's concept, calls the assertive will in modern technological society creates a pathological attitude toward the world that reduces nature to a mere supply store for human wants. The later Heidegger, according to Young, is convinced that only art, in somewhat the way Schopenhauer conceived it as a release from individual willing, can save us from this deplorable state of things through a return to metaphysical at-homeness. Yet Young finds that Heidegger's theory of *technē* provides the basis for two criticisms of Schopenhauer's aesthetics. The aesthetic condition is not necessarily opposed to will without qualification, as Schopenhauer maintains, but more specifically to what Heidegger calls the self-assertive will. The will in general moreover is not essentially excluded from aesthetic activity, but can in principle be embodied in a proper mode of production, and even in an entire culture.

Schopenhauer's philosophy of music is examined in Lawrence Ferrara's and Lydia Goehr's complementary essays. Ferrara discusses Schopenhauer's thesis that music is the direct embodiment of Will, and questions Schopenhauer's knowledge of musical theory. The issue is noteworthy because of Schopenhauer's efforts to seek scientific corroboration for his philosophical conclusions; in this case, for his collateral analysis of both nature and music as direct expressions of Will, from the standpoint of Rameau's formal theory of harmony. The ineffable nature of Will and the inexpressible depth of music show many correspondences in Schopenhauer's analysis, according to Ferrara. The strivings of Will are immediately nondiscursively represented in music by melodic, harmonic, and rhythmic discords and reconciliations. Goehr looks beyond Schopenhauer's theory to his influence on such later composers as Wagner, Schoenberg, Prokofiev, and Rimsky-Korsakov. She presents an interpretation of Schopenhauer's importance for subsequent traditions in terms of three concepts of silence: the inexpressibility of music; the inability of philosophy adequately to describe sound and the musician's art; and the silence with which Schopenhauer's ideas about music have often been received. Goehr interprets silence in the third

29

category, not as disavowal, but as a sign of widespread approval of Schopenhauer's theory by musicians, music theorists, and critics.

The distinctive impact of Schopenhauer's philosophy on writers and painters is documented in essays by T. J. Diffey and Shehira Doss-Davezac. Diffey offers a thorough investigation of Schopenhauer's influence on literature, with special emphasis on the novels of Thomas Hardy as a case study. Diffey notes that Hardy had little or no interest in Schopenhauer's aesthetics, but responded in his fiction to what he found of value in Schopenhauer's metaphysics and ethics. Diffey's research on Schopenhauer's importance for Hardy raises more general questions about the extent and manner in which philosophy can shape the art of literature, particularly when a philosopher is also as talented a literary stylist as Schopenhauer. Doss-Davezac examines an exciting period in art history to uncover Schopenhauer's role as intellectual patriarch of the dominant trends of nineteenth-century French painting, literature, and criticism. The Decadents and Symbolists self-consciously acknowledged their debts to Schopenhauer, and Doss-Davezac identifies the particular editions of selections from Schopenhauer's writings that circulated widely among such artists and authors of the time as Theodule Ribot, Jean Bourdeau, Baudelaire, and Mellarmé, and locates specific references to Schopenhauer's ideas in their paintings, poetry, and critical reviews. She sees resonances of neoplatonism and the popularity of Plotinus in Schopenhauer's appeal in the Paris art scene of the 1860s as a reaction to the prevailing contemporary positivism.

The stratification of higher and lower artforms in Schopenhauer's aesthetics is critically evaluated by Mitchell Schwarzer in his essay on Schopenhauer's philosophy of architecture. In defiance of the three traditional Vitruvian categories of durability, convenience, and beauty, Schopenhauer's theory of architecture as a fine art led the way for the overt structuralism heralded by Michel de Klerk and Hans Scharoum, and in the twentieth-century Modern Movement of LeCorbusier and Mies van der Rohe. Schwarzer traces Schopenhauer's denial of artistic significance to the functional utility of architecture from its roots in eighteenth-century German aesthetics. He considers Schopenhauer's argument that architecture is the lowest of the fine arts, that the proper aesthetics of building concerns the expression of loads and supports within a space-enclosing structure, and that the appreciation of architecture as a fine art has as its purpose the sense of release from the conflicting strivings of gravity and rigidity.

SCHOPENHAUER'S AESTHETIC LEGACY

The Schopenhauerians of the nineteenth and twentieth centuries, those through whom Schopenhauer's thought changed not only the theory but the practice of fine art, were almost cultish in their aesthetic worship of Will, and in their attitudes, imbibed from *The World as Will and Representation,* toward death, suffering in the world, and even the moral and intellectual inferiority of women. Yet the romantic conception of the aesthetic genius, the true artist as a figure of special suffering, misunderstood by lesser minds in the most painful struggles to express difficult ideas, is an enduring legacy of Schopenhauer's ideas about art and the difficulties of working toward perfection in art.

With its roots firmly embedded in a particular interpretation of Plato, Kant, and Asian philosophy, Schopenhauer's theory sheds light on these important intellectual and mystical religious traditions. Through its diffusion into the history of post-nineteenth-century art, especially idealism, symbolism, romanticism, and certain phases of naturalism and gothic and neoclassical revivals, Schopenhauer's aesthetics provides the philosophical subtext for major artistic movements, as it does for particular psychological and philosophical developments. It is consequently no exaggeration to say that Schopenhauer's aesthetics is central to understanding the history of modern and contemporary art and philosophy of art.

What else can we learn from Schopenhauer? What value beyond its purely historical connotations can we derive from his reflections on the nature and evaluation of art, if we are not persuaded by his idealist metaphysics of the world as Will and idea?

Schopenhauer discovers something immensely revealing about the relation of perception and will in aesthetic appreciation, and about the distractions of appetite and desire in the contemplation of beauty and the sublime. The distinction might be drawn without the trappings of Schopenhauer's metaphysics of the world as Will and idea in terms of aesthetic and extra-aesthetic or even anti-aesthetic aspects of experience. Schopenhauer also recognizes that there is something special about music among the other arts. He may not have quite put his finger on what it is that makes music different. But many theorists share his intuition that music belongs in a unique category, that it is an art more of time than space, more directly in tune with the emotions, with a life of its own, unlike the solid stationary plastic arts of painting, sculpture, architecture, or even

31

(printed) poetry and literature. To have intuited this distinction and offered a powerful explanation of the nature of music in terms of the metaphysics of Will and idea is an impressive achievement, worthy of serious reflection, and suggestive of other approaches to the problems of music to be explored independently of Schopenhauer's idealism.

If we want to appreciate a great work of art, Schopenhauer may be on the right track to maintain that we must lose ourselves in the experience, to become so absorbed that we distance ourselves at least for a few moments from petty business and social and personal concerns. Such stirrings of will cloud our appreciation of beauty in art, just as it obscures our experience of nature to consider a majestic rocky shoreline's commercial real estate value. They detract from the most rewarding aesthetic experience, even for those with more refined or better disciplined aesthetic sensibilities. To have a richly satisfying aesthetic experience, Schopenhauer seems justified in demanding that we allow nothing but the artist's presentation of natural forms to occupy our full attention. Equally, if we want to create or encourage great art, Schopenhauer with qualifications is undoubtedly right again that we must receive ideas (if not Ideas), modify them to make them our own through imagination, and acquire techniques whereby our thought in its most essential forms can be communicated to others. We can adapt many features of this model of aesthetic creativity from Schopenhauer without admitting that Will lurks behind the veil of Maya, or that Platonic Ideas are partly perceivable and partly the product of imagination.

To advance a philosophy of fine art as Schopenhauer does from within an idealist metaphysics of appearance and Will as thing-in-itself is an audacious and fascinating proposal. Whether it is also fruitful for those standing outside his system in understanding and appreciating the beauty and sublimity of nature and art is a question the following essays on Schopenhauer's aesthetics may now help us to consider.

Notes

1 *WWR* 1, Appendix, "Criticism of the Kantian Philosophy," 417–425.
2 Friedrich Nietzsche, "Schopenhauer as Educator," in *Untimely Meditations*, R. J. Hollingdale, trans. (Cambridge: Cambridge University Press, 1983), p. 134: "Schopenhauer's way of expressing himself reminds me

here and there a little of Goethe, but otherwise he recalls no German model at all. For he understands how to express the profound with simplicity, the moving without rhetoric, the strictly scientific without pedantry: and from what German could he have learned this?" See also James Snow, "Schopenhauer's Style," *International Philosophical Quarterly*, 33, 1993, pp. 401–412.

3 Schopenhauer regards the distinction between *phenomena* (the world as it appears), and *noumena* (the real world as it is in itself) as the most important achievement of Kant's critical idealism. He writes (*WWR* 1, 417–418): "*Kant's greatest merit is the distinction of the phenomenon from the thing-in-itself,* based on the proof that between things and us there always stands the *intellect*, and that on this account they cannot be known according to what they may be in themselves." Kant's slogan that reason without intuition (sense experience) is empty, and intuition without concepts (innate forms of intuition or categories of pure understanding) is blind, summarizes the (Copernican) revolutionary synthesis of rationalism and empiricism. See Immanuel Kant, *Critique of Pure Reason*, Norman Kemp Smith, trans. (New York: St. Martin's Press, 1965), A51/B75. In providing a critique of pure reason, Kant attempts to set limits to the pretensions of reason alone as a method of disclosing the synthetic *a priori* truths of metaphysics. Reason within its bounds nevertheless accomplishes much for Kant, provided it does not try to extend knowledge of phenomena beyond what the understanding can make of experience.

4 *Critique of Pure Reason*, "The Refutation of Idealism," A275–276.

5 *WWR* 2, 191–200. *FFR* 119–120: "In my chief work I have shown that, on the path of the representation, we can never reach the thing-in-itself, i.e., that which exists generally outside the representation, but that for this purpose we must take quite a different path leading through the heart of things and opening for us the citadel by treachery so to speak."

6 *FFR* 41–42. See F. C. White, *On Schopenhauer's Fourfold Root of the Principle of Sufficient Reason* (Leiden: E. J. Brill, 1992), for a comprehensive exposition of Schopenhauer's application of the principle in its limited application to phenomena or the world as idea. Whether Schopenhauer according to his own theory of knowledge says more than he is entitled to say in characterizing thing-in-itself as Will may be irrelevant, since epistemology for Schopenhauer has application only to phenomena in the world as idea. Dale Jacquette, "Schopenhauer's Circle and the Principle of Sufficient Reason," *Metaphilosophy*, 23, 1992, 279–287.

7 Plato, *Republic* 514a–b4.

8 See Kant, *The Critique of Judgement*, James Creed Meredith, trans. (Oxford: The Clarendon Press, 1952), "Introduction," p. 11, for an account of Kant's later position that the concept of freedom "makes the supersensible cognizable by means of formal laws." Also, Part Two, "Critique of Teleological Judgement," pp. 144, 160. But see p. 14:

"Albeit, then, between the realm of the natural concept, as the sensible, and the realm of the concept of freedom, as the supersensible, there is a great gulf fixed, so that it is not possible to pass from the former to the latter (by means of the theoretical employment of reason), just as if they were so many separate worlds ..." If Freedom is the supersensible thing-in-itself for Kant, to which the concept and feeling of freedom gives cognitive access, then Schopenhauer's concept of (absolutely free) Will (beyond the limits of natural and conventional law), to which the concept and act of individual willing gives cognitive access, is not so far removed at least from Kant's later epistemology as Schopenhauer maintains. Schopenhauer comments on the similarities of freedom and Will in *WWR* 1, 272: "But in the light of our whole view, the [W]ill is not only free, but even almighty; from it comes not only its action, but also its world; and as the [W]ill is, so does its action appear, so does its world appear; both are its self-knowledge and nothing more."

9 Schopenhauer rails against the mindless distractions of the greater part of mankind in *WWR* 1, 314: "But purely intellectual pleasures are not accessible to the vast majority of men. They are almost wholly incapable of the pleasure to be found in pure knowledge; they are entirely given over to willing ... [T]his need for exciting the will shows itself particularly in the invention and maintenance of card-playing, which is in the truest sense an expression of the wretched side of humanity."

10 "Schopenhauer as Educator," p. 160.

11 An inference I draw from the subtitle of Nietzsche's *Twilight of the Idols; Or, How to do Philosophy with a Hammer*.

12 Here in Schopenhauer's idealism we discover the origin of Wittgenstein's early identification of ethics and aesthetics as one, in Ludwig Wittgenstein, *Notebooks 1914–1916* (G. H. von Wright and G. E. M. Anscombe, ed.; Anscombe, trans. (Oxford: Basil Blackwell, 1969)), 8.1.16, p. 79, and *Tractatus Logico-Philosophicus* 6.421 (C. K. Ogden, ed. (London: Routledge and Kegan Paul, 1922)). Aesthetics for Schopenhauer is indistinguishable from the moral duty to place knowing above willing and to perfect natural forms in art. On Schopenhauer's influence on Wittgenstein, see Erik Stenius, *Wittgenstein's "Tractatus": A Critical Exposition of its Main Lines of Thought* (Ithaca: Cornell University Press, 1960), Chapter XI, "Wittgenstein as a Kantian Philosopher," pp. 214–226. Benjamin R. Tilghman, *Wittgenstein, Ethics and Aesthetics: The View from Eternity* (Basingstoke: Macmillan, 1991). A. Phillips Griffiths, "Wittgenstein, Schopenhauer, and Ethics," in Godfrey Vesey, ed., *Understanding Wittgenstein* (London: Royal Institute of Philosophy, 1974), pp. 96–116. But see also Rudolf Haller, "Was Wittgenstein a Neo-Kantian?", *Questions on Wittgenstein* (Lincoln: University of Nebraska Press, 1988), pp. 44–56.

13 *The Critique of Judgement*, "Analytic of the Beautiful," pp. 41–89; "Analytic of the Sublime," pp. 90–203.

14 Plato, *Parmenides* 130e.

15 *WWR* 2, 374: "For the beauty with which ... objects present themselves rests precisely on the pure objectivity, i.e., disinterestedness, of their perception ..." Kant had earlier written, in *The Critique of Judgement*, "Critique of Aesthetic Judgement," pp. 42–43: "Now, where the question is whether something is beautiful, we do not want to know, whether we, or any one else, are, or even could be, concerned in the real existence of the thing, but rather what estimate we form of it on mere contemplation (intuition and reflection) ... Every one must allow that a judgement on the beautiful which is tinged with the slightest interest, is very partial and not a pure judgement of taste."

16 *Critique of Judgement*, "Critique of Aesthetic Judgement," pp. 94–117.

17 Jean-Jacques Rousseau offers an evocative image of the sublime in describing the waterfalls at Chailles, near the Pas de l'Échelle, in *The Confessions*, J. M. Cohen, trans. (London: Penguin Books, 1953), Book Four (1732), pp. 167–168.

18 David Hume, in *A Treatise of Human Nature* (second edition by L. A. Selby-Bigge, revised by P. H. Nidditch (Oxford: The Clarendon Press, 1978)), explains the sublime in terms of the triumph of the imagination over the challenges of great distances in space and time or the terrifying. Hume writes, pp. 433–434: " 'Tis a quality very observable in human nature, that any opposition, which does not entirely discourage and intimidate us, has rather a contrary effect, and inspires us with a more than ordinary grandeur and magnanimity. In collecting our force to overcome the opposition, we invigorate the soul, and give it an elevation with which otherwise it wou'd never have been acquainted. Compliance, by rendering our strength useless, makes us insensible of it; but opposition awakens and employs it."

19 *Critique of Judgement*, "Critique of Aesthetic Judgement," pp. 109–114.

20 I hazard this figure even while recognizing that Schopenhauer vehemently disliked Wagner's music. See Ronald Gray, "The German Intellectual Background," in *The Wagner Companion*, Peter Burbridge and Richard Sutton, ed. (London: Faber and Faber, 1979), p. 39. Byron Nelson, "Wagner, Schopenhauer, and Nietzsche: On the Value of Human Action," *The Opera Quarterly*, 6, 1989, pp. 24–32. For similar reasons, Schopenhauer would undoubtedly reject comparisons of his aesthetic genius with Goethe's Faust or young Werther as too clumsily self-conscious in their dramatic advocacy of philosophical propositions to make interesting art or competent philosophy. Art is supposed to embody or portray the perfected forms of nature, not the abstruse conclusions of metaphysics. Faust, Werther, and Wagner's Teutonic gods and heroes are nevertheless almost irresistible icons in thinking of Schopenhauer's aesthetics.

21 Nietzsche, *The Genealogy of Morals*, in *The Complete Works of Friedrich Nietzsche*, Oscar Levy, ed., Horace B. Samuel, trans. (New York: Gordon Press, 1974), Vol. XIII, p. 132. The anti-erotic elements of Schopen-

hauer's aesthetics are discussed by Iris Murdoch, *Metaphysics as a Guide to Morals* (London: Penguin Books, 1993), pp. 61–62; 67–70.

22 *The Genealogy of Morals*, pp. 131–132.

23 I offer a more expansive treatment of these topics in Jacquette, "Schopenhauer on the Antipathy of Aesthetic Genius and the Charming," *History of European Ideas*, 18, 1994, pp. 373–385.

The work of art
Schopenhauer on the nature of
artistic creation

The origin of the fundamental idea for a work of art has been very appropriately called its *conception*; for it is the most essential thing just as is procreation to the origin of man; and like this it requires not exactly time, but rather mood and opportunity.

Schopenhauer, "On the Metaphysics of the Beautiful"
Parerga and Paralipomena

Knowledge and tranquility: Schopenhauer on the value of art

CHRISTOPHER JANAWAY

SCHOPENHAUER AND PLATO

Bertrand Russell claimed that Schopenhauer owed less to Plato than he thought he did.[1] I want to begin by challenging that judgment. On the surface there appears little doubt as to which of Schopenhauer's revered predecessors, Plato and Kant, exerts the greater influence. A large part of Schopenhauer's philosophical vocabulary is appropriated from Kant, and he engages with him in a prolonged, detailed dialogue (seen in most concentrated form in the "Critique of the Kantian Philosophy"). There is no parallel debate with Plato.[2] And yet a case can be made for saying that Schopenhauer's philosophy, at a deeper level, is more Platonic than it is Kantian. First, we must hold ourselves back from two related errors. We must see the invocation of "Platonic Ideas" in the third of the four books which make up *The World as Will and Representation* not as a kind of afterthought, but rather as a carefully prepared revelation of one of the work's most fundamental points. And we must resist the temptation to hive off this Third Book from the rest as a self-contained and subordinate piece concerning "merely" Schopenhauer's aesthetics. The Third Book must hold centre stage once we appreciate that aesthetics is at the heart of philosophy for Schopenhauer: art and aesthetic experience not only provide escape from an otherwise miserable existence, but attain an objectivity explicitly superior to that of science or ordinary empirical knowledge.

The *Early Manuscripts*[3] give a fascinating insight into the genesis of a great philosophical work. We begin with the thoughtful, versifying youth of 1806, and proceed through his encounters with university philosophy, his creative synthesis of diverse sources, his doubts and reformulations, to longer essays which form the basis for

The World as Will and Representation. If there is an underlying agenda which can be called Platonic, we may hope to trace it here. The earliest notes (1808–10) already contain some clues. One aphorism reads:

All philosophy and all the consolation it affords go to show that there is a spiritual world [*Geisterwelt*] and that in it we are separated from the phenomena of the external world and from an exalted seat can view these with the greatest calm and unconcern, although that part of us, belonging to the corporeal world, is still pulled and swung around so much in it

(*MR* 1, p. 8)

The terminology is not that of the final published work, but the pattern is unmistakable: despite our nature as bodily beings, belonging to the world of empirical objects, we can rise to the contemplation of something higher, beyond the empirical.

The young Schopenhauer is preoccupied with the issues of suffering and tranquility. His conviction is already that life is miserable, and his quest is for some consolation lying beyond finitude and corporeality – for otherwise (as he puts it) "we must ask: what is the point of the mockery and sham of the world?" (ibid., p. 10). At the same time, art is never far from his concerns. Tragedy, in particular, acts as the messenger which tells us "We are not meant to thrive and flourish like the plants of the earth" (p. 8), and as the mediator of the higher realm: "as all poetry is the image of the eternal in time, *the (Platonic) Idea of . . . real, inexplicable and unconditioned evil* is awakened by images of earthly misfortune, and an awareness of eternity is thus brought home to us. This is the tragedy" (p. 9).

Schopenhauer allies himself at this stage with Plato "the divine"; he initially calls Kant only "acute and clever" in contrast to Plato, who really "knows the truth." Kant's defects can also be expressed by saying (pertinently) that "he was not acquainted with contemplation."[4] What Schopenhauer looks for in vain in Kant is what he calls the better consciousness [*besseres Bewußtsein*]" – the conception which becomes the pivot for his evolving philosophy during 1813. What is the "better consciousness" better than? It is better than empirical, spatio-temporal consciousness, to which it is fundamentally opposed. The world of empirical consciousness is associated with "a wrong direction from which virtue and asceticism are the return journey," which is why Plato "calls the entire life of the sage a long dying, i. e. a breaking away from such a world."[5] This better consciousness is a supersensuous and extratemporal consciousness (pp. 43–44), which has moral or religious significance, but it is also

40

aroused when something affects us aesthetically, and in art it expresses itself as genius.[6] Art, whether in a still life painting or in a tragedy, enables the better consciousness, and does so by revealing some "Platonic Idea" (p. 43). The better consciousness is connected "indissolubly" with Ideas (p. 83). Thus, even before the end of 1813, the core of Schopenhauer's theory of art is already in place. He will re-work a great deal before the publication of *The World as Will and Representation*. The "better consciousness" will lose its name, and gain more careful formulation. But the position in the completed work is not different in motivation and overall shape from the thoughts of those early years.

Commentators have said that in the main work Schopenhauer "suddenly and surprisingly introduces the notion of Platonic Ideas,"[7] that they "suddenly, disconcertingly, claim a pivotal function" in his aesthetic theory.[8] The Ideas, as used in the aesthetic theory of the Third Book, do surprise the unsuspecting reader of *The World as Will and Representation*. In the drama of the work as a whole,[9] the Kantian subject, the centre of empirical knowledge, is at first apparently sovereign, but in the Second Act (as it were), its claim is challenged by a revelation of its less than noble origins: the subject is explained as a secondary outgrowth of the Will as it manifests itself in the body. In the Third Book both the Will and the Kantian subject with its ordered world of mere empirical objects are "suddenly" shown to be hindrances standing in the way of something higher. But we now know that the Ideas, as objects of a timeless, painless consciousness, were not *ad hoc* extras, but one of the earliest and firmest parts of the whole system. The notion that Schopenhauer's motives were ever genuinely Kantian ought, therefore, to come under suspicion. It is not only that *The World as Will and Representation* challenges Kant by treading an unashamed path towards a metaphysical account of the essence which lies behind the whole world of appearances.[10] More important is the fact that its author always believed the mind could be conscious of a timeless sphere beyond the empirical, and wanted to reveal how the individual who is otherwise rooted in the body is transformed into a pure, will-less intellect in which the body's desires are stilled. The system's underlying aspiration is much closer to Plato, and the machinery of representation and thing-in-itself, subject and object, space, time and causality, serves only as a vehicle to take us somewhere Kant thought it was not even possible to go.

So far I may have shown that from early on in his career

Schopenhauer strove for an unKantian account of a timeless trans-empirical consciousness, and that he borrowed the term "Ideas" from Plato to apply to its supposed objects. But that is not especially Platonic, the objector may say. Two relevant points which have frequently been raised about Schopenhauer's doctrine of Ideas are its failure to cohere with other central elements of his metaphysics, and its degree of divergence from the Platonic conception of Ideas or Forms. To take the latter point first, Schopenhauer's Ideas are in some manner perceptible by the senses, whereas Plato consistently denies this of his Forms. Furthermore, while Plato's Forms must be equated with ultimate reality ("what truly is"), Schopenhauer cannot equate his "Platonic Ideas" with the thing-in-itself in his system. If Schopenhauer's Ideas are perceptible to the senses and not metaphysically fundamental, then it becomes dubious whether they are Platonic in anything but name.[11]

Accepting that these divergences are genuine, my central claim is nevertheless largely unaffected. For there are deeper Platonic motivations at work in Schopenhauer's opposition between empirical and timeless knowledge, and between will-bound and will-free modes of considering the world. Plato has a notion of "viewing the objects themselves" – Ideas or Forms – "with the soul by itself" – independently of the body – and Schopenhauer can be seen as adopting a variant of this, for reasons similar to Plato's. Plato wanted there to be genuine, secure knowledge of entities not infected by appearance and change. But his quest for knowledge was also a search for peace for the soul itself. The body, Plato says, "fills us up with lusts and desires, with fears and fantasies of every kind, and with any amount of trash," and is wont to "intrude everywhere in our researches, setting up a clamour and disturbance, and striking terror, so that the truth can't be discerned because of it."[12] By contrast, for Plato, purifying the soul of its contamination by the body will bring it the tranquility of apprehending the "being itself" of the eternal Forms. Schopenhauer's notion of freeing oneself from the Will bears a close similarity to this, as he himself recognized: when Plato deplores the soul's connection with the body and wishes to be liberated from it, Schopenhauer comments: "we understand the real and true meaning of this complaint, in so far as we recognize ... that the body is the Will itself, objectively perceived as spatial phenomenon."[13] The freeing of the "better consciousness" which Schopenhauer associates with the cessation of willing is akin to the "purification"[14] from desires and other hindrances which Plato expects the soul to enjoy on disembodiment. When Schopenhauer's "pure subject of knowledge" becomes free of the will, it attains "knowledge of the object not as individual thing, but as Platonic *Idea*" (*WWR* 1, p. 195) – no surprise from a Platonic point of view, since from that point of view the notions of a timeless, painless self freed from its attachment to the body, and of a realm of timeless realities for the self to know, are of a piece. This completes my case for saying that the underlying pattern of Schopenhauer's philosophy should be viewed as Platonic.

We should now return briefly to the second of the customary worries about Schopenhauer's Ideas which I mentioned above: that they are an anomaly within his own system. A common way of reading Schopenhauer has it that Ideas are distinct both from the thing-in-itself, and from empirical objects.[15] If that is right, then Ideas do not fit comfortably into the Kantian framework of representation and thing-in-itself, and are something of an embarrassment. This, however, is not an objection to my reading. If we are satisfied that the Ideas are at odds with the Kantian division of reality into representations and thing-in-itself and with the ban on knowledge outside space, time, and causality, we may regard the embarrassment in different ways. It is customary to write as if Schopenhauer's philosophy is Kantian, and the Ideas a disruptive oddity. My argument in this section would have it the other way round: if there is a disruption, it is because Schopenhauer's long-standing attempt to show how we could transcend empirical consciousness in aesthetic experience fell foul of the Kantian machinery he felt obliged to employ in order to explain empirical consciousness.[16]

DEFENDING ART AGAINST PLATO

There is one drastic divergence from Plato that we cannot ignore. Schopenhauer invokes "Platonic Ideas" as the entities revealed to the mind *by art in aesthetic experience*, thus setting himself indeed in head-on collision with Plato, as he sees:

[Plato] teaches (*Republic*, X [601], p. 288) that the object which art aims at expressing, the prototype of painting and poetry, is not the Idea, but the individual thing. The whole of our discussion so far maintains the very opposite, and Plato's opinion is the less likely to lead us astray, as it is the source of one of the greatest and best known errors of that great man, namely of his disdain and rejection of art, especially of poetry. His false judgment of this is directly associated with the passage quoted.　　　(*WWR* 1, p. 212)

Plato's supposed "error" lies in assigning no positive value to poetry. Schopenhauer, in common with many modern readers, is prepared to see in this an implicit attack on *art*. There is some justice in this view. Plato assimilates the poet, in particular the writer of tragedy and epic (who most concerns him[17]) to the painter of an object such as a bed. He unites them both under his concept of *mimêsis*. And although Plato does not say anything about banishing painters from his model city, painting scarcely emerges from his account as a very important or worthwhile activity. Someone will disagree with Plato if, wishing to assign a high value to poetry and painting, they invoke the concept of art. Schopenhauer does, then, oppose Plato over a substantive issue.

It will be worth trying to state succinctly some of Plato's main charges against mimetic poetry.[18] They can be grouped under two main headings, that of cognitive deficiency, and that of psychological harmfulness. Poetry of the kind produced by Homer and the tragedians is generally lauded for its insight into "all human affairs concerned with virtue and vice, and all about the gods as well,"[19] and people argue that the poet must know all manner of things in order to produce fine poetry. Plato claims that this is false. Fine poetry is the production of a pleasing appearance, and does not require knowledge of the subject-matter which it produces an appearance of. Poetry is not a route to knowledge, but can masquerade as one, because the world it creates in appearance is so comprehensive and so convincing to the observer. This is the point of the comparison of tragedy with painting, which presents to us only the way an empirical object appears, making not a real bed, but an "appearing bed,"[20] and having no contact with any eternal Form.

The other factor which Plato especially notes about mimetic poetry is its capacity to give pleasure. He asks whether the pleasure in witnessing representations of people playing out their lives full of action, suffering, and emotional turmoil, appeals to the "better" or "worse" part of the soul. He argues that such things, presented in poetic image, appeal irresistibly to an undisciplined emotional part of our nature, by-passing the rational control and concern for the overall good which should rule in the healthy soul. By nurturing the other part of the soul continually, we put this rational and best part of ourselves at risk of overthrow. After "banishing" mimetic poetry, Plato welcomes the possibility of a proper defence of poetry, but not simply on the grounds of harmlessness. Only if poetry could be shown to be beneficial to human life ought it to be re-instated.[21]

If Plato commits an error, how should the philosophy of art correct it? In broad terms, two strategies suggest themselves. One, which we might call a cognitivist strategy, is to accept that Plato's criterion of value for the arts – whether they provide knowledge – is the correct yardstick, and to pursue the thought that the arts rate highly by this criterion. Possibly the arts will give knowledge of a kind that is unique to them, and in a way which makes them approach philosophy in significance. In saying that he maintains "the very opposite" to Plato, this is what Schopenhauer has in mind. He wants to show not only that Plato went wrong in denying knowledge to the poet, but that art is *par excellence* the locus of something like the knowledge Plato himself sets up as an ideal. As Julian Young has put it, "Schopenhauer's endeavour is to refute Plato by describing art in just those terms which, for Plato, render an activity respectable and important."[22]

Another strategy, however, is what I shall refer to as the "aesthetic experience" strategy. This would argue that the arts can be defended as beneficial, but only once the Platonic criterion of knowledge has been abandoned as wrongly constraining the terms of the debate. What appears to be lacking in Plato, it might be said, is any thought that there is a peculiarly aesthetic state of mind which gives our pleasure in the arts a value of its own. In one way, Schopenhauer embarks on this strategy too: the tranquil contemplation of art gives us a pleasant and valuable aesthetic *experience*. Dwelling in the perception of some particular thing's beauty is therapeutic because it frees the mind from the pains and strivings associated with the body, albeit temporarily. This defence in terms of therapeutic experience is one whose broad terms Plato could also understand. If this is what aesthetic experience is like, and if art is an especially good way of attaining aesthetic experience, then art will emerge as something beneficial. For this strategy, however, art will not necessarily be a channel to knowledge at all; it will be valuable on its own terms, without having to compete in the arena of cognitive supremacy.

While we are speaking in this schematic way, a further alternative to the first strategy should be noted. One may hold out *for* the cognitive importance of the arts, while *resisting* the domination of Plato's transcendent conception of knowledge. Art may be of value to the extent that it presents to the objective gaze the very surface and particularity of "this" world, the world of appearance which Plato disparages. To borrow Nietzsche's image, the artist need not be conceived as "a telephone from the beyond"[23] in order to be acknowledged as a transmitter of something worth knowing. In opposing Plato there are thus choices to be made: whether to concede to Plato that the debate is about knowledge or to locate art's value elsewhere, in aesthetic experience; and whether – if knowledge is relevant – to acquiesce in Plato's conception of knowledge or to re-assert the claims of the realm of appearance and defend art in relation to it.

Now officially Schopenhauer does not separate out these strategies, largely because of his persisting allegiance to the Platonic vision. For him, the will-less contemplation of the beauty of a particular thing transforms the individual into a pure subject of knowing (*Erkennen*) and is "at one stroke" also the apprehension of an Idea which gives us our most objective contact with reality.[24] His thought is that, whenever we have the pleasure of will-less contemplation of some empirical thing, we penetrate beyond the merely empirical and attain knowledge of an Idea. But does this produce a convincing unitary theory?

My starting-point is a revealing passage prior to Schopenhauer's discussion of the several arts, where, despite his conviction that every instance of will-less contemplation is an instance of knowing an Idea, he makes a subtle qualification:

Knowledge of the beautiful always supposes, simultaneously and inseparably, a purely knowing subject and a known Idea as object. But yet the source of aesthetic enjoyment will lie sometimes rather [*mehr*] in the apprehension of the known Idea, sometimes rather [*mehr*] in the bliss and peace of mind of pure knowledge free from all willing, and thus from all individuality and the pain that results therefrom. ... Thus with aesthetic contemplation (in real life or through the medium of art) of natural beauty in the inorganic and vegetable kingdoms and of the works of architecture, the enjoyment of pure, will-less knowing will predominate, because the Ideas here apprehended are only low grades of the Will's objectivity, and therefore are not phenomena of deep significance and suggestive content. On the other hand, if animals and human beings are the object of aesthetic contemplation or presentation, the enjoyment will consist rather in the objective apprehension of these Ideas that are the most distinct revelations of the Will. For these exhibit the greatest variety of forms, a wealth and deep significance of phenomena; they reveal to us most completely the essence of the Will, whether in its violence, its terribleness, its satisfaction, or its being broken (this last in tragic situations) ... Historical painting and the drama generally have as object the Idea of the will enlightened by full knowledge.

(*WWR* 1 pp. 212–213.)

Schopenhauer speaks of aesthetic enjoyment (*Genuß*) or pleasure (*Wohlgefallen*).[25] Though it is characterized by the cessation of willing and the cessation of the possibility of suffering, the "peace" in question is not a mere absence, or a neutral state lacking both pain and pleasure. It "revives," "cheers," and "comforts" (ibid., p. 197). These notions need not conflict with his vivid claim that in aesthetic contemplation "happiness and unhappiness have vanished" (ibid.), provided that we understand happiness, in one sense at any rate,[26] as a state essentially related to motives or ends we strive for, and enjoyment as not so related. When the usual satisfaction of achieving ends has disappeared, there may still be will-less enjoyment.

In the above passage Schopenhauer presents us with opposite ends of a spectrum. Sometimes, he explains, our enjoyment of art is principally an enjoyment of this enriching state of tranquility. But then are not the "low grade" Ideas which we supposedly apprehend in depictions of the inorganic and the vegetative ultimately dispensable in Schopenhauer's account of the value of art? Since such Ideas have no "deep significance and suggestive content," the value of contemplating a depiction of apples or flowers must lie predominantly in the enjoyment experienced by the subject in will-less contemplation. And if predominantly, why not wholly? Even if some other instances of aesthetic experience require a correlative Idea, may not the Ideas in this case be an idle addition? Does tranquility entail knowledge? And even if some species of "knowing" is involved in peacefully contemplating a still-life, must it be knowledge of a Platonic character?

At the other end of the spectrum, does knowledge entail tranquility? Schopenhauer mentions tragedy, drama in general, and historical painting. In these cases it seems sensible to claim that art not only brings knowledge of something objective, but reveals some essence lying behind particular human acts. Calling this the apprehension of an Idea is at least prima facie intelligible, and we might consider ourselves on the scent of a plausible defence of tragedy with the thought that in tragedy we come to know general truths about human life and the terrible Will which drives it. But how plausible is it to say that we learn these truths in peaceful, will-less contemplation? Is it not rather that this process of learning may be distressing, or at least that it works by inviting and stirring up emotion?

The quoted passage, then, encourages us to think that in accounting for the value of art, the two components of aesthetic experience, will-less tranquility and knowledge of Ideas, may float free of one another. Some art may be valuable because it induces contemplative tranquility, but its associated Ideas may be unimportant, indeed redundant, in an account of its value. Some art may be valuable because it puts us in contact with disturbing general aspects of humanity, but it seems questionable whether it leaves us enjoying an experience of will-free tranquility. Later, by examining Schopenhauer's claims about the two ends of the spectrum in the arts, we shall seek to discover to what extent he succeeds in holding together a single, plausible theory.[27] Before that, let us make a few remarks of a more general nature.

AESTHETIC OBJECTIVITY

Schopenhauer's account of art and aesthetic experience has a certain thesis about objectivity built into it. Consider firstly his notion of *genius*. Schopenhauer makes genius a necessary condition for the existence of art. It is a persistent natural capacity of the mind, which only relatively few human beings possess, and is defined as

the capacity to remain in a state of pure perception, to lose oneself in perception, to remove from the service of the will the knowledge which originally existed only for this service ... the ability to leave entirely out of sight our own interest, our willing, and our aims ... in order to remain *pure knowing subject*, the clear eye of the world. (*WWR* 1, pp. 185–186)

The gift of genius is, then, "the most complete *objectivity*, i. e. the objective tendency of the mind, as opposed to the subjective directed to our own person, i. e. to the will" (ibid., p. 185). Without this capacity to achieve an objectivity not present in everyday perception, there would be no art for Schopenhauer. The same applies to the receptive side of aesthetic experience. If the observer could not attain in some degree the kind of objectivity constitutive of genius, there would be no possibility of an observer's having an aesthetic experience of an artwork. In the well-known passages in which Schopenhauer introduces us to aesthetic experience, he stresses once again the way of considering things "without interest, without subjectivity, purely objectively" (p. 196).

So is the objectivity of aesthetic experience, in Schopenhauer's account, simply its will-free nature? An examination of his metaphorical descriptions of aesthetic contemplation suggests that it is. "We *lose* ourselves entirely in this object" and "continue to exist only as pure subject, as clear mirror of the object"; "we are no longer able to separate the perceiver from the perception, but the two have become one" (pp. 178–9). This indicates an experience in which we are not aware of any relations between the perceived object and desires, needs, or interests of our own, because we are not aware of having any desires, needs, or interests of our own. The object does not present itself as related to ourselves in any particular way, but perception of it nevertheless continues. We consider "solely the *what*" of the object before us, "devote the whole power of our mind to perception … and let our whole consciousness be filled by the calm contemplation of the natural object actually present, whether it be a landscape, a tree, a rock, a crag, a building, or anything else" (p. 178). What Schopenhauer means by the objectivity of such contemplation is that in it we can perceive purely "what is there" in front of us, undistorted by desires of our own or by any thought of the thing's relation to our will.

But what is the object of contemplation? If suspending my will when I am perceiving a tree leaves me in a more objective state with regard to it, aesthetic experience ought to be a will-free, heightened perception of the tree – *of the ordinary empirical object*. Yet Schopenhauer says that something else occurs which he admits is "remarkable" and "surprising":

If, therefore, the object has to such an extent passed out of all relation to something outside it, and the subject has passed out of all relation to the will, what is thus known is no longer the individual thing as such, but the *Idea*, the eternal form, the immediate objectivity of the Will at this grade.

(p. 179)

Schopenhauer appears to commit himself to an ontological distinction between empirical things and Ideas, and to the thesis that aesthetic experience is not really the experience of an empirical thing, but of an Idea. But what justification could he have for saying that will-free contemplation must be of an Idea thus conceived?

If this is Schopenhauer's view, we can explain (if not justify) it in terms of the clash between his Platonic and Kantian commitments. He believes that experience of empirical objects is necessarily governed by the principle of sufficient reason and involves the imposition by the subject of the *a priori* forms of space, time, and causality. He goes along with Kant in saying that without these forms, no experience of empirical objects is possible. Yet at the same time he holds the anti-Kantian belief that if we dispense with these subjective forms, an experience closer to "what truly is" can come about. Within empirical consciousness Kant's rules must apply;

when they cease to apply, it is not just that empirical consciousness is impossible – rather, the door opens to another "less subjective" form of consciousness. Since consciousness must be *of* something, and since *this* consciousness cannot be of empirical objects, another, non-empirical object must be found. Ideas thus enter because Schopenhauer's basically Kantian account of empirical consciousness intersects with his continuing conviction that a distinct and "better" consciousness is possible.

But what argument could lead us from the will-free nature of aesthetic experience to the conclusion that its proper objects are always distinct from empirical, spatio-temporal individuals? If we consider the most obvious argument, we find that it is flawed. To say that aesthetic contemplation of an object is will-free is to say that none of the individual subject's desires govern the manner in which the object is perceived. In one sense of "objective," such contemplation is more objective than perception upon which the individual's desires do intrude. But in order to convince us that will-free contemplation *must not* have a spatio-temporal thing as its object, Schopenhauer would have to rely on the thought that all perception of individual spatio-temporal things is "in the service of the will." He has argued at length that the *capacity* for perception of empirical objects is subservient to certain ends of the organism, and that for perceivers the usual way of regarding things is permeated with their desires and interests. From these points it follows that an episode of experience in which an individual spatio-temporal object is perceived without the intervention of the will is (1) an unusual episode, and (2) at odds with the will-governed nature of the capacity for perception. But none of this shows that there *cannot be* an episode of empirical perception in which, even though the individual's will is suspended, an ordinary spatio-temporal object is nevertheless perceived. To think otherwise is to confuse the claim that the *capacity* for perceiving spatio-temporal objects is in the service of the will, with the claim that every *episode* of experience which exercises that capacity is in the service of the will.

Schopenhauer appeared not to be making this mistake when he referred to genius "removing from the service of the will the knowledge which originally existed only for this service." This is most naturally taken to mean that an episode of straightforward perception need not be will-governed, even though the general capacity for such perception is will-governed. But if this is Schopenhauer's view, then will-free contemplation of something may be recognized as more "objective" than ordinary perception, without our having to say that anything distinct from an ordinary empirical object is contemplated. We lack any reason for thinking that will-less contemplation must latch exclusively on to timeless, non-empirical entities if it is to occur at all.

Apart from these considerations, Schopenhauer's examples make it tolerably clear that what he is describing *is* perception of an individual empirical thing. In Patrick Gardiner's admirable words, "he did not wish to hold that artistic knowledge is wholly independent of normal sense-perception of particular things, and it would have been odd, to put it mildly, if he had done so."[28] In perceiving an Idea, we do not cease to perceive a tree, rock, or crag. Rather, we perceive the empirical thing in a particular, significant way. This Schopenhauer strives to express by saying that the individual thing we are perceiving "is raised [*sich erhebt*] to the Idea of its species," that it becomes a "representative" [*Repräsentant*] of its Idea, or that it "expresses" or "reveals" the Idea to us.[29] There is at least one parallel in Plato, admittedly from a different context. Mathematicians, says Plato, study visible diagrams which are images or resemblances of other entities such as triangles and circles, or the odd and the even. "They use visible figures and talk about them, but ... they are making their points about the square itself, the diameter itself, not about the diameter which they draw."[30] A Platonic mathematician sees a particular empirical thing inscribed on a particular surface, but from this seeing learns about universals. I suggest that Schopenhauer's aesthetic theory is best viewed as having this general structure.[31] The objectivity of aesthetic experience does not require the empirical object's disappearance from view.

IDEA AND INDIVIDUAL

In the very act of portraying some individual thing, then, the artist reveals an Idea. But I shall suggest that this, taken as a wholly general claim, is implausible. Consider the following passage from *Parerga and Paralipomena*:

[B]oth poetry and the plastic arts take as their particular theme an *individual* in order to present this with the greatest care and accuracy in all the peculiarities of its individual nature down to the most insignificant ... But the essence of art is that its one case applies to thousands, since what it implies through that careful and detailed presentation of the individual is the revelation of the (Platonic) *Idea* of that individual's species.

(*PP* 2, p. 420)

Why? From a picture's portraying an individual in accurate detail we can make no inference to its revealing the essence common to everything of a certain species. On the contrary, the two features seem in danger of excluding one another at least sometimes, since many of a thing's peculiarities will precisely be peculiar to it alone. The leap from individual to Idea here is enormous and perverse.

This, together with Schopenhauer's admission that the Ideas we encounter at the subjective end of his spectrum of cases are of no great significance, should prompt us to wonder what would be lost by removing the Ideas from this part of the account. In cases where, as he puts it, "the enjoyment of pure, will-less knowing" predominates, the following revisionary version of Schopenhauer's theory would surely suffice: "In aesthetic experience of a simple inorganic or vegetative object, or in the aesthetic experience of an artistic representation of one, we are conscious of a particular empirical thing, but our will is suspended, so that we experience the thing objectively, rather than in connection with any ends, needs, or interests that we as subjects may have. We become temporarily unaware of ourselves, and are lost in objective contemplation of the particular thing, which reveals more of its nature to our mind because we cease to impose our own will on it. This state of contemplation is one of tranquility, and we find great enjoyment in being in it." The revisionary account itself makes some assumptions that we may question. It assumes that we can completely suspend our will in contemplating something, and that to do so is likely to bring enjoyment. But these are not obviously fatal flaws (or, if they are, then Schopenhauer's theory will emerge as hopeless on any interpretation).

As an apology for some forms of art, our revisionary account implements what I called the "aesthetic experience" strategy. We enjoy responding in a peculiarly aesthetic way to the perception of some artwork, and that we enjoy this is a source of the value of that artwork. But could Schopenhauer's aim of engaging with Plato on the battleground of cognitive value be fulfilled if we adopted the revisionary account? This will depend on what the "objective" aesthetic mode of contemplation reveals to us about the object's nature. Julian Young, having jettisoned from Schopenhauer's theory the notion that the Ideas constitute an "ontologically distinct realm,"[32] nevertheless insists that "in Schopenhauer's conception, art, good art, that is, is a cognitively important enterprise. It communicates knowledge to us, knowledge moreover of universal application … In this he is surely right and Plato wrong. For only this view can account for the deep significance art has, and is accepted as having, in human life."[33] The claim made in the last sentence quoted is disputable. For, as I have suggested, the significance of *some* art might be accounted for non-cognitively, for example in terms of our enjoying the tranquil contemplation it affords. If the Schopenhauerian theory of art is to show *all* art as a cognitively important enterprise, it will still have to tell us what the cognitive importance of will-less contemplation of a thing is. Young offers the following: "[T]he Ideas might just be ordinary perceptual objects … their universality having to do … with the selectiveness of attention paid to them by the observer … [P]erceiving an Idea … is a matter of perceiving an ordinary object but with one's attention focussed on its essential, and away from its inessential aspects."[34] Later he speaks of "consciousness of an ordinary object, with, however, one's attention focussed upon the significant rather than the trivial in it."[35]

A problem here, however, is that the "significant," the "essential," and the "universal" in an object of perception may fail to coincide. From the point of view of aesthetic contemplation, what is significant may be, for example, the way a thing's form is brought to prominence by the fleeting effect of light playing over it at the moment of perceiving it. This may be neither essential to the particular thing, nor universal to things of its kind. It may apply only to the perception here and now of one aspect of this one thing. Again, what is universal to all apples may be the least engrossing feature of any particular apple one contemplates. And in an object depicted in a painting, it may be deviations in form from what is essential or universal that attract aesthetic contemplation. For example, in a print of orchids by Hokusai, the contingent and imperfect jagged edges of a broken leaf make a contribution to the aesthetic interest taken in the leaf's form. If the artist, in pursuit of botanical exactitude about the species, had depicted only what was essential to an orchid leaf or universal to all orchid leaves, it is not clear that we would have taken the same kind of pleasure in our "pure perception" of the picture. We might conceivably learn from Hokusai's print about orchids in general, or the universal nature of the orchid, or of the world of plants. The question is: must we, as a prerequisite of our contemplation's being a pleasurable will-free experience, learn anything at all of universal application? Surely not.

Think here of Schopenhauer's description of "those admirable Dutchmen who directed such purely objective perception to the most insignificant objects, and set up a lasting monument of their objectivity and spiritual peace in paintings of *still life*" (*WWR* 1, p. 197). The will-free contemplation of these artists is supposed to exemplify the aesthetic state, so Schopenhauer's unrevised theory has it that they *must* not only have perceived a particular empirical object, but had an Idea revealed to them. But the last step does not really add anything here. Schopenhauer's description as just quoted is surely adequate as an account of the value of this genre of painting, without needing any mention of the Ideas. The opportunity to explore the particular object of perception, regardless of all else, is often highly pleasurable. But the cognitive importance of such a practice need not be especially great. What we learn may amount to no more than the intriguing detail of how the particular thing depicted looks. So, in those cases where the subjective pleasure of will-less contemplation dominates, there is no need to think that any special cognitive significance must attach to art. Schopenhauer says of these cases that what we enjoy is "pure will-less *knowing*" – which is fine if "knowing" may include "finding out about the appearance of an object by perceiving it." But otherwise "knowing" is tendentious here. For the kind of case under discussion gives little scope for a Platonic answer to Plato. We should avoid falling into the trap of thinking that, if Plato is wrong about the value of art, then all art has to be defensible in terms of a massive cognitive importance.

TRAGEDY AND THE IDEA OF HUMANITY

Let us now move to the opposite end of Schopenhauer's spectrum of cases, where we enjoy "the objective apprehension of those Ideas that are the most distinct revelations of the Will," in art forms which "reveal to us most completely the essence of the Will, whether in its violence, its terribleness, its satisfaction, or its being broken." The topic that will concern us here is tragedy. Tragedy is Plato's main quarry among the arts – that which, above all else, he wishes to brand as cognitively deficient and psychologically harmful. It is fair to say that Schopenhauer aims to present tragedy as cognitively profound and psychologically beneficial. The question is: how

closely does his account of the value of tragedy fit into that single
garment – Platonic Ideas as the object of contemplation and will-less
knowing as the state of the subject – which he would like all the arts
to wear? Let us take the subjective state first. In the account of
tragedy in Volume 1 of *The World as Will and Representation* the
state of the onlookers at a tragic drama appears to be anything but a
calm, will-less contemplation. The best kind of tragedy, according to
Schopenhauer,

> shows us those powers that destroy happiness and life, and in such a way
> that the path to them is at any moment open even to us. We see the greatest
> suffering brought about by entanglements whose essence could be assumed
> even by our own fate, and by actions that perhaps even we might be capable
> of committing, and so we cannot complain of injustice. Then, shuddering,
> we feel ourselves already in the midst of hell.   (*WWR* 1, p. 255)

Does Schopenhauer believe that spectators at a tragedy feel fear?[36]
Never mind whether that belief is true or false[37] – can he integrate
such a powerful emotional response into his theory of aesthetic
experience? For to "shudder" at the precariousness of one's own
position, and even to relate what is portrayed in the drama intimately to one's life and possible actions, is surely to show interest in
it. It is not to contemplate the performance, or the fictional scene it
presents, in a state of elevated will-less objectivity. Indeed, there is
even nothing especially "aesthetic" about the state of mind Schopenhauer here describes. So what has this shuddering insight to do
with the calm contemplation of a still life? How can a single account
fit them both?

Tragedy is concerned with loss of will and attainment of a
viewpoint higher than that of individuality, according to Schopenhauer. He speaks of a resignation and a turning away from the will
to life. But he first thinks of these effects as occurring *within the
scene that tragedy depicts*: "Thus we see in tragedy the noblest
men, after a long conflict and suffering, finally renounce for ever all
the pleasures of life and the aims till then pursued so keenly, or
cheerfully and willingly give up life itself" (*WWR* 1, p. 253). So far
it looks as if tragedy depicts resignation but arouses consternation,
and it is hard to see how this will fit the general aesthetic account.
In the treatment of tragedy in Volume 2, however, Schopenhauer's
emphasis has changed. Now he says that "the summons to turn
away the will from life" is the "true tendency of tragedy ... *even
where this resigned exaltation of the mind is not shown in the hero
himself, but is only stimulated in the spectator.*"[38] This formulation

has two advantages. It lifts the excessively narrow requirement that the best tragedies must *depict* their central character achieving a state of will-less resignation, thus enabling Schopenhauer implicitly to reclaim into his account many of the finest tragedies which are not of this type.[39] It also makes the essential factor of tragedy reside in the subjective state of the spectator, which must be a "turning away of the will" – hence we have some hope that the general account of the aesthetic experience as a beneficial, will-free contemplation is going to apply to tragedy too.

However, Schopenhauer still appears to insist that the spectator must *feel* emotions of fear and pity, which in themselves are painful. His argument for saying that the bringing about of resignation is the true tendency of tragedy relies on this as a premise:

[I]f this ... were not the tendency of tragedy, then how would it be possible generally for the presentation of the terrible side of life, brought before our eyes in the most glaring light, to be capable of affecting us so beneficially, and of affording us an exalted pleasure? Fear and sympathy, in the stimulation of which Aristotle puts the ultimate aim of tragedy, certainly do not in themselves belong to the agreeable sensations; therefore they cannot be the end, but only the means. (*WWR* 2, p. 435)

So it looks as if tragedy can eventually induce a state of elevation above the will, a state from which human life can be contemplated with a detached and resigned eye – but that it does so by initially provoking the will with the portrayal of sufferings which cause horror in the spectators themselves.

Still I do not think that this is the most coherent way of interpreting Schopenhauer. We have left out one crucial element: the feeling of the sublime. By subsuming tragedy under the sublime Schopenhauer makes the subjective reaction to tragedy an intelligible part of his aesthetic theory.[40] The peace of contemplation may be attained either with or without a struggle. If it is attained with a struggle, we have the feeling of the sublime, where what we contemplate has a destructive or threatening relation to the will, which we are aware of, but from which we wrest ourselves free.[41] What the sublime demands is that I recognize a situation as threatening or distressing – but without feeling personally threatened or distressed. Schopenhauer puts this by saying that I may recognize an object as having a hostile relation to "human willing in general," but without "a single, real act of will" entering my own consciousness. If I really felt fear for myself, I would become incapable of feeling the sublimity of what is before me. So the "shuddering" which is said to characterize our experience of tragedy cannot, after all, be our feeling fear for ourselves. It is our comprehension of the depicted events as terrible for human feeling in general. That we thus comprehend the drama in emotional terms, and can yet remain in a state of objective contemplation of it, explains the *pleasure* we take in tragedy, and does so in a way which preserves the unity of Schopenhauer's aesthetic theory.[42]

Schopenhauer says that our enjoyment at the "objective" end of the spectrum, where tragedy lies, comes from our apprehension of Ideas. It is a familiar thought, going back again to Aristotle,[43] that tragedy allows us to see, in represented form, not just some particular set of actions, but something universal about all humanity. Schopenhauer's version of this thought is that tragedy presents us with the Idea of humanity. All the Ideas are manifestations of the underlying Will, but Schopenhauer is able to call tragedy the highest and most significant form of poetry because, firstly, the Idea of humanity is the highest of the Ideas, and secondly, the ebb and flow of desire, wickedness, and suffering which he thinks reflects our true nature (and that of the world) is the stuff of tragedy rather than any other literary form. "It is the antagonism of the Will with itself which is here most completely unfolded at the highest grade of its object-ivity" (*WWR* 1, p. 253). Is it then pleasurable to learn of "the unspeakable pain, the wretchedness and misery of mankind, the triumph of wickedness, the scornful mastery of chance, and the irretrievable fall of the just and the innocent"? To learn that this is how things stand (if they do) will no doubt be a valuable cognitive gain, but why a source of *pleasure*? Is it not rather that, to quote Flint Schier, "we value tragedy for the kind of knowledge which it gives us; ... some of the elements in our experience of tragedy are *unpleasant*, because it is a natural fact about us that quite often a knowledge of how things really are is *painful*"?[44]

If knowledge of the Idea of humanity rates as painful, then the pleasure in tragedy cannot come solely from an objective apprehension of the Idea. It is essential to this pleasure that we turn our backs on the world that tragedy reveals to us. It is essential, in other words, that we contemplate the misery of existence from within the security of a resigned, will-free state. For Schopenhauer it is only the production in us of a resigned attitude to real life and real humanity – the "true tendency" of tragedy – that can account for there being a pleasure in it. So once again it is the tranquility of escaping from our attachment to life that brings this form of art its value in Schopenhauer's account – a value which lies in the detached nature of aesthetic *experience.*

CONCLUSION

I conclude that the truly unifying notion in Schopenhauer's aesthetic theory is that of tranquil, will-less contemplation, a state of non-identification with the striving, suffering, bodily individual that one is. It is this that gives him a single account which assigns value to the arts at both ends of his spectrum of cases – albeit with the one qualification that aesthetic pleasure can be either in the beautiful or the sublime. The Ideas testify to the endurance of his Platonic ambitions, but they do not really produce a convincing theory. At one end of the spectrum of the arts, the Ideas are otiose: pleasure is in the tranquility of contemplation, which may perfectly well be of an empirical object in all its individual peculiarity. It is debatable whether in these cases the value of art is cognitive at all; but there is at least no requirement that what is significant in the object of tranquil contemplation be something universal. At the other end of the spectrum, apprehension of the Ideas serves an all-important cognitive function, but our pleasure cannot stem from our knowing the horrifying Idea of humanity *per se.* Rather, the key to the satisfaction we take in tragedy is, in Schopenhauer's account, the will-lessness of sublime resignation in the face of the Idea.

Schopenhauer is deeply committed to answering Plato in Platonic terms, yet the attempt to provide that answer does not ultimately provide him with a unified and plausible aesthetic theory. It is not that he spoilt his theory by branching off in a Platonic direction that was alien to it. If anything, he clung too tenaciously to his juvenile understanding of the revelatory consciousness that would transport us beyond the empirical realm, and did not sufficiently question the assumption that a defence of art against Plato must at every point engage Plato on his own high ground.

Notes

1 *A History of Western Philosophy* (New York, 1960), p. 753. The judgment is supported by Hilde Hein, "Schopenhauer and Platonic Ideas," *Journal of the History of Philosophy*, 4, 1966, pp. 133–144.

2 This point is made by D. W. Hamlyn, *Schopenhauer* (London: Routledge and Kegan Paul, 1980), p. 41.

3 *HN* 1.

4 See ibid., pp. 12–13.

5 Ibid., p. 43. Schopenhauer refers here to *Phaedo* 64a.

6 See ibid., pp. 27, 47.

7 D. W. Hamlyn, *Schopenhauer*, p. 103. Cf.: Patrick Gardiner, *Schopenhauer* (Harmondsworth: Penguin Books Ltd., 1967), p. 203: "... this new category, so suddenly introduced."

8 Bryan Magee, *The Philosophy of Schopenhauer* (Oxford: The Clarendon Press, 1983), p. 239.

9 Julian Young also uses the notion of a drama to locate Book III in relation to what goes before it. *Willing and Unwilling: A Study in the Philosophy of Arthur Schopenhauer* (Dordrecht: Martinus Nijhoff, 1987), p. 81. For the idea that the unity of Schopenhauer's main work is an artistic or dramatic one, see my *Self and World in Schopenhauer's Philosophy* (Oxford: The Clarendon Press, 1989), pp. 12, 285–288.

10 See esp. *WWR* 1, 426–428. The view I give here of Schopenhauer's metaphysics is, I assume, the "standard" view – though it has been questioned by Young, *Willing and Unwilling*, Ch. III. My own account of Schopenhauerian knowledge of the thing-in-itself is in *Self and World in Schopenhauer's Philosophy*, Ch. 7.

11 See Hein, "Schopenhauer and Platonic Ideas."

12 Plato, *Phaedo* 66b–e; David Gallop trans., *Plato: Phaedo* (Oxford: The Clarendon Press, 1975).

13 *WWR* 2, 608–609. Schopenhauer is again referring to the *Phaedo* here.

14 See esp. *Phaedo* 66b–67c.

15 Thus Copleston calls them a "half-way house." *Arthur Schopenhauer: Philosopher of Pessimism* (London: Burns, Oates, and Washburne, Ltd., 1946), p. 106. Similar views are taken by Gardiner (p. 203) and Magee (p. 239).

16 When Schopenhauer first broaches the relation of Kant and Plato in the early manuscripts, he tends to think that Kant's thing-in-itself and Plato's Ideas are the same (see *HN* 1, 204–206). He quickly works through to the realization that this cannot be right (see, e.g., *HN* 1, 247). In the finished *WWR*, he still cannot resist assimilating Ideas and thing-in-itself as closely as possible: they are "not exactly identical, but yet very closely related" (*WWR* 1, 170), "the inner meaning of both doctrines is wholly the same" (*WWR* 1, 172). This is a symptom, in my view, of Schopenhauer's continuing desire to say that aesthetic experience penetrates to what truly is (*ontôs on*) – something which he cannot, however, quite bring himself to say in a Kantian accent. A view with some similarity to mine is expressed by William Desmond, "Schopenhauer, Art, and the Dark Origin," in Eric van der Luft, ed., *Schopenhauer: New Essays in Honor of his 200th Birthday* (Lewiston, NY: Edwin Mellen Press, 1988), p. 118: "With respect to the Idea, Schopenhauer is a *return* to Plato ...

complicated (some might say infected) with ill-digested Kantian notions."

17 See my "Plato's Analogy Between Painter and Poet," *The British Journal of Aesthetics*, 31, 1991, pp. 1–12.

18 I deal with one of these charges in "Plato's Analogy Between Painter and Poet." A discussion of the different arguments of *Republic* 10 can be found in chs. 5 and 6 of my *Images of Excellence: Plato's Critique of the Arts* (Oxford: Clarendon Press, 1995).

19 *Republic* 598e.

20 Ibid., 596e.

21 Ibid., 607d.

22 "The Standpoint of Eternity: Schopenhauer on Art," *Kant-Studien*, 78, 1987, p. 436.

23 *On the Genealogy of Morals*, III, 5, Walter Kaufmann, trans. (New York: 1967).

24 *WWR* 1, 179. Young, "The Standpoint of Eternity," p. 428, clears up any doubt there might be, from Payne's translation, that the transformations of subject and object are claimed by Schopenhauer to be inseparable.

25 See *WWR* 1, 212, 196.

26 However, Schopenhauer allows himself to speak even of aesthetic joy (*Freude* – translated by Payne as "pleasure"), which occurs in our most blissful (*sälig*) moments (*WWR* 1, 390). In *PP* 2, 415–416, he notes the popular view that joy (*Freude*) and pleasure (*Wohlgefallen*) depend on a relation to the will, but affirms that they are possible once the will has been suspended and with it the possibility of suffering.

27 We may think either that such lack of unity would be a bad thing ("it destroys the *oneness* of beauty, of aesthetic experience" – Israel Knox, *The Aesthetic Theories of Kant, Hegel, and Schopenhauer* (New York: The Humanities Press, 1958), p. 134), or that it saves him from a stiflingly monolithic theory ("In practice ... Schopenhauer applies his conception of the Ideas to the interpretation of the plastic and pictorial arts with greater flexibility than might have been expected from the initial very bare and abstract formulation of the theory." – Gardiner, p. 216.)

28 *Schopenhauer*, p. 206. I have also benefited here from Young, "The Standpoint of Eternity," pp. 434–436.

29 See *WWR* 1, 197, 200, 210.

30 *Republic* 510d–e.

31 Hamlyn (*Schopenhauer*, p. 104) and Young ("The Standpoint of Eternity," p. 434) also make parallels between Schopenhauerian Ideas and the objects that mathematics studies.

32 "The Standpoint of Eternity," pp. 433–436.

33 Ibid., p. 437.

34 Ibid., p. 434.

35 Ibid., p. 436.

36 Cf.: Flint Schier, "The Claims of Tragedy: An Essay in Moral Psychology and Aesthetic Theory," *Philosophical Papers*, 18, 1989, pp. 19–20: "I

think Schopenhauer's theory is sub-Aristotelian; it shares with Aristotle the false belief that tragedy somehow involves arousing emotion only to annihilate it."

37 We cannot debate the general issue here. One much-cited paper on this much-discussed topic is Kendall Walton, "Fearing Fictions," *The Journal of Philosophy*, 75, 1978, pp. 5–27. Walton argues that we do not really fear fictions.

38 *WWR* 2, 435 (my italics).

39 Nevertheless, he complains that ancient tragedies do not very often display the spirit of resignation. *WWR* 2, 434.

40 See esp. *WWR* 2, 433. Schopenhauer's notion of the sublime is quite closely based on Kant's, which he considers "by far the most excellent thing in the *Critique of Judgement*" (*WWR* 1, 532). Favourable judgment on Kant's doctrine of the sublime dates back to 1813 (see *HN* 1, 48ff). For some reservations, see *WWR* 1, 205.

41 See *WWR* 1, 200–202.

42 Young, "The Standpoint of Eternity," p. 432, suggests that for Schopenhauer the sublime involves feeling emotions which are "depersonalized" or "disassociated." I do feel fear, say, but am elevated above myself and do not identify myself with the individual who is threatened.

43 See *Poetics*, Ch. 9 (1451[a–b]).

44 "The Claims of Tragedy," p. 21 (my emphases).

3

Schopenhauer and the aesthetics of creativity

LUCIAN KRUKOWSKI

GENIUS AND WILL

Schopenhauer's account of the artistic process is an early contribution to the study of creativity. This account extends his analysis of art beyond the philosophical role typically assigned it at the time – that of providing privileged images of an otherwise inaccessible reality – into the psychological and social characteristics of the artistic personality. This move introduces the creative process as a major subject for aesthetics.[1] In the philosophies of Kant and Hegel, the artist is identified by the term "genius," and is pictured as a gifted but remote creature who is remarkable through achievements that, for theoretical purposes, are independent of biography. The only characteristic of the genius that is of philosophical importance in these theories is the capacity to produce great art. Analysis of this capacity, however, if not relegated to a philosophically "irrelevant" psychology, is accounted for only in general if sometimes heroic terms. For Kant, the status is impersonal and cosmological: Genius, marvelously anointed as "nature's voice," provides a rational face for the noumenal world through the purity and completeness of its representations, and thereby offers us hope of a continuity between the world and our perceptions. The function of genius is a matter of avoiding the commonplaces of both subjective caprice and repetitive craft, thereby channeling the free imagination into forms that are novel as well as exemplary.[2] For Hegel, the status of genius is impersonal and historical: Endowed with telic foresight, his artist provides not so much a glimpse of nature's rationality, as a premonition of spirit's historical future, thereby documenting the ascending stages of cultural progress.[3] But the nature of this status remains as obscure here as it does with Kant, and in neither theory does the

62

artist escape the restrictive domination of genius. Whatever value the creative process may have in other contexts and for other persons, its philosophical importance lies solely in the production of masterworks, because only such works have epistemic force – are revelatory for the system of inquiry.

It must be said at once that Schopenhauer theorizes this way as well. His concern, like those of Kant and Hegel, is with knowing and symbolizing the nature of reality. "Genius" and "masterwork," given their philosophical utility for these ends, are his main aesthetic values, and he is not ready to replace them with such other values as social criticism or psychological deviance. The philosophic valorization of discord between the aesthetic and social belongs to a later period, that of romanticism and its modernist progeny.

A key difference, however, between the aesthetic theories of Kant and Hegel and those of Schopenhauer lies in the tendency of the former, but not the latter, to take the workings of genius as a mystery that is not properly a philosophical concern. With its facticity put aside as irrelevant, genius can be treated as a theoretical entity, a convenient epistemic mechanism borrowed from another discourse. Schopenhauer, to the contrary, in keeping with his interest in the ecstatics of Christian and Hindu saints, is not as fastidious about the purview of philosophy, and so is willing to follow genius into other forms of explanation. It is this turn of theory that opens to the later romantic linkage of aesthetic value with the creative act and marks Schopenhauer as a bridge between the enlightenment and these later periods.

Schopenhauer's sustained scrutiny of artistic creativity extends his aesthetic analysis from the symbol to the conditions of its making. In the course of this analysis, he casts the artist as both prophet and victim of the larger society, and he thus lays the theoretical groundwork for the now familiar conflicts between the aesthetic and conventional – "art and life," "bohemian and bourgeoise," "avant-garde and academy" – that mark the romantic reaction to the enlightenment. Also, in his search for the etiology of this conflict, he anticipates the psychological theories that link creativity and mental illness.[4]

Much of Schopenhauer's interest in the adversarial nature of creativity can be traced back to the conflict implicit in his metaphysics. His thing-in-itself, the will, is both the world's reality and antagonist to the truly human – moral – life. Despite its metaphysical dominance, however, there is an alternative to will, namely, the life of contemplation and quietude that eschews the very processes – drives and ambitions – of willed becoming. Given this alternative, we see that Schopenhauer's system is not built upon, nor reducible to, a single underlying principle. The will does not transcend its opposing principle in due course, as does Hegel's "spirit" in its historical triumph over "matter." Nor is Schopenhauer's alternative realm of quietude a purely rational, although systematically necessary, aspect of an inclusive reality, as is the Kantian "thing-in-itself." Schopenhauer's dualism persists throughout his system – the will, given its negativity, cannot become all that there is – and this leads him to hypothesize a realm outside the scope of his thing-in-itself. This is the realm of the Platonic forms, the locus of both beauty and morality, and it is epistemically accessible to both philosophical contemplation and art. Schopenhauer gives art the capacity to image what the philosopher can contemplate, so these join in providing an alternative epistemology, one that describes a world of stasis and essence in which the temporality of will is replaced by an eternal present.[5]

Because the will is "insatiable" – systematically incapable of resolution – it requires such an alternative, if not for completeness then for balance. In general, a dualistic metaphysics, if it is not to incessantly tilt towards resolution in one unifying principle, requires an equilibrium between those principles it has in opposition. The wanted unity can then be sought within each principle rather than between them. In Schopenhauer's theory, artworks are symbols that evoke one of his opposed principles. They do so by countering the process accounts of causality, the "principles of sufficient reason," that operate within the natural world, with images of an ideal world independent of willed process, the "forms" or "ideas." These function, much as they do with Plato, to present reality's entities in their completeness, undistorted by the ambiguities that Plato blames on subjectivity and Schopenhauer on the will. Unlike Plato, however, Schopenhauer makes this ideal world accessible to art by assigning art the capacity to produce images of the forms. Further – and here the gap with Plato widens – Schopenhauer's artworks enjoin us, through the requirements of their appreciation, to align our moral selves with those quiescent images rather than with the unrequitable drives that characterize the human will.[6]

Through such specifications, Schopenhauer's theory also goes beyond his contemporaries in the philosophical weight it places on art. That art will not succeed in its didactic task – ambition and desire being forever renewed – is, paradoxically, a sign both of Schopenhauer's pessimism and his success at maintaining equilibrium between the divisions in his theory. For, if the one part of his system, the ideal, came to dominate, Schopenhauer would be pressed to characterize its triumph through something like the historicity of Hegel: a telic working out of oppositions in time. If, on the other hand, priority were given to the will – all actions in the world only being versions of its exhaustion and renewal – then this emphasis would anticipate the Dionysian Nietzsche.

Although Schopenhauer has good reason to not wish victory for either side of his world, the equilibrium he erects makes the task of accounting for this world a precarious undertaking. The lessons contained in art, those glimpses of the possibility – and rewards – of a contemplative life, may secure art's philosophical value, but they place the artist in a dilemma that is as personally insoluble as it is vocationally necessary. The dilemma is this: artists, like philosophers, must face the "true nature" of will in order to reveal it; but unlike philosophers, artists cannot then escape the will by withdrawing from its imperatives, for artistic creativity is action in the world. Schopenhauer's philosopher has good reasons to deny the value of action: Ambitions are never fully realized; happiness is a chimera just beyond reach; progress is a coercive illusion; and there is no God to help one along. The artist's product – the artwork – shows us the tranquil alternative to the will through images of the world of forms, a world where there is no inadequacy to instigate action. Yet the completeness of art's content must take shape – be created – within the world of will, and here we find the dilemma Schopenhauer gives to creativity. Artists cannot deny ambition or the hope of progress if they are to fashion the images that, viewed philosophically, provide good reasons for just such denials. In this sense, the didactic import of art's content cannot be applied to the actions that lead to its creation – nor can it inform the lives of its artists.[7]

Schopenhauer joins art and philosophy together in a common task: the exposition of an ideal that is also an achievable virtue. Philosophers, heeding Socrates' recognition of philosophy as a way of life, see through the will's duplicities and reject them. But artists create precisely within the world of ambition and desire, and so must persist in that world – notwithstanding the content of art – if art's images are to be achieved at all. So the artist remains divided, much like Schopenhauer's ontology; and the conflicting demands of content and creation give rise to the personal costs which, in later theories, become familiar signs of the artistic vocation. Schopenhauer presciently identifies these signs – of social alienation and mental imbalance – as conditions of artistic creation, and devotes much of his aesthetic theory to their analysis.

CREATIVITY AND MADNESS

While Schopenhauer stays with the term "genius" as a metaphor for artistic creativity, he does not thereby place that activity outside the range of philosophical scrutiny. His concern with the epistemic function of artworks extends to an interest in the lives and actions of artists, and from his observations on this score he proposes a new interpretation of artistic genius. This interpretation does not suppose the Kantian link between genius and the intuitions of nature's completeness, nor Hegel's link with the premonitions of history's direction, but rather the astonishing link between genius and a pattern of behavior that Schopenhauer identifies through the catch-all word of his time, "madness." The manner in which he brings these together can be shown through the following passages. First, on madness: "Mad people do not generally err in the knowledge of what is immediately present; but their mad talk relates always to what is absent and past, and only through these to its connection with what is present. Therefore, it seems to me that their malady especially concerns the memory. It is not, indeed a matter of memory failing them entirely ... Rather, it is a case of the thread of memory being broken, its continuous connection being abolished, and of the impossibility of a uniformly coherent connection with the past."[8] Second, this passage on genius: "The individual object of (the genius's) contemplation, or the present which he apprehends with excessive vividness, appears in so strong a light that the remaining links of the chain, so to speak, to which they belong, withdraw into obscurity, and this gives us phenomena that have long since been recognized as akin to madness. That which exists in the actual individual thing, only imperfectly and weakened by modifications, is enhanced to perfection, to the very Idea of it, by the method of contemplation used by the genius. Therefore everywhere he sees extremes, and on this account his own actions tend toward extremes."[9]

Schopenhauer's correlation, here, between genius and madness is not an identity claim – not all who are mad are geniuses. Nor, although this is less clear, is it the claim that all geniuses are mad. But it is at least the claim of a special affinity between madness and genius, a noting of similarities in the ways the world is experienced and responded to. Schopenhauer locates these similarities in the experience of time, a skewing of the connection between past and future into an inordinate focus on the present. For the genius, this supposes a capacity to view a moment of reality as if it were the whole of experience. For those who are mad, this capacity robs them of the capacity to order the transitions in their lives. In the artist, the two come together.

In Schopenhauer's view, madness is a condition arising from the attempt to reconcile what is unalterably opposed and the failure to discard what cannot be reconciled. In one sense, this opposition is basic to Schopenhauer's philosophy; it is the one between will and idea. It manifests itself here in the artist's attempt to find, within the ongoing instantiations of will, the still images of will's perfection – its "adequate objectifications." But such finding is also a denial of the will, for perfection nullifies reasons for further action. This is as true for the self as for the world, for the will is located equally in both. So creative action, the act of making images, is also a self-denial, for the artist knows the reasons – they are there in the work – that speak against continuing to act.

Schopenhauer locates madness in the opposition between immediate attention and the patterns of memory, between the still intensity of a single moment and its diffusion through the movement that comparison requires. In this sense, the opposition is also between the artist and the artwork, for the product of creative action, while exemplifying the process that creates it, also denies it. Artworks, even the arts of time – music, drama – are about stillness, when stillness is understood in its metaphysical sense, as completeness and perfection. This content reveals the degenerate status of action, even – perhaps especially – the action required for its own creation.

The artist's heroism lies in the persistence of such action in the face of such content: "He himself bears the cost of producing that play; he himself is the will objectifying itself and remaining in constant suffering." The gesture is not empty, for it fulfills the philosophical task of marking the way from one realm to the other; it facilitates abandoning the will. The benefits of this heroism, however, accrue to others, to those for whom the ideal content of art can be reached through understanding rather than creation, to such a one who, "tired of the spectacle, seizes the serious side of things."[10] Creative action cannot be serious because it responds to a single event as if it were all there is, and this formal encapsulation in turn demands a totality of affective response – a complete attention. Such action mimics the self-sufficiency, the temporal stillness, of the forms, and the links of memory break.

When artists mistake the revelatory actions of art-making for the practical tasks of coping with the world of ordinary affairs – the world of competitive accomplishment – they become its victims. Action that images the world through the self-sufficiency of the Platonic forms cannot sustain the continuity and reciprocity required by communal experience. Unlike the artwork, the artist does not inhabit the world of art, and action whose consequence is isolation from other action is pathological. In a "normal" life – that life which, paradoxically, Schopenhauer sees as subject to the demands of will – the episodes of experience remain fluid and incomplete, and psychic control extends over the flow of events even as it avoids the intensity that can be provided by the singular event. Such control – the classic virtue of "moderation" – gives hope that this flow is compatible with the cadences of happiness, even if, under deeper scrutiny, the achievements of happiness and control are both illusions.[11]

Schopenhauer's artist struggles to produce images of timelessness in time; and the special time of creativity, accordingly, is a hybrid of the two. As a consequence of living this time, the artist fails as both an empirical and an ideal existent – both as actor within the world, and as its pure knowing subject. The failure, of course, is not a philosophical one, for creative madness is redeemed by its symbolic capacity to render the will transparent to the reality that lies beyond it. This, after all, is what Schopenhauer wants of art, but in putting things the way he does he creates a singular opening in aesthetics for the irrational.

HEGEL'S ALTERNATIVE

Not all alienations deserve to be branded as irrational, nor need they be suffered in solitude. There is a sense of artistic alienation that is collective, and this sense leads to a theory quite alien to Schopenhauer's: art as anticipation of the future. An echo of this can be discerned in Schopenhauer's own distaste for the manners and conventions of his day, but the theory more properly belongs to

Hegel, for it correlates alienation with historical prescience. A comparison can be useful here in that it helps distinguish between two later views of the artist that are often confused with each other: The artist as hero and as victim.

In Hegel, artistic achievement is one of anticipation, a recognition of patterns that are as yet too ephemeral for the conventional eye. The world revealed by art is the future as it appears in the present, and heeding that revelation has the consequence of hurrying the present into the past. The trauma of this acceleration produces the defensive response of "killing the messenger;" the artwork is rejected and the artist is alienated. Under this theory, artistic alienation is a malaise of the collective not of the individual, for in a static society, accounts of the world that codify the present are given greater credence than those that evoke the future. Such resistance to what can be known of the future (and art, for Hegel, is a way to that knowing) is both a social malaise and historical mistake. "Spirit's progress" is inexorable, and resistance for the sake of present stability ends in repetitive stereotype and social fragmentation.[12] Hegel's world, unlike Schopenhauer's, is holistic. Knowledge is not distinct from process, but is rather formed within it. Artistic alienation, in this world, is a matter of skewed historical tempos, a present antagonism whose content – if not person – will reappear for reconciliation by the future. Accordingly, the artist's difficulties, although they may seem pathological, are actually prophetic, in that they evoke the explanatory norms of the future. This is the artist as hero.

Yet, for all his optimism – perhaps because of it – Hegel shows little interest in the actual condition of artistic creativity. His artist is on the model of his "world-historical-individual" whose philosophical importance is that of an effective instrument, a facilitator of progress in history. The conditions – circumstances and cost – of this effort are irrelevant to the needs of Hegel's theory, and this means that the only creative efforts of value are those vindicated by later events.[13] This particular location of value is a source for later theories that open the boundaries between the aesthetic and the social (as Schopenhauer does between the aesthetic and the psychological) and enlist art in the struggle against inertial social orders. These are modernist theories that take the anticipatory character Hegel assigns to art, and make it into a polemical-didactic weapon of a radical body politic. Here, the factor of alienation is present in a different sense: when art takes on the function of social criticism, it signals an alliance with particular social beliefs and becomes vulnerable to repressive reactions against such beliefs.[14]

Hegel's historicism, however, does give artists a defense of sorts against the hostility that meets their best efforts. Vindication in and by the future may in fact be an impersonal victory, but belief in its possibility – like the possibility of spiritual salvation – changes the present from an ordeal into a task. This construal of creativity is a staple of the modernist avant-garde, and it helps clarify the rapidity and scope of stylistic dislocation that characterize the arts of that recent period. Belief in one's sense of the future is an antidote against the fear that the extremities of the present are merely psychopathic in origin. In this sense, Hegel's historicism is a safeguard against Schopenhauer's pessimism, and against the existential impasse into which the latter's divided ontology places the artist. Radical art reverses the diagnosis that links creativity and madness and directs it back against its social origins. The artist is not mad – only prescient. The suspension of disbelief that supports appreciation of such art is justified through the possibility, marked above, that the new images hold pragmatic as well as aesthetic values. One consequence, then, of Hegel's aesthetic theory is that epistemic precocity – art that shows the future in the present – counts as the value that is competitive with Schopenhauer's emphasis on creativity in their challenge to the traditional aesthetic of beauty.

Schopenhauer, given his dim view of his own thing-in-itself, puts little stock in premonitions of the future. For him, the future remains normatively constant with both present and past, and value lies not in embracing it but in being indifferent to its promises. Also, given his dim view of Hegel, Schopenhauer does not countenance the very notion of teleology, whether historical or metaphysical. Accordingly, in his aesthetic there is no pattern of historical change that would valorize the insights of artists through a belated later recognition. This is because these insights are not actually novel; they point to an unchanging truth, the nature of the ideal, and their essential function, therefore, is not to anticipate historical change but to reveal this truth. Artworks – throughout their history – are about "the same old thing;" they show how the world is when undistorted by the illusions of the will, of which one of the more pernicious is the illusion of social – and aesthetic – progress.[15] If Hegel's artist is a bridge between present and future, Schopenhauer's spans the world of events and the world of essences. In the first case, art documents what is already implicit in the entire pattern of teleological change;

in the second, art provides the possibility, limited to the human in nature, of discarding one form of reality for another. On this reading, Schopenhauer's artist has the weightier task, for in his universe there is no general principle, nothing inevitable in the nature of nature, that requires or even promotes the crossing to the world of forms. For philosophical reasons that might justify this crossing, Schopenhauer leans on Kant. These reasons, as with the Kantian moral imperative, are both rational and self-given. They are based on the awareness of the normative difference between a heteronomous will and the autonomy gained by its denial. Schopenhauer presumes, as does Kant, that if that difference can be known, there ought be no doubt about the choice.[16] But, as I point out above, his artist cannot complete this crossing from will to idea.

Yet, there is some comfort to be found in the comparison with Hegel. Schopenhauer's artists, unlike Hegel's, are free of history's imperatives and thus are in no danger of epistemic irrelevance, for there is no cultural sea change in the offing for which some – and eventually all – artistic symbols will no longer be adequate. The other side of this, however, is the intractability of the conflict that is the condition of art. Will and idea are in equilibrium because they do not transcend their mutual opposition – neither in principle nor in historic time – and it is the ongoing elucidation of this equilibrium that is both the role and content of art. The artist in expressing this content remains positioned between these antithetical worlds, functioning in effect as the span between them. Although artistic reference is to the idea, art is created within the world of action, the world of will – even if its imperative is to deny that world's adequacy for the human psyche. This is Schopenhauer's sense of the artist as victim.

Perhaps it is the very permanence of this conflict that sparked Schopenhauer's interest in creativity, for it works out that aesthetic accomplishment exacerbates the artist's dilemma while any resolution of this dilemma is at the expense of aesthetic value. Bad art is less painful to make but it does not do the philosophical job; it does not challenge the partiality of will's presentations. Such art is motivated, so to speak, by the same ambitions that characterize the world of will, and these ambitions do not recognize the aesthetic completeness that is both fulfillment and perfection. This is because the ambitions of bad art are fulfilled through the very conventions the will uses to mask its own incompleteness, and these conventions are neither difficult nor painful to follow.

Will's objectifications, conventionally seen, group in normative hierarchies, the higher and lower of things – but this grouping is only residue of the will's programmatic incompleteness. On the other hand, the "adequate objectifications" of will – things as Platonic forms – are not so graded, for their completeness gives them the metaphysical equality that makes them, interchangeably, proper subjects for art.[17] It is the artist's task to transform the one into the other – thing into form – and thus to give sensate support for Schopenhauer's philosophical repudiation of will. To do this, the artist's action must retain the contents of both worlds – and the pain of the transformation – without escaping into either one. Enduring this instability amounts to a personification of its metaphysical source, and thus it is that artistic creativity becomes an affective sign of aesthetic value. The other face of this endurance, as we have seen, is creativity as a symptom of psychological malaise.

In this theory, then, it is the conflicted genius that gains philosophical unity – an ideological if not psychological redemption – by being, qua artist, a model of the dualistic equilibrium through which Schopenhauer measures the world. It is the artistic act – creativity not artwork – that straddles the worlds of will and idea.

SCHOPENHAUER AND FREUD

In tracing the influences that Schopenhauer has on later theories of artistic creativity, we follow his view to the historical locus where the concept of will loses its metaphysical force and becomes identified with a specifically human function. Taken this way, the will relinquishes its status as explanatory principle for cosmic process, and becomes rather a principle of behavior in psychology and medicine. With this contextual shift, the role of will in aesthetic theory also changes. The pressures that the will exerts on the content of art no longer present us with a noumenal revelation but only with the revelations of a self, and this gives rise to a new aesthetic centered on the value of artistic expression.

The exercise of will, in its new guise as specifically human volition, is now linked directly with the work of art as its content; and this turns willing into a virtue. The new aesthetic concern is not with setting aside the will in favor of its ideal alternative – as Schopenhauer would have it. Rather, it is in volition's claim to be a human function that is internally unique and externally demonstrable, that makes it valuable as aesthetic content. In this turn of theory, the mission that Schopenhauer assigns art: the affirmation of rationality through presentations of the ideal, is abandoned for another, philosophically more modest, mission: the presentation of the nature and varieties of human subjectivity. With this historical shift, however, the concern arises to show what is so rich in the concept of will as human volition as to make it, so to speak, competitive with its role as universal force in the earlier theories. A major contribution to this turn of thought is to be found in the work of Sigmund Freud, and I continue my study by tracing some continuities between Freud's theories and Schopenhauer's.[18]

For Schopenhauer, the will is divided: there is the universal will, which is his principle of the thing-in-itself; and there is human volition, which is a proper part – a "grade" – of the universal. But then there is that volition he does not so name, that which lies outside the will, the human capacity to deny the will and separate from its world. This is a capacity which, quixotically, is engendered within the world-as-will even as it becomes the instrument of that world's denial. For Freud, there is only one will, that aspect of personality which is human volition, and he thus rejects both Schopenhauer's metaphysical thesis and its normative consequences. Despite this difference in basis, however, there are important similarities to be noted in the way both theories are constructed.

Schopenhauer presents the world as a stratification – a grading of the will's objectifications – in which the glacial forms of geology support the layers of accelerating change that move through the plant and animal kingdoms and culminate in the human being.[19] Freud's theory is also a stratification, although it is doctrinally limited to a parsing of Schopenhauer's end point, the human psyche. This theory moves its subject from the private recesses of the id through sub and pre-conscious layers into the public domain of the ego and super-ego.[20] In both theories a play between hidden and overt factors can be found: Schopenhauer's will is hidden in the sense that it is masked by the illusions of progress which both energize human actions and endanger their search for meaning. The Freudian psyche, in a parallel sense, is divided between unconscious and conscious aspects, the former constituting the origins of individual identity but also a source of danger, for a skewed transition between the two aspects results in a neurotic distortion of identity. The occlusion or mischanneling of the unconscious sources of personality is, in fact, the general account that Freud gives of neurosis.[21] Here, a difference between theories emerges.

73

With Schopenhauer, where value is divided between accomplishment in a causal world, and the rejection of this world for the sake of a non-evolving ideal, insight into the hidden realm of will results in embracing the value of withdrawal rather than accomplishment. In a Freudian context, however, such a move would be a characteristic of neurosis, for the healthy personality is measured through accomplishment, and withdrawal is but a symptom of the inability to cope.

In Schopenhauer's theory, I have identified the dilemma of the artist as a consequence of the needs of creativity: the process of art-making must incorporate the processes of a world that art's content gives reason to abandon. This is the basis for Schopenhauer's correlation between creativity and madness as distortions of time and memory. In this account, the extreme focus on immediate events that generates artistic content is achieved at the expense of the durational control of experience, a loss in the memory of sequential events. In Freudian theory, neurosis is similarly associated with the distortion of memory, particularly with the mechanism of repression, which is a defensive forgetting, levelled primarily at childhood traumas. Freud's neurotic attempts to resolve later manifestations – or replicas – of these traumas but without the continuity of insight that would lead to their original sources. As in Schopenhauer, each such attempt is an event of extreme focus, and the succession of events lacks the durational controls – here, the causal awareness – that would lead memory back to the early events and to the resolution of trauma.

In Freudian theory, the search for the origins of neurosis centers around childhood experiences, particularly those concerned with infantile sexuality, and it is toward the nature of these early experiences that much of his therapy is directed.[22] Here, another difference between the two theories is to be found. In his later commentaries, Schopenhauer modifies his preoccupation with genius and madness by making another correlation, this time between genius and the child. Children, for Schopenhauer, are "pre-sexual" beings in which the cognitive faculties outweigh the affective ones, and the advent of sexuality is held off until the beginnings of puberty. So this correlation – between child and genius – is based upon a model of childhood that is free of the traumas and confusions of the sexual drive and, consequently, of the distortions that will imposes on psychic development. On this issue Schopenhauer writes: "The genital system is one with the most vehement of all desires. I have

74

thereby called this the focus of the will. Just because the terrible activity of this system still slumbers, while that of the brain already has full briskness, childhood is the time of innocence and lost happiness, the paradise of life, the lost eden ...''[23]

Before the appearance of the sexual drive – this inevitable intrusion of the will upon cognition – Schopenhauer's child enjoys the clarity of vision and intensity of focus that makes it capable of seeing the world in singular terms: the uniqueness of things rather than relationships. This capacity anticipates the special perception of artistic genius and, thus, the two – genius and child – share access to the realm of the Platonic ideas. While Schopenhauer does not sufficiently anticipate modern concerns to extend this insight to the art of children, he nevertheless places the seeds of creativity in that early stage. Presumably, as with Plato's doctrine of "recollection," maturity is a kind of forgetting – to which most children succumb but which the genius avoids. Schopenhauer remarks: "Every genius is already a big child, since he looks out into the world as into something strange and foreign, a drama, and thus with purely objective interest. He who throughout his life does not, to a certain extent, remain a big child ... will never become a genius."[24]

So "childlike innocence" is the Enlightenment virtue with which Schopenhauer belatedly softens his earlier account of creativity – the correlation with madness – and brings it closer to the peace of philosophical contemplation, that innocence of old age achieved by the mastery – or waning – of sexuality. For Schopenhauer, the denial of the will is a virtue, achieved through a philosophical substitution of ideality for action, or it is a gift, given to children and, in part, to artists. His compartmentalization of developmental stages: the pre-sexual child, the obsessed adolescent, the striving adult, the disengaged philosopher, is more like a series of normative choices between alternatives than a continuing process. The philosopher makes the choice; for the child it is a gift. For the artist, qua genius, it is also a gift, but one that has the taint of its alternatives. In contrast, Freud's categories of psychic development are not so discrete. Because he locates the origins of sexuality – and neurosis – in early childhood, he does not give the psyche a time of respite from its dynamics. Causal links tie together the events that emerge in a given personality, and early childhood events, given the vulnerabilities at that stage of experience, have the primary impact on the conformation – the absence, strength and turn of neurosis – that marks the adult. The particular development that is the artistic personality is identified as that special kind of neurosis in which disorder is compensated for by the capacity to symbolically defuse its content.[25] Here, artistic content is not an image of a will-less reality; it images the effects of will. Nevertheless, in Freud's theory, there is a sense in which art shows an alternative to will: the creative process substitutes an imaginative construction for a real but untenable action. While artworks do not reveal a metaphysically sanctioned reality, they do reveal ways – often marvelous ones – in which the human psyche can defuse pain through its representations.

For Schopenhauer, making art has undoubted, if primarily philosophical, value. Whether it has value for Freud depends on how one regards the Freudian alternative: the therapeutic replacement of representation by reality. This alternative indicates a problematic aspect of Freud's linkage between neurosis and creativity: if art is a substitute for psychic reality, the therapeutic achievement of such reality would result in the corresponding loss of the impetus to art. Presumably, with the source of neurosis reached and understood, its share as both reason and mechanism in the creative process diminishes. There is then no longer a pressing reason to make art, and if the richness of the artistic content is proportionate to the degree of psychic distortion, that value also diminishes.[26] This conjecture has an independent history, but here it brings us back to the juncture between will and idea where Schopenhauer situates his artist, that balance-point of tension which permits the forming of an ideal content within the dynamics of willed process.

The needs of Schopenhauer's theory has him ask artists for a sacrifice that Freud would have them reject: the endurance of personal disorder for the sake of a representation. But we remember that, for Schopenhauer, the representation is not of that disorder but of a world – ontologically real – in which disorder does not occur. Here, psychic content is not important in itself but only as a propaedeutic: the secrets of the psyche unmask the will and are thus enabling towards the glimpse of ideality that art provides. For Freud, on the other hand, the primary consideration in neurosis – artistic or other – is to effect a cure through the psychoanalytic procedures of retrieval and insight. Notwithstanding similarities between the themes of will and id, Freud has no metaphysical allegiance to the id. The subconscious, taken analytically, is an aspect of personality and its processes require integration within the balance of functions that constitutes the normal psyche. So the will is not to be avoided; it can be tamed. There is no special pleading in Freudian theory through which the value of art supersedes the value of psychic wholeness. When such values are medically specified, the artist – qua neurotic – remains a candidate for treatment.[27]

In a more general sense, however, Freud did share the beliefs of his time in the salutary contributions that the beauties of art and the capacity for appreciation make to civilized life. In this reflective sense artistic creativity remains useful, for it encourages a socially desirable form of behavior, namely, the substitution of symbolic representation for direct gratification. Freud's view of civilization – and here he exhibits some of Schopenhauer's pessimism – is that such rechanneling of desire, although itself a form of repression, becomes a social virtue when it succeeds in mitigating the destructiveness that is incestuously linked with desire.[28] So in both theories art defeats the will – if only partially and for the time being.

AFTERWORD

In its historical freshness, the linkage of creativity with subjectivity must have been a compelling notion, with its unplumbed depths and unthinkable contents. Schopenhauer evidently found it so or he would not have given the will such philosophical prominence. But that aspect of the will which is human subjectivity is also the realm in which the first estrangement with the cosmic will takes place. The recognition that that will – after all its eons and strivings – remains indifferent to the human will could only have come as a feeling, first of betrayal, but then of freedom. For this recognition of cosmic indifference acts to give subjectivity its own value: human will is the realm where the alternative to the cosmic will is first imaged, and the autonomy of the human psyche is first evoked.

With all this, however, Schopenhauer remains an elitist in his expectations. Both the imaging and evoking are rare and singular capacities which he does not grant to every subjectivity. In his aesthetic theory, this view makes the creation of art a difficult and exclusive matter – the mysteries of genius – and the apprehension of art only somewhat less so – the restrictiveness of appreciation. While such difficulties reinforce the sceptical cast of Schopenhauer's social views, they also anticipate the antagonisms between artist and audience that characterize romanticism and early modernism.

However, in the later developments of modern art, particularly those which reflect its successes in the post-war years, these antagonisms are eased. The metaphysically victimized artist in Schopenhauer's theory, and the psychically wounded one in Freud's, are transposed into an image of the artist as both existential and social hero.[29] This image reflects the popular belief that the "artist's life" is both a testimonial and a guide to wanted social values. Abetted by the Freudian transfer of creativity into the more manageable realm of psychology, the satisfactions of art-making, now couched in the familiar terms of self-expression, become accessible to larger numbers of people. As part of this transformation, the functional link between creativity and madness is discredited, and the normative dependence of creativity on genius is weakened.

Mapping the historical consequences of this shift is a concern for another study, and I close this one with a few summary observations.[30] When will – creative volition – separates from metaphysical or individual subjectivity and becomes identified with the aesthetic value of collective expression, this generates important new attitudes about practice in the arts: (a) The insights of genius lose their democratic appeal, for these insights would support theories that find subjectivities inherently unequal. (b) Reliance on historical canons of excellence for present artworks diminishes, for these canons only perpetuate the social version of subjective inequality. (c) The view of artistic style as a progression in sensibility is abandoned, for this view stratifies society through its consideration that differences in preference are also normative differences.

All this forces a rethinking of what, by now, has become theoretically suspect: the alliance between subjectivity and art. Such rethinking also challenges, and will perhaps defeat, the influence of both Schopenhauer's and Freud's aesthetic theories on the present period – at least to the extent that they are interpreted as I do here, as theoretical sources of this alliance.

Notes

1 The doctrinal move I attribute to Schopenhauer is the expansion of philosophical concern with art to include the artist's process as well as the artwork. I take Schopenhauer's aesthetic theories to be part of a compressed discussion beginning with Kant and ending with Nietzsche where, despite differences, there is a common concern with both art and the creative process as functional parts of a philosophical system. Schopenhauer's aesthetic writings primarily occur in Book III of each volume of his major work, *WWR*.

2 Immanuel Kant, *Critique of Judgement*, J. H. Bernard, trans. (New York:

Hafner Press, 1951) "Analytic of the Sublime." The designation of genius as "nature's voice" carries with it some general requirements: the products of genius, artworks, must be both novel and exemplary; and while the creativity of genius does not follow extant rules, its procedures nevertheless generate new ones which authenticate its products. However, Kant does not look beyond this at the creative personality. See pp. 151–164.

3 G. W. F. Hegel, *Aesthetics* I, T. M. Knox, trans. (Oxford: Oxford University Press, 1975) "The Beauty of Art or the Ideal." Hegel locates the value of genius in history, not nature, and he gives the artist the insights into "spirit's evolution" that make artworks effective symbols of cultural progress. But, like Kant, Hegel does not elaborate on this capacity. See pp. 280–298.

4 There seem to me two strains here: in Kant, and such others as Schiller and Lessing, the uses of art are directed towards appreciation and its civilizing effects. Here, the opening to beauty is seen as propaedeutic to the capacity for morality. The other strain (which I credit Schopenhauer with instigating) focuses on creativity, self-knowledge, and individual autonomy. It is in this latter strain that the conflict between creativity and social norms is articulated.

5 Schopenhauer's account of the will occurs primarily in the second book of *WWR* 1, 2. He discusses the Platonic Forms through their exemplifications in artworks in Book III, and the question of morality in Book IV.

6 *WWR* 1, Book III, Chs. 33–35.

7 *WWR* 1, 378–398. Schopenhauer gives many examples of the mystic or holy one who escapes the dilemma between action and knowledge through a retreat into contemplation. The artist's condition is less fully documented, perhaps because Schopenhauer had fewer literary models to draw on and depended on his own observations. However, from his discussion of morality and its requirements, it seems clear that Schopenhauer does not include artists among those who have mastered denial of the will.

8 Ibid., 1, p. 192.

9 Ibid., 1, p. 194.

10 Ibid., 1, p. 267.

11 Schopenhauer's much noted pessimism with regard to happiness and accomplishment echoes Kant's thesis that the concept of happiness is indeterminate and cannot be given as an imperative. See Immanuel Kant, *Metaphysics of Morals*, Lewis White Beck, ed. (New York: Library of Liberal Arts, 1990), pp. 34–35.

12 G. W. F. Hegel, *Phenomenology of Mind*, J. B. Baillie, trans. (New York: Harper and Row, 1967). See "Spirit in Self-Estrangement," pp. 507–610.

13 Hegel, *Philosophy of History*, J. Sibree, trans. (London: George Bell and Sons, 1884), pp. 30–39.

14 For a modern analysis of this issue see Theodore Adorno, *Aesthetic Theory* (New York: Routledge and Kegan Paul, 1984), pp. 234–251.

15 The sentiment is attributable to the painter Ad Reinhardt who followed Schopenhauer in his admiration for those schools of Eastern art in which the redoing of ancient forms is the aesthetic virtue of "doing the same old thing," of repeating perfection.

16 Kant, *Metaphysics of Morals* (New York: Macmillan, 1985), pp. 51–2.

17 *WWR* 1, Book III, Ch. 31, p. 32.

18 Freud does not offer an aesthetic theory as such. He identifies the artistic personality with a particularly rich capacity to symbolize (thus sublimate and partially defuse) the psychic origins of neurosis. See Sigmund Freud, "The Relationship of the Poet to Daydreaming," *Collected Papers*, Vol. 4 (London: Hogarth Press, 1934).

19 *WWR* 1, Book II, sections 23, 26; *WWR* 2, Book II, Ch. 23.

20 Sigmund Freud, *The Ego and the Id* (New York: The Norton Library, 1962).

21 Freud, "General theory of the neuroses," in *A General Introduction To Psychoanalysis* (New York: Garden City Publishing Co., 1938), Part III.

22 Ibid., Lectures 20, 21, on Infantile Sexuality.

23 *WWR* 2, 394.

24 *WWR* 2, 395. This image of childhood as paradise is quite compatible with Rousseau's "noble savage" whose pairing of innocence and virtue is contrasted with the veniality and distortions of civilized life. This image is also sharply at odds with the pervasive Victorian one of Freud's time: that of the child as an (ignoble) savage, requiring constraints and discipline from its civilized elders.

25 Sigmund Freud, "Beyond the Pleasure Principle," in *A General Selection From the Works of Sigmund Freud*, ed. John Rickman (New York: Doubleday 1957), p. 148.

26 For a study, within the psychoanalytic tradition, that attempts to disengage creativity from neurosis see Laurence Kubie, *Neurotic Distortion of the Creative Process* (New York: Noonday Press, 1961).

27 For a very different view of the relationships between creativity, sexuality and society, see Herbert Marcuse, *Eros and Civilization* (Boston: Beacon Press, 1955).

28 Sigmund Freud, *Civilization and its Discontents* (New York: Norton 1961), p. 44.

29 This change in the social status of the artist correlates with the post-war valorization of – primarily American – art during the 1950s and 60s.

30 See my discussion of this in *Aesthetic Legacies* (Philadelphia: Temple University Press, 1992), particularly Chs. 7–9.

4

Art as liberation: a central theme of Schopenhauer's philosophy

JOHN E. ATWELL

SCHOPENHAUER AND BUDDHA

In his youth, Schopenhauer accompanied his father and mother on a long trip throughout much of Europe. The extended journey had a powerful, lasting effect on the young man: London, with its teeming masses and 80,000 prostitutes, appalled him; the plight of 6,000 galley prisoners in Toulon horrified him; and the general misery of human life in all of Europe stamped itself on his mind, never to be eradicated. In later years he was to recall:

In my 17th year, without any learned school education, I was gripped by the *misery of life*, as was Buddha in his youth when he looked upon sickness, old age, pain, and death ... and my conclusion was that this world could not be the work of an all-good being, but rather that of a devil who had brought creatures into existence in order to take delight in their suffering; to this the data pointed, and the belief that it is so won the upperhand.[1]

By the time Schopenhauer came to compose his "main work," *The World as Will and Representation* (1814–1818; publication date 1819), he no longer regarded the world as the (causal) work of a devil, but as the (noncausal) manifestation of something just as evil – the nonconscious, insatiable will. Consequently, Schopenhauer inferred, the only "way out" of this world of misery and suffering is the denial of the will (or, as he proceeded to put it, the denial of the will to life).

Recalling the allusion to Buddha, we might divide Schopenhauer's entire philosophy into three main parts: (1) an observation – that animate life is essentially suffering (Buddha's *dukkha*); (2) a diagnosis – that suffering is caused by the will to life (Buddha's *tanha*); and (3) a cure – that cessation of willing life eliminates suffering (Buddha's *nirvana*).[2] For Schopenhauer (departing now from

Buddha's eightfold path), the cure cannot be prescribed to the will: the will (at least as thing-in-itself) is free and self-determining, and (said in direct reference, not to Buddha, but to Kant) "it is indeed a palpable contradiction to call the will free and yet to prescribe for it laws by which it is to will."[3] But the cure (which does occasionally come about) can be described, albeit only negatively, and as such the description amounts to a description of freedom from the will to life and thus, allegedly, from suffering. Freedom, being for Schopenhauer only a negative concept, is therefore "freedom from," which is to say that it is liberation. Liberation (*Befreiung*) has rightly been called "the theme of Schopenhauer's philosophy."[4]

LIBERATION FROM INDIVIDUALITY

Liberation, in the most general formulation, is freedom from the will to life or cessation of the affirmation of the will to life, but this formulation (which Schopenhauer repeats time and time again) tells us very little about liberation in a concrete or specific sense. If we keep in mind, however, that liberation is supposed to be – if not by definition, but at least by (for lack of a better term) "strict inference" – freedom from suffering, and if we recognize, following Schopenhauer, that suffering necessarily depends on the existence of conscious animal and human individuals, we shall come to the inevitable conclusion that liberation is, first and foremost, liberation (freedom) from individuality. (Since the animal is not capable of liberation, it will be set aside in the sequel.) What accounts for individuality in the human being is embodiment: it is the body (*der Leib*) that "roots" the human being in the world[5] – the world subject to the principle of sufficient reason (hence the world of necessity), the world governed by the *principium individuationis* (hence the world of temporally and spatially distinct objects), and finally the world manifesting the will to life in conflict with itself (hence the world of suffering and misery). Consequently, liberation could be characterized as freedom from the body as much as freedom from individuality (and sometimes, particularly in his account of the ascetic, Schopenhauer suggests this very point). Since, however, the body is merely the manifestation of the individual will, that is, the will as localized or particularized in the individual human being, the only way to get free from the body is to get free from the individual will. It is precisely this "getting free" that I shall understand as liberation from individuality. How this liberation is possible and what it involves informs Schopenhauer's discussion of aesthetic contemplation and, more generally, his philosophical account of art. (It also informs his accounts of pity and salvation, but I focus first on the account of aesthetic contemplation; for it is here that he emphasizes the loss of individuality initially.)

With regard to liberation, aesthetic contemplation may be characterized as a "state of mind" (my expression) in which the intellect gets free from the will, but the very possibility of this "state of mind" seems to be precluded by Schopenhauer's contention that the intellect (or knowledge) is originated by the will for the sole purpose of furthering the will's aims and ends. He writes:

> Knowledge in general, rational as well as merely intuitive, proceeds ... originally out of the will itself, belongs to the essence of the higher grades of the will's objectification [i.e., to the essence of animate, and particularly human, beings], as a mere *mēchanē*, a means to the preservation of the individual and the species, just like every organ of the body. Therefore, destined originally to the service of the will, to the accomplishment of its ends, it [knowledge] also remains almost [*fast*] throughout serviceable to it [the will]; so is the case in all animals and in nearly [*beinahe*] all human beings.[6]

Prior to the "advent" of the animal kingdom, Schopenhauer surmises, the will operated in the world merely through causation (in inorganic nature) and stimulation (with the plant kingdom), and that was perfectly sufficient; although natural forces and plant species stood in conflict with each other, there was no consciousness, no error or deception, thus no suffering. But, "with the ever-growing multiplicity of phenomena," the likelihood of acquiring nourishment merely through stimulation became slight, hence the will found it necessary to create (out of itself!) knowledge or intellect: "The will, which hitherto followed its tendency in the dark with extreme certainty and infallibility, has at this state kindled a light for itself."[7] Now movement in consequence of motives and knowledge in general allow the will, in its many individuals, to obtain nourishment from afar, to avoid enemies, and to seek out mates, so that, all in all, animal and human individuals may endure long enough to perpetuate their respective species. "But with this expedient, with this *mēchanē* [with knowledge], the world as representation now stands out at one stroke with all its forms, object and subject, time, space, plurality, and causality." The world is no longer mere will, but also representation. The development of reason in the "complicated," "extremely needy" human being is just a consequence of the will's need to survive.[8]

WHAT LIBERATION INVOLVES

It appears from this (fanciful) story that the intellect could never get free from its maker and master (the will), hence that nothing like aesthetic contemplation could ever occur. But, with the words "almost" and "nearly," in the passage quoted just above, Schopenhauer indicates that the intellect's servitude to the will is not absolute and unremitting, at least not in all human beings all the time. And he holds, of course, that aesthetic contemplation – liberation from the normal mode of knowledge – is an undeniable fact. It is another one of those facts that Schopenhauer fully acknowledges, even when doing so threatens to pose a contradiction to his original and perhaps basic account of things – in this case, his account of the origin of knowledge. What this undeniable fact demands, just as, for example, what genuine compassion and saintliness (also abnormal states) demand, is philosophical interpretation and, so far as possible, elucidation.

In the fulfillment of this particular demand, Schopenhauer introduces the Platonic Ideas and, correlatively, the "*pure*, will-less, painless, timeless *subject of knowledge.*"[9] In aesthetic contemplation the pure subject of knowledge knows Ideas (or "pure objects"), and this requires that individuality in both the subject and the object be set aside. This "setting aside" proceeds only from the subject (the Ideas do not *do* anything), and in this fashion: the subject of knowing severs itself from the subject of willing, and equally it severs itself from the principle of sufficient reason.[10] In virtue of this one, but two-dimensional, severance, the subject of knowing becomes the pure, nonindividual subject of knowing and its objects become the pure, nonindividualized objects of knowing.[11]

Although the severance accomplished by the knowing subject is one thing, namely, loss of individuality, it can be viewed from two standpoints, which means, in effect, that individuality can be understood in two ways. In getting free from the subject of willing, the subject of knowing rids itself of egoistic knowledge; and in getting free from the principle of sufficient reason, it escapes from the body. After reminding us once again that "originally and by its nature, knowledge is completely the servant of the will," Schopenhauer adds that "like the immediate object," that is the body, knowledge is originally "only objectified will."[12] The knowing subject as individual is embodied; its knowledge passes through the body in virtue of sensation; and since the body is the manifestation of the will, all knowledge of the individual knowing subject affects (and in turn is affected by) the will. In other words, the individual knowing subject, being tied to its will, has an interest in its objects: it is concerned with, and only with, the relations that its objects have with each other, and ultimately with their utility for its will. Indeed, Schopenhauer states, "knowledge that serves the will really knows nothing more about objects than their relations," hence "if all these relations were eliminated, the objects also would have disappeared for [this] knowledge, just because it did not recognize in them anything else."[13] It appears then that pure knowledge would be absolutely impossible, for it would have to be knowledge that sidesteps the medium or "the starting point of knowledge," namely, the body. For precisely this reason, pure knowledge has to do away with the principle of sufficient reason, specifically, with the aspect that places the body in a causal relation to known objects. "Therefore," Schopenhauer says, "if the Ideas are to become objects of knowledge, this can happen only by abolition of individuality [*Aufhebung der Individualität*] in the knowing subject."[14] Or, equally, "if it is possible for us to raise ourselves from knowledge of particular things to that of the Ideas, this can happen only by a change taking place in the subject," specifically, the change by which the subject is "no longer individual,"[15] i.e., no longer embodied.

It is at this point that the second dimension of "losing individuality" comes into play: the loss of egoistic knowing, or the severance of the knowing subject from the willing subject. For the most part, Schopenhauer maintains, human beings intuit objects in the world with the frame of mind typified by the egoist's stance: of what use can this object (or person) be to me? Is this object (or person) a likely benefit or a likely hindrance to me in the pursuit of my aims? Such an individual views every thing (and every other person) solely in terms of personal utility; his or her knowledge is wholly subjective, guided throughout by the powerful demands of the individual will; and what this individual intuits is distorted, obscured, and skewed by the will-dominated mode of knowing. In short, then, individuality in the knowing subject is egoistic (or "practical") knowing; and to lose individuality is to eliminate egoistic (or "practical") knowing. It is indeed a most extraordinary thing.

Nevertheless, there will occasionally occur a "transition from the common knowledge of particular things to knowledge of the Idea" – not a transition that comes about slowly and gradually, but one that "happens suddenly."[16] Schopenhauer describes this transition (as he must) more negatively than positively, saying that "knowledge tears itself from the service of the will, precisely by the fact that the subject ceases to be a merely individual one and is now a pure, will-free subject of knowledge, which no longer follows relations in accordance with the principle of sufficient reason, but rather rests in fixed contemplation of the presented object, outside its connection with any other [object], and merges into it." While acknowledging how astonishing one will find this account – until one grasps "the whole thought to be imparted in this work," upon which the astonishment will "disappear of itself" – Schopenhauer proceeds with a battery of statements and references that are truly amazing. He mentions the "power of the mind" (*die Kraft des Geistes*) raising (*heben*) one above the ordinary way of considering things; he says that "one no longer considers the where, the when, the why, and the whither of things, but only the *what*"; he remarks that "one *loses* oneself entirely in this object," that "one forgets one's individuality, one's will, and continues to exist only as pure subject, as clear mirror of the object, so that it is as though the object alone existed without anyone's perceiving it," that "one therefore can no longer separate the intuiter from the intuition, but the two have become one, since the whole consciousness is completely filled and occupied by a single intuitive image."[17] Finally:

When, therefore, the object has to such an extent passed out of all relation to something outside it, and the subject has passed out of all relation to the will, what is thus known is no longer the individual thing as such; rather it is the *Idea*, the eternal form, the immediate objectivity of the will at this grade. Thus at the same time, the one involved in this intuition is no longer an individual, for the individual has lost itself in this intuition; he [*er*] is *pure*, will-less, painless, timeless *subject of knowledge*.[18]

When the object loses all relation to other objects (and thus is released its temporal, spatial, and causal determinations) and the subject loses (or, actually, "has stepped out of") all relation to the will (and thus escapes its normal enslavement), the known object becomes Idea and the knowing subject becomes pure knower – all at once, simultaneously, and correlatively. That is aesthetic contemplation.

It is at the same time a form of freedom: freedom as knowledge. Aesthetic contemplation is freedom from the world of sensible particulars and thus from the individual will (it is freedom from the world as representation subject to the principle of sufficient reason –

hence from time, space, and causality – and thereby freedom from the individual subject of willing), and it is knowledge of the world as Idea (it is knowledge of the "eternal form" of a thing, hence knowledge of the "immediate objectivity of the will at this grade") and it is knowledge or consciousness of oneself as the pure subject of knowledge. Consequently, aesthetic contemplation delivers one from suffering, for it is freedom from the condition of all suffering, namely, individuality. When the individual loses itself in the object, being then unable to separate itself from the object, it becomes, Schopenhauer says, one with the object, hence it does not want anything of the object.[19]

AESTHETIC CONTEMPLATION AS FREEDOM FROM THE INDIVIDUAL WILL

Several questions arise at this point. One, does Schopenhauer really mean to say that in aesthetic contemplation the "pure" subject becomes one with the pure object, the Idea? Surely not, at least not in the strict sense of "becoming one with," that is, in the sense in which the pure subject and the Idea would become indistinguishable. What he may mean is that the pure subject and the Idea become correlative, hence inseparable, that is, one cannot focus or describe the one without necessarily being led to focus on or describe the other. In other words, the term "subject" is elliptical for "subject-of-an-object," and the term "object" is elliptical for "object-of-a-subject."[20] Actually, aesthetic contemplation would not be knowledge if the pure subject and the Idea literally become one, for knowledge presupposes subject on the one side and object on the other – even if the two sides are correlative. On the other hand, in claiming that in contemplation the pure subject and the Idea "become one," Schopenhauer may mean that the in itself (*das An sich*) of the former is strictly identical with the in itself of the latter: both, in themselves or as such (*an sich*), are (one and the same) will. (See next paragraph.) Two, does Schopenhauer hold that in aesthetic contemplation the will totally drops out of the picture? In at least one passage dealing directly with the issue, the proferred answer is yes: "then [when the pure subject of knowing arises and so on] the world as representation alone remains; the world as will has disappeared."[21] But this is not, and cannot be, Schopenhauer's considered position, for in aesthetic contemplation, he holds, the will knows the will. In the passage just quoted, Schopenhauer has

apparently slipped into a consideration, not of aesthetic contemplation, but of something beyond it, namely, saintly resignation or
salvation (*Erlösung*). Three, how can knowledge or the subject of
knowing "tear itself free from the service of the will," when as pure
it is definitionally "will-less"? What can be meant by "the power of
the mind," raising one above "the ordinary way of considering
things"? The latter two questions point up difficulties that can be
resolved only by attributing to Schopenhauer a distinction between
the individual will and the will.

In accord with "the single thought" to be "imparted" in *The World
as Will and Representation*, namely, that "the world is the self-
knowledge of the will,"[22] Schopenhauer maintains that in both
"common knowledge" and aesthetic contemplation, "the will knows
the will." He writes:

> The will is the in itself of the Idea, which completely [*vollkommen*,
> perfectly] objectifies it; it is also the in itself of the particular thing and of the
> individual that knows it, which [two together] objectify it incompletely
> [*unvollkommen*, imperfectly]. As will, outside the representation and all its
> forms, it is one and the same [will] in the contemplated object and in the
> individual, who soaring aloft in this contemplation becomes conscious of
> itself as pure subject; those two [the contemplated object and the pure
> subject] are therefore in themselves not different; for in themselves they are
> the will, which here knows itself, and only in the way and manner that this
> knowledge comes to it [the will], i.e., only in appearance, in virtue of its
> form, of the principle of sufficient reason, is there plurality and difference.[23]

As long as there is knowledge, there is will: with "subjective"
knowledge, the individual subject of knowing (in the service of the
individual will) knows particular objects (in accord with the full
principle of sufficient reason); with "objective" knowledge, the pure
subject of knowing (freed from the individual will) knows "pure"
objects or Ideas (freed from the subordinate forms of the principle of
sufficient reason, namely, time, space, and causality, but not freed
from "objectness" or "objectity"). Hence, in both "subjective" and
"objective" knowledge, the will knows the will – "inadequately" in
the former case and "adequately" in the latter (to use Schopenhauer's terminology).[24]

It cannot be true, therefore, that in aesthetic contemplation "the
world as will has disappeared" or the will has vanished; for in
aesthetic contemplation the will knows the will, not however as
particular objects – and certainly not as the will in itself (since the
will as thing-in-itself is never object)[25] – but as "immediate objectity

of the will," that is, as Idea or "pure" representation. Nor has the will vanished from the pure subject of knowing, for it is the in itself of the pure subject as much as the in itself of the Idea; otherwise it could not be the case that in aesthetic contemplation the will knows the will. Everything involved in knowledge – whether "subjective" or "objective" – is at bottom will, including the individual subject and its objects, and the pure subject and its objects. So, again, as long as there is knowledge, there is will. And if will should ever vanish or disappear, in every form and in every way, there would be no knowledge at all. But something of will does vanish or disappear in aesthetic contemplation, namely, the individual will (and everything essential to knowledge conjoined to the individual will). Consequently, given the fact of aesthetic contemplation, we have to distinguish the individual will – from which there is liberation – from the will – which remains.

There is another, and extremely important, reason why will cannot totally disappear from that form of knowledge called aesthetic contemplation: it is necessary for the subject of knowing's act of emancipating itself from the subject of willing. In this emancipation (or even "slave revolt") the subject of knowing "tears itself free from" the individual will, and thereby asserts its inherent freedom – a freedom that it has as such, but which can be asserted only by calling upon what it (and everything else) is in itself, namely, will. In the individual the subject of knowing is tied (through "identity," Schopenhauer says in the dissertation)[26] to the subject of willing, but in itself or as such it is free. And it asserts its inherent freedom by ridding itself of individuality, thereby breaking its "tie" to the subject of willing.

Inherent freedom can be attributed to the subject of knowing on two grounds, one stemming from "representation theory" and the other deriving from "metaphysics." The first is that the subject of knowing does not belong to the world governed by the principle of sufficient reason, hence it is not as such subject to the law of causality, indeed, it is not in time.[27] It is free from "the world," and as long as it remains true to its very nature, as it were, it simply knows "the world" – immune to every trace of servitude, compulsion, and determination.[28] That the subject of knowing as such does not belong to the world governed by the principle of sufficient reason constitutes the "theoretical possibility" of its "actual" release from the subject of willing, to which it is "tied" in the individual. But for this release (liberation, emancipation) to come about "in reality," activity or power (what Schopenhauer calls "the power of the mind") is required. Accordingly, the second ground for attributing freedom to the subject of knowing is that this subject is in itself, "metaphysically," will, which is to say that in itself it is absolutely free. Drawing on what it is in itself (will), it asserts what it is as such (the pure subject of knowing) – free from all individuality, and all that belongs essentially to individuality, including the world governed by the principle of sufficient reason in the forms of time, space, and causality, excluding only the form of subject and object. This is precisely what happens upon aesthetic contemplation. The pure subject of knowing knows every object as a grade of the will's objectification, as Idea, and it is conscious of itself as in itself that very same will. In aesthetic contemplation, then, the will knows the will; therein, too, there arises the clearest, most distinct instance of what the world is, "the self-knowledge of the will." Only because contemplation amounts to the will's knowing itself does saintly resignation – the elimination of the will – become possible, as we shall now see.

Freedom, in Schopenhauer's thought, may take (at least) two radically different forms: freedom as pure knowing (found in aesthetic contemplation) and freedom as resignation (found in, say, saintliness). Both are freedom from the will, but the former is freedom from the individual will, and the latter is freedom from the will altogether (or, as Schopenhauer sometimes says, almost altogether). To make this point clear, I return to book two of *WWR*, just following the passage in which Schopenhauer refers to knowledge's original and normal, but not absolute, servitude to the will. He writes there:

> However, we shall see in the third book how, in particular persons, knowledge can withdraw from this servitude, throw off [*abwerfen*] its yoke, and, free from all ends of willing, exist [*bestehen*] purely for itself, as mere, clear mirror of the world – out of which art proceeds. Finally, [we shall see] in the fourth book how, through this kind of knowledge, if it reacts on the will, the self-elimination of the same [the will], i.e., resignation, can occur – which is the ultimate goal, indeed, the innermost essence of all virtue and holiness, and salvation from the world.[29]

This implies that knowledge "out of which art proceeds," namely, aesthetic contemplation, need not "react on the will" and then result in the self-elimination of the will, in resignation. Although knowledge can, and in aesthetic contemplation does, get "free from all ends of willing" (hence, I would say, free from the individual will), that does not amount to, but only prepares the way for, resignation. In other words, aesthetic contemplation is one kind of freedom, namely, freedom from the individual will, and resignation is another kind of freedom, namely, freedom from the will altogether – even if in some general way both are freedom from the will to life, and therefore (allegedly) from suffering.

One might assume that aesthetic contemplation – occurring when knowledge withdraws from servitude to the will, throws off its yoke, and becomes "free from all ends of willing" – is a temporary state of which self-elimination of the will or resignation is an enduring state. Viewed from the standpoint of escape from suffering, this assumption is eminently reasonable: the aesthetic contemplator gets free from suffering momentarily (just as long as contemplation lasts, which is usually not very long), but, say, the saint gets free from suffering enduringly (remaining, quite exceptionally, in contemplation over a long period, perhaps forever); hence, apart from length of time, the two do not differ. On the other hand, from the standpoint of knowledge, the "state" of the aesthetic contemplator differs in kind, and not just in time, from the "state" of the saint: in the former, the will knows the will; whereas in the latter, the will has vanished, along with all knowledge.[30] Although aesthetic contemplation is liberation from suffering (temporarily), it is not devoid of knowledge; indeed, in one of its most poignant instances, it is knowledge of the Idea of life as essentially suffering. Saintly resignation begins with knowledge of the Idea of life, which knowledge then "occasions" the saint's withdrawal from the will, from life, from the world, hence from even knowledge of the Idea of life. I suggest then that contemplation is liberation from the individual will but not from will altogether (else contemplation would not be knowledge in which the will knows itself), while saintly resignation is liberation from the will altogether (thus from every trace of knowledge). This suggestion relies on the distinction urged above between the individual will and the will. It is, I fear, a distinction that will find resistance; so I want to show that it, or something very much like it, figures necessarily in Schopenhauer's account of moral virtue, which is denominated *Mitleid* (pity or compassion).

The pitying agent (*der Mitleidende*) denies or renounces the will to life as belonging exclusively to himself or herself (he or she abandons egoism, the normal incentive for human beings), and, seeing through the *principium individuationis*, "identifies" with the will to life in other animate, suffering creatures. For the pitying agent, any known suffering is taken on as his or her suffering, hence he or she works toward eliminating it wherever it occurs. This agent therefore renounces only the individual will (specifically, the ego-istic will), not the will *in toto*; he or she continues to affirm life as such, for which reason he or she continues to suffer – as the very term *der Mitleidende* ("co-sufferer") indicates. Only by a further step does the pitying agent pass into complete denial of the will, and that is the step "occasioned" by the recognition that suffering, belonging essentially to life, cannot be eliminated from life; in short, that final step, akin to if not identical with resignation, is indifference (*Gleich-gültigkeit*).[31] Equally, I suggest, only by a further step does the aesthetic contemplator reach the "state" of saintly resignation. With that final step, all suffering and all knowledge, strictly speaking, cease – including even knowledge of the Idea of life as suffering.[32] Taking into consideration Schopenhauer's accounts of common knowledge, aesthetic contemplation, moral virtue, and saintly resig-nation, we see the necessity of attributing to him the distinction between the individual will and the will.

THE GENIUS VERSUS THE SAINT

Taking into consideration some of Schopenhauer's remarks on suffering compels us to acknowledge the same distinction. All animate beings – essentially, if not incessantly – suffer. The lower animals suffer the least, higher animals suffer more, and the highest animal – the genius – suffers most. "The person in whom genius is to be found," Schopenhauer asserts, "suffers most of all."[33] When coupled with the claim that in aesthetic contemplation – that state of objectivity attributable to the genius – the individual subject becomes the "*pure*, will-less, painless, timeless *subject of knowl-edge*," there results what may be called the "paradox of the suffering genius": the characteristic state of the genius (objectivity) is immu-nity to suffering, yet the genius suffers most of all.[34] By way of resolving this paradox, one might urge that it is the person "in whom genius is to be found" who suffers immensely, not the genius per se, in other words, that this person suffers, not because of his genius, but because of other factors, for example, his loneliness, his aliena-tion from society, his ineptitude in practical matters (so that he often appears mad), his devotion to the eternal while living in the finite, his great need for but often lack of leisure, and so on.[35] In short, the attempted resolution goes, the person in whom genius appears does not suffer from his genius. Though plausible, indeed though reflecting perhaps a part of Schopenhauer's view on the matter, this suggestion does not do full justice to the crucial fact, also urged by Schopenhauer, that this person would not suffer "most of all" unless he reached aesthetic contemplation (with its serenity, delight, and pleasure) and then voluntarily abandoned that highly felicific state.

At the very end of section 55 (*WWR*, I) Schopenhauer repeats his metaphysical thesis that "the will in all its appearance is subject to necessity, while in itself it can be called free and even omnipotent."[36] Then, at the very beginning of section 56, he continues (partly in my paraphrase) thus: this freedom and omnipotence of the will, which has been lost in "all its appearance," "can now express itself anew," and indeed precisely "where, in its most perfect appearance [ultimately in the genius], the completely adequate knowledge of its own essence has dawned on it."[37] Now, freedom of the will in the genius faces two alternatives: "either it also wills here, at the summit of reflectiveness and self-consciousness, the same thing that it willed blindly and without knowing itself ... or, conversely, this knowledge becomes for it a *quieter*, which silences and eliminates all willing."[38] The genius, through his extraordinary insight into the fact that life (including his own life) is essentially suffering, reaches the point at which the great question of life stands out most vividly – whether to affirm life or deny it – and he chooses to affirm life, knowing full well what his choice involves.[39] Not unlike the Bodhisattva in Buddhism or the universal pitying agent, but unlike the saintly resignator, the genius chooses to participate in the world of suffering and misery (for which he is then fully responsible), sacrificing himself, as it were, for the good of humankind by creating artworks that facilitate apprehension of the Platonic Ideas by others and that, equally, offer others the now-and-again consolation of aesthetic serenity. (None of this will probably occur to the artistic genius, however.)

The paradox of the suffering genius and what differentiates him from the saint receive further elaboration in the final paragraph of section 52, the final section of Book III. There Schopenhauer refers to "the enjoyment of everything beautiful, the consolation afforded by art, the enthusiasm of the artist, which allows him to forget the cares of life," and he claims that this gives the genius the one advantage over others, "compensating him for the suffering that is heightened in proportion to the clearness of consciousness, and for the desert loneliness among a different race of men."[40] The suffering of the genius, as that of anyone involved in life, is due (ultimately) to the fact that "the in itself of life, the will, existence itself is a constant suffering and in part miserable, in part frightful." On the other hand, in reference now only to the genius, the very same thing, "as representation, purely intuited, or repeated through art, free from torment, affords a significant spectacle." The artistic genius becomes so enthralled with the great spectacle of life and existence, which is actually "the objectification of the will," that "he sticks to it, does not get tired of contemplating it, and of continuing to present it [in his works]." But "he himself bears the cost of producing the play, he himself is the will objectifying itself and remaining in constant suffering."

> That pure, true, and profound knowledge of the essence of the world now becomes for him an end in itself; at it he stops. Therefore it [this knowledge] does not become for him a quieter of the will, as ... in the case of the saint who has attained resignation; it does not deliver him from life forever, but only for a few moments. For him it is not the way out of life, but only occasionally a consolation in it ...[41]

The genius experiences only an occasional consolation (*Trost*) in life; he does not, like the saint, attain liberation from life "forever" (*auf immer*); so the genius remains wedded to the will, through his never-tiring contemplation and then repetition of its objectification (life and existence), while the saint renounces the will in the mode of resignation.

THE ACTIVITY OF AESTHETIC CONTEMPLATION

What we have just surveyed provides support for, and explanation of, a number of definite conclusions. First, both the artistic genius and the saint possess that "objectivity of mind" uniquely characteristic of aesthetic contemplation, hence on this preliminary score both possess genius. This quality, significantly, is not voluntarily acquired; it is inborn rather than chosen; consequently, aesthetic contemplation comes over one. What distinguishes the artistic genius from the saint in Schopenhauer's account is the voluntary decision – upon but beyond genius considered as "objectivity of mind" – to remain "in life" (which the artistic genius chooses) or to pass "out of life" (which the saint chooses). Second, the fact that aesthetic contemplation on the part of the artistic genius is typically short term and resignation on the part of the saint is long term (or

94

even "forever") is explained by the fact that in the former case the will has not been abolished while in the latter case it has been abolished. When the will is not abolished, it continues to reassert itself (and regain dominance over the intellect); but when the will has been abolished, it cannot reassert itself. Unlike the intellect, the will never weakens or tires; so as long as it is not abolished, it will persist in demanding its "original and normal" domination over the intellect. Third, the crucial, essential difference between aesthetic contemplation and saintly resignation concerns knowledge: in the former state, the subject of knowing, now pure, knows the grades of the objectification of the will, the Ideas; and in the latter state, knowledge ceases in consequence of the abolition of the will, hence, it may be said, the saint knows nothing (*nirvana*), not even the Ideas.[42]

The above three conclusions appear to be perfectly warranted, but two further contentions, specifically, about aesthetic contemplation, will probably not go unchallenged: (1) Contemplation dispenses with the individual will, but not with the will altogether; and (2) in contemplation the subject of knowing "tears itself away from" the subject of willing, thereby becoming pure, in virtue of a power that it has "in itself," namely, the power of will. The first contention has been defended chiefly on the ground that in contemplation the will knows the will, which is the underlying version of "the pure subject knows the Idea"; alternatively, the in itself of the subject knows, and is identical with, the in itself of the Ideas, and that is will. Since the individual will disappears upon aesthetic contemplation, yet the will remains (quite unlike saintly resignation), there must be a distinction between the individual will and the will. The second contention takes its start from the fact that Schopenhauer uses so many active terms in characterizing the subject of knowing's liberation from the subject of willing. (These terms, occurring mainly in section 34, have been cited above, but the most important ones may be repeated here: *sich losreißen; in fester Kontemplation; die Kraft des Geistes; die ganze Macht seines Geistes; sich ganz in diese Anschauung versenken; sich gänzlich in diesen Gegenstand verlieren; das Subjekt ist aus aller Relation zum Willen getreten; das Individuum hat sich eben in solche Anschauung verloren*; and so on.)[43] Since this activity cannot belong to the individual will, which has been overcome, it must belong either to the subject of knowing or to the will; I suggest that it belongs to the in itself of the subject of knowing, which is the will.

Largely in accord with this suggestion, though couched in rather different terms, Malter writes:

> In [aesthetic contemplation] the subject [of knowing], which ordinarily stands passively over against the determination of its objects, becomes active. It "tears itself loose" from its relationship to the *single* thing, which encounters it in intuition; it acts thereby not in the sense that it changes something in the thing, rather it is acting in that it ignores the singleness of the thing and "loses" itself completely in the opposite matter.[44]

Later Malter remarks that "in aesthetic contemplation there occurs a liberation of the subject by the subject."[45] I would simply add that what gives the subject of knowing the power to liberate itself from the (individual) will is what it is in itself, namely, the will.

INTUITION OF IDEAS

Until Schopenhauer comes to discuss in some detail the intuition of Ideas (in section 35 of Book III) and the nature of the genius (in section 36), he tends to suggest that aesthetic contemplation occurs upon "simply" intuiting a natural object, that is, upon intuiting it "will-lessly." Indeed, he talks as if intuiting an object without the slightest trace of wanting it, fearing it, using it, and so on amounts to intuiting the Idea of the object. Accordingly, sheer indifference to the object brings out, as it were, its Idea. But in sections 35 and 36 Schopenhauer makes clear that this is not his actual position. Not only does he hold, as noted above, that intuiting anything "will-lessly" requires active liberation on the part of the knowing subject whereby it "tears itself away" from the individual will, he also holds that intuiting the Idea of a natural object (for example, the cloud, water, the crystal, humanity, which appear in various and sundry individual forms) requires rapt attention to the object's essential features and dismissal of its inessential features. Moreover, Schopenhauer maintains, aesthetic contemplation requires imagination (*Phantasie*), that quality coupled with pure objectivity making up the genius. Anyone capable of aesthetic contemplation has to possess some degree of imagination, hence will-less or objective knowledge by itself is not sufficient to bring out an object's Idea. Why the genius needs imagination in addition to objectivity is rather easy to see. First, the genius is a person who, as such, has only a limited range of knowledge of things, yet the Ideas extend beyond actual knowledge into "the realm of possibility";[46] consequently, he must, through imagination, reach out beyond personal experience and "construct" (*konstruiren*) Ideas, not every dimension of which he has ever experienced. The genius must somehow "create" the Idea or essence of the type of object that he otherwise views "objectively"; without this construction or creation the relevant Idea will not pass before his "clear eye of the world." Second, since "the actual objects are almost always only very imperfect copies of the Idea that manifests itself in them," "the man of genius requires imagination in order to see in things not what nature has actually formed, but what she endeavored to form, yet did not bring about because of the conflict of her forms with one another."[47]

Imagination is an active faculty. Although it, by itself, is not sufficient for genius, when conjoined with pure objectivity (hence with displacement of the individual will), we have the genius.[48] It follows that imagination in the genius, that is, imagination in conjunction with objectivity, cannot derive from the individual will; but since it is active, it must derive from the will in some way. Genius, then, is a power, not of individuals, but a power that comes over certain individuals (those called geniuses) now and again.

Now this is by no means the case at every moment of their lives, for the great though spontaneous exertion [*die große, wiewohl spontane Anspannung*] required for the will-free apprehension of the Ideas necessarily relaxes again ... On this account, the action of genius [*das Wirken des Genius*] has always been regarded as an inspiration ... as the action of a superhuman being different from the individual himself, which takes possession of him only periodically.[49]

Genius, in other words, is a power of the (human, or even super-human) will, by means of which the will (the in itself of the pure subject of knowing) knows the will (objectified in the Ideas). Apprehension of the Ideas is "will-free" only in the sense of being free from the individual will, and thus not in the sense of being free from the will. Genius is as much a manifestation of the will as anything else (except, possibly, the absolute saint or mystic, who totally escapes the will), indeed, it is the highest manifestation of the will. In aesthetic contemplation the genius gets free from the individual will, in virtue of this objectivity; and he sees in individual objects more than they present, in virtue of his imagination – both objectivity and imagination being highly active powers.

It is well to remember that aesthetic contemplation is apprehension of Ideas, for which activity on the part of the apprehender is required, and upon which pleasure (enjoyment, well-being) comes about. Pleasure, of course, is a feeling; and in Schopenhauer's first account it is the feeling produced by contemplation of the beautiful, that is, of Ideas themselves or of objects (natural or created) that facilitate apprehension of Ideas. Sometimes aesthetic pleasure regarding the beautiful derives chiefly from the contemplated Ideas (as, for example, in historical painting, sculpture, and poetry [*Dichtung*]), sometimes chiefly from the peaceful, "will-free" contemplation itself (as, for example, with inorganic things, plants, and – very differently, it would seem – architecture), but usually from both sides.[50] Following this discussion, Schopenhauer turns to aesthetic pleasure taken in the sublime; accordingly, he makes a highly significant distinction between the feeling of the beautiful and the feeling of the sublime, both of which belong to the subjective side of aesthetic pleasure. (On the objective side of both feelings, there are the Ideas, which as such or strictly speaking do not account for the distinction between the two feelings themselves.)

THE SUBLIME

The feeling of the sublime arises, to start with, when the objects that invite a pure contemplation of them – and which, then, incite the feeling of the beautiful by facilitating apprehension of their Ideas – "have a hostile relation to the human will in general, as manifested in its objectity, the human body."[51] The beholder does not view these objects as a threat to his own individual will (that would be fear or anxiety, which destroys contemplation), but as a threat to "the human will in general." Hence

although perceiving and acknowledging [this hostile relation to his will], he with consciousness turns away from it, forcibly tears himself from his will and its relations, and, giving himself up entirely to knowledge, quietly contemplates, as pure, will-less subject of knowing, those very objects so terrible to the will.[52]

So long as the beholder continues to contemplate their Idea, he is elevated "above himself, his person, his willing, and all willing"; and precisely then "he is filled with the feeling of the *sublime*, he is in a state of exaltation, and therefore the object occasioning such a state is also called *sublime*."[53] The beholder gets free from "all willing," he raises himself up above himself and thereby becomes an objective contemplator, but he is fully aware of the threat posed by the hostile objects – to the (human) will; most assuredly, then, the (human) will has not vanished from, indeed, it is essential for, the feeling of the sublime.[54]

It seems, however, that with the feeling of the beautiful every trace of consciousness of the will has vanished, indeed, Schopenhauer continues:

> What therefore distinguishes the feeling of the sublime from that of the beautiful is this: with the beautiful, pure knowing has won the upperhand without struggle, since the beauty of the object, i.e., its quality facilitating the knowledge of its Idea, removed from consciousness, without resistance and hence imperceptibly, the will and the knowledge of relations slaving in its service; and this same consciousness remains over as pure subject of knowing, so that not even a recollection of the will remains; on the other hand, with the sublime, that state of pure knowing is first of all obtained by a conscious and violent tearing away from the, recognized as unfavorable, relations of the same object to the will, by a free exaltation, accompanied by consciousness, beyond the will and the knowledge relating to it.[55]

In discussing the sublime Schopenhauer appeals to a distinction between the individual will (one's own will) and the human will: he remarks just below the passage just quoted that the exaltation found in or making up the feeling of the sublime must be "won with consciousness" and also maintained, so it is "accompanied by a constant recollection of the will, yet not of a single individual willing, such as fear or wish, but of human willing in general"; and in the next two sentences he notes that "the peace of contemplation," necessary for the sublime, would be lost if "the actually moved individual will" were to gain the upperhand. Both the feeling of the beautiful and the feeling of the sublime involve contemplation of Ideas, release from the individual will, freedom from the principle of sufficient reason, and so on. "The feeling of the sublime is distinguished from that of the beautiful only by the addition, namely the exaltation beyond the known hostile relation of the contemplated object to the will in general."[56] But, although the sublime calls for activity on the part of the contemplator of Ideas, the beautiful apparently does not; and although the sublime dispenses with the individual will, it does not dispense with "human willing in general." Significantly, then, Schopenhauer suggests here that contemplation of Ideas as beautiful is perfectly passive, while he grants that contemplation of Ideas as sublime involves the addition of activity.

Since the feeling of the beautiful occurs only upon contemplation of Ideas, and since contemplation of Ideas occurs only upon the subject of knowing's "tearing itself away from" the individual will and the world of objects subject to the principle of sufficient reason, the feeling of the beautiful occurs only upon the subject of knowing's activity. The person in whom this activity takes place will not be conscious of it; he will certainly not bring it about voluntarily or intentionally; in fact, it is not the person's activity, but rather that of the subject of knowing in virtue of what it is in itself (namely, will); but, after all of this is said, contemplation of Ideas cannot take place without activity. If Schopenhauer denies this conclusion when he comes to distinguish the feeling of the beautiful from the feeling of the sublime, he simply contradicts what he has claimed earlier. He does not contradict himself, however, if he holds that the feeling of the sublime involves an activity beyond that figuring in the feeling of the beautiful. And there is no reason why he cannot hold this very position.[57]

The fundamental feature of the feeling of the sublime is precisely that whereby it goes beyond the feeling of the beautiful, and that is "the exaltation [*Erhebung*] beyond the known hostile relation of the contemplated object to the will in general."[58] This exaltation is free and it is accompanied by consciousness or "a constant recollection" of "human willing in general." (This does not mean, however, that the will disappears from the feeling of the beautiful or from recognition of beauty, but only that consciousness of the will disappears.)[59] What exaltation involves is a twofold, highly contrastive self-realization: that "as individual, as feeble appearance of the will," one feels vulnerable to the awesome powers of nature and no more significant in the vast universe than a single drop of water in the ocean, yet that "as the eternal, serene subject of knowing," one feels oneself to be "the condition of all objects, even the bearer of this whole world."[60] Hence, "our dependence on [the world] is now annulled by its dependence on us," and one reaches "a consciousness, merely felt, that in some sense or other (made clear only by philosophy) one is one with the world, and is therefore not oppressed but exalted by its immensity."[61] The feeling of the sublime "arises through the contrast between the insignificance and dependence of ourselves as individuals, as appearance of the will, and consciousness of ourselves as pure subject of knowing."[62]

TRAGEDY

Schopenhauer believes that the feeling of the sublime is aroused not only by contemplating the hostile, threatening aspects of nature, but also by experiencing "the summit of poetic art," the tragedy (*der Trauerspiel*).[63] He does not literally express this belief in volume one of *WWR*, but he does do so in volume two[64] and in a note written in 1815.[65] In volume one Schopenhauer states that "the purpose of this highest poetical achievement is the description of the terrible side of life,"[66] and indeed that "the presentation of a great misfortune is alone essential to tragedy."[67] Such presentation can be produced in three basic ways: through "extraordinary wickedness of a character" (as Iago in *Othello*), through "blind fate, i.e., chance or error" (as in *King Oedipus*), and through "the mere attitude [*Stellung*, position] of persons to one another through their relations."[68] Schopenhauer, as one might expect, prefers the third kind of presentation, on the ground that it shows great misfortune to be, in a word, normal – hence something that could happen to any of us and be occasioned by actions that any of us might well perform.[69]

Tragedy, according to Schopenhauer, has a definite metaphysical significance. It portrays, if only as a hint, "the nature of the world and of existence"; it reveals "the antagonism of the will with itself"; and it shows, at least in its highest presentation, "one and the same will, living and appearing in [all human individuals], whose appearances fight with one another and tear one another to pieces." Now and again, however, this will is brought to "thoughtfulness" (*Besinnung*) and "softened by the light of knowledge, until finally, in single cases, this knowledge, purified and heightened by suffering itself, reaches the point where appearance, the veil of Maya, no longer deceives it."[70] In short, the will comes to know itself as the one and same will in all appearances. With this self-knowledge, the *principium individuationis* is seen through, egoism expires (*ersterben*), the normally so powerful motives of action lose their force, and "instead of them the complete knowledge of the essence of the world, acting as a *quieter* of the will, produces resignation, the giving up not merely of life, but of the whole will to life itself."[71]

With regard to resignation Schopenhauer proposes in volume two of *WWR* a new classification of tragedies: those in which the tragic hero turns away from the will to life, harboring no additional emotions or sentiments, and those in which the tragic character reaches resignation, joined however with other feelings. In his judgment, modern tragedies fall into the former class (as with Gretchen in Goethe's *Faust*), and ancient ones fall into the latter class (as with Cassandra in *Agamemnon*, who still feels revenge, and with Iphigenia in *Iphigenia at Aulis*, who evinces patriotism).[72] On this ground Schopenhauer prefers modern tragedy to ancient tragedy.[73] In both cases, however, there is an invitation to resignation; and although the tragic hero may not actually reach that state, the suffering he or she experiences invites the spectator to do so.

Thus the summons to turn away the will from life remains the true tendency of tragedy, the ultimate purpose of the intentional presentation of the sufferings of mankind; consequently it exists even where this resigned exaltation of the mind is not shown in the hero himself, but is only stimulated in the spectator at the sight of great unmerited, or indeed even merited, suffering.[74]

When "this resigned exaltation of the mind" (*diese resignirte Erhebung des Geistes*) is aroused in the spectator, Schopenhauer maintains, we have what is called "pleasure in the *tragedy*," which belongs, not to the feeling of the beautiful, but to the feeling of the sublime.[75]

Schopenhauer has to admit, however, that *this* feeling of the sublime differs widely from the feeling of the sublime occasioned by contemplating those aspects of nonhuman nature standing in a hostile relation to "human willing in general." And in fact he does admit this, saying that "at the sight of the sublime in nature we turn away from the interest of the will, in order to behave [*verhalten*] in a purely intuitive way," while "in the tragic catastrophe we turn away from the will to life itself."[76] In other words, the feeling of the sublime regarding nature reaches only a state of contemplation and indeed one in which consciousness of the human will is not lost, but the feeling of the sublime regarding tragedy (at least when tragedy achieves its ultimate purpose) reaches a state, beyond contemplation, in which full resignation comes about. It follows, I suggest, that "resigned exaltation" is self-contradictory: exaltation comes only with contemplation, and resignation goes beyond contemplation; the former may lead to but it does not join with resignation, hence there is only contemplative and not resigned exaltation.

THE INEXPLICABILITY OF SALVATION

Our discussion of Schopenhauer on tragedy has led us to the utmost limit of his entire philosophy: salvation (resignation, denial of the will to life, self-elimination of the will) and consequently complete liberation from suffering. We have seen that tragedy, like philosophy and life itself, can bring one to the threshold of salvation, but we have not "seen" what that "state" consists of. Perhaps quite naturally, we seek further information: we want to know the exact nature of this "state"; we want to know whether it exceeds every conceivable vestige of will; we enjoin Schopenhauer to tell us whether salvation involves a totally new kind of knowledge and a totally new mode of existence, and if so what they could be. Schopenhauer insists, however, that we are demanding of him something that he cannot possibly deliver: he cannot, as a philosopher, provide a positive description of salvation – for, as he often says, that would be to become "transcendent," which has no legitimate place in philosophy.[77] If we nevertheless attribute to the saint some sort of knowledge and some sort of will – as perhaps we, given our point of view, must – we shall have to say that he or she "knows" that life as we know it is "a bad dream from which we have to awake,"[78] and that he or she has come to "will something better."[79] Aesthetic contemplation, and particularly a sensitive reaction to tragedy, can serve as a means to this Buddha-like awakening – but thereof we must be silent.

Notes

1   *HN* 4, Cholera Book, paragraph 36. The impetus to do philosophy, Schopenhauer often says, derives from life, not books.

2   On Buddhism, see Huston Smith, *The Religion of Man* (New York: Harper & Row, Harper Colophon Books, 1964), Ch. III. "*Tanha*," Smith remarks (p. 101) "is a specific kind of desire, the desire to pull apart from the rest of life and seek fulfillment through those bottled-up segments of being we call our selves." It may be that Schopenhauer understands the will to life in very much the same way, as a sort of individual or even selfish willing.

3   *WWR* 1, 262; also *HN* 1, paragraph 591. It is pretty obvious that Kant and Schopenhauer have different notions of the will (*Wille*).

4   Rudolf Malter, *Der eine Gedanke: Hinführung zur Philosophie Arthur Schopenhauers* (Darmstadt: Wissenschaftliche Buchgesellschaft, 1988), p. 67. It will be noticed that I rely heavily on this marvelous little book.

5   *WWR* 1, 99.

6   Ibid., 152; see also 176.

7   Ibid., 150.

8   Ibid., 151.

9   Ibid., 179; see also *WWR* 1, 195, 199.

10 Malter notes that these two severances are "synonymous" (*gleichbedeutend*); see his *Der eine Gedanke*, p. 67.

11 At *WWR* 1, 169, Schopenhauer calls the principle of sufficient reason "the ultimate principle of all finiteness, of all individuation."

12 Ibid., 176.

13 Ibid., 177. For this reason individual objects, unlike the Ideas, can be said not to exist as much as exist. On this score Schopenhauer believes himself to be repeating Plato's position.

14 Ibid., 169.

15 Ibid., 176.

16 Ibid., 178. This transition also happens involuntarily or unintentionally. It comes about, one does not bring it about. This is not to say, however, that "knowledge" is inactive in coming to know the Idea – as the following remarks clearly show.

17 *WWR* 1, 178–179.

18 Ibid., 179. Note Schopenhauer's shift from "one" (*man*) and "the one" (*der*) to "he" (*er*).

19 Schopenhauer apparently holds then that willing presupposes a separation between the willer and what is willed, and that when that separation is closed, willing ceases; see *WWR* 1, 199.

20 For this view, see the early sections of *WWR* 1, where Schopenhauer puts forth his "representation theory."

21 Ibid., 199.

22 See Ibid., xii (preface to the first edition); Ibid., 410; and *HN* 1, paragraph 662. This is the thought Malter has in mind in his *Der eine Gendanke*; see p. ix.

23 *WWR* 1, 180; see also 274–275. Much of Schopenhauer's metaphysics can be summed up in the proposition that the world as representation (whether as individual objects or as Ideas) is that whereby the will comes to know itself – so that, I would add, it may then eliminate itself.

24 The will knows itself "adequately" when it knows its various "grades" or "levels" (*Stufen*) merely as objects (these are the Ideas); and the will knows itself "inadequately" when it knows those "grades" as broken up into temporally, spatially, and causally determined objects (these are, say, perceptual particulars).

25 See, e.g., *WWR* 1, 128, 174.

26 See *FFR*, section 42. This second edition was published in 1847, and it greatly enlarges the dissertation of 1813. Unfortunately, many critics cite the second edition, but give its date as 1813.

27 See book one of *WWR* 1, and also *HN* 1, paragraphs 436, 593.

28 See Malter, *Der eine Gedanke*, p. 61.

29 *WWR* 1, 152. Artists can demonstrate resignation (*WWR* 1, 232–233), but they don't do it (*WWR* 1, 267).

30 See James D. Chansky, "Schopenhauer and Platonic Ideas: A Groundwork for an Aesthetic Metaphysics," in Eric von der Luft (ed.), *Schopenhauer: New Essays in Honor of his 200th Birthday* (Lewiston, NY: The Edwin Mellen Press, 1988), p. 77, n. 11: "... the aims of aesthetics and of asceticism are not merely different but really quite opposed. The former forgets its own willing precisely in order to perceive the will's visibility more clearly, while the latter goes further and does not just forget but

aims to annihilate the will *along with its objectification*. Asceticism, then, is not at all left with the world as representation in any sense, but rather, is left precisely with *nothing*: Without the perceiver, there is no world; without the world, no perceiver; no will, no representation." While Chansky refers to asceticism (as indeed Schopenhauer does, particularly in Book 4), I refer to saintliness (as Schopenhauer does in earlier books). I am just not convinced that the ascetic, as usually described – in his or her efforts to punish the body – has reached the state of saintly resignation. Actually, I think, Schopenhauer is far from clear on the matter.

31 See in particular sections 66–68 of *WWR* 1.
32 See *WWR* 1, 410: "Such a state cannot really be called knowledge, since it no longer has the form of subject and object . . ."
33 *WWR* 1, 310.
34 It might be claimed, however, that the universal pitier suffers most of all, but possibly he or she is reckoned as a sort of genius – at least in the sense of penetrating the *principium individuationis*. I shall ignore this complication.
35 See *WWR* 1, 190–191, and especially Ch. XXXI in *WWR* 2 ("On Genius").
36 *WWR* 1, 307.
37 Ibid.
38 *WWR* 1, 307–308.
39 Compare *WWR* 1, 184: "In this world of appearance, true loss is as little possible as true gain. The will alone is; it is the thing in itself, it is the source of all those appearances. Its self-knowledge and, based on this, its affirmation or denial decided on, is the sole event in itself."
40 *WWR* 1, 267.
41 Ibid. See also *HN* 1, paragraphs 420, 682 and note.
42 See also *HN* 1, paragraphs 96, 234, 250, 253, 337, 593. Incidentally, if any knowledge can be ascribed to the saint (and Schopenhauer suggests that it can, at *WWR* 1, 411: "Only knowledge remains; the will has vanished"), then it is for those still affirming the will to life "nothing." On the previous page he says that the state of the saint cannot really be called knowledge, as cited in note 33 above.
43 Elsewhere I have argued that in his accounts of aesthetics, ethics, and scholarship Schopenhauer tacitly makes a distinction between "objective" willing and "subjective" willing; see *Schopenhauer: The Human Character* (Philadelphia: Temple University Press, 1990), pp. 182–192. There most of my evidence for this distinction derives from works written long after the first edition of *WWR*; here evidence for a similar distinction is cited entirely from the first edition.
44 Malter, *Der eine Gedanke*, p. 61.
45 Ibid., p. 77. I am pleased to see that Malter agrees in the main with the argument mentioned in note 43 above.
46 *WWR* 1, 183.
47 Ibid., 186.

48 Ibid., 186–187.
49 Ibid., 188.
50 See especially sections 42, 43, 45, and 48 of *WWR* 1.
51 Ibid., 201.
52 Ibid.
53 *WWR* 1, 201–202.
54 See Ibid., 204: "The storm howls, the sea roars, the lightning flashes from black clouds, and the thunder-claps drown the noise of storm and sea." Almost exactly this same picture is presented in Joseph Conrad's *Typhoon*; moreover, the mammoth will to live is portrayed most vividly in Conrad's *Falk: A Reminiscence*, in which the main character resorts to cannibalism.
55 *WWR* 1, 202; see also 208–209.
56 Ibid., 202.
57 The two feelings differ by degrees, it may also be noted; see *WWR* 1, 202–203.
58 Ibid., 202.
59 See Ibid., 222.
60 Ibid., 204–205.
61 Ibid., 205. Here Schopenhauer shifts from "we" (*wir*) and "our" (*unser*) to "one" (*man*), but he should use only "one" to indicate the pure subject.
62 Ibid., 206. Again he uses "we."
63 Ibid., 252.
64 *WWR* 2, 433ff.
65 *HN* 1, paragraph 404: "The tragedy is the summit of the sublime."
66 *WWR* 1, 252.
67 Ibid., 254.
68 Ibid.
69 *WWR* 1, 254–255.
70 Ibid., 253.
71 Ibid., 253; see also *HN* 1, paragraph 642. There are two main routes to salvation: one by saintly resignation, which occurs upon the mere knowledge of suffering in the world, and the other by a "broken will," which befalls one personally; see *WWR* 1, 392–393.
72 *WWR* 2, 434.
73 Schopenhauer would have loved Thomas Hardy's *Jude the Obscure*. Through no real fault of his own, Jude's will is broken, leading him to rue the day he was born.
74 *WWR* 2, 435.
75 Ibid., 433.
76 Ibid.
77 For a particularly clear statement to this effect, see *WWR* 2, 642.
78 Ibid., 433.
79 Ibid., 574.

PART

II

The experience of beauty
Schopenhauer's theory of aesthetic
encounter

To become a pure subject of knowing means to be quit of
oneself; but since in most cases people cannot do this, they are,
as a rule, incapable of that purely objective apprehension of
things, which constitutes the gift of the artist.

Schopenhauer, "On the Metaphysics of the Beautiful"
Parerga and Paralipomena

5

Pleasure and knowledge in Schopenhauer's aesthetics

PAUL GUYER

NEGATIVE AND POSITIVE PLEASURE

Schopenhauer is famous for his characterization of aesthetic experience in purely cognitive terms, as an experience in which consciousness of the manifold and ever-changing particulars of ordinary experience is superseded by cognition of the unique and timeless forms of objects of experience or objectifications of the Will,[1] which Schopenhauer calls "Platonic Ideas." In his words, aesthetic experience

Is just the state that I described above as necessary for knowledge of the Idea, as pure contemplation, absorption in perception, being lost in the object, forgetting all individuality, abolishing the kind of knowledge which follows the principle of sufficient reason, and comprehends only relations. It is the state where, simultaneously and inseparably, the perceived individual thing is raised to the Idea of its species, and the knowing individual to the pure subject of will-less knowing, and now the two, as such, no longer stand in the stream of time and of all other relations. It is then all the same whether we see the setting sun from a prison or a palace. (*WWR* 1, 38, 96–97)[2]

However, on first glance the pleasure of aesthetic response associated with this cognition of Platonic Ideas is entirely negative, consisting in relief from the incessant pain of the inevitably unfulfilled desires associated with ordinary consciousness of the manifold particulars of quotidian experience, and in nothing but that relief. But such a purely negative account of the pleasures of such an elevated form of cognition seems disappointing, and to treat aesthetic experience as indeed nothing but an anaesthetic: if all that cognition of Platonic Ideas has to offer us is relief from pain, it is not clear why the most refined art should be in any but merely contingent ways preferable to a good drug. Further, such an account of the aesthetic as offering relief from all effects of the will by means of the contemplation of Platonic Ideas seems to be not merely disappointing but particularly paradoxical when it comes to what Schopenhauer himself clearly regards as the highest of all art-forms and aesthetic objects, that is, music. For Schopenhauer characterizes music as "by no means like the other arts, namely a copy of the Ideas, but [as] a *copy of the Will itself*" (*WWR* 1, 52, 257). But this immediately raises the question, how can experience of a copy of the Will itself produce relief from the will, which is apparently the sole source of pleasure in all aesthetic experience? And if this question cannot be answered, is there then not a contradiction between Schopenhauer's general theory of aesthetic pleasure and the account of the particular art-form which he clearly cherished the most?[3]

To answer this and several other puzzles about Schopenhauer's cognitivist theory of aesthetic pleasure will require seeing Schopenhauer's account of the pleasure of cognition as rather more nuanced and complicated than is often recognized. On the account I will give, Schopenhauer's theory contains a positive element as well as a negative one, that is, a recognition that certain forms of cognitively significant experience are intrinsically pleasurable as well as affording relief from the pains associated with other forms of experience.[4] Recognition of the positive as well as negative element in Schopenhauer's aesthetic cognitivism will also allow us to perceive some of the continuities between Schopenhauer's view and those of some of his most important predecessors, which the customary focus on the purely negative side of his theory may well obscure.

THE COGNITIVIST TRADITION IN GERMAN AESTHETICS

Let me begin, then, with a few words about the sorts of aesthetic theories prior to Schopenhauer's which we might regard as having defined the basic form of aesthetic cognitivism. In Germany, modern philosophy in general as well as modern aesthetics in particular began with Leibniz and Wolff. Neither one of these philosophers developed a free-standing aesthetic theory, but both revealed a certain shared conception of the nature of aesthetic experience and of the pleasure that we take in it in using examples to illustrate more general points in their philosophies, especially general claims about the nature of sensory or empirical knowledge. They appealed to the well-recognized experience of *je ne sais quois* in matters of taste to illustrate what they regarded to be the clear but confused nature of sensory perception in general as a cognitive state in which we have a clear recognition of the difference between one object and another without any distinct awareness of the particular characteristics that actually make the two objects distinct that a more refined or divine intellect than our own might enjoy. At the same time, however, they saw even such a confused form of thought, which might otherwise be thought to be a source only of distress, as a source of pleasure, insofar as it is the way, imperfect as it may be, in which the objective perception of the world can be communicated to us. Thus Wolff offered the famous definition of pleasure as the sensory perception of perfection.[5] Pleasure was thereby defined as the response to the recognition, or more precisely as itself the form taken by the recognition, of objective perfection, primarily in a metaphysical sense but then in a practical sense as well. On this account, however, the pleasurability of sensory experience in general or aesthetic experience in particular was not associated with the form or vehicle of perception as much as with its content or object. Aesthetic experience was not thought of as pleasurable because of its logical or phenomenological features such as its clarity on the one hand but indistinctness on the other, but solely because of its content.

Alexander Gottlieb Baumgarten, usually reputed the founder of modern aesthetics because of his master's dissertation of 1735, *Meditationes philosophicae de nonnullis ad poema pertinentibus*,[6] wrote metaphysics in the Leibnizo-Wolffian vein, but effected a subtle transformation in the Leibnizo-Wolffian conception of aesthetic experience, one that indeed often went unnoticed by his own disciples such as Georg Friedrich Meier. For Baumgarten explained aesthetic pleasure as due not to the *sensory perception of perfection* but rather to the *perfection of sensory perception*. That is, Baumgarten agreed with the basic Leibnizo-Wolffian conception of sensory perception as a clear but confused awareness of that which could at least in principle be represented both clearly and distinctly by a more refined intellect, but did not infer from that characterization that the pleasure associated with sensory perception must therefore arise entirely in spite of the nature of sensory perception itself and only because of the content that is, however imperfectly, perceived. On the contrary, he held that the special nature of sensory perception as clear but confused is not an imperfection at all, but rather that it offers unique opportunities for cognition which could not be replicated by more purely conceptual cognition, and that in aesthetic experience we enjoy the exercise of this unique form of

111

cognition in its own right and not merely because of some valuable content it may happen to convey. "The goal of aesthetics," he wrote, "is the perfection of sensitive cognition as such."[7] And the particular feature of sensory perception that is exploited for the unique pleasure of aesthetic experience, he held, is its *richness*, the possibility of conveying a lot of information through a single pregnant image, a possibility that is sacrificed by logical or conceptual cognition for the sake of greater clarity. "The perfection of every sort of cognition arises from richness, magnitude, truth, clarity, certainty and the liveliness of cognition,"[8] he held, but whereas the richness of conceptual cognition arises from the way in which a concept can apply to many particulars precisely by sacrificing most of the detail that makes each unique, the richness of aesthetic objects arises precisely from the way in which they suggest an inexhaustible wealth of information and ideas that cannot be reduced to any simple concept. Although of course in the end Baumgarten made room for conventional pieties – under the category of "aesthetic magnitude" he explained our pleasure in the uplifting content of works of art – his revolutionary contribution lay in his recognition that aesthetic experience exploits the distinctive character of sensory rather than intellectual representation or cognition, and that we enjoy the exercise of this unique cognitive capacity in aesthetic experience at least as much for its own sake as for the sake of any content that is conveyed.

Much in the aesthetic theory of Immanuel Kant can be construed as an alternative to Baumgarten's conception of aesthetic experience, although there is much else in his theory that is clearly a direct development of Baumgarten's views.[9] Kant may well owe his general insistence on the overarching difference between intuitions and concepts in all knowledge to the example of Baumgarten's distinction between sensory and logical cognition, but he does not follow Baumgarten in associating what is characteristic about aesthetic experience with the unique formal features of intuition.[10] Nor, however, contrary to common characterization of Kant's aesthetics as non-cognitivist, does he dissociate the explanation of aesthetic experience from the value of cognition altogether. On the contrary, the heart of Kant's aesthetic theory is the explanation of aesthetic pleasure as due to the realization of the fundamental goal of cognition under non-standard conditions in which the realization of this goal cannot be taken for granted.

The theoretical foundations of Kant's aesthetics have to be reconstructed from the two different introductions that Kant wrote for the *Critique of Judgment*. Most of the key premises are laid out in the Introduction that Kant published in the *Critique of Judgment*, where he argues that the feeling of pleasure is always connected with the attainment of a goal, and thus that an intersubjectively valid feeling of pleasure such as he will argue the feelings of the beautiful and the sublime to be must be associated with the attainment of an inter-subjectively shared goal, such as he assumes in this context only the goal of cognition itself is. But further, Kant notes, such pleasure is "especially noticeable" only when there is something unexpected about the attainment of the goal in question.[11] And this additional condition is fulfilled when we are in the state which Kant charac-terizes as the "harmony" or "free play" of the cognitive faculties of imagination (which includes sensory intuition) and understanding, because, as Kant perhaps makes clearer in the originally drafted, so-called "First Introduction," which he did not use in the published work allegedly only on the grounds of its length, such a state represents satisfaction of the "subjective conditions for a cognition," or the unification of the sensory manifold presented by an object of experience, precisely in the absence of the condition which ordina-rily guarantees the satisfaction of the goal of cognition, namely the subsumption of the object of experience under some determinate concept.[12] This condition can be understood as one in which we have a sense of the unity of the manifold offered to us by an object that does not flow from the subsumption of that object under any determinate concept, a model which Kant develops for the specific case of art in the form of his theory of aesthetic ideas, which describes the ineffably rich way a work of artistic genius commu-nicates to us an idea that cannot be exhaustively reduced to any ordinary concept.

In this theory, Kant does not follow Baumgarten in linking aesthetic pleasure directly to intuitions rather than concepts, but instead links such pleasure to a special state in which the under-standing's general goal of finding unity in manifolds is felt to be satisfied by the sensory manifold offered to us by a work of nature or of art even and precisely when that manifold cannot be sub-sumed under any determinate concept. So he does not associate aesthetic pleasure with the achievement of a special kind of cogni-tion, but rather with the use of the cognitive faculties and the realization of at least the subjective aspect of cognition under special circumstances, circumstances in which one of the ordinary requisites for cognition, the subsumption of objects under determinate concepts, is lacking. But he shares with Baumgarten the underlying impulse of aesthetic cognitivism, namely the assumption that there is a powerful source of pleasure directly associated with the use of cognitive faculties and the achievement of cognitive goals, independent of any particular content of the object of such exercise of the cognitive faculties (although of course potentially enhanced by further values which may attach to the content). In other words, the key supposition of both of these pillars of the cognitivist tradition in German aesthetics is that the unique uses of our cognitive capacities which are paradigmatic for aesthetic experience are intrinsically and positively pleasurable.

ACTIVE AND PASSIVE CONTEMPLATION

It is precisely this underlying assumption which Schopenhauer's conception of aesthetic pleasure appears to deny. What I shall now argue, however, is that a similar assumption that there is a positive source of pleasure in cognition itself is not absent from Schopenhauer's thought, and some of the puzzles of his aesthetic theory, including the puzzle earlier mentioned about the possibility of our pleasure in music, can be resolved by recognizing this positive aspect of his cognitivism.

The quotation with which we began comes from a point in Schopenhauer's exposition of his aesthetic theory in the Third Book of *The World as Will and Representation* at which he is summing up the first stage of his discussion. This book begins, however, with a general characterization of the Platonic Ideas as the archetypes or forms of the species of particular objects in the world of appearance; those individuals are objectifications of the Will, which is on Schopenhauer's conception the underlying reality of appearance understood in terms of the phenomenon, human will, that most closely approximates it, and the Ideas thus represent the various possible forms or what Schopenhauer calls the "grades" of the objectification of the Will (*WWR* 1, 30, 169). Prior to making the explicit connection between the Ideas and aesthetic experience, Schopenhauer follows this initial general characterization of the Ideas with an initial and equally general characterization of the effect of contemplation of the Ideas on the will that does not yet mention art or the aesthetic. As this initial characterization raises several questions for the subsequent application to the aesthetic, it is necessary to have it before us in detail:

> The transition that is possible, but to be regarded only as an exception, from the common knowledge of particular things to knowledge of the Idea takes places suddenly, since knowledge tears itself free from the service of the will precisely by the subject's ceasing to be merely individual, and being now a pure will-less subject of knowledge ...
>
> Raised up by the power of the mind, we relinquish the ordinary way of considering things, and cease to follow under the guidance of the forms of the principle of sufficient reason merely their relations to one another, whose final goal is always the relation to our own will. Thus we no longer consider the where, the when, the why, and the whither in things, but simply and solely the *what*. Further, we do not let abstract thought, the concepts of reason, take possession of our consciousness, but, instead of all this, devote the whole power of our mind to perception, sink ourselves completely therein, and let our whole consciousness be filled by the calm contemplation of the natural object actually present, whether it be a land-scape, a tree, a rock, a crag, a building, or anything else. We *lose* ourselves entirely in this object, to use a pregnant expression; in other words, we forget our individuality, our will, and continue to exist only as pure subject, as clear mirror of the object, so that it is as though the object alone existed without anyone to perceive it, and thus we are no longer able to separate the perceiver from the perception, but the two have become one, since the entire consciousness is filled and occupied by a single image of perception. If, therefore, the object has to such an extent passed out of all relation to something outside it, and the subject has passed out of all relation to the will, what is thus known is no longer the individual thing as such, but the *Idea*, the eternal form, the immediate objectivity of the Will at this grade. Thus at the same time, the person who is involved in this perception is no longer an individual, for in such perception the individual has lost himself; he is *pure*, will-less, painless, timeless *subject of knowledge*.
>
> (*WWR* 1, 34, 178–179)

Here Schopenhauer suggests that because contemplation of the Ideas replaces attention to the particular objects that are the ordinary objects of desire, the subject is freed from desire and the pain attendant upon the impossibility of its fulfillment; and he suggests further that in focussing attention upon the Ideas the subject even loses awareness of its own individual identity, an awareness which Schopenhauer must thus be supposing is always grounded upon recognition of the distinction between the individual self and individual objects of perception, and in so loosing all awareness of its individual identity the self seems to be freed of even the possibility of desire, which is always the desire of an individual subject for an individual object.

Whether it is at all plausible for Schopenhauer to ascribe such effects to the contemplation of Ideas, it seems at least clear what he wants to claim. On reflection, however, there are several puzzles about what he is claiming. First, although the passage ends by describing something like the loss of all individual desire and will, it begins with a description of contemplation as the consequence of an active, even violent adoption of a cognitive attitude by the individual mind – "knowledge tears itself free from the service of the will," and "raised up by the power of the mind, we relinquish the ordinary way of considering things." Yet it seems difficult to understand such decisive mental actions except as at least in part products of the individual will. Thus there seems to be an air of paradox about Schopenhauer's account. It is not mere contemplation which passively frees us from our will; rather we actively will to contemplate in order to free ourselves from our will. Not that there is actually a logical contradiction in such an idea – one could, after all, inflict a great pain upon oneself now in order to be free of all pain later, or freely choose to enslave oneself now and thus loose all freedom later – but there does seem to be something unsettling about it.

Further, the characterization before us seems to have several untoward consequences. First, the idea that we can free ourselves *for* contemplation by actively tearing ourselves away from our ordinary concerns and thus allowing what are ordinarily objects of individual desire to become objects for pure will-less and self-less knowing suggests that, since every object must embody some degree of the objectification of the Will, *any* object could become an object of aesthetic experience as long as our initial will to contemplate is sufficiently strong. Yet the fact that on a proposed characterization of the aesthetic attitude any object at all could become a proper object of this attitude is usually supposed to be a conclusive objection against that account of the attitude, or even against the very possibility of an aesthetic attitude theory altogether.[13] Second, the account appears quite unrealistic in ascribing a sort of mental heroism to all aesthetic transactions, that is, in suggesting that every experience of something beautiful presupposes a violent exercise of the will by means of which the object is mentally wrenched from its ordinary context of desire and the freedom for contemplation created. At one point, Schopenhauer writes that art "plucks the object of its contemplation from the stream of the world's course, and holds it isolated before it" (*WWR* 1, 36, 185); but while that sort of active exercise of the will might be a plausible account of certain moments of genius or artistic revolution, it certainly seems too romantic to characterize every passing experience of natural beauty or art that has already been produced by someone else. On the contrary, it would seem to be the case that at least some if not many beautiful or aesthetically pleasing objects induce their response in us without any effort of our own will at all.[14] In Schopenhauer's own words, indeed, it seems natural to suppose that the "purely objective frame of mind" that he claims aesthetic pleasure to be is often quite passively induced, "facilitated and favored from without by accommodating objects, by the abundance of natural beauty that invites contemplation, and even presses itself on us" (*WWR* 1, 38, 197).

Considering these two objections together suggests that there is a tension or ambivalence in Schopenhauer's account between the idea that aesthetic contemplation is a state which always presupposes an effort of our will to free us from our ordinary concerns and the idea that it is a state that is passively induced in us by external objects and thereby produces rather than presupposes freedom from the will. Postponing consideration of any further objections to Schopenhauer's account, I would now like to turn to his defense by arguing that Schopenhauer is hardly unaware of the possibility of these two alternative interpretations of his basic idea. On the contrary, he clearly exploits the difference between them in order to provide an account of several of the most fundamental distinctions of aesthetic theory. Schopenhauer marks the theoretical distinctions between beauty and sublimity, natural and artistic beauty, and artistic creation and reception, among others, precisely by distinguishing their positions along an axis of activity and passivity. The active and passive conceptions of contemplation are thus not two incompatible conceptualizations of a single sort of experience, but are rather distinct but related phenomena that fall under Schopenhauer's general model of aesthetic experience even though they differ in important ways.

SCHOPENHAUER'S RECONSTRUCTION OF TRADITIONAL AESTHETICS

Let us take first the distinction between the beautiful and the sublime, which was such a prominent feature of aesthetic theory from Addison to Kant. Schopenhauer's way of making this distinction was clearly influenced by Kant's, although it is ultimately set in a very different framework. On the one hand, Schopenhauer characterizes natural beauty precisely by the way in which naturally beautiful objects induce the state of contemplation and will-less knowing without any effort on the part of the individual subject:

> Transition into the state of pure perception occurs most easily when the objects accommodate themselves to it, in other words, when by their manifold and at the same time definite and distinct form they easily become representatives of their Ideas, in which beauty, in the objective sense, consists. Above all, natural beauty has this quality, and even the most stolid and apathetic person obtains therefrom at least a fleeting, aesthetic pleasure. Indeed, it is remarkable how the plant world in particular invites one to aesthetic contemplation ... (*WWR* 1, 39, 200–201)

Here the apathetic person would appear to be precisely the person who does not himself in any way exercise his own will in order to enter into a state of contemplation, but is quite passively induced into that state by the objects presented to him, presumably by the lucidity of form and thus the accessibility of the Ideas in them. On the other hand, Schopenhauer equally explicitly characterizes the experience of the sublime by the effort of will that it takes to be able to contemplate the form of, or Ideas in, sublime objects:

> But these very objects, whose significant forms invite us to a pure contemplation of them, may have a hostile relation to the human will in general, as manifested in its objectivity, the human body. They may be opposed to it; they may threaten it by their might that eliminates all resistance, or their immeasurable greatness may reduce it to naught. Nevertheless, the beholder may not direct his attention to this relation to his will which is so pressing and hostile, but, although he perceives and acknowledges it, he may consciously turn away from it, forcibly tear himself from his will and its relations, and, giving himself up entirely to knowledge, may quietly contemplate, as pure, will-less subject of knowing, those very objects so terrible to the will ... In that case, he is then filled with the feeling of the sublime ... Thus what distinguishes the feeling of the sublime from that of the beautiful is that, with the beautiful, pure knowledge has gained the upper hand without a struggle ... On the other hand, with the sublime, that state of pure knowing is obtained first of all by a conscious and violent tearing away from the relations of the same object to the will which are recognized as unfavorable, by a free exaltation ... (*WWR* 1, 39, 201–202)

The difference between the beautiful and the sublime is then just that the latter requires a distinct, even conscious effort of the will in order to set aside the ordinary concerns of the will and thereby make possible contemplation of forms, whereas in the former the state of contemplation is achieved effortlessly and seems rather to cause than to presuppose liberation from the ordinary concerns of individual will. Schopenhauer does not incoherently suppose that the same state of mind is both active and passive; rather he supposes, quite coherently, that particular states of contemplation which are in some ways similar but in other ways different, and in any case numerically distinct, are sometimes reached more passively, sometimes more actively, and sometimes require more of an antecedent liberation from ordinary desires, and sometimes instead induce such liberation. And while it would in fact be logically possible even for the same objects to have these different effects on different occasions or different persons, assuming perhaps variations in the subjects rather than objects, Schopenhauer naturally enough assumes that these different effects will typically be correlated with phenomenologically different sorts of properties or objects (and thus different Platonic Ideas), such as light and darkness (*WWR* 1, 39, 203) or delicate ice crystals on a window-pane (*WWR* 1, 35, 182) and "immense, bare, over-hanging cliffs" (*WWR* 1, 39, 204) – in other words, typical examples of the beautiful and the sublime.[15]

Schopenhauer also exploits the difference between the active and the passive conceptions of contemplation in order to characterize the difference between aesthetic appreciation of nature and art. This contrast is clearest when we compare his remarks about natural beauty to his remarks about genius. In the case of natural beauty, as we just saw, it is the object itself "that invites contemplation, and even presses itself on us" (*WWR* 1, 38, 197), and the subject need take no active role in preparing for this contemplation. Art, however, is described actively rather than passively: as we also saw earlier, "it plucks the object of its contemplation from the stream of the world's course, and holds it isolated before it" (*WWR* 1, 36, 185). This active rather than passive image of art becomes even more pronounced as Schopenhauer proceeds to describe genius, the concept which, in this again following Kant, he uses as the vehicle for his description of artistic creation. Genius is described precisely as the ability deliberately to disengage the will from its ordinary concerns in order to allow contemplation:

Genius is the ability to leave entirely out of sight our own interest, our willing, and our aims, and consequently to discard entirely our own personality for a time, in order to remain *pure knowing subject*, the clear eye of the world; and this not merely for moments, but with the necessary continuity and conscious thought to enable us to repeat by deliberate art which has been apprehended ... For genius to appear in an individual, it is as if a measure of the power of knowledge must have fallen to his lot far exceeding that required for the service of an individual will ... This explains the animation, amounting to disquietude, in men of genius ... This gives them that restless zealous nature, that constant search for new objects worthy of contemplation ...   (*WWR* 1, 36, 185–186)

Again there is that whiff of paradox in the idea of actively willing to set aside the will that we noticed earlier; but there can be no doubt that Schopenhauer describes genius in active terms: genius is an *ability* to leave ordinary concerns out of sight, to discard our own personality, to repeat by deliberate art, constantly to search, and so on.

The activity of the genius can be broken down into several aspects. First, the genius does not find the Platonic Ideas lying on the surface of things, but he has to seek them out by cognitive activity. "The man of genius requires imagination in order to see in things not what nature has actually formed, but what she endeavoured to form, yet did not bring about ... Thus imagination extends the mental horizon of the genius beyond the objects that actually present themselves ..." (*WWR* 1, 36, 186–7). But further, the work of art does not consist simply in "knowledge of the Idea," but in "communication" of it (187), and the second component of genius is both the will and the ability to find a vehicle for the communication of the Idea that contemplation has revealed to the artist to other persons as well. As Schopenhauer puts it, the genius can "retain that thoughtful contemplation necessary for him to repeat what is thus known in a voluntary and intentional work, such repetition being the work of art. Through this he communicates to others the Idea he has grasped" (*WWR* 1, 37, 195). As voluntary and intentional, the production of a work of art clearly requires an act of will in the ordinary sense, a decision and resolve, and the active exercise of human capacities, whether verbal as in the case of a poem or manual as in the case of a painting or sculpture. Thus even if its ultimate effect is the same sort of release from individual will that is induced by the contemplation of natural beauty as well, there can be no question that the production of artistic beauty is firmly anchored in the sphere of intentional human activity, and that among humans the genius is remarkable for his particularly high degree of both cognitive and indeed in many cases physical activity.[16]

This emphasis on the cognitive as well as the physical activity of the genius also provides the key for Schopenhauer's way of modeling the distinction between the creation and reception of art, or between artist and audience. Schopenhauer assumes that the ability to disengage the will and engage in contemplation must be "inherent in all men" in some degree, "as otherwise they would be just as incapable of enjoying works of art as of producing them" (*WWR* I, 37, 194), but that the difference between artist and audience lies precisely in the activity or passivity that characterizes the exercise of this inherent ability. The genius actively struggles to produce both his insight and the object by means of which to communicate it, but once having struggled to communicate the former through the latter he then facilitates the enjoyment of his knowledge by the rest of us, that is, makes it easy for us to see what was difficult for him, or allows us to be passive in that contemplation in which he had to be active. "The work of art is merely a means of facilitating that knowledge in which [aesthetic] pleasure consists ... The artist lets us peer into the world through his eyes" (195). In other words, the genius and the ordinary person enjoy the same knowledge and ultimately enjoy the same respite from the incessant demands of ordinary desire and will that such knowledge affords, but the genius arrives at this knowledge by means of an active exercise of the will which the rest of us can then participate in passively.

In fact, Schopenhauer finally arrays artistic creation, the aesthetic enjoyment of nature, and the reception of art on a single spectrum of activity. The production of art through genius clearly requires the highest degree of activity; the reception or appreciation of art produced by others, however, requires not only a lower degree of activity than such production of art, but even a lower degree of activity than aesthetic response to nature. This is because in a work of art the Platonic Ideas have already been isolated out by the artist, and are presented to the rest of us on a platter, whereas in the case of natural beauty, although the objects are accommodating and inviting, there is still some work of abstraction to be performed before the Ideas can be entirely willlessly contemplated. In Schopenhauer's words, "That the Idea comes to us more easily from the work of art than directly from nature and from reality, arises solely from the fact that the artist, who knew only the Idea and not reality, clearly repeated in his work only the Idea, separated it out from reality, and omitted all disturbing contingencies" (*WWR* 1, 37, 195). Thus human subjects are most active, both cognitively and otherwise, in the production of art, most passive in the reception and enjoyment of art, and fall in between in the perception of natural beauty because even the latter is not merely a matter of passive response to particulars but requires some cognitive effort of abstraction for the contemplation of pure forms.

Schopenhauer's emphasis on the passivity of the reception of art may not seem flattering to the modernist artist and the modernist critic, both of whom pride themselves on the possibility of artistic form challenging the audience rather than making things easy for it. The truth undoubtedly lies between the two positions: neither art that challenges its audience without gratifying it nor art that gratifies its audience without challenging it is likely to withstand the test of time. The very fact that Schopenhauer can suggest a spectrum of aesthetic response from the most active to the most passive, however, suggests that there may be no reason in principle why both the production and the reception of different works of art should not be seen to call for varying degrees of activity and passivity, thus allowing his theory to accommodate art that calls for both more and less from the audience and interpreter. But my aim here is not to assess the ultimate viability of Schopenhauer's aesthetics (that would obviously require major metaphysical surgery) so much as it is to use what would seem to be some of the most obvious objections to it in order to arrive at a better understanding of its complexity. I trust that it is clear by now, in any case, that Schopenhauer does not simply fail to distinguish between active and passive interpretations of his fundamental idea of the connection between contemplation and release from ordinary willing, but consciously exploits this distinction to provide his version of some of the most basic concepts of aesthetic theory.

Before leaving the issue of the active and passive entirely, I will note one other example of Schopenhauer's conscious exploitation of this distinction. I earlier mentioned a consequence of Schopenhauer's contemplative conception of aesthetic experience that is commonly alleged against it as an objection to any aesthetic attitude theory, namely that on such an account any object is potentially an aesthetic object.[17] Schopenhauer is hardly unaware of this consequence of his basic theoretical model; on the contrary, he draws it quite explicitly himself: "Now since, on the one hand, every existing thing can be observed purely objectively and outside of all relation, and, on the other, the will appears in everything at some grade of its objectivity, and this thing is accordingly the expression of an Idea, everything is also *beautiful*" (*WWR* 1, 41, 210). Given his assumption of the overriding desirability of obtaining relief from the demands of the will by means of will-less contemplation, however, Schopenhauer could hardly see such a consequence as an objection to his theory of aesthetic experience, but would rather regard it as one of the theory's clearest strengths. Nevertheless, like any philosopher advocating a revisionary metaphysics, he does recognize the need to reconcile his theory with common sense, in this case the common assumption that there is a crucial difference between the beautiful and the aesthetically indifferent. He does this by again resorting to the distinction between the active and the passive inducement of contemplation, and recasting the ordinary distinction between the beautiful and the indifferent as a difference of degree rather than of kind: objects range from the most beautiful, which transport us into contemplation with virtually no effort at all, to the least but still potentially beautiful, which transport us into that state only with considerable effort on our own part. Thus he says:

> That even the most insignificant thing admits of purely objective and will-less contemplation and thus proves itself to be beautiful, is testified by the still life paintings of the Dutch ... But one thing is more beautiful than another because it facilitates this purely objective contemplation, goes out to meet it, and, so to speak, even compels it, and then we call the thing very beautiful. (*WWR* 1, 41, 210)

Some things virtually compel us to contemplate them, thus leading us to abnegation of the will with almost no antecedent effort of our will, while other things we have to compel ourselves to contemplate, and they thus offer us relief from our will only after considerable antecedent effort of the will. On this account, then, the difference between what would commonly be regarded as beautiful and what would commonly be regarded as not is noticeable but never insuperable, and that is exactly how Schopenhauer should want it to come out.

In amplifying this point, Schopenhauer argues that the scale of beauty is actually correlated with the scale of cognitive adequacy in the objectification of the Will, a scale on which inorganic or lower forms of organic existence generally have a low degree of beauty because they manifest a relatively low-grade objectification of the Will, but on which the artistic representation of human form and conduct potentially has the highest degree of beauty because what is represented are the highest objectifications of the Will. In constructing such a scale of beauty, Schopenhauer is fulfilling a standard requirement of traditional aesthetic theory.[18] I will not discuss this theme in its own right, however, but only as it bears on the next issue I will take up.

THE PLEASURES OF KNOWLEDGE

Thus I now return to another of the general objections to Schopenhauer's theory that I earlier raised, the objection that it characterizes aesthetic response in purely negative terms merely as relief from pain, and thus credits aesthetic experience with nothing that could not also be obtained from an adequate drug. The standard account of Schopenhauer's theory certainly presents it in this light,[19] and the idea that aesthetic experience is important only for an effect which could readily or perhaps even only potentially be obtained from other sources has certainly been taken to be a problem throughout contemporary aesthetic theory. What I would now like to argue, however, is that although Schopenhauer certainly stresses the negative pleasure of relief from the will that is afforded by contemplation of Platonic Ideas in much of his exposition, this is not in fact the only source of aesthetic pleasure that he recognizes. He also acknowledges an intrinsic and positive pleasure in the contemplation of those ideas themselves, a pleasure which cannot be readily be obtained from anything but aesthetic experience, and this should suffice to spare him from this objection.

Fairly early in his exposition Schopenhauer makes it clear that there are two elements in aesthetic experience:

In the aesthetic method of consideration we found *two inseparable constituent parts*: namely, knowledge of the object not as an individual thing, but as Platonic *Idea*, in other words, as persistent form of this whole species of things; and the self-consciousness of the knower, not as individual, but as *pure, will-less subject of knowledge*. The condition under which the two constituent parts appear always united was the abandonment of the method of knowledge that is bound to the principle of sufficient reason ...

(*WWR* 1, 38, 195–196)

This does not imply, however, that there are two separate sources or kinds of aesthetic pleasure, but only that there are two conditions that need to be satisfied for the one and only kind of aesthetic pleasure to occur. Pure, will-less knowing of Platonic Ideas, this account suggests, produces the negative pleasure of relief from the incessant clamor of the will that has previously been described.

As he continues the present passage, however, Schopenhauer suggests a more complicated picture:

Moreover, we shall see that the *pleasure* produced by contemplation of the beautiful arises from those two constituent parts, sometimes more from the one than from the other, according to what the object of aesthetic contemplation may be. (*WWR* 1, 38, 196)

This suggests that acquaintance with the Platonic Ideas is not merely the necessary condition for achieving the state of pure will-less knowing, which is in turn pleasurable solely because it offers relief from the pain of ordinary willing, but rather that the contemplation of the Platonic Ideas is itself a source of pleasure in addition to being the precondition for pure will-less knowing, and that the pleasure of contemplation is to some degree independent of the pleasure of relief from the demands of desire, at least independent enough so that these two kinds of pleasure can be present in different aesthetic experiences in different amounts even if one never occurs in the total absence of the other.

Schopenhauer does not develop this suggestion in the remainder of his discussion of the beautiful in 38 or in his discussion of the sublime in 39, both of which focus on the negative pleasure of relief from the will whether that is achieved effortlessly or forcibly. Subsequently, however, Schopenhauer makes it clear that he does suppose that contemplation and relief from the will are two distinct sources of pleasure. In 41, he reiterates the distinction between the two components of aesthetic response

By calling an object *beautiful*, we thereby assert that it is an object of our aesthetic contemplation, and this implies two different things. On the one hand, the sight of the thing makes us *objective*, that is to say, in contemplating it we are no longer conscious of ourselves as individuals, but as pure, will-less subjects of knowing. On the other hand, we recognize in the object not the individual thing, but an Idea; and this can happen only in so far as our contemplation of the object is not given up to the principle of sufficient reason ..., but rests on the object itself. (*WWR* 1, 41, 209)

In the next section, he then separates the pleasure of contemplation from the pleasure of relief from the will more fully and more firmly than before:

I return to our discussion of the aesthetic impression. Knowledge of the beautiful always supposes, simultaneously and inseparably, a purely knowing subject and a known Idea as object. But yet the source of aesthetic enjoyment will lie sometimes rather in the apprehension of the known idea, sometimes rather in the bliss and peace of mind of pure knowledge free from all willing, and thus from all individuality and the pain that results therefrom. (*WWR* 1, 42, 212)

Here Schopenhauer does not say that there are two conditions for the occurrence of aesthetic pleasure, but that there are two different sources of such pleasure. Nor does he just suggest that these two sources can be present in different degrees on different occasions of aesthetic contemplation, but he asserts, apparently without qualification, that our pleasure in an aesthetic experience can sometimes be due to one cause and sometimes to the other. This would seem to make sense only if each of these sources can give rise to pleasure by itself, and that there are thus two different although not necessarily phenomenologically distinct sorts of aesthetic pleasure which could be called positive and negative on account of their etiology. And this would imply that there is a pleasure in contemplation which is not merely identical to the pleasure of relief from the will, even if it typically leads to the latter, and thus that aesthetic experience is not simply fungible with anesthesia even if there are other sources of relief from the tyranny of the individual will besides aesthetic contemplation. Thus there is a positive aspect to the cognitivism of Schopenhauer's aesthetics which is clearly in the tradition of such predecessors as Baumgarten and Kant, even if Schopenhauer's conception of the ethical significance of the aesthetic – his account of the negative pleasure of relief from individual will, that is – is radically different from anything they would have contemplated or accepted.

Again Schopenhauer confirms his recognition of the complexity of aesthetic experience for us by grounding his version of a traditional contrast in aesthetic theory precisely on a distinction that we might initially have overlooked. In this case, he uses the distinction between negative and positive pleasures in cognition to differentiate lower and higher forms of beauty. The natural beauty of the inorganic and vegetable kingdoms as well as the beauty of forms of art rank relatively low, he argues, because in those cases the pleasure that predominates is just the negative pleasure of pure will-less knowing, that is, relief from the tyranny of will, whereas "if animals and human beings are the object of aesthetic contemplation ... the enjoyment will consist rather in the objective apprehension of these Ideas that are the most distinct revelations of the will" (*WWR* 1, 42, 212). This ranking would be impossible if the objective apprehension of Ideas were merely the necessary condition for relief from the will. On the contrary, this ranking suggests that in the end relief from the will is not the most important benefit of aesthetic experience, but that the pleasure of contemplation is at least as great if not greater than the pleasure of mere relief.

THE PARADOX OF MUSIC

We are now in a position to consider the final question that was initially raised about Schopenhauer's apparently merely negative account of aesthetic pleasure, the paradox that aesthetic pleasure is supposed to arise entirely from relief from the pain of willing, but that music, which Schopenhauer clearly regards as the highest form of art and thus of all beauty, is nothing less than "a *copy of the Will itself*" (*WWR* 1, 52, 257). By claiming that music is a copy of the Will itself, Schopenhauer aims to avoid a simplistic mimetic theory of music, on which we enjoy flute trills because they imitate rippling streams and timpani rolls because they imitate rolling thunder, while still keeping music in the cognitive ballpark by claiming that it imitates a metaphysically deeper and more obscure reality (see also 261). But this still leaves the question, how can a copy of the Will offer relief from the will?

The complexity we have found in Schopenhauer's cognitivism now allows us to see that this is a question that Schopenhauer can and does answer at several levels. Schopenhauer stresses that music does not represent states of the will as individual occurrences in particular human lives, but as universals. "Therefore music does not express this or that particular and definite pleasure, this or that affliction, pain, sorrow, horror, gaiety, merriment, or peace of mind, but joy, pain, sorrow, horror, gaiety, merriment, peace of mind *themselves*" (*WWR* 1, 52, 261). This implies, first, that responding to a piece of music need not involve or invoke the individual will of the particular listener, perhaps even that it can distract the listener from the pains attendant on his own will. And there is no doubt that Schopenhauer does attribute such a palliative effect to music:

The inexpressible depth of all music, by virtue of which it floats past us as a paradise quite familiar and yet eternally remote, and is so easy to understand and yet so inexplicable, is due to the fact that it reproduces all the emotions of our innermost being, but entirely without reality and remote from its pain.
(*WWR* 1, 52, 264)

But as we have now seen, Schopenhauer does not in fact limit the pleasure of aesthetic experience to relief from one's private pain, so there is no reason why such negative pleasure should be the whole story about our enjoyment of music. And in fact what Schopenhauer clearly stresses the most in his account is not this sort of negative pleasure but the intrinsic pleasure of contemplative knowledge of

127

the nature of Will and thus metaphysical reality itself. Thus, in discussing the contrast between harmony and melody in music, Schopenhauer stresses its necessity for understanding the complexity of reality, and in his treatment of melody in particular he gives a particularly intellectualist account, which asserts not that melody gives us greater relief from pain than any other aspect of music but that it gives us greater insight: "In the *melody* ... I recognize the highest grade of the Will's objectification, the intellectual life and endeavour of man ... In keeping with this, *melody* alone has significant and intentional connection from beginning to end" (*WWR* 1, 52, 259). Ranking melody over harmony on this ground would make no sense at all if intellectual insight itself were not a positive source of pleasure. And the claim that music is remote from the pain of reality which was cited a moment ago is only the preface to a description of the value of music in purely cognitive terms:

In the whole of this discussion of music I have been trying to make it clear that music expresses in an exceedingly universal language, in a homogeneous material, that is, in mere tones, and with the greatest distinctness and truth, the inner being, the in-itself, of the world, which we think of under the concept of Will, according to its most distinct manifestation.

(*WWR* 1, 52, 264)

Here there is no reference at all to music's power to alleviate pain, but a description of its cognitive significance which makes sense only on the assumption that cognition of universals is itself not just a source of pleasure but ultimately the source of the highest form of pleasure.

Schopenhauer's penultimate word on art in general further stresses the cognitive value that has become predominant in his account of music: "If the whole world as representation is only the visibility of the Will, then art is the elucidation of this visibility, the *camera obscura* which shows the objects more purely, and enables us to survey and comprehend them better" (*WWR* 1, 52, 266–267). Certainly such a remark makes sense only on the assumption that there is an intrinsic value, which within Schopenhauer's psychology can only be an intrinsic pleasure, in comprehension itself. Added to his account of how music can turn one's focus away from his own individual will, this is more than enough to resolve the apparent paradox in Schopenhauer's account of music.

But I think there is one more thing to be said about the paradox of will in Schopenhauer's account of art in general, something which is not explicitly mentioned in the account of music but which would apply to it above all else. This is a point which Schopenhauer makes, not repeatedly like most of his other points, but just once, in his treatment of the sublime. Here he suggests that there is a pleasure which is not just the cognitive pleasure of contemplation of the nature of reality through universals nor just the negative pleasure of relief from ordinary willing but a pleasure in the recognition of and indeed affirmation of the individual's underlying identity with a greater reality:[20]

The vastness of the world, which previously disturbed our peace of mind, now rests with us; our dependence on it is now annulled by its dependence on us. All this, however, does not come into reflection at once, but shows itself as a consciousness, merely felt, that in some sense or other (made clear only by philosophy) we are one with the world, and are therefore not oppressed but exalted by its immensity.   (*WWR* 1, 39, 205)

Here, like his nemesis Hegel but unlike the more Romantic Schelling, Schopenhauer does not suppose that art actually supersedes philosophy, but rather that aesthetic experience gives us an adumbration of truth which must ultimately be clarified by philosophy. But the truth of which philosophy thus gives us an adumbration is a truth about an identity with reality which is deeper than the superficial appearances which separate us from reality. And Schopenhauer does not characterize the recognition of this identity as merely relieving us from oppression, but as positively exalting us; we are not just relieved from the pain of being, but positively rejoice in being part of being itself. Thus the experience of art does not just allow us to escape from the pain of reality, like a drug, but occasions a joyful affirmation of our identity with reality that cannot readily be obtained anywhere else. And insofar as this account applies to music in particular, then, we would there enjoy not just relief from ordinary willing nor contemplation of the nature of Will in general but also, and perhaps above all, the identity of our individual selves and our individual wills with reality and Will in general.

Whether plausible or not, this is surely no merely negative account of aesthetic pleasure, but a complex and ultimately affirmative account. Such an account of the complexity of Schopenhauer's aesthetic cognitivism would link it more closely to his successor Nietzsche's conception of the contrast yet equally inseparable connection between the Apollonian and Dionysian than might otherwise be thought. But that connection must be a story for another occasion.

Paul Guyer

Notes

1 I capitalize "Will" when referring to the supra-individual metaphysical substratum of the world as Schopenhauer conceives of it, but use the lower-case "will" when referring to the phenomenon of individual volition as it presents itself through ordinary consciousness in the phenomenal realm. In fact, references to will in this ordinary sense of individual volition, which I will sometimes also designate as "our will" or "individual will," numerically predominate the other usage in this essay.

2 References are to and translations from Schopenhauer's *WWR* 1, 2. References to Kant's *Critique of Judgment*, also to be cited frequently, are given by section number, followed by volume and page as in *Kants gesammelte Schriften*, edited by the German Academy of Sciences (Berlin, 1900 –).

3 Such a tension must be obvious in, for example, the otherwise helpful exposition of Schopenhauer's aesthetics in Bryan Magee, *The Philosophy of Schopenhauer* (Oxford: The Clarendon Press, 1983), pp. 164–188. Magee claims that on Schopenhauer's view music "is the only art that articulates the noumenal will directly" (p. 184), but also describes Schopenhauer as holding that "we care so much about art" only "because it provides us with a release, if only momentary, from the prison we ordinarily inhabit" (p. 170), and does not ask whether knowledge of the noumenal Will as thing-in-itself provides such relief or, if not, whether there is some other pleasure inherent in it.

4 In recognizing both negative and positive pleasures, Schopenhauer's aesthetics is part of a well-established tradition. Both Burke and Kant had used versions of such a distinction to explain the distinction between the beautiful and the sublime. See Edmund Burke, *A Philosophical Enquiry into the Origin of our Ideas of the Sublime and Beautiful*, Adam Philips, ed. (Oxford: Oxford University Press, 1990), Part I, sections III–IV, pp. 31–35; Immanuel Kant, *Critique of Judgment* §23, 5: 244–245. As we will see in the fourth section below, Schopenhauer has a different way of explicating the distinction between the beautiful and the sublime, and uses the distinction between positive and negative pleasure much more broadly.

5 *Vernünftige Gedanken von Gott, der Welt, and die Seele des Menschen* (Halle, 1720) §404.

6 This work earns Baumgarten the status of founder because it was the first to introduce the term "aesthetics" (*aesthetica*) as a name for a special philosophical discipline; but that discipline had already been a recognized subject in professional philosophy in Britain for at least a decade, since the publication of Francis Hutcheson's first *Inquiry Concerning Beauty, Order, Harmony, Design* of 1725. While Baumgarten's work certainly constituted a major innovation in the German philosophical tradition and was to be of enduring influence for the better part of a

century, the lively debate on the foundations of taste that had already begun in Britain means that his invention of the name for the new discipline cannot earn him credit for the invention of the discipline itself.

7 *Aesthetica* §14; in Hans Rudolf Schweizer, *Ästhetik als Philosophie der sinnlichen Erkenntnis: Einer Interpretation der "Aesthetica" A. G. Baumgartens mit teilweise Widergabe des lateinischen Textes und deutscher Übersetzung* (Basel: Schwabe, 1973), p. 114.

8 *Aesthetica* §22; Schweizer, p. 118.

9 In particular, the theory of aesthetic ideas in §49 of the *Critique of Judgment*, which presumably must have been at least an initial impetus to Schopenhauer's theory of the role of the Platonic Ideas in aesthetic experience, is a direct development of Baumgarten's leading idea of the richness of clear but confused sensory perception.

10 That association had been reserved, after all, to explain the unique contribution of space and time to all theoretical cognition; this is what underlies Kant's rejection of Baumgarten's conception of aesthetics as a special discipline concerning the beautiful at *Critique of Pure Reason* A21/B35–36.

11 *Critique of Judgment*, Introduction, Section VI, 5:187.

12 *First Introduction to the Critique of Judgment*, Section VIII, 20:224.

13 See for example George Dickie, *Art and the Aesthetic: An Institutional Analysis* (Ithaca: Cornell University Press, 1974), p. 77. Of course, the potential ubiquity of the aesthetic attitude will be an objection against an account of it only if one supposes that the account is supposed to play some role in grounding some extensional distinction, such as that between art and non-art. Otherwise, the potential ubiquity of the aesthetic attitude implied by a given theory of it might well be thought to be a recommendation of that theory.

14 This was precisely the reason for Hutcheson's classical characterization of the response to beauty as an internal sense. See *An Inquiry into the Original of our Ideas of Beauty and Virtue* (London: first edition, 1725; fourth, corrected edition, 1738), *Treatise I: Concerning Beauty, Order, Harmony, Design*, Section I, §§xiii–xiv.

15 This is not the place for a detailed contrast between Schopenhauer's conception of the sublime and its Kantian antecedent. It will have to suffice to say that although Schopenhauer's account bears a great similarity to Kant's conception of the dynamically sublime (*Critique of Judgment* §28), they nevertheless differ in that for Schopenhauer the sublime frees one from concerns of the will altogether, while for Kant it is precisely the moral will, or the determination of the will by pure practical reason, which frees one from concerns that could influence the will only by inclination. The Schopenhauerian sublime, in other words, is an experience of liberation from the will altogether, while the Kantian sublime is an experience of the liberation of the will from inclination by pure practical reason.

16 Schopenhauer's conceptions of both art and genius stand squarely in the tradition of Kant. His emphasis on the intentional and voluntary nature of artistic production follows Kant's analysis of the concept of art in §43 of the *Critique of Judgment*, and his twofold analysis of genius as consisting in the capacity to discover both ideas and the forms for communicating them closely follows Kant's characterization of genius in §49 of the third *Critique*, where he stresses that genius consists in a talent for both the conception of aesthetic ideas as well as the expression of such ideas in "material, i.e., intuition for the exhibition of this concept" (5:317). The main difference between the two accounts is that Kant stresses the genius's *invention* of aesthetic ideas, whereas for Schopenhauer the genius uses all of the effort of his will ultimately to *discover* the Platonic Ideas that are inherent in the appearances of things.

17 It should be clear now that this would not imply that on Schopenhauer's account any object can therefore become a *work of art*; his account of art has held that works of art are products of voluntary and intentional human activity aimed at the communication of Platonic Ideas, a definition that is not satisfied by any natural or found object no matter how beautiful it might be.

18 Both Kant and Hegel, for example, construct scales of the significance of art, Kant on the basis of the expressive potential of various artistic media (*Critique of Judgment* §51), though this has only a minor part in his aesthetic theory or even in his discussion of fine art, and Hegel on the basis of the cognitive potential of the different fine arts as stages in the sensuous embodiment of the Idea, the organizing thought of his entire *Lectures on Fine Arts*.

19 See, for instance, D. W. Hamlyn, *Schopenhauer* (London: Routledge and Kegan Paul, 1980), p. 111; more recently, Terry Eagleton, *The Ideology of the Aesthetic* (Oxford: Basil Blackwell, 1990), pp. 162–163; and most recently, A. L. Cothey, *The Nature of Art* (London: Routledge, 1992), pp. 70–71. Two writers who come closer to recognizing the complexity I will now portray are Patrick Gardiner, *Schopenhauer* (Baltimore: Penguin, 1963), p. 196, and Michael Podro, *The Manifold in Perception: Theories of Art from Kant to Hildebrand* (Oxford: The Clarendon Press, 1972), pp. 100–104. Neither of these authors, however, is quite as explicit about Schopenhauer's positive theory of aesthetic pleasure as I am about to be.

20 This point is also suggested by Podro (*The Manifold in Perception*, p. 106), although without citation of this or any other supporting passage.

6

Schopenhauer and aesthetic recognition

CHERYL FOSTER

INTRODUCTION

Nature and art exist on an aesthetic continuum for Schopenhauer, but one that splinters, much like the straws of a broom, along subtly different trajectories. As with straw tethered to a broom handle, artworks find their anchor in nature, fastened to it by the vision and imagination of genius. In what follows it is suggested that Schopenhauer's philosophy of art grows out of his views on our aesthetic engagement with and general indebtedness to the natural world. This reading of Schopenhauer poses an intriguing challenge to category-relative and institutional theories of art, where history, criticism and convention determine the framework for accurate aesthetic assessment. Before considering this challenge, however, the approach here taken to Schopenhauer's aesthetics requires justification and clarification: justification of its disregard for questions concerning the aesthetic function of metaphysical Ideas and clarification of the relationship between nature and works of art, mediated as they are by the natural capacities of artistic genius.

EXCLUDING IDEAS

Because Schopenhauer's aesthetic observations are sandwiched between and imbued with the details of his metaphysical system, we tend to interpret his views on art, beauty and genius exclusively through the filter of that system. Indeed, Schopenhauer presents his aesthetic theory as a companion to his metaphysical view of the world and indeed promotes it as one of two avenues of salvation from the tumult of Will, the author of our earthly predicament. Yet, much of Schopenhauer's theory strikes us as being at odds with

133

itself. Sometimes he seems to favor art as being the quickest route to attaining pure subjectivity, while at other times he privileges nature for the same task.[1] Ideas are supposed to be objectifications of Will at *definite* grades, reflective of species-type, but appear at the same time to be infinitely multi-sided. The artist has an apprehension of the Idea in nature but the precise relationship between Schopenhauer's Ideas and their Platonic counterparts remains in dispute.

Excellent attempts have been made to resolve some of these problems or at least to explain the reasons for their occurrence. James Chansky, for example, has argued against the verdict that the Ideas are "sudden, surprising and disconcerting," proposing instead that Schopenhauer's entire metaphysical system requires the Ideas as a way of apprehending objects "free of the influence of both a co-opting reason and a hungry Will, free of all considerations which render it this or that thing, yet which is still a determinate object with specific characteristics and qualities."[2] While Chansky succeeds in accomplishing his stated purpose by elucidating the metaphysical motivation for the introduction of Ideas in Schopenhauer's aesthetic theory, we are nevertheless left with the minutiae of applying Ideas in critical aesthetic practice. Disagreements and confusions abound over issues such as the universality of the Idea and the contradictory implications of creating a hierarchy of Will's objectification.[3]

Furthermore, Schopenhauer's metaphysical views themselves have not been immune from widespread criticism, even if they are judged to be consistent within and around his aesthetic theory. Frederick Coppleston has asserted that "if Schopenhauer's philosophy of art and aesthetics was marred through its relationship to his philosophy in general, this was not because of the relationship as such, but because his general philosophy was so largely false."[4] Bryan Magee observes that Schopenhauer's descriptive, metaphorical perceptions about the relationship between aesthetics and the world seem distorted by the imposition of his metaphysical system.[5] Despite multifarious interpretations of Schopenhauer which might themselves have merit, Schopenhauer's metaphysical system, manifested in part by the aesthetic use of Ideas, contains many perplexities and flaws. It is possible, however, to view the introduction of Ideas into Schopenhauer's aesthetics as a subsidiary, technically configured dimension of an otherwise illuminating theory; and one may do so in concert with Schopenhauer's own opinions.

Genius, claims Schopenhauer, arrives like inspiration. A gift of nature, it transcends ordinary human capacities when it is active but must also endure "long intervals during which men of genius stand in very much the same position as ordinary persons, both as regards merits and defects."[6] As a result of such lapses, works of genius will be a blend of greatness and misguided mediocrity.

Understanding, technical skill, and routine must fill up here the gaps left by the conception and inspiration of genius, and all kinds of necessary subsidiary work must run through the really only genuine and brilliant parts as their cement. This explains why all such works, with the sole exception of the most perfect masterpieces of the very greatest masters ... inevitably contain an admixture of something insipid and tedious that restricts enjoyment of them to some extent. (*WWR* 2, 410)

It might be countenanced that some of the less tenable passages in Schopenhauer's aesthetic writings adumbrate the Ideas as they play themselves out in the artistic world and that many theoretical headaches have been launched by efforts to disentangle the inconsistencies and opacities resulting from Schopenhauer's use of Ideas. The Ideas serve as a tenuous link between the philosophy of art and the more problematic metaphysical system. Yet, as Bryan Magee asks, has Schopenhauer not always appealed more fully to the artistically inclined among us, than to the philosophical? Might not his most enduring accomplishments be aesthetic rather than strictly metaphysical?[7]

Although Schopenhauer's comments on genius and its limitations, quoted above, refer to artistic genius, art and philosophy are but two sides of the same coin for Schopenhauer. "Not merely philosophy but also fine arts work at bottom towards the solution to the problem of existence" (*WWR* 2, 406). Schopenhauer's sense of continuity between philosophy and the arts goes even further.

The works of poets, sculptors, and pictorial or graphic artists generally contain an acknowledged treasure of profound wisdom, just because the wisdom of the nature of things themselves speaks from them ... all wisdom is certainly contained in the works of the pictorial or graphic arts, yet only *virtualiter* or *implicite*. Philosophy, on the other hand, endeavors to furnish the same wisdom *actualiter* and *explicite*; in this sense philosophy is related to these arts as wine is to grapes. (*WWR* 2, 407)

Therefore, as every artistic apprehension of things "is an expression more of the true nature of life and of existence, more an answer to the question, 'What is life?'" (*WWR* 2, 406), so too is philosophy a more conceptual response to this same question. Thus, the limits of artistic genius apply to philosophical or aesthetic genius as well.

The Ideas, on this view, may be interpreted as a limited dimension of Schopenhauer's aesthetics, governed by technical skill rather than inspired perception.

To defend this conception of Schopenhauer, where the most aesthetically compelling aspects of his work are disengaged from the more laborious passages on Ideas, we need to discern not only what we take to be Schopenhauer's crystalline, genuine perceptions, but also whether or not those perceptions hang together as something more than a series of wryly expressed aphorisms. To begin, the marginalization of Ideas in the sections that follow is justified by Schopenhauer's own views on genius and creativity. In Schopenhauer's own thinking about aesthetics, the expression of metaphysical truth – Will – through its representation in Ideas detracts from what can be construed as Schopenhauer's more compelling and empirical observations about the nature of life, and the life of nature, and the art that reflects it. These observations stand apart from the Platonic scaffolding Schopenhauer erects to support his aesthetic theory within his larger metaphysical scheme.

After all, Richard Taylor tells us, Schopenhauer's "thought was empirical and down to earth. He was an observer of the world, constantly reflecting on even its smallest processes, as exhibited in the lives of animals, for example. His views of human nature were derived not so much from reading, but from the daily observation of people and from divining their conscious and unconscious motives."[8] A richer appreciation of the Schopenhauerian aesthetic requires an acknowledgment of our status as living creatures, as *beings* at home in an extended environment, though the character of this extension shifts as we leave the realm of sufficient reason for that of the aesthetic, away from practical relations and purposes and towards the apprehension of relational representation. Early in *The World as Will and Representation*, Schopenhauer notes that we require the body to know Will in our individual selves (*WWR* 1, 19). The body as our link to nature and the primacy of nature in both aesthetic understanding and artistic creation will forge the key needed to unlock the continuity between nature, artist and art in Schopenhauer's aesthetic theory. In addition, the acknowledgment of ourselves as living creatures allows us to reinterpret Schopenhauer's aesthetic theory as a reflection on the relation between beauty and truth. Beauty promotes the recognition of our kinship with the natural world and with other human subjects. Nature furnishes knowledge of our kinship with other beings and systems, while art provides knowledge of ourselves as members of a species united by Will. Schopenhauer reclaims for aesthetics the quest for truth, albeit not a scientific, quantitative truth,[9] but a truth backlit and hallowed by beauty.

Both art and nature give rise to knowledge but in a perceptual, rather than conceptual manner. In this way, aesthetic experience is at heart a perceptual recognition of our earthly predicament. In nature, it is direct and often inspiring of devotion, peace of mind or awe. In art, it is allusive and relational but not in a culturally dependent or conceptual/allegorical fashion. Rather, art alludes to the living and lived human being as it confronts, struggles with, succumbs to or triumphs over its world. As a corollary to this, Schopenhauer's aesthetic theory implies that art furnishes knowledge about *human* nature most effectively, while knowledge about Will in the natural environment itself is most readily grasped in direct contact with the constituents of the natural world. Nevertheless, experiences of art and nature are preserved as continuous aspects of one aesthetic whole – the perceptual recognition of our earth-rootedness, or worldliness, the near-constant tempo of Will within and without the drama of living characters on the stage of their environment.

Even Ideas, bypassed on this reading of Schopenhauer, maintain a link to the wider natural environment they are meant to transcend. On several occasions in *The World as Will and Representation* Schopenhauer proclaims that Ideas are a representation of Will as species-type or natural kind (*WWR* 1, 197; 210; 235). Ideas are said to convey the *inner life* of all things rather than the relations of particular things (*WWR* 1, 233). The reading made here of Schopenhauer's aesthetics, however, relies upon acquiescence to the claim that the nature of the truth conveyed in aesthetic experience is of more importance, than the vehicle Schopenhauer devises for conveying it. As such a vehicle, Ideas obscure rather than clarify Schopenhauer's aesthetic observations. It is possible to appreciate and perhaps enhance our understanding of Schopenhauer's aesthetic vision without them.

NATURE

Natural beauty, for Schopenhauer, serves as an instantaneous and powerful mode of transport away from the daily and distracting details of life, even for the most ordinary among us.

natural beauty ... invites contemplation, and even presses itself on us. Whenever it presents itself to our gaze all at once, it almost always succeeds in snatching us, although only for a few moments, from subjectivity, from the thralldom of the will, and transferring us into the state of pure knowledge. This is why the man tormented by passions, want or care, is so suddenly revived, cheered, and comforted by a single, free glance into nature.   (*WWR* 1, 197)

The plant world everywhere offers itself for aesthetic contemplation without the medium of art (*WWR* 1, 218) and promotes a state of pure knowing when beheld by us in contemplation, as does the animal world, the objective contemplation of which "is an instructive lesson from the great book of nature; it is the deciphering of the true *signatura rerum*" (*WWR* 1, 219–220). The emphasis here is not only on the pleasurable affects of nature's aesthetic contemplation but also on what such contemplation may reveal to us or teach us, indicating the degree to which Schopenhauer sees aesthetic experience as *instructive* for human beings. It unveils some truth about ourselves and the natural world in which we dwell. Aesthetic relations bear us, if only momentarily, away from our wills and Will and into a state of pure perception. "Above all, natural beauty has this quality, and even the most stolid and apathetic person obtains therefrom at least a fleeting, aesthetic pleasure" (*WWR* 1, 210). The universal truth and consistency of nature combine to make beautiful landscapes so delightful to us (*WWR* 2, 403), and at any level of the natural world, the inner being of that world, Will, may become apparent to us. "Therefore we lose nothing if we stop at any particular thing, and true wisdom is not to be acquired by our measuring the boundless world ... it is acquired by thoroughly investigating any individual thing, in that we try thus to know and understand perfectly its true and peculiar nature" (*WWR* 1, 129). Aesthetic contemplation of an object's inner, essential relations is one such mode of investigation, holding the object or scene up for inspection free of its contingent particularities.

Yet, when it comes to the revelation of pure relations, of representation in the absence of self-interest or will, Schopenhauer sometimes appears to prefer art as the mode of transport into pure knowing. Art, he claims, greatly facilitates aesthetic pleasure and attains with greatest certainty "absolute silence of the will, required for the purely objective apprehension of the true nature of things ... " (*WWR* 2, 370). Nature, he claims, must be understood from ourselves, and not ourselves from nature (*WWR* 2, 196). It would appear that, just as we know Will most immediately in ourselves as will, so too might we know Will in nature by its representation and focus in art, which has a human genesis.

Here as elsewhere, Schopenhauer contradicts himself over the greater power of art or nature to facilitate aesthetic apprehension. Furthermore, when he claims that we must know nature from ourselves, he does not intend to say that all knowledge yielded by human products exceeds that furnished by the natural world. On the contrary, there is utter continuity between art and nature insofar as they encourage the pure knowing of the aesthetic consciousness; *any* particular object in the world has the potential to reveal metaphysical truth. The tendency for us, as human beings, to encounter this truth most pressingly in our individual wills does not then cast a hegemonic glaze over all particular items associated with our authorship. Will courses through *all* worldly veins, human or otherwise, and proper aesthetic appreciation reveals this to be the case.

Any appearance of contradiction in Schopenhauer's aesthetics over the issue of whether nature or art promotes the state of pure knowing most effectively disappears once the common metaphysical root of natural and artistic products becomes apparent. The contradiction emerges almost entirely from difficulties surrounding the interpretation and gradation of Ideas. Once Ideas are marginalized in a reading of Schopenhauer's aesthetics, the common metaphysical ancestry of art and nature emerges from Schopenhauer's text. From the very earliest pages of *The World as Will and Representation*, Schopenhauer stresses that the one-sided investigation of will in ourselves – which is immediate and in seeming contrast to the mediate awareness of Will in the representation of other objects – is a necessary abstraction and a "forcible separation of two things that essentially exist together" (*WWR* 1, 19). Not only are all objects indebted to the same metaphysical source; "aesthetic pleasure is essentially one and the same, whether it be called forth by a work of art, or directly by the contemplation of nature and of life" (*WWR* 1, 195). Even if the force of intellect rises as we move from the plant world through the animal kingdom and into the human community, the presence of will at each of these levels remains undiminished. "[T]he will everywhere retains its identical nature, and shows itself as a great attachment to life ... " (*WWR* 2, 206). Therefore, since aesthetic pleasure arises in the pure contemplation of the representation of

Will in particular objects or places, free from the usual tug of our daily and egoistic concerns, art essentially achieves the same thing as the visible world itself but perhaps with more focus on the universal relations revealed at hand (*WWR* 1, 266).

This continuity of aesthetic effectiveness between nature and art, as well as our place as artists on this continuum, point to several important but sometimes overlooked dimensions of Schopenhauer's aesthetic theory. Consider Schopenhauer's assertion of the twofold existence of human beings, who, when acting as mere individuals, encounter the world in the mode of suffering through the egoistic demands of the individual will. These same creatures, transformed by aesthetic consciousness, apprehend the world not as a place of suffering but as truth represented. "As such he is *all things*, in so far as he perceives them, and in him their existence is without burden or hardship" (*WWR* 2, 371). In aesthetic contemplation, our unity with the world becomes apparent. To the beholder of the world's beauty, information about the inner nature of that world is given in an epiphany of kinship, namely, "This living thing art thou" (*WWR* 1, 220).

In this sense, poetry that sings the praises of nature is just as much about the pure subject of knowing, the natural, human creature in a state of aesthetic consciousness, as it is about the environment that calls forth this pure knowing (*WWR* 2, 370). Art's proper end emerges not as a rendering of particular things but as a revelation of the common truth and ancestry beneath all earthly things. The real object of art, of the genius who creates it, "is only the essential nature of things in general, the universal in them, the totality" (*WWR* 2, 379). When knowing becomes free from the aims of will, contemplation can be pure, and "for this reason the result of every purely objective, and so of every artistic, apprehension of things is an expression more of the true nature of life and of existence, more an answer to the question, 'What is life?'. Every genuine and successful work of art answers this question in its own way quite calmly and serenely" (*WWR* 2, 406).

At its root, *art's* concern is to reveal the heart of *nature.* Art paves an avenue into the inner workings of the world, which can also be glimpsed directly in the natural environment itself. Natural and artistic beauty reveal the same thing, the primacy of Will at all levels of life and the world, and the aesthetic pleasure drawn from them is both alien to sensual hedonism and akin to a serene form of knowing. While natural beauty promotes the serenity of this knowl-

140

edge directly and immediately for most subjects, art requires the handiwork of genius to unveil the course of particularly *human* nature. The transition from one to the other – from the vistas of the natural environment to the concentrated focus of art – occurs on the crest of activities themselves born of a natural phenomenon: genius.

ARTIST

Genius, claims Schopenhauer, is the capacity for heightened contemplation of objects themselves, "the ability to leave entirely out of sight our own interest, our willing, and our aims, and consequently to discard entirely our own personality for a time, in order to remain *pure knowing subject*, the clear eye of the world ... " (*WWR* 1, 185–186). This capacity for sustained contemplation, for transcending the demands of sufficient reason, exists in all humans to some degree but reaches its productive pinnacle in genius, the source of artworks. Schopenhauer emphasizes that genius cannot be learned. Studying the products of art and the history of artistic creation may refine the abilities of the artist but this process cannot impart that ability in the first instance. Genius is indelibly a natural phenomenon, a gift of nature.

Only the genius ... is like the organic body that assimilates, transforms and produces. For he is, indeed, educated and cultured by his predecessors and their works; but only by life and the world itself is he made directly productive through the impression of what is perceived; therefore the highest culture never interferes with his originality.   (*WWR* 1, 235)

Emphasized even by this organic metaphor, the direct lineage from nature to genius manifests itself throughout Schopenhauer's characterization of genius as inborn (*WWR* 1, 195), an instinctual necessity (*WWR* 2, 382), a phenomenal aberration and an excess of reasonable intellect (*WWR* 2, 387–388). While echoing Kant on the natural originality of genius and the non-rule-governed genesis of its works, Schopenhauer nevertheless imparts to genius the crucial function, in his own aesthetic theory, of serving as a turnstile between the natural world and artistic products.

Just as genius itself occurs naturally, the process of creating artworks is naturally engendered. Schopenhauer's account of artistic creation stresses "the rapture of the moment, of the inspiration, of the free impulse of genius, without any admixture of deliberation and reflection" (*WWR* 2, 409). The most salient features of any artwork will hearken back to the moment of unmannered and almost uncontrollable urges of instinct. Of course, gaps between inspiration and technique will haunt any work and, as cited earlier, "all kinds of necessary subsidiary work must run through the really only genuine and brilliant parts as their cement" (*WWR* 2, 410). Still, genius, when most active, functions not only as a creature of nature but as "the clear mirror of the inner nature of the world" (*WWR* 1, 186). Its products reveal truth not through the talented deployment of concepts but through the expression of inspired, imaginative *perception*. In this way, one particular kind of natural object may be represented over and over again, for genius creates imaginative variations on natural themes (*WWR* 1, 267; *WWR* 2, 379) and even ordinary, non-inspired observers bring some modicum of imagination to bear in understanding the significance of works of art (*WWR* 2, 407). Unlike the deductions and inferences utilized by persons of talent, the imaginative perception of genius inspires artworks, and imaginative perception is, in turn, inspired by them.

If the contribution of genius to our knowledge rests on perception, however, we are left wondering what role those arts of a conceptual nature might play in the acquisition of knowledge. In the case of poetry, Schopenhauer asserts, an initial reliance on concepts through language leads *away* from the conceptual container in which perceptions are borne and towards more sustained reflection on the expression of perceptions themselves (*WWR* 1, 240). The real threat to genuine perception in art – to directing our focus on art's proper end, the revelation of the inner nature of things – comes not from conceptually embodied arts like literature and poetry but from conceptually interpreted perceptual arts, like painting and sculpture. More will be said about this in the next section, but here it is noted that concepts have little place in Schopenhauer's aesthetic vision. He remains adamant that genius has the capacity for genuine knowledge of the world through imaginative perception. Perceptual knowledge of both nature and art stands in contrast to the contemporary scientism which subordinates notions of truth to quantitative and logical expression, and its value differs from that of the concepts yielded by persons of talent in pursuit of scientific inquiry. The respect for an *aesthetic* way of knowing, as an alternative to the more familiar scientific way of knowing, is one of the most potent but neglected lessons to be drawn from Schopenhauer's work.

On this rests the high value of imagination as an indispensable instrument of genius. For only by virtue of imagination can genius present to itself each object or event in a vivid image, according to the requirements of the connexion of its painting, poetry or thinking, and thus always draw fresh nourishment from the primary source of all knowledge, perception ... Therefore the man without imagination is related to him as the mussel fastened to its rock, compelled to wait for what chance brings it, is to the freely moving or even winged animal. For such a man knows no other perception than the actual perception of the senses; until it comes, he nibbles at concepts and abstractions which are nevertheless only shells and husks, not the kernel of knowledge.   (*WWR* 2, 379)

Aesthetic knowing, then, relies on heightened perception to reveal the kernel of truth beneath conceptual husks. In relation to art, such perception is eased by the products of genius, but the natural genesis of genius and the indebtedness of genius to a gift of nature over which it does not have total control, suggest that imaginative, perceptual knowing is of an entirely different character to that of reasoned, conceptual knowing. In addition, the tight control of scientific ways of knowing serves the needs of will, while the almost spontaneous responsiveness to beauty can neither be willed in itself nor made subservient to will.[10] As a way of transcending the tumult of will, aesthetic perception runs renegade from the very needs of will served by science and other conceptually-oriented ways of knowing nature and the world. Genius, as both natural product and conveyer of nature's truth, preserves the continuity between art and nature not only by being subject to natural impulses and necessities for the creation of its products but also by making the inner nature of things, as harnessed by imaginative perception, the *subject of* its creations. Schopenhauer's art draws inspiration from a vision of nature, comes to fruition through the handiwork of nature's artistic pawn and, finally, reveals the truth of that nature – Will – in perceptually accessible, representative form. Thus does art, when properly construed in Schopenhauer's terms, exert its influence not by means of allusion to history, myth, culture or belief, but by direct and unfettered portrayal of Will in the willing of creatures and objects of the world.

ART

As remarked in an earlier section, art conveys the universality and totality of Will through the creation of representational products. In focusing on the omnipresence of Will in nature, artworks do not feature reference to conceptual schemes, history or cultural matrices but rather to those truths that endure.

> The material of history is the transient complexities of a human world moving like clouds in the wind, which are often transformed by the most trifling incident. From this point of view, the material of history appears to us as scarcely an object worthy of the serious and arduous consideration of the human mind. Just because it is so transitory, the human mind should select for its consideration that which is destined never to pass away.
>
> (*WWR* 2, 442)

Nations, races, tribes; all are mere abstractions from the human individual and as abstractions ought to be ignored as subject matter in the province of art. Conversely, the pure contemplation of any *individual*, human or otherwise, reveals an entire world. Schopenhauer perpetually warns us away from too sweeping a contemplative project, urging us instead to fix our attention upon what is revealed in close, perceptual inspection of single entities.

From the very beginning of *The World as Will and Representation* Schopenhauer prefers direct perception and intuition to inferential abstraction (*WWR* 1, 6). In tune with this he stresses the "inner" rather than the "outer" significance of art, where the "inner" dimension reveals the essential relations of any species-type and the "outer" dimension concentrates on the time-ordered and conventional connections between and among individuals (*WWR* 1, 230). Pictorial and plastic allegory as a mode of focus on the outer, historical dimension of art is particularly rejected by Schopenhauer, for it derives its significance from relations of convention and concept, rather than from the representative portrayal of Will at work in nature: "... through the allegory a concept is always to be signified, and consequently the mind of the beholder has to be turned aside from the depicted representation of perception to one that is quite different, abstract, and not perceptive, and lies entirely outside the work of art" (*WWR* 1, 237). Therefore, allegory stands in direct contrast to the proper end of art as conceived by Schopenhauer: allegorical works refer rather than represent, and do so in connection with human institutions, traditions and practices rather than with nature itself. "Only the genuine works that are drawn directly from nature and life remain eternally young and strong, like nature and life itself" (*WWR* 1, 236). And, as we have seen, Schopenhauer's aesthetics marks a strong preference for the depiction of that which endures, that is, Will, in nature and in natural human creatures.

Especially offensive to Schopenhauer's aesthetic sensibility is that degenerate mode of allegory known as symbolism, for in its practice, art veers entirely off course from perceptual contemplation into territory through which one must be guided by concepts alone. Foreshadowing contemporary semiotic concerns, Schopenhauer complains that "if there is absolutely no connexion between what is depicted and the concept indicated by it ... the sign and the thing signified are connected quite conventionally by positive fixed rule casually introduced" (*WWR* 1, 239). In plastic and pictorial art especially, "allegory leads away from what is given in perception, from the real object of art, to abstract thoughts ..." (*WWR* 1, 240). Because allegorical symbols force consciousness away from what can be known in direct perception and towards the conventional connection of that perception with conceptual considerations, art which features allegory or relies upon conventional matrices for its interpretation and appreciation will constitute, for Schopenhauer, a degenerate form of art.

Far from serving as a web for the play of signs and conventions of signification, art reaches its apex in the depiction not merely of nature but in the revelation of nature in its human incarnation (*WWR* 1, 210). Plant forms and even animal behavior can be observed most fruitfully in direct contact with nature, without human intervention (*WWR* 2, 404), though they also lend themselves to the pictorial and plastic arts. For the pure contemplation of human nature, however, art and especially poetry become necessary to reveal "not only ... the form, but ... the action, position, and deportment, though always only as the character of the species, not of the individual" (*WWR* 1, 219). This is required because of the dramatic character of human willing in the world and also because it is more difficult for the observer to achieve aesthetic consciousness of a human being in direct contact with that human being: so many practical, instinctual and willful drives interfere! While Schopenhauer sometimes equivocates over whether it is best to appreciate the non-human environment directly or through art, he never oscillates on the question of how human beings *qua* species-type ought to be approached aesthetically. The dramatic character of the human animal requires an art form to evoke the presence of Will and so "the presentation of man in the connected series of his efforts and actions, is thus the great subject of poetry" (*WWR* 1, 244). Poetry not only mimics the sense of movement and progress characteristic of human action; it requires the imaginative input of the perceiver to bring its vision to fullness and in so doing provides an aesthetic parallel to the discovery of Will through our individual wills.

Poetry achieves its impact in a perceptual manner. The reader or listener develops a *sense* of human character as it plays itself out in metaphorical narrative. Metaphor, unlike allegory, creates new visions of relations. Allegory substitutes denotation for visions and relies less upon imagination and perception than upon cultural acquaintance. Metaphor draws directly on perceived experience, allegory on learned conceptualization. When Will in human nature, as will, is portrayed pictorially or in the plastic arts, its strength will derive from the capacity of these arts to foster a direct perception of Will in the willing of the portrayed subject. If a work requires some translation of a cultural, conceptual or historical allusion, it degenerates as art and falls away from the potency reserved for what Schopenhauer thinks of as genuine art – art that seeks to promote serene, will-less knowledge of Will through direct perception of the beautiful. Similarly, poetic strength derives not from complex allusion and symbol but rather from the vivid depiction, in metaphorical narrative, of the struggles of human creatures in their earthly environment. We need not know who, in the individual sense, is struggling in a poem – as with pictorial allegory, such necessity guarantees the degeneration of art – but, through metaphor employed to capture and ignite imagination, we perceive the willful wrestling characteristic of the human species-type.

While genius possesses the capacity for heightened perception of the natural environment and human nature, and conveys that perception in works of art, even ordinary observers have some potential for aesthetic observation of art and nature, if only for a fleeting moment. The ability to contemplate the world aesthetically relies, however, not upon acquaintance with and dexterity in the application of cultural symbols, art history or conceptual analysis, but rather upon the mere possession of human senses, will-lessly employed. Aesthetic perception consists of attaining a serene level of contemplation of the world such that this world appears clearly in virtue of its representative relations and not as an extension or object of our individual wills. This clarity of perception allows us to *apprehend*, sensorially, the true nature of the world and its beings, the character of Will in its variously graded manifestations. There-fore, what art uncovers is not its own properties and places as elucidated by institutions, theories or histories of human endeavor, but enduring natural truths which at once encompass and work within all worldly things.

In light of this, Schopenhauer's philosophy serves as a mild corrective to any theory of art that might overemphasize the necessity of convention and category in aesthetic appreciation. While contemporary aesthetic theory privileges those approaches which make the interpretation and evaluation of art dependent upon all variety of conceptual matrix – categories of art, institutions of art, artworld theories, sign and signification – Schopenhauer's aesthetics reminds us that many avenues lead to beauty's door. Making the apprehension of beauty a passenger on the coach of academic discourse robs aesthetic experience of its multi-hued complexity. Institutional or category theories of art may function well as frameworks through which to clarify and preserve our aesthetic traditions, but limiting art's value to its placement in such frameworks contravenes the *actual* aesthetic experiences of *actual* human persons. Every day in galleries in every city all over the world, and every night in woods, on mountains and at sea, persons untutored in the history and categories of art find themselves in the midst of aesthetic emotion. Surely art and nature have the power to move us, have the strength to imply the presence of true apprehension, for reasons other than their allegorical and conventional significance.

In nature, manifold beauties reveal themselves unfettered by the bonds of art and by such revelation allow us to consider them for what they themselves are, rather than for their usefulness or relationship to us. In art, perceptions of others unfold to widen our understanding of nature at work in the world, including human nature, its environs and struggles within and beyond itself. One need not know *whom* a portrait represents to see *what* it portrays. Human dramas and natural forms can bypass the web of instruction and appeal directly to the senses and understanding of the creature who knows his or her world and recognizes its portrayal. For Schopenhauer, art maintains a direct line to nature *via* the works of the natural genius. Genuine artworks unveil, in overtly sensuous fashion, the tumult of Will as the cauldron encompassing life.

For this reason, aesthetic perception does not occur when one has made the correct appellation of subject to symbol, or when one has acknowledged a work's possession of the standard features of its category, or when one comprehends a work due to its initiation into an esoteric artworld. Such practices, while valuable for pedagogical and theoretical endeavors, are not, on Schopenhauer's view, perceptual aesthetic engagements but abstract conceptual ones. Rather, aesthetic perception occurs when one *recognizes* the presence of Will in the world, and recognizes it free from the movement of will itself. All things, everywhere, stand in thrall to Will, to the course of nature, and perceiving this truth provides us with one of our few respites from that fact as it shapes and shifts events in our own lives. Whether we meet with Will in the harmonious forms of the natural environment or in the artistic expression of human dramas, the character of what is met with and recognized never changes. The ever-changing face of nature itself, as well as the embodied flexibility of artistic imagination, snatch our attention and realign our focus on the kinship of all earthly life. Aesthetic experience, for Schopenhauer and perhaps, at times, for us, is valued not for the moments of pleasure it brings but for what the pleasurable abatement of will allows us to *know*: the truth of our earthly predicament.

Notes

1 Details of this ambiguity in Schopenhauer have been explored elsewhere in articles by T. J. Diffey and me. See T. J. Diffey, "Schopenhauer's Account of Aesthetic Experience," *British Journal of Aesthetics*, 30, 1990, pp. 132–142; Cheryl Foster, "Schopenhauer's Subtext on Natural Beauty," *British Journal of Aesthetics*, 32, 1992, pp. 21–32.

2 James D. Chansky, "Schopenhauer and Platonic Ideas: A Groundwork for an Aesthetic Metaphysics," in Eric von der Luft, ed., *Schopenhauer: Essays in Honor of his 200th Birthday* (Lewiston, NY: The Edwin Mellen Press, 1988), p. 72.

3 For an excellent treatment of the particular problem of the gradations of Will in Schopenhauer's aesthetic theory, see T. G. Taylor, "Platonic Ideas, Aesthetic Experience, and the Resolution of Schopenhauer's Great Contradiction," *International Studies in Philosophy*, 19, 1987, pp. 43–53.

4 Frederick Copleston, *Schopenhauer: Philosopher of Pessimism* (London: Burns, Oates, and Washburne, Ltd., 1946), p. 141.

5 Bryan Magee, *The Philosophy of Schopenhauer* (Oxford: The Clarendon Press, 1983), p. 174.

6 *WWR* 1, 188.

7 Magee, p. 114.

8 Richard Taylor, "Forward," von der Luft, ed., *Schopenhauer*, p. xxiii.

9 William Desmond, "Schopenhauer, Art and the Dark Origin" in von der Luft, ed., *Schopenhauer*, p. 102.

10 Schopenhauer's treatment of the sublime suggests that some sort of aesthetic consciousness can in fact be willed. But it is not entirely clear whether the character of such consciousness is truly aesthetic in the sense of its engendering the pure subject of knowing who transcends the tug of practical need. What we can be certain of here is that the aesthetic response to beauty cannot be willed, where beauty differs from the sublime in nature primarily by virtue of its spontaneous grasp on our attentions.

7

Schopenhauer on beauty and ontology

NATHAN ROTENSTREICH

THE JUDGMENT OF TASTE

We begin our exploration of Schopenhauer's conception of beauty by summing up some components of Kant's system related to that subject. This is done, not because of the chronological or historical sequence but because of the built-in relation of Schopenhauer to Kant on that issue. We may say already here that Schopenhauer integrated several of Kant's components of the exploration and gave them a new dimension and status.

Kant says that the beautiful is that which pleases in the mere estimate of it; it is not in sensation or by means of a concept.[1] From the position of judgment related to the beautiful, it is said that the judgment of taste determines its objects in terms of delight – as a thing of beauty. Though these components, both of taste and delight, are prominent, there is a claim to the agreement of everyone just as if it were objective. An example is that to say that this flower is beautiful is tantamount to repeating its own proper claim to the delight of everyone.[2] An additional characteristic of art is that the work of art is organized or a self-organized being. An organized being possesses inherent formative power. It is a self-propagating formative power, which cannot be explained by any mechanism.[3]

The conjunction of delight on the one hand and the inner structure of the work of art on the other becomes manifest in the absense of interest, that is to say of taking advantage of the work of art. Every interest vitiates the judgment of taste and robs it of its impartiality. It is a pure judgment of taste, uninfluenced by charm or emotion. The determining ground is the finality of form.[4] An empirical interest in the beautiful exists only in society – but that interest is of no importance for the placement of the work of art which has to be evaluated beyond its empirical usage. The judgment which is called aesthetic refers to the representation by which an object is given. Yet, it refers solely to the subject and does not describe the quality of the object. It describes only the final form in the determination of the powers of representation. The determining ground is the feeling of the internal sense. It refers to a thing which is capable only of being felt. "For I must feel the pleasure immediately in the representation of the object, and I cannot be talked into it by any grounds of proof."[5] Hence it is the reflection of the Subject upon his own state to the exclusion of precepts and rules.[6]

FINALITY OF FORM

This closed character of the work of art on the one hand and its relation to the responding subject and his judgment of taste on the other – is manifested in the finality of the work of art. When an object contains the grounds of the actuality of itself, it is called its end. The agreement of a thing with the constitution of things which is only possible according to ends, is called the finality of its form.[7]

The self-contained essence of the work of art or of the beautiful in general is identical with the finality of itself. The finality pointed to is merely a subjective formal finality of the object. The grounds of pleasure reside merely in the form of the object. Consequently, it resides not in any sensation of the object or in any reference to a concept. A representation of finality on the part of the object is in respect to the cognitive faculties of the Subject.[8] We can say that for Kant the work of art is beautiful. The attribution of beauty to parts of nature is tantamount to the self-contained character of the object perceived as beautiful. There is no reference to other objects. Hence the isolation of the beautiful is related only to the responding subject in his delight and negatively to overcoming any particular interest in the state of affairs evoking his delight. Because of these characteristic features, Kant dealt with the beautiful in the context of his theory of the faculty of judgment, being a kind of in-between link between knowledge and practice. There is no constitution of the object in the sense present in knowledge, neither is there a shaping of the object, as inherent in ethical acts. There is merely a looking at accompanied by delight and evoking a particular mode of judging – the judgment of taste. We have to move now to two additional components in Kant's conception which are not that central but have to be mentioned anticipating Schopenhauer's position.

SCHOPENHAUER'S CONCEPT OF GENIUS

The first point to be mentioned here is the status of the genius. For Kant, genius is a talent and as such a natural endowment which gives the rule to art. Genius is the innate mental aptitude.[9] Fine arts must necessarily be regarded as arts of genius, because fine arts do not derive as a product of any rule. A genius is a talent which gives a rule but does not follow it. The individual as such by his natural endowment lays down the rule of art. Thus, fine art is only possible as a product of genius. The products of genius are exemplary. This relation between genius and art cannot indicate scientifically how it brings about its product. Thus, genius is not guided by any method, as it is not guided by any rules. Nature prescribes the rule through genius, but not to science. It prescribes it to art, insofar as it is to be fine art. Eventually there is a complete opposition between genius and the spirit of imitation, since imitation is inherently an attitude of following something which is beyond the creativity of the individual.[10]

Within the sphere of art, Kant refers to several modes like painting and architecture. We have to pay special attention to his description and evaluation of music, because of the centrality of music in Schopenhauer's system. Kant speaks about the relation between music and what he calls a sense of vitality (*Vitalsinn*).[11] The term employed here refers to Kant's basic position that music has to be viewed on the level of sensation or vitality grounded in sensation. Indeed, music is the art of tone, and speaks, in Kant's description, by means of mere sensations without concepts. It does not, like poetry, have any good for reflection behind it. It moves the mind, being more a matter of enjoyment than of culture. Music, according to Kant, advances from sensations to indefinite ideas while other art advances from definite ideas to sensation. Hence, the impression of music is only fleeting and does not evoke a lasting impression.[12] Put differently, the course of playing music ranges from bodily sensation to aesthetic ideas.[13]

These descriptions which are just the same evaluations of music lead us to the conclusion that music is not on a high level of art activity but rather on a low level, because the emphasis is laid on the component of sensations or even of the body. It will be evident that Schopenhauer's analysis of music and its evaluation is basically different because Schopenhauer takes music to be the highest manifestation of artistic activity and brings it rather close to philosophy. This will be our concern later.

152

In the last part of the first volume of *The World as Will and Representation*, Schopenhauer deals extensively with a critique of Kantian philosophy. Schopenhauer stresses the impact of Kant's philosophy, mainly Kant's distinction between the phenomenon and the thing-in-itself, and, even more so, the opposition between the two. Schopenhauer analyzes these differences in the two editions of the *Critique of Pure Reason*. Our concern is with Schopenhauer's comments on the Third Critique, precisely because the essence of art is dealt with in this context.

According to Schopenhauer, Kant did not start with an analysis of the beautiful, but with judgment of the beautiful and therefore reached toward judgment of taste. Schopenhauer stresses the concept of finality which is for Kant the key to the essence of the beautiful. Without going into some critical remarks at this point, it can be said that in Kant there is a correlation between judgment and finality. Thus there is a correlation between the approach of the subject and the object of his approach. When Schopenhauer takes advantage of Kant's concept or term "the faculty of judgment," he speaks about the faculty of intuitional knowledge (*anschaulich*). He says that he wants to employ this concept in the direction of a positive part of his system. At this point we can deal with some aspects of Schopenhauer's philosophy of the beautiful.

Schopenhauer integrated into his system some of the basic descriptions and analyses of beauty and the work of art. This integration led to some systematic consequences which went beyond Kant's descriptions and system. We can already say at this point that Schopenhauer's integration has to be viewed within the context of the world as "will and representation"; we have to be aware that the term "representation" is not fully adequate for the German term *Vorstellung* because of the difference between the prefixes "re" and "vor." We start with one of Kant's descriptions of the essence of representation. Kant says that whatever the origin of our representations, namely, whether they are due to the influence of outer things or are produced through inner causes, whether they arise *a priori* or as appearances, and have an empirical origin, they must as modifications of the mind (*Geist*) belong to inner sense. What is significant in terms of our exploration is that Kant gives a very large scope of meanings or directions to the representations. Therefore he describes them as modifications of the mind (*Geist*) to emphasize this broad scope of meanings attributed to them. In addition, as we notice, there is a relation between representations

153

and inner sense, though Kant does not articulate that relation more specifically.[14]

When we look at some of the descriptions of Schopenhauer's exposition of the concept of representation, we notice that he considers representations to be the first fact of consciousness. There are essential basic forms of the fact, namely the split between object and subject. The realm of object is guided by the principle of sufficient grounds. The whole class of objects is related to that principle. Time as succession and space as well as matter – are all manifestations of representation in its various directions.[15] It is therefore essential for Schopenhauer, within the scope of representation, to ask whether there is some essence or structure to representation. Indeed, we find that Schopenhauer employs in this context the term *Gestalt*, that is to say that there is an underlying structure to all of these manifestations of representation.[16] In the context of our analysis of these philosophical explorations of the essence of music, we notice that Schopenhauer speaks about music as representation.[17] These descriptions lie within the comprehensive scope of representation, and are not just a modification of consciousness or of the mind. Representations are foci of different interpretations of that which is given to consciousness, including space and time. This points to the basic issue, namely that Schopenhauer deals with representation within the dichotomy or duality between will and representation. Relational components of data are within the structure of representation and are not to be listed with conceptual or categorical statements as Kant conceived this.

OBJECTIVITY AND PURITY OF PERCEPTION

The second point to be mentioned at this stage of our analysis is the interpretation offered by Kant of the finality of works of art or of the beautiful. Schopenhauer employs the term "idea" even in its Platonic sense in relation to the object of art or that which is beautiful. Within the reference to the beautiful, we know the object not only as a particular thing, but we know also the Platonic idea, that is to say the permanent form of the whole species of things. Schopenhauer considers that relation not only as one referring to the individual spectator of beauty but to the pure subject of knowledge. That subject is in Schopenhauer's terminology "without will."[18] The two poles of that characterization are significant for the shape of Schopenhauer's system. He wants to stress the purity of the representation inherent in the work of beauty because that work is separated from reality and its disturbing accidental events. The artist lets us look through his eyes in the world. He recognizes the essential beyond all accidental relations of things. This is indeed the gift of the genius who combines in his essence that which is innate and that which he acquires as a technical component of art.[19] Because of that isolated element of art, Schopenhauer speaks even in this characterization about the beatitude of spectating without being motivated by will.[20] This is for Schopenhauer the basic manifestation of subject delight, and, indeed, he uses here Kant's term "delight," though he gives it an interpretation which goes beyond Kant's interpretation of art. It is not by accident that Schopenhauer uses the term "aesthetic contemplation,"[21] pointing again to the correlation between the idea and the pure subject of knowing.[22] The idea of man in general is fully expressed in the form which is to be spectated.[23] Schopenhauer speaks about the objective expression; it is obvious that the "objective" does not connote the placement within relations of different objects. It connotes that which is perfectly expressed.[24] Hence the idea amounts to the status of being objective, but that status is immersed within the work of art or of that which is beautiful. By this, Schopenhauer stresses the inherent synthesis between expression in the sensuous stratum or component and that which is in ideational character. Probably Schopenhauer's analysis of music and its evaluation, to which we shall return presently, is related to that isolated character of the work of art which has its own structure within its own scope. Coming back to Kant's description of finality, we can say that for Kant a thing exists as a physical end if it is both cause and effect of itself. An example which Kant presents in this context is rather telling: "A tree produces, in the first place, another tree, according to a familiar law of nature. But the tree which it produces is of the same genus. Hence, in its *genus*, it produces itself. In the genus, now as effect, now as cause, continually generated from itself and likewise generated itself, it preserves itself generically."[25] This example shows that finality though related to a particular tree has its impact on the relations between particular trees. Thus, it cannot be seen in its isolation or to put it differently we have to distinguish between being particular and being final. Because for Schopenhauer finality is synonymous with separation and isolation, we shall deal now with that aspect, because it amounts to what is in Schopenhauer's own terminology the metaphysics of art, that is, music.[26]

BEAUTY IN THE SELF-ENCLOSED ARTWORK

The self-enclosed character of the work of art shaped by beauty is more prominent than beauty inherent in natural phenomena. Those phenomena are connected with the environmental framework of natural phenomena. Only the beholder isolates them from their built-in context. In terms of the work of art, the self-enclosure is prominent, because that work is particular and it is established by the activity of a person or persons. For Schopenhauer, the finality inherent in the work of art is a reinforcement of the self-enclosed character. Here again we can ask whether natural phenomena can be seen as containing a formal finality in themselves. This finality emphasizes the separation of the work of art from the infrastructure of reality because that structure is one of relations, that is to say, does not point to the separated character of any event or phenomenon. In terms of Schopenhauer's system, that isolation amounts to the basic fact that the work of art is not prompted by sufficient reason or by causality, since both principles point to the relation between events and phenomena and do not enable the separation of a single phenomenon from its context. Obviously, the work of art even as established is still present in the total environment of the surrounding world. But that presence is not of a shaping character as it occurs within the boundaries of the singular work of art. The singularity of the work is the other side of isolation or the other way around. Thus, even when Schopenhauer accepts Kant's description of the work of art and its relation to representation, he moves forward to the position of the work of art within the surrounding world as not being interrelated with occurrences or phenomena of that world. Thus, the work of art grounded in beauty occupies a semi-ontological position by being present in the environmental world but still separated from it. To employ, in this context, the term not employed by Schopenhauer, estrangement or alienation – we could say that the work of art embodies in itself the alienation from the surrounding world. Schopenhauer employs the term 'objectification," but in a more precise sense, we may say that objectification amounts to estrangement or alienation. We do not deny that the creator of the work of art belongs to the world at large, but that what he creates is estranged from that world.

Schopenhauer agrees with Kant about the relation between judgment and beauty, but he separates the phenomenon of beauty from being dependent on a judgment only. In a rather extreme formulation, he says that he denies the whole doctrine of the categories.[27] The mode of looking at things independent of the proposition of sufficient reason, is described by Schopenhauer even as a complete objectivity or objective direction of the spirit. This is so because it is opposed to the subjective direction pointing to one's own person. That pointing is essentially one directed toward will. Geniality of the person is again understood as the most complete objectivity.[28]

We already mentioned that Schopenhauer speaks in this context about the beatitude of *Anschauen* lacking will – in order to stress that there is a response to that self-enclosed work of art.[29] That response can be described as beatitude or blessing because of the detachment from reality, driven by urges grounded in will. Beatitude apparently implies a kind of tranquility, and tranquility again can be attributed to the impact of that which is self-enclosed, that is, remains within its own boundaries. This component of objectivity applies even to human beauty as an objective expression containing in itself the idea of man in general.[30]

It is in this context that we have to consider the most eminent position attributed to music in Schopenhauer's system. We don't have to deal with possible personal predilections. We have to consider the systematic aspect of Schopenhauer's view. Schopenhauer deals with different modes of art, like poetry, architecture, and so on. Yet music has a special status, because, as Schopenhauer says,[31] music is not an image of ideas like the other arts. It is an image of the will itself. The other arts speak about shadows while music speaks about essence. Music is an immediate objectification and image of the complete will the way the world itself is.[32] Apparently, Schopenhauer thought that the position of the image of the will can be understood as a total separation from the quotidian impact of the will. Thus, self-enclosure is not one of particularities, but of the will as such. This radical statement points to the relation between music and the structure of the universe and its underlying force and still separates music from the pressure of will in its expressions. Because of that total separation, we find in Schopenhauer's description of the position of music, the statement that music expresses the quintessence of life.

Schopenhauer attributes to the delight of all that is beautiful the conciliation or tranquility[33] which are meant to overcome the pressure of day-to-day reality. Again, we notice that Schopenhauer is not satisfied with the response to the work of art as being beautiful, but adds to that response a kind of a repentance (*Trost*), thus going beyond the limited scope of delight to something which is akin to the beatitude to which he referred already. Why music is of this particular character as a kind of an isolated island *par excellence*, is perhaps not explained by Schopenhauer himself. We can say that looking at some of the philosophical explorations of music, like, for instance, that of Hegel, we notice that Schopenhauer, in a very pointed way, goes beyond the placement of music within the inner aspect of the subjective. Hegel emphasizes the relation of the subjective inner component with time, as the universal element of music. Schopenhauer goes beyond these descriptions in order to place music as the highest manifestation of artistic creativity and perhaps the only way to understand this conception is by trying to interpret it.

IMAGE AND CREATIVITY

One cannot but wonder about the use of the term "image" – *Abbild* – in the context of an analysis of the position of works of art. The same question applies to the metaphor used by Schopenhauer – *camera obscura*. After all, *Abbild* is the German translation of the Greek term *eidolon*. We notice that in the context of his analysis, Schopenhauer refers to the position of ideas with reference to works of art; ideas are related to *eidos* and obviously not to *eidolon*. One does not find an explanation of the employment of these terms or metaphors in the text. Hence, we have to present a conjecture.

Probably, the term *Abbild* does not connote the content of the work of art. If the work of art is a product of creativity and as such is prompted by the finality without end and contains that finality in itself, it is not an image of a reality outside it. Moreover, if the work of art lacks will, it cannot copy will which is the basic factor or force of reality at large. To emphasize this even more, the work of art, as we have seen, is isolated from reality and will. Thus, it cannot represent it in the strict sense of the term, that is to say, refer to it and present an image of it in its own orbit. On the other hand, a work of art is particular and its isolation is possible on the basis of its particularity. Hence, it cannot represent will or reality at large.

Our conjecture would be that the work of art being self-contained, is considered by Schopenhauer as an ultimate structure, ultimate in its own boundaries, that is to say, created and not given – unlike the givenness of the will or the universe at large. The work of art cannot be reduced to any orbit or factor outside itself. Schopenhauer apparently makes the step from being self-enclosed to being ultimate and in this sense within the plurality of works of art – and there is no way but to point to that plurality – each one is ultimate. The plurality is *post-factum*, and does not anticipate the product of creativity. Perhaps Schopenhauer wanted to point to a kind of positional parallelism between every work of art and the ultimate factor of reality, will and reality as prompted by it.

Again, as a conjecture, the special or superior position of music is grounded in these deliberations. Music, unlike, for instance, poetry or painting, is self-contained to such a degree that even its components and not only its structure is self-enclosed. Music does not structure words like poetry where the words are given and therefore precede the creative approach to them and their created structure. Colors are present in nature and to some extent painting is an *Abbild* in the basic sense of that term of the colors encountered. Music does not take advantage of words, neither does it relate to colors. Music is self-enclosed, *par excellence*. Its components are created and its structure is correlated to the components; we cannot separate the particular tones and the rhythm of a symphony or of an opera. Indeed, when music is performed, the performance takes place within a certain space. It occurs in the sequence of time and thus is brought into the structure of reality at large, even when that framework of its performance is a limited structure or a partial one. It is expressed through instruments, and these are physical objects. But we apparently have to distinguish between music and its performance, whereby the performance is dictated by the music, though it may be an interpretation of it. Probably, this position of music which is correlated to its intrinsic structure, the self-enclosed correlation between tones, rhythm, and the final expression of the two, enabled Schopenhauer to attribute to music this superior position within the scope of works of art. That superior position makes the quasi-parallelism between art and will as the prompting factor of reality more prominent, whereby Schopenhauer does not erase the difference between reality and art, but attempts possibly to emphasize that on the top level the work of art is so prominent that it can be seen as being not only independent of reality, but also parallel to it in its status.

We can sum up by saying that for Kant the work of art is correlated to judgment, and, for that basic consideration, Kant dealt with art in the context of his Third Critique. Schopenhauer is not oblivious to these reflective or reflectional aspects of the work of art and taste.

Yet, by dealing with the position of the work of art within the broadest scope of reality, he considered the metaphysics of art, and thus its position as an ultimate mode of reality, precisely by being created and not given or preestablished. At this point, we can say that Schopenhauer attempted to bring about a synthesis between reflection and metaphysics, that is to say, between reflection and a kind of ontology of beauty. Beauty is not only in the eyes of the beholder, but is inherent in the "partial islands" of that which is created by the creator, that is, by the agent of art. Whether what we refer to as estrangement or alienation permits that ontological approach is an open question.

We employed the term "alienation" to describe the process inherent in creating the work of art. It is a term with negative connotations, and Schopenhauer wanted to express the positive aspects of the process. The term "estrangement" is more positive, and, in Hegel's system, the external spirit is a stage toward the absolute spirit. In a sense, Schopenhauer considered the objectification as being consonant with the absolute status of the work of art, since that work is absolved, that is to say, separated. Its separation is not given in the first place, but it becomes someone's creation.

It is not clear whether Schopenhauer considered the result of the process as a deliberate goal. If so, he could attribute an intention to the overcoming of will, the deliberate direction of will overcoming its primary drive. Or the outcome containing in itself the element of repentance is an outcome in the sense of externalization whereby it is objective without the grounds in subjectivity.

Still, that status of the outcome is for Schopenhauer the background for this consideration of the work embodying beauty.

Notes

1 Immanuel Kant, *Kritik der Urteilskraft*, in *Kants gesammelte Schriften*, königlich Presussischen Akademie der Wissenschaften (hereafter *Akademie Ausgabe*) (Berlin: G. Reimer, 1902–1910), vol. V, p. 306. The English translation is referred to after the semicolon, from *The Critique of Judgement*, James Creed Meredith, trans. (Oxford: Clarendon Press, 1964), p. 167.
2 Ibid., p. 282; p. 136.
3 Ibid., p. 246; p. 92.
4 Ibid., p. 223; pp. 64–65.
5 Ibid., pp. 285–286; p. 141.

6 Ibid.; ibid.
7 Ibid., p. 180; p. 19.
8 Ibid., p. 190; p. 31.
9 Ibid., p. 307; p. 168.
10 Ibid.; ibid.
11 *Akademie Ausgabe*, p. 155.
12 Ibid., p. 195.
13 Kant, *Kritik der reinen Vernunft, Akademie Ausgabe*, vol. III, p. 99; p. 131.
14 Schopenhauer, *Die Welt als Wille und Vorstellung* (Leipzig: P. Reclam, 1890), p. 71.
15 Ibid., p. 264.
16 Ibid.
17 Ibid., p. 288.
18 Ibid., p. 280.
19 Ibid., p. 285.
20 Ibid., p. 259.
21 Ibid., p. 290.
22 *Kritik der Urteilskraft*, p. 371; trans. Part II, p. 18.
23 *WWR* 2, 447ff.
24 *WWR* 1, 576.
25 *WWR* 2, 252.
26 *WWR* 1, 268.
27 Ibid., 295.
28 Ibid., 340.
29 Ibid., 8.
30 Ibid., 55.
31 Ibid., 151.
32 Georg Wilhelm Friedrich Hegel, *Vorlesungen über die Aesthetik*, III, Glockner, ed., vol. 14, p. 151. Hegel considered art to be within the scope of absolute spirit, as the first stage of it, implying representation or *Anschauung*. The notion of objectivity could not be applied to a stage of absolute spirit.
33 Paul Oskar Kristeller deals with systems of aesthetics up to Schopenhauer. See his "The Modern System of Arts," *The Journal of the History of Ideas*, 12, 1951, pp. 496ff; 13, 1952, pp. 17ff. Otto Poggeler, "Schopenhauer und das Wesen der Kunst," *Zeitschrift für Philosophische Forschung*, 14, 1960, pp. 353ff.

8

Schopenhauer, Heidegger, art, and the will

JULIAN YOUNG

INTRODUCTION

The question of the relationship between Schopenhauer and Heidegger has been, in English at least, virtually untouched. This is somewhat odd given the evident fact that Heidegger read Schopenhauer and the rather striking affinities between the two. No doubt this neglect has been encouraged by the fact that Heidegger's explicit references to Schopenhauer are, almost without exception, contemptuous. (For example: "[Schopenhauer's discussion of art] stumbles about aimlessly ... It cannot be called an aesthetics that would be even remotely comparable to that of Hegel. In terms of content Schopenhauer thrives on the authors he excoriates, namely Schelling and Hegel. The one he does not excoriate is Kant. Instead he thoroughly misunderstands him.")[1] This, however, should by no means be taken as decisive. Wittgenstein, for example, having plundered, almost plagiarized, Schopenhauer in the *Tractatus* later judged (employing, paradoxically, a characteristically Schopenhauerian metaphor) that "where true depth begins Schopenhauer's runs out." And Nietzsche, of course, having plundered Schopenhauerian philosophy in *The Birth of Tragedy* spent the rest of his life protesting that Schopenhauer has always been his "antipode."

To speak of the influence of Schopenhauer on Heidegger raises difficult questions concerning the genesis of Heidegger's ideas which, on this occasion, I do not wish to investigate. I shall speak, therefore, merely of *affinities*. In this essay I propose to begin (but by no means complete) the task of studying the affinities between Heidegger and Schopenhauer. In particular, I want to look at those

162

which concern a topic crucial to both philosophers, the relationship between art and the will.

Heidegger divided his philosophy into early and late in terms of a "turning" (*die Kehre*) that occurred in about 1930. While there is a great deal of debate as to the radicalness and uniqueness of this "turning," a rough and ready division of his philosophy into early and late is universally accepted. In this essay I want to postulate an extremely bold two-part hypothesis. (i) Early Heidegger, in particular the Heidegger of *Being and Time* (1927) = the Schopenhauer of, roughly, Books I and II of *The World as Will and Representation*. In a different sense of "early" one could speak of "early" Schopenhauer and say that early Heidegger = "early" Schopenhauer. (ii) Late Heidegger = the result of adding Books III and IV of *The World as Will*, in particular, the discussion of art, to Books I and II. (Late Heidegger = "late" Schopenhauer.) This hypothesis is certainly false. There is, however, enough truth in it to make its exploration fruitful both in terms of illuminating the affinities between the two philosophers and in terms of illuminating the issues themselves with which both are concerned.

INTERESTED PERCEPTION

I begin with the relationship between "early" Schopenhauer and early Heidegger, with the affinities between Schopenhauer's account of our everyday (in Heidegger's language) being-in-the-world and that offered by *Being and Time*.

Consistent with the central concept of his general metaphysics, the heart of Schopenhauer's account of everyday existence is the concept of will. The human essence is, he says, to will. From this it follows that we do not view the objects of our world with the detached curiosity traditionally ascribed to the "theoretical" observer. Rather, we regard them essentially "in relation to the will," in their bearing, that is, to our "interest" (*WWR* 1, 177), our concerns as practical agents. This perpetual relating of things to the willing self, this all-prevailing "subjectivity," is not, says Schopenhauer, a matter of making judgments concerning the relation of "objectively" perceived objects to the self. Rather – at this point Schopenhauer makes his decisive break with the understanding of the *Lebenswelt* common to all his Cartesian predecessors – subjectivity affects (*WWR* 2, 373) "even the original perception of things":

In the immediate perception of the world and of life, we consider things as a rule merely in their relations, and consequently according to their relative, not absolute essence and existence. For example, we regard houses, ships, machines, and the like with the idea of their purpose and suitability therefore; human beings ... according to their position and vocation ...

(*WWR* 2, 372)

In ordinary consciousness we always encounter objects under functional or instrumental concepts. A paradigm of such consciousness is the way in which an absorbed chess player apprehends the chess pieces as mere function-fulfillers and is entirely unaware of their non-functional qualities (*PP* 2, 69).

This means, as one may put it, that ordinary consciousness *etiolates* things, drains them of their fullness of being, of in particular, that being which they have independently of human interest. For example,

... a traveller who is anxious and in a hurry, will see the Rhine and its banks only as a dash or stroke, and the bridge over it as a line intersecting that stroke. In the head of a man filled with his own aims, the world appears just as a beautiful landscape does on the plan of a battlefield.   (*WWR* 2, 381)

Being and time

Turning now to early Heidegger, to *Being and Time*, we find him, too, insisting that the way things "show up" in the world of "Dasein" is in terms of interest. Things, that is, show up as "equipment" (*Zeug*) or (a roughly equivalent concept) "ready-to-hand" (*Zuhanden*).[2] Like Schopenhauer, Heidegger insists that objects do not first show up as neutral "things" that are subsequently "invested with value" (instrumental relevance). Rather, they are given immediately as equipment. But this means that the intrinsic, Dasein-independent character of a thing, its "present-at-handness" (*Vorhandenheit*) (what Schopenhauer calls its "absolute essence") normally speaking "withdraws." As Heidegger puts the thought in a later work, the autonomous, intrinsic character of a piece of equipment "disappears into usefulness."[3]

Heidegger develops the idea that things only show up in terms of Dasein's interests with a thoroughness and refinement not present in Schopenhauer. Thus, for example, nature, he says, may show up either as raw material – "the wood is a forest of timber, the mountain a quarry of rock; the river is water power, the wind is wind 'in the sails' "[4] – or as "equipment" whose use does not involve alteration, as when we use the sun's motion as a clock.[5] Of course, he concedes, we are not always unaware of the "present-at-hand" in things, but even this shows up in terms of the category of "ready-to-handness."[6] We are aware, for example, of the car as a heavy chunk of metal precisely when it "obstinately"[7] refuses to move – when, for example, we have lost the keys. The "present-at-hand' shows up, in short, as the "*un*ready-to-hand."

This brief excursion into *Being and Time* makes clear the striking affinities between the Schopenhauerian and Heideggerian analyses of human being-in-the-world. One apparent difference, however, is that whereas Schopenhauer only purports to be talking about how things, most of the time, *appear* to us – will-moulded consciousness, he says, "falsifies" (*WWR* 2, 373) the nature of things – Heidegger purports to be doing ontology: the equipmental character of things is not, he insists, a matter of an "aspect" or "subjective colouring" given to "some world-stuff" whose being is independent of Dasein and its concerns. Rather, "readiness-to-hand is the way in which entities, as they are 'in themselves' are defined ontologic[ally]";[8] it constitutes their "being." This is true not merely of artifacts but of natural entities too. Of the south wind, for example, which shows up to the farmer, Heidegger claims, only as a sign of rain, he says that "only by the circumspection with which one takes account of things in farming, is the south wind discovered in its being."[9]

In a lecture series given in 1927 (the year in which *Being and Time* appeared) and later published as *The Basic Problems of Phenomenology* Heidegger moves to counter the suggestion of a radical Berkeleyan immaterialism contained in the above remarks. Nature, he now observes, is of course an "intraworldly" entity: it shows up in the world of Dasein's practical concerns. Yet "for all that intraworldliness does not belong to nature's being." The decisive reason for this is that "world" is a "cultural," Dasein-dependent entity while nature is not: "world is only if and as long as Dasein exists. Nature can also be where no Dasein exists."[10]

The considered position of the early Heidegger thus seems to amount to a kind of Kantianism. Kant, that is, used "metaphysics" (he could have said "ontology") in two senses: one to refer to the (in his view futile) study of ultimate reality – the "in itself" – the other to refer to the study of *structural* ("*a priori*") features of the world of human experience. Similarly (if we assume the *Basic Problems* passage to be explicating rather than simply contradicting the position of *Being and Time*), Heidegger seems to use both "ontology" and "being" in two senses: one to refer to the being of things in themselves, the other to refer to structural features they must have in so far as they show up in the world of Dasein. In the light of *Basic Problems* it seems we must understand *Being and Time* to be claiming that only being in this second sense is dependent upon Dasein and its practical interests. But in this second sense Schopenhauer, too, could have spoken of himself as offering an "ontology" of the human *Lebenswelt* and of human interest as constitutive of the "being" of entities in that world.

Or rather he could have done so had he believed that ready-to-handness really is structural with respect to human experience, had he believed that things *only* show up in terms of human interest. But, of course, Schopenhauer does *not* believe that. For rare and brief though those episodes may be, he believes that we all have the capacity to transcend the categories of instrumental consciousness and to experience the world "will-lessly," free of "interest." We have the capacity, that is, to experience it aesthetically. Early Heidegger on the other hand is committed to denying this: things can *only* show up for us in terms of the category of ready-to-handness and its variants. Here, then, we arrive at the real difference between Schopenhauer and the early Heidegger. The real conflict, that is, is not between an ontologist and an epistemologist but rather between Schopenhauer's (correct) view that things show up only *for the most part* in terms of instrumental categories and Heidegger's (incorrect) view that they always do so.

In attributing this position to Heidegger I do not wish to deny the existence of a certain internal conflict within *Being and Time* itself, a conflict, one might feel, between the observations of the careful phenomenologist on the one hand, and the reductionist drive of the "ontologist" on the other. Qua phenomenologist, that is, early Heidegger sensibly distinguishes from both nature as it appears to practical interest and nature as it appears to theoretical science "the nature which 'stirs and strives,' which assails us and enthrals us as landscape."[11] This is nature as it appears to primitive people[12] and poets (later Heidegger will call it nature as *physis*). Of it he says, equally sensibly, that "perhaps even readiness-to-hand and equipment have nothing to contribute as ontological clues in interpreting ... [it]"[13] Elsewhere, however, the reductionist drive takes over: "even the phenomenon of 'nature' as it is conceived in ... romanticism can be grasped ontologically only in terms of the concept of world – that is to say in terms of the analytic of Dasein."[14] In other words, Heidegger promises (without giving any indication of how the promise might be fulfilled) that even the nature of primitive people and poets can be accounted for in terms of the categories of practical interest.

Is there an actual self-contradiction contained in these passages? It seems so. What is clear, however, is that the main stress needs to be placed on the last. For *Being and Time* repeats time after time that the "being" (that is, the being for Dasein) of every entity is determined by Dasein's practical concerns. This is the central theme of Division I. The reference to the nature of art and of primitive peoples is best regarded as a lacuna, an unsolved problem for the early Heidegger for whom (qua philosopher) art held no interest. (Later Heidegger, however, for whom art is extremely important, as we shall see, exploits this gap as part of the process of overthrowing the "ontology" of his earlier self.)

Notwithstanding the obscurities and conflicts present in early Heidegger, what emerges from the discussion to date is the essential truth of the first part of our exploratory hypothesis: early Heidegger = Schopenhauer minus art. For what early Heidegger in effect does is to take the discovery of the instrumentality of ordinary perception, for which Schopenhauer surely deserves the major credit, and turn it (in fact, exaggerate it) into a structural account of human world-experience as such.

INTERESTED PERCEPTION AS PROBLEMATIC

I turn now to the second part of my hypothesis: late Heidegger = "early" Schopenhauer plus the discussions of art and salvation. The hypothesis, in other words, is that late Heidegger came to see the error of his early philosophy and altered it in such a way as to end up in an essentially Schopenhauerian position.

To explore this hypothesis we need to ask, first of all, what it is that "late" adds to "early" Schopenhauer. The first thing he does, it seems to me, is to transform the analysis of the relation between will and experience which appeared in the first half of *The World as Will* as a neutral account of the way things are, into a *problem*. Physiology, as it were, is recast as pathology. He does this in two ways. First, he points out that if the effect of the will is to substitute "relative," instrumental essences for "absolute" ones, then it follows that the human intellect, in at least its normal functioning, presents us not with reality as it is but with merely an instrumental interpretation, in fact misinterpretation, of it. As a "medium of motives" which is "thoroughly practical in tendency," the intellect is "by no means intended to present the true, absolutely real inner nature of ... things to the consciousness of the knower" (*WWR* 2, 284–286). The earlier account of the human experiential situation thus comes to present itself as *epistemologically* problematic: if all we apprehend is a subjective appearance of things then the human intellect seems to be inadequate as an instrument of knowledge.

The second way in which Books III and IV transform the earlier account of human being-in-the-world into a problem can be described as *existential*. Since ordinary consciousness places objects "in relation to the will," we confront them always from the standpoint of willing. But according to Schopenhauer's pessimism, to will is to suffer. Generally speaking, that is, there is a disjunction between the will and the world: the way the world is is rarely the way we want it to be. And if it happens that it is then we suffer the terrible penalty of "boredom": a frustrated "pressure" of the will which lacks any object upon which to express itself (*WWR* 1, 364). Hence ordinary consciousness is suffering consciousness.[15]

The second half of *The World as Will* thus turns the content of the first half into a double problem. But it also provides a double solution – a solution through art or, more exactly, aesthetic perception.

Aesthetic consciousness comes about, says Schopenhauer, when "our whole consciousness is filled with the calm contemplation" of an object so that "we *lose* ourselves entirely in this object" (*WWR* 1, 178). When this loss of self-consciousness occurs we are no longer aware of ourselves as inhabiting a common world with the object of perception. We cease to be aware of the spatial, temporal, and causal relations in which we stand to the object, with the result that it passes out of all relation to our individual will. The consequences of this are twofold. First, since the object is perceived out of relation to the will the "subjectivity" of ordinary consciousness falls away to be replaced by pure "objectivity." The object now stands before us free of the distorting mechanisms of instrumentality. In particular, it is free of the mechanism of etiolation so that it stands before us in the "inexhaustible" (*WWR* 2, 408) richness of its being, unviolated and undiminished by the will. This means that the epistemological problem posed by ordinary consciousness finds, in art, its solution. Since the knowing subject has become the "clear mirror" of the object it has revealed to it no longer "relative" but rather "absolute essences," "no longer ... the where, the when, the why and the whither of things, but simply and solely the *what*" (*WWR* 1, 178).

The second consequence of the will-lessness of aesthetic perception constitutes a solution to the existential problem posed by ordinary consciousness: since the will is entirely "forgotten" in aesthetic consciousness and since suffering is unsatisfied willing, it follows that in the aesthetic state we achieve that "painless state, prized by Epicurus as the highest good and as the state of the gods," a kind of "peace, always sought but always escaping us on the ... path of willing" (*WWR* 1, 196).

Schopenhauer does not consider the possibility that the aesthetic state could find embodiment in an entire life-form or culture – a point to which I shall return. For him, that which embodies it is always individual consciousness. Given this, he reasonably considers the state to be invariably brief, a "peak experience" in which, for a moment, "we celebrate the Sabbath of the penal servitude of willing" (*WWR* 1, 196). For this reason art, for Schopenhauer, cannot constitute a substantial or final solution to the existential problem. Its significance, rather, is as an intimation of, a pointer towards, final "salvation" from the pain of existence, a salvation that consists in asceticism or "denial of the will": from the blissful will-lessness of aesthetic contemplation "we can infer how blessed must be the life of a man in whom the will is silenced not for a few moments, as in enjoyment of the beautiful, but for ever" (*WWR* 1, 196).

MODERNITY AS PROBLEMATIC

I turn now to the later Heidegger. As with the "later" Schopenhauer here, too, we find physiology transformed into pathology. The account of being-in-the-world which early Heidegger had presented as neutral ontology is transformed by the later Heidegger into a problem.

To understand the character of this problem it is necessary, first, to call to mind the essential feature of the "turning" which separates late from early Heidegger. This feature consists in what we might call the historicization or Hegelization of Heidegger's philosophy. Like his mentor Husserl, and like Schopenhauer, early Heidegger had operated within the Kantian conception of the task of philosophy as that of laying out the timeless, *a priori*, structure of human existence. Late Heidegger, however, takes the view that there is no such structure:[16] human being-in-the-world is radically diverse from one historical epoch to another. The importance of this with regard to our present topic is that it requires us to observe that while late Heidegger transforms *Being and Time*'s analysis of being-in-the-world into a problem, it is taken to be a problem not for all people at all times but one, rather, specific to the world of post-industrial-revolution technology. What appeared in *Being and Time* as physiology is transformed by late Heidegger into a pathology *of modernity*. This important difference between late Heidegger and "late" Schopenhauer, the difference between the historical relativity of his account of the will-moulded world and the omnitemporal character of Schopenhauer's account, is one to which I shall return.

When I say that late Heidegger reproduces essentially *Being and Time*'s ontology of human being-in-the-world as a pathology of modernity what I have in mind is the fact that central to both accounts is the idea that things only show up in the human world in terms of categories determined by human interest. It should be noted, however, that there is a considerable change in the vocabulary of description. Thus, whereas early Heidegger spoke of the reduction of everything to "equipment" or "ready-to-hand", late Heidegger speaks of everything showing up as *"Bestand"* – "standing-reserve" or "resource".[17] And whereas early Heidegger spoke of everything showing up in terms of Dasein's "circumspection" or "concern," later Heidegger speaks of the "enframing" (*das Ge-stell*)[18] of everything by the "self-assertive will"[19] that reduces nature to "a gigantic gasoline station."[20] Furthermore, whereas early Heidegger spoke of the "withdrawal" of the intrinsic being of things used as equipment, late Heidegger speaks of the disappearance of "the image which [things] offer to sensible intuition,"[21] the "fading away" of their intrinsic being,[22] and of "the injurious neglect of the thing" (*Verwahrlosung* – a noun which might also be translated as failure to "keep," "guard," "protect," or "secure").[23]

Why is the world of modern technology problematic? Why does Heidegger speak of us as living in "destitute"[24] times? To this question he gives a number of interrelated answers. I shall focus on two of them. The first consists in the claim that the world has become levelled, homogenized, claustrophobic,[25] flat, stale, "dreary,"[26] "boring."[27] The reduction of the world to *Bestand* is not merely its physical but also its conceptional devastation. For those in the grip of the technological will, the will to the domination and exploitation of nature, the environment – including the human

170

environment – is reduced, conceptually, to the one-dimensionality of resource. The rich and varied being of the world disappears as objects are made to report in the monotonous categories of calculating instrumentalism.

Heidegger's second and, in his own eyes, most important account of the destitution of our times consists in the claim that the reduction of the world to resource is, in a metaphysical (though also sociological) sense, the loss of *Heimat* – of "home," rootedness. Modern humanity is homeless in the sense of having lost that groundedness in Being common to earlier historical epochs. Worse, save for those rare, marginalized spirits, the poets, we have lost the ability to be aware any longer of our own homelessness.[28] Nietzsche articulated the groundlessness Heidegger has in mind (and so must count, for him, as a poet) in a famous evocation of the metaphysical consequences of the "death of God":

What were we doing when we unchained the earth from its sun? Wither is it moving now? Wither are we moving? Away from all suns? Are we not plunging continually? Backward, sideward, forward, in all directions? Is there still any up or down? Are we not straying through an infinite nothing! Do we not feel the breath of empty space! Has it not become colder![29]

Heidegger accepts that the phenomenon Nietzsche described as the death of God is the event of humanity's becoming homeless but provides a more fundamental description of it. The death of God or, Heidegger's preferred description, "flight of the gods,"[30] is really the destruction of our ability to sense the world as poetic, awesome, as "holy." The reduction of everything to resource is the destruction of that "space" within which alone a god or gods can appear: "The ether ... in which alone the gods are gods ... is the holy."[31] Elsewhere he puts the point in terms of a phase from Holderlin: "Man dwells poetically." To the extent, therefore, that the possibility of a poetic environment is destroyed man can no longer "dwell."[32]

A DIFFERENCE

I have observed that one difference between Heidegger and Schopenhauer's treatment of the will-governed world as problematic consists in the historicism of the former as opposed to the ahistoricism of the latter. Another consists in the fact that whereas Schopenhauer identifies two *distinct* problems as generated by the willing stance to the world, one epistemological the other existential, for Heidegger, the epistemological problem *is* the existential problem. For him, that is, it is not the case that in the willing stance we (a) reduce things to equipment or resource thereby preventing the object from appearing to us as it is in itself and (b) suffer. It is rather that in willing we reduce things to the sensuously and spiritually impoverished condition of resource and *hence* suffer from an underlying boredom and homelessness.

This, surely, is a more plausible approach to the Schopenhauerian intuition that there is an essential connexion between willing and suffering than Schopenhauer's own attempt to establish the connexion independently of a consideration of the effects of willing on perception. For that attempt, Schopenhauer's effort at establishing an inescapable polarity between the pain that comes from there being an object that is willed (dissatisfaction), and the boredom or pain that comes from there being no such object (satisfaction), while not without interest, is open to well-known objections, many of which are raised, in his less systematic moments, by Schopenhauer himself.[33]

THE BEAUTIFUL AND THE SUBLIME

Like Schopenhauer, the later Heidegger does not merely display the world of "human self-will"[34] as a problem. He also seeks to provide a solution.[35] He speaks of the need for a "turning" (one which will mirror the turning in his own philosophy) in which humanity, or at least the individual, will be saved from the desecrated world of the self-assertive will. And like Schopenhauer he looks to art to "foster" the "saving power."[36] What he looks to art to do is to rescue what he calls "the Thing" (*das Ding*) from the "injurious neglect" it has suffered in the world of resource.

What does this saving of the Thing amount to? In his earliest reflections on art and technology, *The Origin of the Work of Art* (1935), Heidegger at least sometimes seems to recognize that the restoration of the sensuous presence of an object, its true "weight,"[37] its "constancy and pith" or "sensuous pressure,"[38] constitutes a legitimate and important sense in which art might be said to have the capacity to foster the restoration of the Thing. Sometimes, that is, in that seminal but confused work, he identifies the "thingness of the Thing" with its "earthly," that is, sensuous character, and says that in contrast to the "assault" made on the Thing by its treatment as resource, art "lets the earth be an earth."[39]

Nietzsche applied the word "beautiful" to that kind of art – "Apollonian" art, he called it – which is a celebration, transfiguration, apotheosis of the sensuous reality of things. We might think of French Impressionism, of Monet or Renoir, as post-Nietzschean paradigms of Apollonian art. Following this conception of beauty we may say – though Heidegger in fact, does not – that in the above usage, restoring the "thingness of the Thing" is a matter of restoring its beauty. In a world grown dreary and desolate through its reduction to resource, an artist's sense of the sensuous beauty of the world can play an important role in overcoming the "destitution" of our age.

Unfortunately, however, having in 1935 glimpsed the restorative power of art that consists in its openness to, and ability to communicate, the sensuously beautiful, Heidegger proceeded to forget about it. The notion of "saving the Thing" came to have a quite different meaning determined by the dominant position occupied by the "default of God"[40] in his analysis of the destitution of modernity. After 1935 the sensuous and the beautiful suffer serious neglect in Heidegger's discussions of art.[41] The "highest possibility of the essence of art"[42] comes to be seen as lying not in an Apollonian celebration of the sensuous image but – again in Nietzsche's rather than Heidegger's language[43] – in its "Dionysian" capacity to take us "behind" that image. The task of art is to restore that ancient Greek sense of nature as *physis*, as the "great ... world epiphany"[44] of "the overpowering,"[45] of "the boundless,"[46] of "Being." The task of art, in other words, is to re-establish our ability to sense nature as awesome, poetic, holy, to re-establish that "space" within which, one day, the "fugitive gods" might return. For it is only then, remember, that humanity, which can "dwell" only in a poetic "ether," can once again be at home.

Though he never uses it, it is clear which term from traditional talk about art is appropriate to Heidegger's conception of its essential task: it is the term "sublime." After 1935 the beautiful disappears from Heidegger's discussions of art in favour of the view that the business of art is to foster the recovery of the ability to experience the world as sublime.[47]

After about 1950 Heidegger begins to identify nature as *physis* – sublime nature – with what he calls "the fourfold" (*das Geviert*), an indissoluble unity of mutually implying elements, earth, sky, mortals, and immortals. The "Thing" is identified as that which "gathers" the fourfold together.[48] In the pouring of wine from a humble earthenware jug mortals are gathered together in an act of reverence before the divinities, while in the wine itself is present its nurturing forces, earth (rock, soil) and sky (climate, rain).[49] Metaphysical at-homeness, Heidegger now says, is only possible in, and so requires the return of, the fourfold.

HEIDEGGER'S NEGLECT OF THE BEAUTIFUL

I have no wish to deny the importance of Heidegger's connexion between the possibility of metaphysical *Heimat* and the ability to experience nature as sublime.[50] It seems to me quite true that "man dwells poetically," or at least that the possibility of *metaphysical* dwelling in the world requires that world to reveal itself as poetic, holy, pregnant with divinity, sublime. And conversely, that one will be metaphysically homeless in a world physically and conceptually ravaged by the technological will. (A grove of trees cannot be experienced as the seat of a demi-god if it presents itself as a thousand cubic meters of timber.) It is certainly true that to sense the sublime is to oppose the physical and conceptual ravages of that will.

On the other hand, it does seem to me that later Heidegger's discussion of art – of fine art, at least – is marked by an "injurious" neglect of the beautiful, a neglect of the fact, as I shall shortly show, that it, too, provides resistance to the physical and conceptual assaults of the technological will. The beautiful, of course, does not supply us with a *metaphysical* homeland above and beyond the sensuous world. But to experience the world as beautiful does away, perhaps, with the need to ask for one. Perhaps, that is, in Wittgenstein's words, "The solution of the problem of life is seen in the vanishing of the problem" (*Tractatus Logico-Philosophicus* 6.521).

THE BEAUTIFUL IN LIFE

Schopenhauer, of course, was well aware that the beautiful, as well as the sublime, is the antithesis of the reduction of the world to equipment or resource. Consistently, that is, it is the "*beautiful* landscape" that is reduced to a "plan of a battlefield" in will-governed consciousness (*WWR* 2, 381), the "*beautiful* and artistically carved" chessmen that are reduced to mere functions in absorbed chess-playing (*PP* 2, 69). On the other hand, as we have noted, Schopenhauer views the aesthetic in general and the beautiful in particular as at best a brief holiday from the work-a-day world of willing. If he is right, therefore, the beautiful cannot be offered as a genuine solution to the problem of living in the flat unloveliness of the world of resource.

But is he right? I believe not. And I believe that the wrongness of his relegation of the aesthetic in general and beautiful in particular to a brief lyrical refuge from the world of business can be seen by attending to the later Heidegger's discussions of the will and of *technē*.

As we have seen, Heidegger, like Schopenhauer, criticizes the willing attitude that is responsible for the reduction of the world to resource. When he does so, however, he is always careful to make it clear that it is not willing *uberhaupt* that is responsible for the devastation of our world. In *Gelassenheit*, for example, explicitly distinguishing himself from Schopenhauer, he says that though "releasement" from enslavement to the technological view of things does require a kind of "non-willing,"[51] this is *not* to be understood as a matter of "float[ing] in the realm of unreality ... lacking all power of action ... a will-less letting in of everything and basically, the denial of the will to live."[52] What is "denied," rather, is a specific kind of willing: "self-assertive" willing, "human self-will,"[53] or as he often says, the "will to power." What we need in place of this is a willing that is "stronger than any self-assertion,"[54] a willing that "manufactures nothing," that "accomplishes but does not produce."[55] The essence of this willing lies in "insight"[56] or "open-ness,"[57] an openness that allows Being to appropriate us, allows our goals and actions to flow from the nature of the world rather than constituting the demand that the world should accommodate itself to us. Even in *Being and Time*, Heidegger reflects retrospectively, the seemingly assertive concept of *Entschlossenheit* (resoluteness) was actually written as *Ent-schlossenheit* (un-closedness). There already, the "essence of willing" was understood as a matter of "letting be."[58]

What would be an example of this non-aggressive, "letting-be" kind of willing? One conspicuous example of what he has in mind is to be found in his discussion of pre-industrial, in particular Greek, craftsmanship, a kind of *technē* starkly different to modern tech-nology. Greek craftsmanship, says Heidegger, is "more than practical diligence; it is a matter of composed, resolute openness to beings.[59] In what does such openness consist? It consists, for example, in the way a true cabinet maker ... makes himself answer and respond to all the different kinds of wood and to the shapes slumbering within

175

wood – to wood as it enters into man's dwelling with all the hidden riches of its nature. In fact, this relatedness to wood is what maintains the whole craft."[60]

Though Heidegger himself appears not to be fully aware of this point, it seems to me that a mode of production or life-form which is, in this way, sensitive to the possibilities and limitations inherent in nature and in natural materials, is one that is open to what I have been calling the beautiful. Only someone who is open to the full sensuous being of a material is capable of responding to the range of potentialities "slumbering" within it. And only someone who delights in that sensuous being will be thus open. Notice the difference between "riches of ... nature" and "resources of nature": only someone who experiences the riches of nature *as* riches will be sensitive to their variety and will wish to conserve, preserve, and to celebrate them.

SCHOPENHAUER'S NEGLECT OF THE BEAUTIFUL IN LIFE

From Heidegger's discussion of the will and of craftwork it seems to me that two criticisms of Schopenhauer's philosophy of art can be derived. First, the aesthetic state, and in particular apprehension of the beautiful is not, of necessity, opposed to the will. It is not the case that the beautiful can appear only under the "complete silence" of the will. What must be silent is the "self-assertive" will that reduces everything to resource; but not that will which is, in fact, the visible expression of openness to the beautiful. This observation provides substance to the often-made criticism of Schopenhauer's aesthetic theory that by demanding will-lessness it reduces the aesthetic to pure contemplation and cannot account for the executive aspect of art.

The second criticism that emerges is that the aesthetic state, the experience of the beautiful (but also, to concede to Heidegger the importance of his discussion, the experience of the sublime) need not be a mere "Sabbath" from the "penal servitude" of willing but can, on the contrary, find embodiment in a mode of production and even, perhaps, in an entire culture. Once this point is grasped – essentially Nietzsche's point that we need to become "wiser" than the artists and become artists of *our lives* [61] – then art, the aesthetic, becomes much more significant than even Schopenhauer allows. Rather than being a mere intimation of the real *Erlösung* from the destitution of our world, "denial of the will," art contains within itself the outline of a possibility of overcoming that destitution.

A third criticism of Schopenhauer can be derived from Heidegger's discussion of technology. If we accept, as I believe we plausibly should, the general validity of Heidegger's suggestion that there is a distinction in kind between modern technology and pre-industrial craftmanship, if we accept as historical fact that there really was a time when technological activity displayed a sensitivity to the possibilities and limitations inherent in nature which sets if radically apart from the world-stance of modernity, and if, moreover, we accept that a high degree of truth is contained in Heidegger's characterization of the world of modern technology as the world of resource, then it follows that the account of the will-moulded world which Schopenhauer offers as an omnitemporal, structural account of quotidian being-in-the-world is not that at all, but is rather, in embryo, a description of the condition of modernity. If, that is, we are persuaded to view the history of technology in an at least generally Heideggerian fashion, then there was – and might again be – a time and a mode of (in Heideggerian language) being-at-work when viewing things "in relation to the will," rather than draining them of their fullness and autonomy of being, was actually an affirmation of that fullness and autonomy.

CONCLUSION

I have derived a number of criticisms of Schopenhauer from reflection upon the work of the later Heidegger, criticisms which make it clear that the accuracy of the first part of our exploratory hypotheses – Heidegger = Schopenhauer minus art – is not matched by the second part – Heidegger = Schopenhauer plus art. I do not wish, however, to end on a note of criticism. Rather, I should like to conclude by emphasizing both the originality of Schopenhauer's break with the Cartesian separation between will and experience, a break which flowed into the work of Nietzsche (even at his most anti-Schopenhauerian) he still paid tribute to Schopenhauer's "immortal doctrine" of the "instrumental character of the intellect"[62] and, by one route or another,[63] into the work of Heidegger. One should also emphasize the validity of Schopenhauer's perception that the effects of the will upon experience are highly problematic and that art might have something to do with overcoming those effects. Finally, one

Julian Young

should emphasize the contemporary relevance of Schopenhauer's reflections upon art and the will, relevance not merely to the topic of art but to critical issues, too, concerning the topics of technology and ecology.

Notes

1 Martin Heidegger, *Nietzsche* (New York: Harper and Row, 1979), vol. I, p. 107.
2 Heidegger, *Being and Time*, J. Macqarrie and E. Robinson (Oxford: Basil Blackwell, 1973), p. 68 (page references are to the seventh German edition given in the margins of this translation).
3 Heidegger, "The Origin of the Work of Art," in *Poetry, Language, Thought* (New York: Harper and Row, 1975), p. 46.
4 *Being and Time*, p. 70.
5 Ibid., p. 71.
6 Ibid.
7 Ibid., p. 74.
8 Ibid., p. 71.
9 Ibid., pp. 80–81.
10 Heidegger, *The Basic Problems of Phenomenology* (Bloomington: Indiana University Press, 1982), pp. 169–170.
11 *Being and Time*, p. 70.
12 Ibid., p. 82.
13 Ibid.
14 Ibid., p. 65.
15 There is a certain idealization in my account of the content of *WWR* terms in its two halves. For elements of Schopenhauer's argument for pessimism emerge at the end of Book II and the epistemological inadequacy of the intellect is also noted in Book II. It remains true, nonetheless that these problems only become fully *pressing* in Books III and IV.
16 Or at least it is a very "thin" one possessing none of the richness or detail attributed to it by the author of *Being and Time*.
17 See Heidegger, "The Question Concerning Technology," in *The Question Concerning Technology and Other Essays* (New York: Harper and Row, 1977), *passim*.
18 Ibid.
19 Heidegger, "What Are Poets For?", in *Poetry, Language, Thought, passim*.
20 *Discourse on Thinking* (New York: Harper and Row, 1966), p. 50.
21 "What Are Poets For?", p. 127.
22 Ibid., p. 130.
23 Heidegger, "The Turning," in *The Question Concerning Technology and Other Essays*, p. 45.

24 "What Are Poets For?", *passim.*
25 Heidegger, "The Thing," in *Poetry, Language, Thought*, p. 165.
26 Heidegger, *Introduction to Metaphysics*, R. Manheim, trans. (New Haven: Yale University Press, 1959), p. 37.
27 Heidegger, *Gesamtausgabe* (Frankfurt: Klosterman, 1975 –), vol. 29/30, p. 12.
28 "What Are Poets For?", p. 93.
29 Nietzsche, *The Gay Science*, Walter Kaufmann, trans. (New York: Vintage Press, 1966), §125.
30 *Introduction to Metaphysics*, p. 38.
31 "What Are Poets For?", p. 94.
32 See Heidegger, " ... Poetically Man Dwells ...," in *Poetry, Language, Thought, passim.*
33 See my *Willing and Unwilling: A Study in the Philosophy of Arthur Schopenhauer* (Dordrecht: Martinus Nijhoff, 1987), Ch. X.
34 "The Turning," p. 47.
35 In popular interviews Heidegger consistently denied the presence of any constructive or remedial element in his later philosophy. But these denials, I believe, were devices intended to ward off crude misunderstanding of his philosophy. In particular, later Heidegger was highly sensitive to the paradox contained in "Yes, I see that the problem is all to do with willing. Now what shall we *do* about it." Tentative and subtle though it is, it seems to me quite clear that there is a remedial element in Heidegger's later philosophy.
36 "The Question Concerning Technology," p. 35.
37 "What Are Poets For?", p. 135.
38 Heidegger, "The Origin of the Work of Art," in *Poetry, Language, Thought*, p. 26.
39 Ibid., p. 46.
40 "What Are Poets For?", p. 91.
41 His consistent hostility to the "aesthetic" enjoyment of art (e.g., at "The Question Concerning Technology," p.34) seems to do the double duty of rejecting both the sidelining of art into "cultural activity" and the importance of the sensuous enjoyment of art and nature.
42 "The Question Concerning Technology," p. 34.
43 See Nietzsche, *The Birth of Tragedy*, Walter Kaufmann, trans. (New York: Vintage Press, 1966), § 17.
44 *Introduction to Metaphysics*, p. 63.
45 Ibid., p. 151.
46 "What Are Poets For?", p. 120.
47 Notice that this lopsided view of art – reflected in Heidegger's disposition to treat poetry as the only serious art form – is prefigured already in *Being and Time* where the aesthetic experience of nature is identified with experience of "nature that stirs and strives," of, that is, "the nature of romanticism" (see pp. 166–167 above).
48 See "The Turning," *passim.*

49 Notice that "earth" no longer refers to the sensuous as such but has been poetically anthropomorphized into a nurturing force.

50 That being said, it is also true that the transformation of the sublime into the nostalgia of the fourfold carries with it a certain whiff of Tolkien-esque kitsch. One worries that the late Heidegger's *Heimat* sounds more than a little like "the Shire" and his "mortals" like hobbits. (More appropriately, perhaps, one should speak of Black Forest kitsch.)

51 Heidegger, *Discourse on Thinking*, p. 79.

52 Ibid., p. 80.

53 "The Turning," p. 47.

54 "What Are Poets For?", p. 120.

55 Ibid.

56 "The Turning," p. 47.

57 *Discourse on Thinking*, p. 81.

58 *Introduction to Metaphysics*, p. 21; compare *Discourse on Thinking*, p. 81.

59 *Nietzsche*, vol. 1, p. 164.

60 Heidegger, *What is Called Thinking?*, F. D. Wieck and J. Glenn Grey, trans. (New York: Harper and Row, 1968), pp. 14–15.

61 See *The Gay Science* §299.

62 Ibid., §99.

63 Heidegger's access to Schopenhauerian ideas may have been primarily direct. Or it may have been primarily through Nietzsche or through Kierkegaard. A still further channel of communication may have been the poet Rilke who was (a) a sympathetic reader of Schopenhauer and (b) greatly admired and studied by Heidegger. As I have indicated, however, it lies beyond the scope of this essay to engage in serious speculation concerning the causal relation between Schopenhauer and Heidegger.

Schopenhauer's enduring influence on the arts: idealism and romanticism

Consequently, really to exist and live, a fine work requires a sensitive mind, and one well conceived needs a mind that can think. But afterwards the man who presents such a work to the world, may only too often feel like a maker of fireworks who has enthusiastically let off the fireworks that took him so much time and trouble to prepare, only to learn that he came to the wrong place and that all the spectators were inmates of an institution for the blind.

Schopenhauer, "On Judgement, Criticism, Approbation and Fame,"
Parerga and Paralipomena

9

Schopenhauer on music as the embodiment of Will

LAWRENCE FERRARA

INTRODUCTION

Schopenhauer's metaphysics of music is based on two presuppositions: (1) music is the embodiment of the Will and (2) music and nature (the world as representation) share certain parallel features. Schopenhauer readily admits that his metaphysical conception of music as the embodiment of the Will cannot be logically demonstrated.[1] Evidence for this metaphysical vision of music as Will is provided by the comparative analysis of the parallel constitution of music and nature, the latter being the objectification of the Will (*WWR* 1, 258–259). But Schopenhauer's evidence – his comparative analyses of the structures of nature and music – is in the mode and tone of (an additional) metaphysics without proof, logical or empirical. After all, Schopenhauer argues that the depth of the Will and music is ineffable. He warns about the conceptual constitution of discursive descriptions of music; descriptions fettered in conception are not freed by the pure "will-less" perception that he argues is required for a meaningful musical experience. Therefore, how can one ever know whether a discursive description of music or the Will is uncorrupted and thereby valid if not certain?

Schopenhauer turns to laws of acoustics to authenticate his collateral analysis of music and nature, and in so doing, to validate his metaphysical vision. In the recitation of those laws he is on solid and verifiable ground: Pythagorean principles of sound vibrations and laws of "harmonics" are immutable as he recounts them. However, Schopenhauer ventures from the surety of mathematics to the frailty of music theory. Here, Schopenhauer chooses the work of Jean-Philippe Rameau (1683–1764) as the basis for his understanding and explanation of musical syntax. The choice of Rameau places the question of the degree of success or failure, fecundity or impotence in Schopenhauer's metaphysics of music into a music historical context. Understanding the impact (on his metaphysics of music) of Schopenhauer's historical selection of Rameau as his portal into musical syntax is crucial to the determination of the strengths and weaknesses of Schopenhauer's theory of music. An examination of Schopenhauer's use of principles of the mathematics of sound in addition to Rameau's approach to music analysis provides a focus with which to penetrate his highly varied writings on music.

Schopenhauer's writings on music move in a multitude of directions, cover plenteous issues connected (more or less) to music, and in that process provide insights that range from those of a profound philosopher to those of a cavalier dilettante. While his use of laws of acoustics and (Rameau's) rules of harmony will be an effective axis for this inquiry, important aspects of his metaphysics of music are not directly tangential to these subjects. Therefore, in addition to (1) acoustics and (2) Rameau's music theory, a third theme in his theory will be explored: (3) the relationship between formalism and referentialism. These three themes, not unrelated, will encompass and allow for a broad yet focused engagement of Schopenhauer's metaphysics of music.

First, in order to recreate and evaluate the music historical spirit and moment in Schopenhauer's metaphysics, we must briefly contextualize it within his contiguous conceptions of the Will, aesthetic experience and the arts.

THE WILL, AESTHETIC EXPERIENCE, AND THE ARTS

Schopenhauer embraced much of the transcendental idealism in Kant's *Critique of Pure Reason* with an emphasis on the division between phenomena and the thing-in-itself. Phenomena are objects perceived by a mediating subject. The subject experiences its body in much the same way as it experiences phenomena (read representations). It also experiences itself in a deeper way: we experience our inner selves as Will. Comparable to Kant's thing-in-itself, the Will exists independently of the perceiving mind and its imposition of Kantian categories of reason. Thus, like Kant's bifurcation of the world, Schopenhauer's world involves two levels of existence: a perceived world of representation and a deeper world of the Will.

Schopenhauer's Will is a world of struggle and discord, an incessant flux driven by a "blindly urging force" (*WWR* 1, 117) which underlies the world of phenomena and remains subservient to this instinctive force of desiring, yearning and "endless striving" (*WWR* 1, 164). While intellectual understanding can penetrate the world of phenomena or representation, Schopenhauer did not agree with Kant's contention that the thing-in-itself is unknowable. This deeper level of the world as Will can be experienced through aesthetic contemplation.

The Will "objectifies" as a hierarchy of grades: in stones, plants, animals and humans. The multitude of particular objects in each grade of objectification in the world of representation "exist as ... the eternal forms of things" (*WWR* 1, 129). Although these archetypal grades, understood as Plato's Ideas, are not known in the normal willful activities of existence, during an aesthetic experience we engage the purity of the Platonic Idea. In this case, the aesthetic object is reflected upon for its own sake, as an ideal object. In order to effect such a view of an object, a purposeless, disinterested subject is released from willful wants, cravings, and longings: one is freed "from the service of the will" and is thereby "will-less, painless, timeless *subject of knowledge*" (*WWR* 1, 178–179). In this state of "aesthetic pleasure," one forgets oneself so that the perceived, pure aesthetic object alone is left in consciousness.[2]

The arts exemplify an analogous grading to the Platonic Ideas (objectified as stone, plant, animal, human) (*WWR* 1, 212–255). Each fine art exemplifies a specific stage in the objectification of the Will. The lowest stage is architecture which, according to Schopenhauer, embodies Ideas of "gravity, cohesion, rigidity, hardness, those universal qualities of stone, those first, simplest, and dullest visibilities of the will, the fundamental bass-notes of nature" (*WWR* 1, 214). Higher grades of art capture the inner and deeper meanings of human life. Moving through landscape painting, sculpture, historical painting, poetry and tragedy, Schopenhauer's theory of fine art is a highly idiosyncratic (although at times insightful) collection of essays pressed into conformity with his grand metaphysical design. This purposeful development of a theory of art for the corroboration of his metaphysics continues in Schopenhauer's "metaphysics of music."

SCHOPENHAUER'S SECOND THEORY OF ART: MUSIC AS THE WILL

In Schopenhauer's key writings on music,[3] music "stands quite apart" from the other arts because it does not represent any singular grade of the Will's objectification as Platonic Ideas, but directly "refers to the innermost being of the world and of our own self" (*WWR* 1, 256). Music bypasses the Ideas and is "independent of the phenomenal world." It is not "like the other arts, namely a copy of the Ideas, but a *copy of the will itself*" (*WWR* 1, 257). While the other arts speak of the shadow (as in Plato's cave), music speaks of the essence and is directly expressive of, "the most secret history" of the Will: satisfaction, desire, nobility, suffering, anxiety, convulsion, lament, attainment, "affliction, pain, sorrow, horror, gaiety, merriment or peace of mind" (*WWR* 1, 261). Music embodies these dimensions of the Will in "their essential nature," purely in their quintessence and extracted immediately from the Will. Music "expresses the metaphysical to everything physical in the world, the thing-in-itself to every phenomenon. Accordingly, we could just as well call the world embodied music as embodied will" (*WWR* 1, 262–263).

Schopenhauer attempts to circumvent the intractability to logical argument or empirical evidence in his metaphysics of music with his conception of "a parallel, an analogy, between music and the Ideas" (*WWR* 1, 258). He identifies parallels between grades of the objectification of the Will in nature and the syntax of music as it is understood by Schopenhauer, a lay musician. The lowest bass tones of musical harmony correspond to "inorganic nature, the mass of the planet." The tenor and alto (middle voices or instruments) correspond to the vegetable and animal ("brute") kingdoms, respectively. Finally, the soprano (the highest tones providing the melody) represents the knowing subject. The graded texture of music from the lowest voices to the highest correspond to "the whole gradation of the Ideas in which the will objectifies itself ... The definite intervals of the scale are parallel to the definite grades of the will's objectification, the definite species in nature" (*WWR* 1, 258 and *WWR* 2, 447). While interesting, many of his analogies between music and nature are little more than myth or lore. One must question whether his comparison of "impure discords" (musical dissonance) to "monstrous abortions between two species of animals, or between man and animal" (*WWR* 1, 259) discloses anything of import concerning musical dissonance or the other. The evidence for this alleged parallelism lies in acoustics and "rules of music."

ACOUSTICS AS THE GROUND FOR A METAPHYSICS

Schopenhauer's acoustical understanding of music is grounded in Pythagorean laws, "the natural origin of the tonal system" (*WWR* 2,

447). The key aspect in Schopenhauer's usage is that as one shortens or lengthens an object (for example, a string), the frequency is in inverse proportion to the vibrating length. The following principle also results: if the frequency of a tone is n, then that of the octave is 2n, that of the fifth is 3/2n, that of the fourth is 4/3n, that of the minor third is 5/3n, and that of the major third is 5/4n. These intervals – the third (and the inverted third, a sixth), the fourth, the fifth and the octave – are the "consonant" intervals and are based on relationships of "small numbers" (each of their correlative numbers are 5 or less). "Dissonant intervals such as the second (9/8n) and seventh (15/8n) are based on larger correlative numbers" (above 6). Schopenhauer grounds his theory of consonance and dissonance in music on this acoustical law, a law which certainly impacted on the aesthetics of musical consonance and dissonance in music through the nineteenth century.

One can also add "harmonics"[4] and its key ingredient, the overtone series, to Pythagorean principles as a seminal structure in Western tonal music. When one hears a particular musical tone – for example, a middle C on the piano – in addition to hearing the main sound or fundamental, one hears a number of overtones which are exact multiples of the frequency of the fundamental. An instrument producing a middle C frequency n actually produces vibrations (overtones) of the frequences n, 2n, 3n, 4n, ... beyond 20n. These overtones are not heard clearly because their amplitude is much less than that of the fundamental tone (n). The human ear can hear the fundamental (n) plus four overtones: an exact double of the previous overtone, 2n is the octave, 3n is the fifth, 4n is the octave and 5n is the major third. By 6n (another fifth), hearing overtones becomes very fuzzy and by 7n it becomes nearly impossible. When one hears the tone, C, one actually hears, through faint overtones, a C major chord (made up of a C, E and G). Thus, major tonality in music (for instance, being in the "key of" C or G major as opposed to being in the "key of" C or G minor) is based on nature's acoustics.

Schopenhauer declares that he will show the connection of the "metaphysical aspect of music with the physical" (*WWR* 2, 450). The nearest consonant ("harmonic") intervals that sound with a fundamental note "by means of secondary vibrations" are the octave and its fifth (*WWR* 2, 447). A consonant or "rational" relation between two notes sounding together (harmoniously) is based on the fact that their vibrations are "expressible in small numbers" (*WWR* 2, 450). In this recitation of an aesthetics of consonance in tonal music based on natural law, the small number vibrations to which he refers are those of the octave 2n, major third 5/4n, minor third 5/3n, fourth 4/3n, and fifth 3/2n. On the other hand, "if that relation is an irrational one, or one expressible only in large numbers ... they resist" being joined together "in our apprehension, and accordingly are called a dissonance" (*WWR* 2, 450). Based on natural law, these intervals produce wider, less related vibrations from the consonant intervals and are therefore deemed, dissonant.[5]

In the same paragraph from which the citations immediately above are taken, Schopenhauer steps out of the "physical" aspects of music and back into his metaphysical discussion:

The connexion of the metaphysical significance of music with this its physical and arithmetical basis rests on the fact that what resists our *apprehension*, namely the irrational relation or dissonance, becomes the natural image of what resists our *will*; and, conversely, the consonance or the rational relation, by easily adapting itself to our *apprehension*, becomes the image of the satisfaction of the *will*.   (*WWR* 2, 451)

This citation seems to present a contradiction: if the Will is marked by continuous, blind craving and discord and remains quite separate from the objectifications of those emotions and states of being in the world of representation, why would this deeper world of eternal strife be in any way harmonious with the rationality of consonance? One would expect that such musical and rational consonance would be repelled by the Will. One would also expect that the inherent numerical "irrationality" in tonal dissonance would be drawn to the Will like metal to a magnet. It is clear from Schopenhauer's metaphysics that life is marked by striving and reaching, tensions and resolutions. Those resolutions are often short and fleeting, however, and yearning continues in all grades of the objectification of the Will. Thus, the "will-less" aesthetic experience of music brings satisfaction in the form of a brief respite from the otherwise continuous strife and urge that characterize existence: "satisfaction is of a *negative* nature, that is, simply the end of a suffering, whereas pain is that which is positive" (*PP* 2, 416). There is a necessary correlation between the perception of the Platonic Idea and a "will-free subject of knowing" in the aesthetic experience. In being purpose-less and will-less there is a "disappearance of all willing from consciousness." In this aesthetic experience "the pure subject" and "the pure object" arise (*PP* 2, 416–417).

Thus, Schopenhauer's rationale for the apparent contradiction runs as follows. His pessimistic view of life is characterized by suffering and strife; this is the normal (or "positive") way of being. Releasing the Will from consciousness during the moments of an aesthetic experience negates the normal "pain and woes" of life. Harmonic dissonance in music strikes discord in our consciousness because of its numerical relations to large numbered vibrations as calibrated in acoustics. Dissonance is resisted by our will. On the other hand, consonance, "the natural image," satisfies the Will. This explanation seems to remove the problem of self-contradiction. However, as a world of craving and pain in its normal and positive disposition, *how can the Will "resist" its normality and accept its negation unless the Will has consciousness?* While a knowing subject could certainly transcend the ("positive" and normal) world of suffering it does so only through acts of consciousness. Schopenhauer's "blind" Will is without consciousness and therefore without the ability to accept or reject consonance or dissonance. Only the Will as human can make such ethical judgments. This contradiction in the status of the Will as blind and yet conscious exposes a fundamental omission in his exegesis of the Will: there is an absence, in Schopenhauer's overall metaphysics, of a substantive discussion of the relationship between the subject and the Will. While he makes it clear, if not always convincing, how the subject fits as mediator into the world of representation (phenomena are there for and through the subject), he does not systematically bridge the Will to a knowing subject. Although he provides a few interesting metaphors, there are only two distinct worlds: the world of a subject's representations and the world of the Will. To state that the subject is the Will itself does not clarify the relationship. Ultimately, as noted in the opening of this chapter, the ineffable nature of the Will and the "inexpressible depth of all music" (*WWR* 1, 264) remain the barrier to the logical resolution of this fundamental omission in his metaphysics of music. In this form and on this point his metaphysics of music is relegated to mysticism.

Schopenhauer provides an embellishment on his mathematical ground for his metaphysics of music in the remainder of the original paragraph in question (*WWR* 2, 450–451). Because the "numerical relations" in musical consonance and dissonance allows for "innumerable degrees, nuances, sequences, and variations," music "faithfully" portrays "all movements of the human heart ... in all their finest shades and modifications." Recall that this paragraph under study opens with a recitation of Pythagorean principles, continues with the implication of those principles in the form of an aesthetics of consonance and dissonance, and moves (or leaps) into a discussion of the myriad variations of "numerical relations" in music. It does not necessarily follow (from Schopenhauer's presentation of Pythagorean principles or an aesthetics of consonance and dissonance derived thereof) that innumerable variations of numerical relations in musical vibrations provide "physical" evidence for the allegedly correlative (metaphysical) position that a multitudinous number of human emotions exemplified in music are essentially congruent, or as Schopenhauer would say, analogous. At best, Schopenhauer might suggest a loose analogy between his physical and metaphysical views of music. In fact, one could furnish instances of substances and systems that imbue myriad numerical relations and that could be related, somehow, to music. Once again, the ineffable nature of music and the Will remain the obstacle for the kind of substantiation that Schopenhauer is attempting here.

Finally, the following passage reads like Helmholtz half a century before the latter's codification of the overtone series:

high notes ... may be regarded as resulting from the simultaneous vibrations of the deep bass-note. With the sounding of the low note, the high notes always sound faintly at the same time, and it is a law of harmony that a bass-note may be accompanied only by those high notes that actually sound automatically and simultaneously with it (its *sons harmoniques*) through the accompanying vibrations. (*WWR* 1, 258)

Although interesting, more important than Schopenhauer's preemption of Helmholtz's work is Schopenhauer's continuation of the citation above with the following:

all the bodies and organization of nature must be regarded as having come into existence through gradual development out of the mass of the planet. This is both their supporter and their source, and the high notes have the same relation to the ground-bass ... just as a certain degree of pitch is inseparable from the tone as such, so a certain grade of the will's manifestation is inseparable from matter. (*WWR* 1, 258)

The poetic flavor of these coincidental similarities provide only superficial insight into nature and music. No logical bridge is built between the two. Representative of Schopenhauer's use of music acoustics,[6] the citations above demonstrate his competent recounting of acoustical theory but also belie his inability to transform the "physical" side of music into a logical basis for his metaphysical view of music. We turn now to the second non-metaphysical basis for his metaphysics of music, the music theory of Rameau (*PP* 2, 430).

190

SCHOPENHAUER ON RAMEAU

The choice of Rameau's theory as the foundation of Schopenhauer's understanding of musical syntax is among the most consequential of his theoretical commitments in his essays on music. Schopenhauer, in 1819, finds himself at a watershed moment in the history of music theory. Rameau's system takes command around this time and overshadows much of nineteenth-century music analytical practice. It prevailed over the approach espoused in Johann Fux's *Gradus ad Parnassum* (1725), which continued to be studied and practiced by the master composers of Western music throughout the eighteenth and nineteenth centuries but was not widely used as a music analytical tool in the nineteenth century. Schopenhauer's embrace of Rameau's approach, instead of that of Fux, causes significant damage to his understanding and explanation of musical syntax as a foundation for his metaphysics of music.

Rameau's *Traite de l'Harmonie* (1722) is symptomatic of the Age of Reason in its presentation of a rationally based, logical harmonic disposition rather than the more empirically based practice of the realization of chords over a "figured bass" and species counterpoint codified in the music theory of Fux. Rameau advocated a "vertical" (harmonic) method; Fux championed a blending of "vertical" (through realization of "figured bass") with "horizontal" (through "species counterpoint") approaches in the teaching and analysis of music composition. In a C chord, the constituent notes are C, E and G: C is the root, E is the third and G is the fifth. Any one of these three notes could be the bass or lowest note of this chord on a piano, in a choral piece for four parts, or in an orchestral piece for twenty parts. Distinctive in Rameau's approach is that the bass note is always understood in terms of the root (in this case, C) and music is conceived as a progression of "vertical" states that imply a "functional harmony." From Rameau's viewpoint, music analysis should move up and down, building chords on thirds based on the root, in a series of "now" points. This can be likened to a cloth sewn only of vertical threads, disconnected by a horizontal texture. The effect of Rameau's analysis is that of a dissection of a musical work in which one might say the musical cloth falls apart as a series of disconnected vertical threads.

In this century, especially through the work of Heinrich Schenker and his students, a theory of free composition developed from eighteenth century Fuxian contrapuntal theory of the sort that was actually practiced by the masters of Western music (including Telemann, J. S. Bach, C. P. E. Bach, Haydn, Mozart, Beethoven, Schubert, Berlioz, Chopin, Rossini, Bruckner and Brahms among others). In fact, there is evidence that Rameau's theory of composition was disparaged by J. S. Bach, C. P. E. Bach, Haydn, Mozart and Beethoven.[7] Schenker concludes that Rameau's harmonically based approach misses the linear, in contrapuntally directed lines which combine and express harmony. Schenker sought to disentangle the "vertical" from the "horizontal" for the clarification of each in order that they could blend into the flow of musical time. Without a view of the "horizontal" movement of contrapuntal lines, Rameau's analytical method is dislocated from motivic development within the temporality of music. Schenker's post-Fuxian approach attempts to leave the musical cloth, constituted of both "horizontal" and "vertical" threads, intact against a canvas of musical time. Recognizing Schopenhauer's partiality for melody over harmony – "I ... regard melody as the core of music to which harmony is related as the sauce to roast meat" (*PP* 2, 431) – it is exceedingly unpropitious that Schopenhauer embraced the non-linear, harmonic approach of Rameau.

It is important to understand that Rameau's prescriptive rules for composing and analyzing music are based more on music of French Baroque composers than the generally more contrapuntal seventeenth and eighteenth-century German composers, and that his rules precede the mature period of the Classic Era in music, approximately from 1750 through 1820 (there is an obvious overlap with other style periods). The four-part Chorale "form" is the most applicable to Rameau's rules. The chorale probably reached its highest degree of perfection under the pen of J. S. Bach. But when one attempts to apply Rameau's vertical rules to Bach's Chorales, the rules do not obtain! In what should be his best forum, the analysis of Bach four-part chorales, Rameau's approach is insufficient and often wrong-headed. Furthermore, Rameau's rather pedantic approach to chorale writing was generalized by later music theorists and analysts for all types of tonal music composition. Schopenhauer, following music analysts of his century, broadened the purview of Rameau's rules to include Classic and early Romantic music. The application of harmonic method demonstrates that his restrictive principles do not manifest in the works of three centuries of master composers.

Schopenhauer declares that Rameau has "laid the foundation" for "the most precise rules" of music (*PP* 2, 430) and he insists that

Rameau's theory "is by no means arbitrary, but has its root in the natural origin of the tonal system" (*WWR* 2, 447). Schopenhauer announces the "fundamental rule of music ... that the bass should remain at a greater interval below the three upper voices or parts than these have between themselves" and that the bass should never be within one octave of the other parts (*WWR* 2, 447). Furthermore, the upper voices should be in the third octave above the bass and in their preferred form should remain in "extended" (open) position rather than "close" position. In contrast to a highly "flexible soprano," the bass is described as "inflexible and rigid." The bass "moves heavily, rises and falls only by large intervals, thirds, fourths, and fifths and is guided here by fixed rules in each of its steps" (*WWR* 2, 452). The bass "can never rise by *one* tone" especially from the fourth to fifth scale step.

One need only play through the four-part chorales of Bach or one of his fugues to discover less than an octave distance between the bass and tenor and "close" position in countless musical moments. One consistently hears a non-rigid, flowing bass which moves *stepwise* as well as in larger intervals. The bass is often considered the second melody to the soprano. Furthermore, the interval of a third is not a "large interval" but is understood as abbreviated stepwise motion; the ear perceives the middle tone in a linear, stepwise effect. The statement that stepwise bass movement from the fourth to the fifth of the scale causes "the incorrect fifth or octave sequence" (*WWR* 2, 452) in the upper voices is half right. With a small number of notable exceptions, two voices in four-part chorale writing generally do not move in parallel motion when they are (and therefore remain) a perfect fifth or octave apart. Such a part-writing "rule" does exist and this is a correct reading of the compositional aesthetic of most seventeenth and eighteenth-century composition. However, the movement of the bass from the fourth to the fifth step of the scale hardly guarantees such a parallel movement. Even if one of the upper voices formed a perfect fifth or octave with the bass note on the fourth step, when the bass moves from "the fourth to the fifth" the upper voice could simply move in contrary motion. This would block parallel fifths or octaves. Furthermore, bass notes are not always the root of the chord; many chords are in inversion. In such a case and in the key of C, the bass could be the third of the chord (the F of a Dm chord) and move from the fourth step (F) to the fifth step (G), as the bass and root of a G chord. Not only does this not have to result in parallel fifths or octaves, this "fourth to the fifth" bass movement would set up the most common cadential chord progession (ii6, V, I) and *stepwise bass movement* in seventeenth, eighteenth and nineteenth-century music composition. One might also add that the use of inversion in the bass in the Baroque period is most often for melodic reasons, not wholly harmonic ones. In such a case, the bass line displays stepwise motion in order to assure melodic continuity, and uses intervallic leaps for variety, not as a rigid rule of limited motion. Schopenhauer's recitation of Rameau's vertical view of harmony, always in relation to the root position chord, misses the richly linear (horizontal) movement in much bass writing. Indeed, for melodic purposes, sometimes bass notes work at cross-purposes to chord roots.

Schopenhauer's low opinion of the bass line in music carries over to vocal music when he states: "solo arias with orchestral accompaniment are suitable only for the alto or soprano." Bass and tenor arias stand out "like an arrogant and conceited voice" (*PP* 2, 434) and cannot reach "the pure and perfect delight of a soprano aria" (*WWR* 2, 452). These condemnations fly in the face of countless low-voice arias by Bach, Mozart and Beethoven (Rameau makes no such judgment concerning bass arias). Schopenhauer's idiosyncratic censure may be more a function of his need to press music into conformity to his metaphysical position than his lack of a musical ear. The bass, after all, is declared to be analogous to the inorganic kingdom, a grade of the objectification of the Will which "is devoid of feeling" and is inaccessible to nuance (*WWR* 2, 452). This asserted parallel to inorganic nature forbids and ignores Jon Vicker's *Otello* and Pavarotti's *La Boheme*.

Schopenhauer divides melody into two elements, rhythm and harmony (*WWR* 2, 452–456) (and thereby leaves out a third important element, "contour"). Rhythm depends on the "perpendicular" lines and harmony on "the horizontal lines" ("horizontal" understood in his usage as a series of "now points" running from left to right in the score) in a "symmetrical rhythm." Schopenhauer's usage of "rhythm" shifts between what would more accurately be termed "meter" and musical "form" or "structure." His second usage is more interesting. He captures the essential idea of formal growth in most seventeenth- and eighteenth-century music as he merges his use of rhythm with harmony. Musical form is the alternation of "*discord* and *reconciliation*": a progress from consonance (of the original key center), to dissonance (of a competing key center), and to resolution (back to the original key center) (*WWR* 2, 452). Musical "periods" or formal sections are marked by modulation (a change of key) "to the dominant" (the key of the "discordant" v chord built on the fifth step of the scale in the original key) and then "sinking, calming, and finding again the fundamental note" (*WWR* 2, 453), that is, modulating back to the original key. Thus, a typical piece might start off in C major, modulate to G major, its fundamental "discord," then through a series of modulations, find its way back to C major. The experience of this piece is therefore mostly "discordant," that is, dislocated from and then in search of the consonance of the original key center. The "reconciliation" results from a merging of rhythmic (as form and meter) and harmonic satisfaction in the form of the return to the original key in a symmetrically correct moment of the work and on a strong beat of the final measures (*WWR* 2, 454–456). While more could be said, as general descriptions of two centuries of music go, this segment of Schopenhauer's explanation of musical syntax (which moves beyond Rameau) is an accurate account of the nature of formal growth in much of seventeenth and eighteenth-century European music.

Nevertheless, Rameau's theory (the basis for most of Schopenhauer's "rules") and Schopenhauer's adaptation of it are, for the most part, not congruent with the way the great masters of seventeenth through nineteenth-century Western music learned how to compose, nor are their "rules" congruent to the compositions by the great masters. Had he embraced Fux rather than Rameau, Fux's system would have supported Schopenhauer's propensity for melody as Rameau's harmonically based system could not. Of course, it is somewhat anachronistic to fault Schopenhauer's acceptance of Rameau; as noted above, Rameau's was the dominant music analytical approach at the time. One can only guess how differently Schopenhauer's theory of musical syntax might have better informed his metaphysics had he chosen Fux at that wonderful music historical moment.

THE MERGING OF FORMALISM AND REFERENTIALISM

Schopenhauer's formalism is conspicuous in his approach to musical syntax. His formalism is not limited to Rameau's dissecting practices. He goes beyond Rameau (but not to Fux) in his analysis of phrase structures and overall form (the alternation of "discord and reconciliation"), a nineteenth-century preoccupation in music analysis. In addition to his method of music analysis, Schopenhauer's philosophical commitment to formalism can be readily uncovered in his writings on the aesthetic experience and the arts.

Schopenhauer's theory of an aesthetic experience presents a will-less subject who remains tacit in favor of an objectified and timeless object. "The pure subject" experiences "the pure object," perceived as Platonic *Idea* (*PP* 2, 417). The Platonist modality of Schopenhauer's formalism lies in a belief in a world of Ideas (which for Schopenhauer is a middle ground between the world of representation and the world as Will) that transcends particularism. In this experience, the "power of representation then becomes at once perfectly *objective*" as aesthetic contemplation allows for the "disregard" of an object's "position in time and space and thus its individuality" (*PP* 2, 416–417). Able to "disregard time and space," a pure knowing subject intuits "the *Idea,* that which endures and is permanent in all change" (*PP* 2, 417). The Platonic Idea "constitutes the real material and kernel, as it were the soul, of a genuine work of art." Art separates the "form from the matter" and leads us away from "the individual to the mere form," to the universal Idea: "It is, therefore, *essential* to the work of art to give the form alone without matter" (*PP* 2, 422). In so doing, music's universality "is like geometrical figures and numbers, which are the universal forms of all possible objects of experience" (*WWR* 1, 262). Thus, Schopenhauer's aesthetics are marked by the acceptance of the objectivist possibility of an ahistorical subject with the apodictic power of the "pure" peception of "pure" musical form. The conception of a tacit knower who can objectively engage a purified musical object in the pursuit of "pure" form is a true formalism.

Schopenhauer's philosophical aim in all of this is to use the explanation of musical meaning as a paradigm example for his general metaphysical vision. Uncovering the inner meaning of music as the embodiment of the Will and in parallel to nature and the Ideas is vital to the success of his metaphysics. Thus, irrespective of his highly formal approach to musical syntax and his commitment to the uncovering of "pure form," Schopenhauer must allow music to break out of its *formal* significance and erupt into its *reference* understood as the exemplification of the structures and innermost essence of the world as representation and Will.

An important and telling aspect of this deep reference is the explicit interpretation of the manner in which music exemplifies emotions:

rapid melodies without great deviations are cheerful. Slow melodies that strike painful discords and wind back to the keynote only through many bars, are sad ... The *adagio* speaks of the suffering of a great and noble endeavour ... the entrance of a minor third instead of a major, at once and inevitably forces on us an anxious and painful feeling ... The *adagio* in the minor key reaches the expression of the keenest pain and becomes the most convulsive lament.   (*WWR* 1, 260–261)

What is of particular interest is Schopenhauer's merging of formalism with referentialism as it relates to his theory of emotion in music. Music does not express an actual or definite emotion but emotion in abstraction and in its "essential nature." Emotion in music is experienced in its pure or "mere form without the substance" of actual "joy, sorrow, love, hatred, terror, hope" (*WWR* 2, 450). He warns that there is a *tendency* to add "flesh and bone" to the "form" of feelings exemplified in music which would prohibit the apprehension of emotion in music "purely and in its immediacy" (*WWR* 2, 450 and *WWR* 1, 261).[8] This "tendency" may be ancillary to a more serious problem. The ineffable nature of music disrupts Schopenhauer's Newtonian dream to provide physical evidence for his metaphysical vision. Even if music is expressive of the universal quality of emotion, that expressivity cannot be translated into a conceptually based discursive language according to Schopenhauer. He writes that while music discloses the "true nature of all things" in their "most secret meaning, and appears to be the most accurate and distinct commentary on it," music remains "inexpressible" and as such is "quite familiar and yet eternally remote," so "easy to understand and yet so inexplicable" (*WWR* 1, 262–264). What keeps music so "eternally remote" is its ineffability, a barrier to the physical (based in acoustics) and logical (based in Rameau) bridges that Schopenhauer hoped to build to his metaphysics of music.

Schopenhauer's discussion of rhythm understood as musical form is, like his summary of acoustical principles, competent. But he bypasses this analytical aspect of the obvious structure of music (ABA, Rondo, and so on) and moves to a more important and compelling discussion of the purity of "mere" form, that is, music experienced as the logical form of emotion.[9] This philosophically and historically generative insight undermines the empirically corroborable status of his discussion of musical form as obvious structure (and "rhythm") and replaces (or grounds) it in a metaphysical and rich Platonic interpretation of music as the "pure form" of emotion. Emotion in music, a referential level of musical significance, is clarified in musical form. With this astute interpretation, he at once merges his formalism with his referentialism but puts both outside the reach of discursiveness.

The fecundity of Schopenhauer's legacy in music certainly lies in his metaphysics for their own sake, not in his unsuccessful attempt to provide physical evidence for them or in his highly idiosyncratic and often uninformed pronouncements about music. His cardinal accomplishment in this aspect of his philosophy is bringing formalist and referentialist positions in proximity to each other. Thus, the key to understanding the merging of Schopenhauer's formalist and referentialist views of music is also the key to understanding the essence of his metaphysics of music: music, as the "pure form" of the ineffable world of human emotion and the embodiment of the Will, provides the only direct and immediate publicly communicatable and accessible portal into the essential structures of the Will itself.

Notes

1 *WWR* 1, 257.
2 *PP* 2, 416–417.
3 *WWR* 1, Section 52, pp. 255–267; *WWR* 2, Ch. 39, 447–457; and *PP* 2, 415–452.
4 It is a guess as to whether Schopenhauer was knowledgeable of the details of "harmonics," later codified by Hermann Helmholtz (1821–94) as the "overtone series." The idea and use of "harmonics" was known in Schopenhauer's time, though admittedly not codified.
5 I will not engage the ongoing debate on consonance and dissonance in music in this chapter. The merit of the historical relativist position (that consonance and dissonance are culturally and temporally based) notwithstanding, the significance of considering Schopenhauer's recitation of a naturalistic definition of consonance and dissonance in music is that this position historically locates Schopenhauer's musical aesthetics.
6 Schopenhauer also invokes the practice of temperament, the accepted system of tuning since around 1700, as comparative evidence for the flexibility of types and classifications of natural species (*WWR* 1, 258–259). Whereas harmonics are in the domain of the science of sound, temperament moves toward the musician in sound.
7 Johann Fux, *The Study of Counterpoint from Johann Fux Gradus ad Parnassum*, A. Mann, ed. (New York: W. W. Norton, 1971) Intro-

duction, pp. xiv–xv; Heinrich Schenker, *Counterpoint,* Book 1, trans. John Rothgeb (New York: Schirmer Books, 1987), Author's Preface, pp. xxvii–xxx; and Heinrich Schenker, *Harmony,* Oswald Jonas, ed., Elizabeth Mann Borgese, trans. (Cambridge, MA: MIT Press, 1973), p. 176.

8   Well-known formalist art critic, Clive Bell, urges art critics to engage "significant form," the essential focus of his theory. Bell's description of "significant form" is remindful of Schopenhauer's discussion of "mere" or "pure form." And like Schopenhauer, Bell is also cognizant of emotion: "The starting-point for all systems of aesthetics must be the personal experience of a particular emotion" (London: Chatto and Windus, 1914, p. 6). The emotion to which he refers is one's response to the intellectual yet intuitive experience of "significant form" stripped of representation and actual emotion. Bell likens this experience to that of the mathematician who revels in the beauty of form in mathematical formulae. This is certainly close to the formalist dimension of Schopenhauer's aesthetics.

9   This more abstract view of music understood as the "logical form" of feeling (as Susanne Langer would say and very much in the spirit of her rootedness in Schopenhauer) is several cuts above the nineteenth-century Romantic version: music understood as presenting the *actual* emotions of the composer.

10

Schopenhauer and the musicians: an inquiry into the sounds of silence and the limits of philosophizing about music

LYDIA GOEHR

" ... the rest is silence"   (Shakespeare)

"Science has laid bare to us the organism of speech; but what she showed us was a defunct organism, which only the poet's utmost want can bring to life again; and that by healing up the wounds with which the anatomic scalpel has gashed the body of speech and by breathing into it the breath that may animate it with living motion. This breath, however, is – music."

(Richard Wagner)

INTRODUCTION

Schopenhauer did not write very much about music. His musical remarks take up surprisingly little space in his otherwise lengthy, but classically pellucid, philosophical corpus.[1] Even granting that the remarks are intended only to make sense as part of a total metaphysical system, they are, critics have found, frustratingly incomplete. Nevertheless, no philosopher's writings about music have proved more influential. Exploited, as Thomas Mann thought, by "enthusiastic admirers and fanatical converts," Schopenhauer was not wrong in believing that musickind would learn something from him it would never forget.[2] Almost the mere mention of his name has come to stand for an entire worldview about the status, meaning, and value of classical music. He articulated what modern commentators sometimes call "the Idea of Music."[3] Deservedly or not, he has become to musical aesthetics what Beethoven has become to classical music itself – a central reference point in a range of historically momentous debates. That Schopenhauer was largely

200

responsible for providing the rationale behind the canonization of Beethoven only renders this comparison more fitting.[4]

This essay seeks to comprehend the limits of Schopenhauer's philosophy of music. It asks whether the limits are a sign of music's inexpressible profundities, of philosophy's apparent failure to describe musical meaning, or merely a sign of incompetent theorizing.

Consider the latter option first because it is the least fertile. Perhaps Schopenhauer's remarks are limited because he was a musical amateur and couldn't say more than he did. Schopenhauer, however, knew quite a lot about music and was thought sensitive to its concerns. According to Dahlhaus, Schopenhauer "knew music more comprehensively and fundamentally than some people believe."[5] Wagner appreciated Schopenhauer for having "recognized the true nature of music" and for having been the first to define "the position of music among the fine arts with philosophic clearness," though he does surmise that Schopenhauer knew music only as a layperson.[6] Mahler found Schopenhauer to have written one of "the profoundest" things about music he had ever read, and commentators Israel Knox and Georg Simmel judge Schopenhauer's account of music to be, respectively, "one of the triumphs of his book," and "perhaps ... the most meaningful that has ever been given."[7] Other readers regard the musical remarks as the culmination of Schopenhauer's treatise: they even say his feeling for music pervades his entire philosophy and that a musical quality characterizes his prose.[8] With thoughts like these, Thomas Mann concludes that "Schopenhauer was very musical." "I have often called his great work a symphony in four movements," he continues, "he celebrates music as no other thinker has ever done."[9]

If Schopenhauer's remarks are not interestingly limited by ignorance or amateurship, then one might judge them limited on philosophical grounds, as many have, as "deeply inconsistent" or "glaringly contradictory." Following a judgment of this sort, Malcolm Budd concludes that although "Schopenhauer is the musician's philosopher," his "philosophy of music is not a fitting monument to the art."[10] Clearly a philosophy's influence need not correlate with its coherence. In that Budd and I probably agree. However, in my view, given a metaphysical reading which takes seriously the idea of limits, Schopenhauer's philosophy of music can be interpreted as a deliberately unfitting, and hence, if successful, a perfectly fitting, monument to the musical art.

To sustain this odd conclusion, I shall offer a three-dimensional interpretation of the limits of Schopenhauer's philosophy of music. I shall argue that these limits are best comprehended by reference to three conceptions of silence, the first two rather more interesting than the last. These conceptions show themselves, respectively, in Schopenhauer's view of music's nature, in the philosophical form in which this view is presented and, finally, in how this view was received by musicians. Let me briefly describe each.

The first dimension of silence captures the meaningful silence of the musical language. Unable to speak discursively or conceptually, music, Schopenhauer argues, nonetheless speaks – and it speaks not merely volumes but "everything." One purpose of my inquiry is to unravel in Schopenhaurean terms the apparent paradox that the fine art of sound is essentially silent, or that the purpose of the musical art is to express the inexpressible.

The second dimension of silence is a meta- or philosophical silence. It captures the inability of philosophy – at least in its traditional forms – to adequately describe the musical art. This silence derives from philosophy's own theoretical limits. Another purpose of my inquiry is to highlight how necessarily dependent Schopenhauer's philosophy of music is upon indirect, analogical description. Apart from the undoubted and explicit influence of Plato and Kant upon Schopenhauer's metaphysics, Schopenhauer works also within an age-old tradition of German anagogical mysticism and philosophical anxiety that utilizes claims of transcendence to find a sacred realm or refuge for the individual, be it in God or music. Like Augustine, but more explicitly like Aquinas, Schopenhauer demonstrates the use to which arguments by analogy (comparison, proportion, and negation) can be put if philosophers are to say anything about that which, in the strictly philosophical terms of rational explanation, cannot be spoken about.

These first two dimensions of silence have been interwoven together in the last two centuries within the romantic-modernist aesthetic. As so interwoven, they have become linked to other conceptions of silence which capture desires for protection, refuge, and purification. All these conceptions assume a fundamentally dualistic metaphysics which requires that its claims about moral, scientific, religious, artistic, and political judgment be characterized as falling either within or beyond the bounds of cognitive sense or the limits of conceptual sayability or expressibility.

One will surely be reminded immediately of the plethora of critical writings about the unwritten side of Wittgenstein's *Tractatus*, and the related development of the aphorism culminating in the concise Viennese architectural, literary, and musical expressions of Loos, Kraus, and Schoenberg. But perhaps one would not think so immediately of how the same metaphysics of unsayability has shaped the major debates over the meaning, autonomy, and power of music in which so many composers and music theorists – roughly from Richard Wagner to John Cage – have engaged. Nor perhaps would one immediately comprehend how this metaphysics illuminates the limits of philosophizing about music or, indeed, why Schopenhauer says so little about music.

The romantic-modernist musical debates have traditionally focused on the following questions: does musical meaning reside in music's form, in its representational depth or surface content, or in its expressive effect? how does purely instrumental music differ from opera? how does absolute music differ from program music? why is the language of music able to speak purely through feeling, symbol, and gesture in ways other languages cannot? how is music related to other arts? how in song and opera is melody related to text? in how concise and non-ornamental a form can musical meaning be encapsulated? how does music achieve absolute autonomy? and, finally, how can "celestial music" be prophetic and articulate a politics for the future? These questions acquire new dimensions of significance (even if not coherence) when investigated as part of a metaphysical aesthetics of unsayability which Schopenhauer articulated through his analogical narrative of "the musician's world."[11]

The third dimension of silence concerns the reception of Schopenhauer's musical remarks. Unlike Schopenhauer's more general writings on suffering and redemption, freedom and genius, pity and love – writings that influenced musicians at least as much as his musical remarks – Schopenhauer's specifically musical remarks pervaded musical discourse amidst an aura of silence. Incorrectly I believe, some commentators interpret this silence as indicative of neglect. "Schopenhauer is ... one of the most neglected figures in the history of thought as distinct from the history of gas (Hegel)," remarks music critic Hans Keller while discussing Pfitzner's opera *Palestrina* – an opera that uses a quotation from Schopenhauer as a motto.[12] Contra Keller I shall suggest that, regarding Schopenhauer's specifically musical remarks, the fact of their silent reception was indicative not of neglect, but of a pervasive and uncritical approval.

SCHOPENHAUER'S MUSICAL REMARKS

Schopenhauer begins his remarks on music by insisting that music stands apart from all other fine arts insofar as "we do not recognize the copy, the repetition, of any Idea of the inner nature of the world."[13] Familiar with claims about music's failure to articulate any determinate particularity in the world, Schopenhauer does not conclude as others did that music is therefore devoid of meaning or to be placed at the bottom in a taxonomy of the fine arts. Music, he writes, is "a great and exceedingly fine art." Indeed, he continues, music has so great effect on "man's innermost nature" and is "so completely and profoundly understood by him in his innermost being," that "we must attribute to music a far more serious and profound significance that refers to the innermost being of the world and of our own self."

To differentiate music from the other arts, Schopenhauer reminds us that the latter are geared towards stimulating knowledge of (Platonic) Ideas. Ideas are the adequate representations of the (universal) Will. Music, by contrast, passes over the Ideas: it communicates no direct knowledge about them.[14] There is "no [literal] resemblance between [music's] productions and the world as representation." Music could exist in a certain sense even if there was no representation. Why? Because music (conceived here as a language of harmonies) is an immediate copy or manifestation of the Will itself. However, as Schopenhauer also argues, where there is Will there is also representation, so music, after all, must be related to representation – but how?

Schopenhauer realizes immediately that the relation is "abstract," "very obscure," and "essentially impossible to demonstrate," because to do so would be to establish "a relation of music as a representation to that which . . . can never be representation." "In the explanation of this wonderful art," he thus remarks, the concept or explanation soon shows "its inadequacy" and "limits." From this he concludes with a sentiment that later becomes identified more closely with Wittgenstein than with himself: if readers wish fully to understand these remarks, they should not try further to philosophize; they should just go *listen* to music with the remarks in mind. ("Whereof one cannot speak . . .")[15]

But in what can Schopenhauer's musical remarks now consist? Schopenhauer answers: since we want to know about music, but we do not have a language that can "unmask" or "reveal" information about music as the manifestation of the Will directly, other than music itself,[16] we can proceed only by drawing analogies to things we can talk about, to phenomena belonging to the world as representation. But he reminds us: "[W]e must never forget" that "when referring to all these analogies ... music has no direct relation to them, but only an indirect one; for [music] never expresses the phenomenon, but only the inner nature ... of every phenomenon." With this warning Schopenhauer proceeds to describe music indirectly – by analogy.

Unlike other arts that communicate Ideas at a specific level of objectification, music responds to every level. "I recognize," Schopenhauer writes, "[i]n the whole of the ripienos that produce the harmony, between the bass and the leading voice singing the melody, ... the whole gradation of the Ideas in which the Will objectifies itself." With the bass corresponding to the lower grades and the higher (tenor, alto, and soprano) voices to the plant, animal, and human worlds, Schopenhauer deliberately restores a view emanating as much out of ancient Western philosophy as from Eastern wisdom about music's literally being at one with the universe. Music is not a universal language just because its meaning is available to all regardless of cultural difference, but because it is the only language which mirrors the Will without mediation. "We could just as well call the world embodied music," he concludes, "as embodied Will."

As a universal language, music finds its profound meaning: it captures the entire endeavor of humankind – all "the deepest secrets of human willing and feeling." Schopenhauer explains: our nature consists in the fact that our (individual) wills strive. After each striving is satisfied, our wills strive again. Our happiness (rarely achieved) consists in a constant transition from desire to satisfaction. The more normal condition of our desires' being frustrated leads to suffering; our constant "empty longing" for new desires results in languor and boredom. Music's patterns, Schopenhauer now claims, are structurally analogous to these patterns of desire, frustration, and fulfillment. "[T]he nature of melody," he writes,

is a constant digression and deviation from the keynote in a thousand ways, not only to the harmonious intervals, the third and the dominant, but to every tone, to the dissonant seventh, and the extreme intervals; yet there always follows a final return to the keynote.   (*WWR* 1, 260)

Melodies of different tempi and keys parallel the different forms and moments of our satisfactions or frustrations. "The inexhaustibleness of possible melodies corresponds," as Schopenhauer puts it, "to the inexhaustibleness of nature in the difference of individuals, physiognomies, and courses of life." Israel Knox illuminates Schopenhauer's position here with poetic clarity:

Music peals forth the metaphysics of our own being, the crescendo, the climax, the crises, the resolutions, of our own striving, impetuosity, peace, and the retardations and accelerations, the surging and passivity, the power and silence of things.[17]

Schopenhauer recognizes that music's meaning is constituted entirely through activities of creation and reception, but requires that these activities realize a uniquely transcendent form. Music is the product of genius, Schopenhauer explains, but it requires more genius than does the production of the other arts. The same dualism which separates the Will from representation, the universal from the particular, the metaphysical from the physical, music from the plastic and literary fine arts also separates the composer-genius from the embodying (phenomenal) person. Composing music is far removed from all conscious intention or reflection, Schopenhauer argues, it is the product of inspiration and imagination. The composer "expresses the profoundest wisdom in a language that his reasoning faculty does not understand." In the composer, "the man is distinct from the artist."

What, now, of music's expressive potential and understanding? Despite the apparent ease with which theorists have been able to attribute expressive or emotive qualities to music – of happiness, sadness, gaiety, and sorrow – music, in Schopenhauer's view, fails to express the materiality and particularity of any emotion. From the perspective of Will, music "means" or "expresses" *abstractly, universally,* and *essentially.* Music is pure temporal process, the dynamics of which directly correspond to the flow of the Will's emotional life. So, if music expresses the different emotions at all, it expresses them "in-themselves," abstracted from any ordinary human motives that might generate their particularized instantiation. Emotions, Schopenhauer again argues by negation, are given as "mere form without the material, like a mere spirit world without matter."

Correspondingly, music speaks to its listeners purely – through non-conceptual activities of the imagination, unmediated by and abstracted from individual and ordinary interests. At this level of disinterested or aesthetic contemplation, music speaks through the purely temporal and audible patterns of melody and harmony of an invisible spirit world and of the quintessence of life.

Such an experience or understanding of music is, however, attained by relatively few persons. Schopenhauer criticizes composers and critics who try "pathologically" to pull music down into the phenomenal world by subordinating it to the sentimental expression of an ordinary person's individual emotions, interests, and concerns; or by associating it with words (this attempt, Schopenhauer says, is the origin of song and later of opera); or by making music imitate programmatically (as Haydn attempted in *The Seasons* and *Creation*). Against this, Schopenhauer claims that the most genuinely universal music is purely instrumental. "[I]f music tries to stick too closely to the words, and to mould itself according to the events [of the phenomenal world]," he writes, it is endeavoring to speak a language not its own. Only composers like Rossini (one of his favorite composers), who can keep "free from this mistake," allow music to speak "its *own* language ... distinctly and purely." Thus, "[f]ar from being a mere aid to poetry music is certainly an independent art; in fact, it is the most powerful of all the arts, and therefore attains its ends entirely from its own resources."

Of course Schopenhauer does not want to dismiss opera or song as altogether without value; after all, Rossini primarily composed operas. Still, he is very disparaging:

Strictly speaking one could call opera an unmusical invention for the benefit of unmusical minds, in as much as music first has to be smuggled in through a medium foreign to it, for instance as the accompaniment to a long drawn out, insipid love story and its poetic pap.[18]

But, in so criticizing opera, Schopenhauer is dismissing only the operas which subordinate melody to words or actions (especially when the latter are trivial). Schopenhauer would eventually dismiss Wagner's Ring cycle as such an example: Wagner "should give up his music, he has more genius as a poet!"[19] Only by giving priority to music, Schopenhauer argues, as in Rossini's or Mozart's operas, can we encounter the most profound information expressed by the opera's words or dramatic actions, for music "stands to the text and the action in the relation of universal and particular, of rule to example." Music, in other words, gives opera its soul. True opera, therefore, is essentially a genre of music and must be composed according to the principles of purely instrumental music. In this way, opera, can also be absolute and autonomous. Schopenhauer even suggests that, contrary to the traditional composition of song, the melody should be composed prior to the words, since what expresses the interior Will should guide that which represents the exterior world.

Readers might think that, by being removed from the sphere of local human interests, and by being put into the autonomous and transcendent aesthetic sphere, music thereby loses its connection to what matters to human beings. But for Schopenhauer the opposite is true: the really "serious" side of life is that of the Will and music traverses the course of that life. "[M]usic is essentially serious even when it is serene," Georg Simmel explains, "because its realm is that of Will itself, the original of the image prior to its diffraction and reflection. And Will is the most serious thing of all, because everything depends on it."[20] Schopenhauer intends to show that music is "rooted in the real nature of things and of man;" its autonomy is not meant to deprive it of a metaphysical and moral involvement with the world. This claim is corroborated by Schopenhauer's insistence that he is always offering a view of transcendence as existing not independently from the phenomenal world, but immanently within it. "My philosophy," he wrote on one occasion, "is never concerned with cloud-cuckoo-land but with this world."[21] Despite the dualistic description, there is only one world – the world is truly a *uni*verse and music is part of it.

Readers might also think that because Schopenhauer conceives of the Will as a blind impulse that forever strives because it cannot achieve final satisfaction, then our experience of music must also be frustrating. But, again, Schopenhauer concludes the opposite. The experience of music, as the highest form of aesthetic experience, is "remote from pain" because it is without phenomenal reality. Unlike in our everyday existence, in music we experience the life of the Will without bearing the full pessimistic brunt of its associated frustrations. Music offers us, therefore, even if for just a brief moment, a redemption from our perpetual suffering.

So conceived, it comes as no surprise when Schopenhauer surmises that music, in its purely metaphysical state, is the true philosophy:

[P]hilosophy is nothing but a complete and accurate repetition and expression of the inner nature of the world in very general concepts ... Thus whoever has ... entered into my way of thinking will not find it so very paradoxical when I say that, supposing we succeeded in giving a perfectly accurate and complete explanation of music which goes into detail, and thus a detailed repetition in concepts of what it expresses, this would also be at once a sufficient repetition and explanation of the world in concepts, or one wholly corresponding thereto, and hence the true philosophy. (*WWR* 1, 264)

Parodying Leibniz's assertion that music is "an unconscious exercise in arithmetic in which the mind does not know it is counting," Schopenhauer characterizes music as "an unconscious exercise in metaphysics in which the mind does not know it is philosophizing."

The hope, however, that Schopenhauer might actually provide what he has just called a "perfectly accurate and complete explanation of music" is immediately thwarted. Could it be otherwise? Necessarily not. Schopenhauer's argument is based on a supposition he knows cannot be sustained, but which he knows needs to be made explicit to show that, conceived as pure and unconscious philosophy, music must proceed in conceptual "silence" (that is, through its own medium of sound), and, furthermore, that if we must speak about music then we must speak about it indirectly. Put otherwise (and to demonstrate the interplay of musical and philosophical silence), music shows its meaning transcendentally through revelation and intuition, and, *therefore*, cannot be translated to, or fully described by, a rational, conceptual, empirical language. Anything, Schopenhauer writes at the end of his treatise, which lies before or beyond the [phenomenal] world "is open to no investigation."[22]

Schopenhauer must decide: either he can stop writing about music altogether or he can continue to write indirectly. He chooses the latter option, but only, he says, to demonstrate further just how tight the analogy is between music and the phenomenal world. Indeed, since Will and representation are two perspectives taken on the same world, there must hold between them a perfect "parallelism."

Having earlier established in Book II that moral human beings cannot exist without the lower-order natural world, or that if the Will is objectified at one level it must be also at the other levels, Schopenhauer now claims that melody (as the highest expression of the Will) cannot exist without complete harmony beneath it. "The high voice, singing the melody, is," he writes:

at the same time an integral part of the harmony, and in this is connected even with the ground-bass. This may be regarded as the analogue of the fact that *the same* matter that in a human organism is the supporter of the Idea of man must nevertheless at the same time manifest and support the Ideas of gravity ... , hence the Ideas of the lowest grades of the Will's objectification.

(*WWR* 2, 448)

Schopenhauer takes the parallelism further. Just as one cannot find perfect harmony in the objectified world, just as there is unending conflict or inner contradictions between individuals at and between different levels of objectification, so comparable "insoluble irrationalities" exist in music:

> No scale can ever be computed within which every fifth would be related to the keynote as 2 to 3, every major third as 4 to 5, every minor third as 5 to 6 .... For if the tones are correctly related to the keynote, they no longer are so to one another, because, for example, the fifth would have to be the minor third to the third, and so on. For the notes of the scale can be compared to actors, which have to play now one part, now another.   (*WWR* 1, 266)

Schopenhauer concludes, therefore, that "a perfectly correct music cannot even be conceived, much less worked out; and for this reason all possible music deviates from perfect purity."

That any manifestation of music is imperfect does not detract in this view from the depth or redemptive quality of music's meaning when music is understood as a universal language. As the Will's unmediated expression, music points to a true and profound knowledge of the world. But that this inner nature is also the source of our constant suffering forces us never, in the larger perspective, to be wholly persuaded by utopian visions of perfect harmony or happiness in our world. We are left only with the sublime (and therefore, double-edged) knowledge of the unavoidable suffering of our insatiable wills but also of our desire and ability to escape this realization by any means possible – even if only temporarily. Music ultimately symbolizes in a way no other fine art can the essential tension between, and mutual involvement of, knowledge and desire.[23]

Unfortunately, given Schopenhauer's pessimism, any such knowledge or temporary alleviation from the world cannot do anything to change the condition of the world. It can only hint at what the world would be like if our experience were different – if we had no illusions and no unfulfilled desires. But, for most of us, this is merely an empty hint.

SCHOPENHAUER'S RECEPTION

Theorists have criticized Schopenhauer's musical remarks from numerous standpoints.[24] Some just reject out of hand his fundamentally dualistic conception of the world and thus the entire basis for drawing analogies between music and the world as representation.

These critics see no good reason to believe that perfect parallelisms obtain either between harmonic structures and the forms of nature, or between the dynamic structure of music and the emotional life of human beings.[25] Other critics object to describing music as radically different from the plastic and literary fine arts – an objection connected to what they take to be an unconvincing use of mediating "Ideas."[26] Some reject Schopenhauer's pessimism and music's role in it. Others protest against his treating music too much as part of a metaphysical system and not enough on its own terms.[27]

These criticisms are not exhaustive. Indeed, one gets the impression that critics are fighting hard to counter the verdict that Schopenhauer's metaphysical aesthetics is nonsense. "A philosophic and many-sided work," began Jean-Paul in an early review, "full of genius and penetration but with depth often bottomless, akin to a sunless Norwegian lake barred by stern ramparts of beetling crags, in whose depth only the starry night is reflected, whose surface no bird skims, no wave upheaves."[28]

Fortunately nonsense takes different forms. Critics mostly try to show that Schopenhauer's nonsense is not empty, but metaphysical and poetic. Serious and penetrating it is therefore, and influential it certainly has been. "Before [Schopenhauer's view] is dismissed as fanciful nonsense," Brian Magee writes,

serious attention must be paid to the fact that it is remarkably similar to something written by Wagner ... When two of the most insightful of all theorists of music bring forward ... related formulations independently ... it cannot be assumed ... that there is nothing to what they say.[29]

As mentioned earlier, one way to assess Schopenhauer's work is to fathom his arguments, to distinguish the valid from the invalid. Another is to judge Schopenhauer's musical view on the basis of its influence on musicians. For if it significantly influenced musicians, then the philosopher's worry that it is nonsensical impinges less directly than it might on its value as a contribution to the history of musical thought.

For nearly forty years following the publication of *WWR*, Schopenhauer was almost entirely ignored. His reputation as a bitter and arrogant critic of nearly everything far surpassed any judgment that he had something to contribute to philosophy. His positive reputation began to grow in the early 1850s when, for example, on the recommendation of German poet George Herwegh, Wagner first read Schopenhauer. "I have of late occupied myself exclusively with a

man who has come like a gift from heaven … into my solitude,"
Wagner wrote to Franz Liszt on December 16, 1854:

> This is Arthur Schopenhauer, the greatest philosopher since Kant, whose
> thoughts, as he himself expresses it, he has thought out to the end. The
> German professors ignored him … but recently, to the disgrace of Germany,
> he has been discovered by an English critic.[30]

In the following decades Schopenhauer's work began to be read
widely and interpreted as meeting contemporary intellectual needs.
Responding to the growing discontent with the dominant "soap
bubble" of "Fichte-Schelling-Hegel" philosophy, Schopenhauer
announced himself, and was accepted as, the philosopher most able
to burst the bubble. "All the Hegels, etc.," wrote Wagner, "are
charlatans by the side of [Schopenhauer]."[31] Regarded the passionate critic of, and outsider to, academic and institutionalized philosophy, he was appreciated – notably by Nietzsche – for the way he
lived his philosophical life in essential honesty, freedom, and
truthfulness.[32] Readers gradually began to judge Schopenhauer the
true representative and culminating philosopher of German romanticism, especially given the romanticists' "exalted intoxication with
music."[33] Readers also agreed with Schopenhauer that he was the
true heir not only to the two most important philosophers in history,
Plato and Kant, but also more particularly to Goethe, Tieck, and
Wackenroder. Simultaneously, they judged him the first philosopher
of irrationalism and of the unconscious and quickly deemed him, as
Mann later put it, "the most rational philosopher of the irrational."[34]

Schopenhauer's reputation did not stop there. Readers began to
see him as the authentic representative of modernity – the pessimist
who dealt most honestly with the loss of absolute values and sought
to find order and value in an ultimately meaningless world.[35] He
also became known as the first philosopher to consider the mind as
biological, to introduce the body into philosophical discourse, to
give priority in his views to concepts of metaphysical and physical
love, and to develop the beginnings of clairvoyance and dream
theory.[36] He became well-known also for his controversial, anti-
revolutionary political views of apolitical quietism and for his
equally ardent anti-Christian views influenced by Indian and
Chinese philosophies. Ultimately, he was rated *the* philosopher of
atheism, asceticism, mysticism, and eroticism – at least until
Nietzsche achieved that rank.

In aesthetics Schopenhauer was appreciated for giving more

credence than Kant had to romantic views of artists and their works. These views presuppose the basic romantic dualism that not only allows but requires the withdrawal or separation of universal art from the mundane, ordinary world: the artist-genius necessarily has an antagonistic and critical relationship to society;[37] with its trans- cendent qualities art serves as the proper secular substitute for religion;[38] works of art are not utilitarian or ordinary, but are aesthetic objects existing for "their own sake."[39]

All of Schopenhauer's views on aesthetical and other subjects entered immediately into the musician's world with a mixture of positive and negative endorsements. Alma Mahler reported that one of Gustav's favorite quotations was taken from Schopenhauer's treatise: "How often have the inspirations of genius been brought to naught by the crack of a whip!"[40] Gustav Mahler himself employed a Schopenhauerean image in describing his relationship to Richard Strauss, the image of "two miners digging a shaft from opposite ends and then meeting underground."[41] Even if Strauss had approved the image, he likely would have dismissed Mahler's desire to quote Schopenhauer. In 1925 Strauss wrote to Hofmannstal: whereas one could seriously discuss the nature of artistic creation with "Goethe, Schiller, ... Wagner, and possibly with Nietzsche," one could hardly do this either "with Eckermann or Schopenhauer."[42]

In personal correspondence, Liszt found himself deeply troubled by Schopenhauer's views, notably his views on legal justice and atheism.[43] Dvorak worried as well about the impact of Schopen- hauer's anti-religious proclamations. On hearing Brahms discuss his agnosticism by reference to Schopenhauer, Dvorak exclaimed (about Brahms): "Such a man, such a fine soul– and he believes in nothing, he believes in nothing!"[44]

Examples like these abound. But this fact is not surprising: by the time his century drew to a close, Schopenhauer's reputation (nega- tive and positive) had thoroughly permeated the culture. Schopen- hauer had in fact become a comfortable reference point in common intellectual discourse.

Thus, consider Prokofiev's memory of a conversation with his friend Maximillian Anatolyvich Schmidthof: "Max found an area where he could attack me," Prokofiev recalled:

quotations from Schopenhauer. Either I wouldn't know how to object or the replies that I improvised would not always be successful. / "Can it be that you haven't read him?" / "That's right, I never have. But I know from my parents that to read through Schopenhauer is like taking a cold bath in pessimism." / "I took that bath two years ago," Max said .... "And on the bottom I found some brilliant ideas."[45]

Rimsky-Korsakov likewise recalled a conversation that took place in a concert intermission in 1902. It was agreed that the symphony just heard composed by Scriabin was "so boring and lifeless," Rimsky-Korsakov commented, "that it fits Schopenhauer's well-known aphorism ... regarding the voluminous but talentless creations of most learned craftsmen."[46] The point is that both Prokofiev and Rimsky-Korsakov were able to converse about and even to quote Schopenhauer with a kind of ease that typifies "cocktail party knowledge" – a kind of knowledge for which serious engagement with the philosopher's writings is not required.

The more relevant feature, however, of all the many random references to Schopenhauer's work is how few of them bear on strictly musical matters. Certainly, musicians were familiar with Schopenhauer's basic view about music, but there is little debate about it in the general musical culture. This is not because musicians didn't read Schopenhauer's work; some engaged with it seriously and passed the word around: Mahler gave an edition of *WWR* to Bruno Walter as a Christmas present. Wagner concluded a letter to Hans von Bülow by earnestly inquiring as to whether he was reading Schopenhauer.[47] Nevertheless, though musicians generally found Schopenhauer's views on most other subjects – including aesthetical ones – deeply controversial and problematic, they seemed to have far fewer qualms specifically about his basic musical view. They seem to take to this view, to use Hans Keller's words, as fish take to the "best water."[48] Schopenhauer's "idea of music" thus pervaded general musical discourse in silence, without a struggle. Certainly, it was not neglected.

The quiet reception of Schopenhauer's musical view had a notable consequence. The view entered the general musical culture sometimes in adapted and subverted forms. Lacking critical scrutiny of a view, corrupted versions can become widespread. Mann actually concludes that artists are generally prone to misuse philosophy because they are attracted more by its passion than its wisdom. Budd comments similarly: "the better we understand [the view] the less likely it is to cast a spell over us."[49] Of course, any corruption of Schopenhauer's view was not due only to the fact of its silent reception. Schopenhauer's two "disciples" Wagner and Nietzsche mediated Schopenhauer's influence in ways that were to that influence as much detrimental as beneficial.[50] Ultimately, however, and disregarding this mediation, what seemed to influence musical culture was much more an "Idea of Music" than a theoretical package of claims seriously contextualized by a philosophical system.

However, as already noted, some composers took Schopenhauer's musical remarks very seriously and used them to help articulate their own views concerning a whole range of musical matters. But to understand fully this side of Schopenhauer's influence, we must first return to our basic question: how did Schopenhauer manage to convey so much while *saying* so little?

"A METAPHYSICAL AESTHETIC OF SILENCES"

Schopenhauer revealed more about music through silence than speech, through what he showed indirectly by analogy than through what he was able to say literally. In this view, speech and silence, like saying and showing, are mutually dependent or correlative concepts. Accordingly, what cannot be said or what belongs to silent discourse is revealed only by contrast to what can be said. The limits of what can be said determine the limits of what can be shown; or, the world of speech delimits the boundaries which the world of silence must transgress. Silence, philosopher Lie Kuen Tong writes, "is not conceived as the mere absence of speech, but rather as its transcendence."[51]

When Schopenhauer employed Shakespeare's expression "the rest is silence" to end to his *Parerga and Paralipomena*, he was probably not thinking about the possible future reception of his life's work, but more likely about how the world as representation admits a form of description which the world as Will does not, and that, consequently, when one reaches the limits of that description one enters the realm of silence. What is useful about the phrase "the rest is silence" is precisely the relative and negating phrasing: it is not just that the two worlds are inherently related, but also that the one world is known in its difference from the other. "Behind our existence lies something else that becomes accessible to us only by our shaking off the world," Schopenhauer writes. The point is that something has to be shaken off.[52] Regarding music, the transcendent feature of the musical experience is a negating experience of that which must be transcended. The musical experience refers to a human condition to be gotten beyond.

215

Philosophers have long distinguished different worlds – transcendent and phenomenal – and different discourses – silence and speech. They have used these distinctions to generate a whole slew of dualisms: knowledge/opinion; fact/value; reason/passion; sacred/secular. These dualisms reflect a desire to determine the limits of what can be known and described. This desire is tied to an assessment of the value of different worlds or forms of discourse. One mode of philosophical discourse investigates in empirical, logical, or rational terms the limits of its subject matter. Usually, however, this investigation excludes the languages of human communication judged most valuable. Involved in this exclusion is another mode of philosophical discourse which regards that which lies beyond reason, logic, and speech – the discourse of the unsayable – to be freer, more truthful, essential, and spiritual. The two modes of philosophical discourse work in tandem, but the result is enigmatic and paradoxical. Just as Schopenhauer's musical remarks are paradoxical, so are claims about philosophical ignorance (Socrates), or that, out of respect, knowledge should not be spoken aloud (Confucius), or that truth and value lie at or beyond the limits of language (Wittgenstein). For each renders philosophy itself a silent discourse and, once this is established, not subject or reducible to further investigation. Not only, therefore, does philosophy historically provoke mutually excluding limits between speech and silence, but it also paradoxically situates itself on both sides of the fence simultaneously.[53]

Why philosophical traditions have supported their fundamental dualisms is a similarly complex matter. Fortunately, one reason can be singled out as most relevant to our inquiry. This reason recalls a fundamental distrust of humanity which reflects an anxious impulse towards perfection and purification: human beings are regarded as living in and responsible for – given their ignorance and existential delusion – an imperfect, disordered, and corrupt world, a world described by Nietzsche as occupied by "weeds, rubble and vermin."[54] No philosopher gave this distrust a gloomier expression than Schopenhauer. But I am concerned less with Schopenhauer's gloom *per se* than with his antithetical or conciliatory positing of a spiritual musical world that provides him a metaphysical and existential escape from base humanity.

That Schopenhauer *says* so little about music *directly* now becomes ever more significant. For his mode of description fundamentally protects music from being reduced to or translated into, and thus perhaps forever corrupted by, mundane and empirical description. As the language of the universal Will, music is the pure language of free subjectivity, feeling, spontaneity, and gesture; it is conceptless, non-intentional, and of preterlinguistic significance. It is protected from base concepts and feelings, common judgments and desires. Not limited by the usual systematic or scientific laws of order and meaning, it succeeds on its own unspoken or unexplained terms in revealing the spiritual meaning of the world. Silence, here, is revelatory, purifying, and protective.[55]

With his positing of an essentially musical world, Schopenhauer also reveals the full meaning of the philosopher's intoxication with music. He shows the extent to which instrumental music serves as the most successful example of a kind of speech unhampered by the "bounds of sense." Instrumental music is the perfect language that speaks temporally from within itself; it is unsullied by empirical content. It gives us access to that which is ordinarily and otherwise unreachable. In forwarding these claims, Schopenhauer helps formulate not only a view of the abstraction from materiality into a world of pure form and spirituality which persuades other arts during the 1800s increasingly to approximate to the condition of music, but also a basic philosophical view about philosophy itself – that it too should approximate to the condition of music. Like philosophy, music occupies no particular place in the world, or as Nietzsche writes in discussing Wagner and Schopenhauer:

Has it been noticed that music liberates the spirit? gives wings to thought? that one becomes more of a philosopher the more one becomes a musician? – The gray sky of abstraction rent as if by lightning: the light strong enough for the filigree of things: the great problems near enough to grasp; the world surveyed as from a mountain.[56]

The claim regarding philosophy's identity with music has not lost any of its impact: it carries as much weight today under the pressures of poststructuralist analyses of "negative theology," absence, presence, and infinite interpretation, as it carried in German Romanticism. The link in the theoretical tradition is captured perfectly by Adorno: "Music is called upon to do nothing less than retract the historical tendency of language, which is based on signification, and to substitute expressiveness for it."[57]

Of course, it is not just philosophers who have constantly pursued the related themes of the silence and transcendence of the musical language, but musicians (mostly in or coming out the German tradition) as well. Engaging in the central debates of musical discourse, not only have musicians consciously employed a particular "Idea of Music" that regards music as the transcendental language of the inexpressible relatively positioned in its difference from ordinary languages of the expressible, but they have also been explicitly aware of the related paradox of trying to philosophize about the inexpressible. For the remainder of this essay, I will briefly record how the two conceptions of silence – musical and philosophical – have entered into the musical debates, noting at the same time the claims explicitly influenced by Schopenhauer.

THE MUSICIANS' DEBATES

When musicians have thought about the particular paradox of trying to philosophize about the inexpressible, they have often referred to Schopenhauer. In "The Artwork of the Future," Wagner writes:

Though Schopenhauer propounds this theory of music as a paradox, since it cannot strictly be set forth in logical terms, he also furnishes us with the only serviceable material for a further demonstration of the justice of his profound hypothesis.[58]

Schoenberg makes a similar mention:

Even Schopenhauer, who at first says something really exhaustive about the essence of music in his wonderful thought, "The composer reveals the inmost essence of the world and utters the most profound wisdom in a language which his reason does not understand," ... loses himself later when he tries to translate details of this language *which the reason does not understand* into our terms. It must, however, be clear to him that in this translation into the terms of human language, which is abstraction, reduction to the recognizable, the essential, the language of the world, which ought perhaps to remain incomprehensible and only perceptible, is lost. But even so he is justified in this procedure, since after all it is his aim as a philosopher to represent the essence of the world, its unsurveyable wealth, in terms of concepts whose poverty is all too easily seen through.[59]

Schoenberg is interested, however, less in philosophy's limits than in music's inexpressible character. His aim is to warn his readers of the disasters of over- or mis-describing music. "There are relatively few persons who are capable of understanding, purely in terms of music, what music has to say," he writes. This is why program notes are handed out to the audience at concerts. "Wagner," he writes, "when he wanted to give the average man an indirect notion of what he as a musician had looked upon directly, did right to attach programmes to Beethoven's symphonies."[60] But, given these notes, one should not thereby confuse musical meaning with the described programmatic content, images, or associations, just as one should not, when listening to a song, believe that the "extra-musical" lyrics exhaust its meaning. On the contrary, in both cases the meaning of the melody and harmony should guide the writing of programs or lyrics and be recognized thereafter as having done such. For in the melody and harmony lies the real meaning.

Rather than differentiating the composition of purely instrumental music from that of opera, song, and program music, Schoenberg is identifying them. And he does so entirely in the tradition of Schopenhauer, Wagner, and Mahler. Though composers wavered over granting music a supreme value above the other components or associations of opera, song, and program music, they all, following Schopenhauer, eventually concluded that the musical component of any genre of composition must ultimately constitute, as Schoenberg describes it, "the real language." The lyrical, dramatic, and programmatic components illustrate the music's meanings but do not produce independent ones. One motivation for holding this view is the conclusion it prompts, that like instrumental music, opera, song, and program music can all be regarded as absolute, in the sense of genuinely or "squarely" musical, despite the fact that, either in sound or in conception, they are not purely instrumental.[61]

One way to understand how the normally extra-musical elements – lyrics, say – become musical in the context of their use in music is by employing the concept of transfiguration. Wagner describes music as a transfigured and transfiguring language: in the context of opera, words and actions are aestheticized, ennobled, and thereby transfigured through their alliance with melody. So allied they are released (though not completely) from their ordinary meanings and connected to transcendent ones. Through this alliance, they acquire the status of being musical.

Thus, transfiguration plays a key role in the development of autonomous and absolute music. Music, Wagner states categorically does not belong to the empirical world – (and nor apparently does its creator: "My kingdom is not of this world.")[62] However, in positing a transgression of the empirical world through transfiguration, there is no suggestion, as for Schopenhauer there is none, that music loses its connection to the highest moral and political concerns of humanity. Under the guise of "aesthetic theology" music is regarded as a thoroughly spiritual language through which we find a redemption from suffering.[63] The significant claim here is not that autonomous music has purely musical meaning, but that autonomous music has spiritual and universal meaning achieved entirely through a transgressive and purified musical language.

When Ernst Bloch writes that the "inward nature of music has a subterranean relation to the exterior which is not just outward," and "music is the melody to which the world *in its entirety* is finally the text,"[64] or when Schoenberg determines that music must "abandon all imaging" because, like truth, it is "purely self-related,"[65] each composer captures the idea that even when music is utterly void of conceptual content it still can point to something beyond itself. It is just that the relation between music and that to which it points is utterly interior or "inwardly corresponding." Schopenhauer argues similarly, as does Wagner: in the transcendental sphere, there is a fundamental identity between the musical and the so-called "extra"-musical; they are related wholly by interiority and thereby require no phenomenal, external relation. Music apprehends the essence of world directly or self-referentially in sounds. Or, as Wagner writes, music is "subject to aesthetic laws quite distinct from those of every other," because it arises from an "immediate consciousness of the oneness of our inner essence with that of the outer world."[66]

By distinguishing a transcendent interior relation from an empirical external relation, musicians approach their solution to two of the hardest questions in the philosophy of music: how can music have extra-musical significance without that significance compromising its autonomy or muddying its squarely musical meaning? And how can music be considered representational without its having to "imitate"? Being a language of pure subjectivity, musicians answer, music communicates in freedom purely through its own materials and not through representation. However, when they answer this way, they are referring only to the phenomenal mode of representation. They are forgetting momentarily, as Peter Kivy reminds us in aptly titled *Music Alone*, that music can have representational depth (read, transcendent depth) beneath its non-representational (empirical) surface.[67]

As long as musicians employ the dualism between two worlds, they can also employ the associated dualism between the sayable and the unsayable – and this they do. Wagner reminds us, however, that unsayability only means unsayability in the cognitive or conceptual terms associated with words:

[T]he essence of higher instrumental music consists in uttering in tones a thing unspeakable in words ... The orchestra indisputably possesses a *faculty of speech* ... In the symphonies of Beethoven we have seen this faculty develop to a height whence it felt thrust on to speak out that which, by its very nature, it cannot speak out ... : now, we have plainly to denote this speaking faculty ... as the faculty of uttering the unspeakable ... [T]his unspeakable is not a thing unutterable per se, but merely unutterable through the organ of understanding.

The orchestra, Wagner continues, speaks the unspeakable through gesture and feeling. Beethoven's symphonies reveal to us through our feelings, Wagner writes:

a schema of the world's phenomena quite different from the ordinary logical scheme ... [I]t thrusts home with the most overwhelming conviction, and guides our feeling with such a sureness that the logic-mongering reason is completely routed and disarmed.

The purely musical, Wagner concludes, speaks to us of "the world outside us" and "in terms intelligible beyond compare." But it is intelligible to us not through logic, but because "its sounding message to our ear is of the selfsame nature as the cry sent forth from the depths of our own inner heart."[68]

Schoenberg also describes his music – specifically, the "free form" in the "obbligato recitative" of his *Five Orchestral Pieces*, Opus 16 – as a means to express the inexpressible. Dahlhaus has already made this point:

That [Schoenberg] took the musically binding statement as an expression of the "inexpressible" is to be understood in the light of Schopenhauer's metaphysics of music ... : the more rigorously music becomes committed to itself as a language in its own right, ... the more clearly it "reveals the innermost essence of the world," which the language of words cannot reach ... This is the essence of the obbligato ... : it is a question of eloquent music, music that "speaks," without the *Hauptstimme* of the piece bearing the least resemblance to recitative in the usual sense of the word.[69]

For Schoenberg as for Wagner, Dahlhaus explains further, music "must at every moment be 'significant' – 'eloquent' in a sense reaching beyond the limits of verbal language, at least this must be so if Schopenhauer's metaphysical claims are to be satisfied." "Nothing should be tolerated," Dahlhaus continues, "that does not justify itself as a musical idea: formulas, padding and ornament are judged empty and insignificant, and are thus excluded from the binding compelling style which both Schoenberg and Wagner had in mind."[70]

The moral imperative not to misuse the language of music is not an isolated expression of the connection between music and morality, but part of a larger view. Accordingly, music is not only essentially moral and truthful, but also prophetic. Nietzsche provides a crucial metaphysical tenet for this view by speaking of the fundamental non-simultaneity and incommensurability between music and the phenomenal world. By surveying the world "as from a mountain," music is released from the conditioning of particular time and place. So positioned, it can carry out what Bloch, for example, under Nietzsche's influence calls its utopian role. "Music [is] an inwardly utopian art," Bloch writes, "completely beyond the scope of anything empirically verifiable." In the "richly intense" experience to which music gives rise, we are taken beyond the "limits" that define "the world of man."[71] "Music," Schoenberg writes comparably, "conveys a prophetic message revealing a higher form of life towards which mankind evolves."[72]

Both Schoenberg and Bloch are again influenced here by Wagner – but this time only to a limited extent. Although Wagner followed Schopenhauer's lead in aestheticizing politics in general, and in attributing to music a purifying force in particular, Wagner developed these thoughts in profoundly disturbing directions, directions eventually associated with an aestheticized politics and a politicized aesthetics. Such developments have severely complicated the development of musical discourse and our understanding of Schopenhauer's influence upon it. For whether and how Wagner's associations with a deeply racist ideology extend to his musical views and even more specifically to his basic Idea of Music remains a deeply troubling question.[73] And whatever we decide about this question will directly affect how we ultimately judge the ideological bias or neutrality of Schopenhauer's musical view.

But the ideological content of Schopenhauer's musical remarks is not the primary focus of this essay. This essay has really had only one focus, to inquire into the multi-dimensional limits of Schopenhauer's philosophy of music. Most interestingly, we now know, these limits are the product of a metaphysically-dualistic conviction that philosophers should not try to say what cannot be said, and that what philosophers can say about what cannot be said can be said indirectly through analogy. For Schopenhauer, philosophizing via analogy has this point: it helps inexpressible languages be *understood* even if they are not adequately (philosophically) *explained*.

But did Schopenhauer draw the right analogies? Many critics think he did not. But if not, did he nonetheless open up a new path to musicians? It seems clear that he did. Perhaps, then, one should conclude about Schopenhauer what he himself concluded about Kant, that "it is the privilege of the real genius, especially one who opens up a new path, to make great mistakes with impunity." Of course this conclusion has its own logical limits, for, even if the mistakes of geniuses are excused because geniuses open up new paths, not all who open up new paths – as the case of Schopenhauer might well show – are geniuses.[74]

Notes

1 Cf.: Thomas Mann's reference to "classic, pellucid prose" in "Schopenhauer," *Essays of Three Decades*, H. T. Lowe-Porter, trans. (New York: A. A. Knopf, 1947), p. 409.

2 See Mann, "Schopenhauer," pp. 374, 393. Cf.: Helen Zimmern's judgment that "Schopenhauer's general treatment of art had a marked influence on later aesthetic theory, especially in its reference to music" (*Schopenhauer: His Life and His Philosophy* (London: G. Allan and Unwin Ltd., 1876; rev. 1932), p. 182; and Ernst Bloch's judgment that without Schopenhauer, "there would have been neither Nietzsche nor Freud ... Marcuse or Adorno" (*Essays on the Philosophy of Music*, Peter Palmer, trans., David Drew, ed. (Cambridge: Cambridge University Press, 1985), p. xxiv.

3 Cf.: *The Idea of Music: Schoenberg and Others*, in which author Peter Franklin investigates Schopenhauer's influence on Richard Strauss, Mahler, and Schoenberg (London, 1985).

4 Wagner was largely responsible for Beethoven's canonization, but used Schopenhauer's arguments to achieve this end. Beethoven, Wagner said, was the perfect demonstration of the Schopenhauerian thesis (Albert Goldman and Evert Sprinchorn, eds., *Wagner on Music and Drama: A Compendium of Richard Wagner's Prose Works*, H. Ashton Ellis, trans. (New York: E. P. Dutton, 1964), p. 179). Robin Wallace writes also: "Thanks in part to Schopenhauer's glorification of instrumental music ... Beethoven has in our own time been considered to be the hero of abstract thought in art, and ... of German idealist views about music" (*Beethoven's Critics: Aesthetic Dilemmas and Resolutions During the Composer's Lifetime* (Cambridge: Cambridge University Press, 1986), p. 70). In the nineteenth century, Schopenhauer was often compared to Beethoven, even regarding their looks (see Alfred Einstein, *Music in the Romantic Era: A History of Musical Thought in the 19th Century* (New York: W. W. Norton and Company, 1947), pp. 44–46, and Bryan Magee,

The Philosophy of Schopenhauer (Oxford: The Clarendon Press, 1983), p. 18).

5 Carl Dahlhaus, *Esthetics of Music*, trans. William W. Austin (Cambridge: Cambridge University Press, 1982), vii. Cf.: Peter le Huray and James Day: "[Schopenhauer] had a very practical understanding and love of music" (*Music and Aesthetics in the Eighteenth and Early-Nineteenth Centuries* (Cambridge: Cambridge University Press, 1981), p. xiv); and Rudiger Safranski, *Schopenhauer and the Wild Years of Philosophy*, Ewald Osers, trans. (Cambridge, MA: Harvard University Press, 1990), pp. 17, 29, 42, 236–237.

6 Wagner, *On Music and Drama*, p. 179: Schopenhauer did not pursue his hypothesis about music more closely "perhaps for the simple reason that as layman he was not conversant enough with music."

7 Knud Martner, ed., *Selected Letters of Gustav Mahler* (New York: Farrar, Straus, Giroux, 1979), p. 412; Israel Knox, "Schopenhauer's Aesthetic Theory," in *Schopenhauer: His Philosophical Achievement*, Michael Fox, ed. (Sussex: Harvester Press, 1980), p. 145; Georg Simmel, *Schopenhauer and Nietzsche*, Helmut Loiskandl, Deena Weinstein and Michael Weinstein, trans. (Amherst: University of Massachusetts Press, 1986), p. 93.

8 See Knox, "Schopenhauer's Aesthetic Theory," p. 145, and Malcolm Budd, *Music and the Emotions: The Philosophical Theories* (London: Routledge and Kegan Paul, 1985), p. 76.

9 Mann, "Schopenhauer," p. 394.

10 Budd, *Music and the Emotions*, p. 103. On p. 96 he writes: "Unfortunately, there is very little truth [in Schopenhauer's theory of music]."

11 The phrase "the musician's world" is Wagner's (*On Music and Drama*, p. 186). For details of the debates, see Dahlhaus, *Nineteenth Century Music*, J. Bradford Robinson, trans. (Berkeley: University of California Press, 1989); Leonard B. Meyer, *Style and Music: Theory, History, and Ideology* (Philadelphia: University of Pennsylvania Press, 1989), and my *The Imaginary Museum of Musical Works: An Essay in the Philosophy of Music* (Oxford: The Clarendon Press, 1992).

12 "Schopenhauer's 'Palestrina,'" *The Listener*, 23, May 1968, p. 676. Philip Alperson comments comparably regarding Schopenhauer's reception among philosophers, whom, he says "have paid less attention to his particular discussion of music – this despite the fact that it is one of his most intriguing analyses." ("Schopenhauer and Musical Revelation", *The Journal of Aesthetics and Art Criticism*, 40, 1982, p. 155.)

13 *WWR* 1, 255–267; *WWR* 2, 447–457.

14 Alperson reminds us that one should more accurately describe music in this view as beyond rather than at the top of the fine arts hierarchy ("Schopenhauer and Musical Revelation," p. 157).

15 Alperson notices the difficulty of Schopenhauer's strategy, but does not pursue it further. Schopenhauer "wants to say that musical revelation is otherwise ineffable and yet he wants to philosophize about it" (ibid., p. 162).

16 Whether the musical language is unique in its capacity to express the Will is a topic also taken up by Alperson (ibid., pp. 159–160).

17 Ibid., p. 144.

18 *Essays and Aphorisms* (Harmondsworth: Penguin Books Ltd., 1970), p. 163.

19 See Safranski, *Schopenhauer and the Wild Years of Philosophy*, p. 347, and John Chancellor, *Wagner* (London, 1978), p. 132.

20 Simmel, *Schopenhauer and Nietzsche*, p. 93.

21 See Safranski, *Schopenhauer and the Wild Years of Philosophy*, p. 329. Although Schopenhauer actually describes his philosophy as immanent, not transcendent, he argues, as critical theorists did later on, that one seeks transcendence in immanence, the universal in the particular. Cf.: Simmel, *Schopenhauer and Nietzsche*, pp. 84ff.

22 For more general discussion of philosophy's limits, see *WWR* 2, pp. 640–646 ('Epiphilosophy').

23 Cf.: Adorno's expression of this point: "the entanglement in the banal is as total as the flight from it" (*In Search of Wagner*, Rodney Livingstone, trans. (London: NLB, 1981), p. 105).

24 Cf.: Budd, *Music and the Emotions*, p. 96, and Magee, *The Philosophy of Schopenhauer*, pp. 240–243.

25 Cf.: Lucian Krukowski, *Aesthetic Legacies* (Philadelphia: Temple University Press, 1992), pp. 61–62, and Alperson, "Schopenhauer and Musical Revelation," p. 161.

26 Cf.: Knox, "Schopenhauer's Aesthetic Theory," p. 145.

27 Cf.: D. W. Hamlyn, *Schopenhauer: The Arguments of the Philosophers* (London: Routledge and Kegan Paul, 1980), p. 119.

28 Quoted in Zimmern, *Arthur Schopenhauer*, p. 90.

29 Magee, *The Philosophy of Schopenhauer*, pp. 186–187.

30 John Oxenford, "Iconoclasm in German Philosophy," *Westminster and Foreign Quarterly Review* (April 1853). Wagner's letter is reprinted in *On Music and Drama*, p. 271.

31 Wagner, *On Music and Drama*, p. 271. The soap bubble metaphor is borrowed from Zimmern, *Arthur Schopenhauer*, p. 121.

32 "Schopenhauer as Educator," *Untimely Meditations*, R. J. Hollingdale, trans. (Cambridge: Cambridge University Press, 1983), pp. 135, 152, and 182–184.

33 Safranski, *Schopenhauer and the Wild Years of Philosophy*, p. 64.

34 Cf.: Hans-Georg Gadamer: "It was the romantic and idealist concept of unconscious production which lay behind [the] development [of the concept of genius] and acquired, through Schopenhauer and the philosophy of the unconscious, enormous popular influence," *Truth and Method*, Garrett Barden and John Cumming, trans. and ed. (New York: The Seabury Press, 1975), p. 54.

35 Cf.: Simmel, *Schopenhauer and Nietzsche*, p. xxvii.

36 Cf.: Terry Eagleton: "[Had Schopenhauer] not studied medicine and physiology … , the course of Western philosophy, all the way from

Lydia Goehr

Nietzsche's praise for the *Buffo* to Jean-François Lyotard's points of libidinal intensity, might have been different." ("Bakhtin, Schopenhauer, Kundera", in Ken Hirschkop and David Shepherd, eds., *Bakhtin and Cultural Theory* (Manchester: Manchester University Press, 1989), p. 179. Eagleton further writes that Schopenhauer was "perhaps the first major modern thinker to place at the centre of his work the abstract category of *desire itself* ... Freud ... was said to consider Schopenhauer one of the half-dozen greatest individuals who had ever lived" (*The Ideology of the Aesthetic* (Oxford: Basil Blackwell, 1990), pp. 158–159). For Wagner's discussion of Schopenhauer's clairvoyance and dream theory, see *On Music and Drama*, pp. 181–186.

37 Nietzsche articulates the thought perfectly: "The genius must not fear to enter into the most hostile relationship with the existing forms and order if he wants to bring to light the higher order and truth that dwells within him" ("Schopenhauer as Educator," p. 137).

38 Cf.: Dahlhaus: "The extent to which the aesthetic categories of the eighteenth, nineteenth and twentieth centuries are secularised theological concepts has never been underestimated" (*Schoenberg and the New Music, Essays*, Derrick Puffett and Alfred Clayton, trans. (Cambridge: Cambridge University Press, 1987), p. 83; also Safranski, *Schopenhauer and the Wild Years of Philosophy*, pp. 62–65.

39 *WWR* 2, 388: "The work of genius may be music, philosophy, painting, or poetry; it is nothing for use or profit. To be useless and unprofitable is one of the characteristics of the works of genius."

40 Alma Mahler, *Gustav Mahler, Memories and Letters*, Basil Creighton, trans. (London: J. Murray, 1946), p. 44.

41 Letter to Arthur Siedl, February 17, 1897 (*Selected Letters of Gustav Mahler*, p. 212).

42 *The Correspondence Between Richard Strauss and Hugo von Hofmannstal*, Hans Hammelmann and Ewald Osers, trans. (Cambridge: Cambridge University Press, 1980), p. 404.

43 *The Letters of Franz Liszt to Olga von Meyendorff, 1881–1886*, W. R. Tyler, trans. (Cambridge, MA: Harvard University Press, 1979), pp. 420–421, 167.

44 *Antonin Dvorak: Musician and Craftsman* (New York, 1966), p. 22.

45 *Prokofiev by Prokofiev: A Composer's Memoir*, David H. Apel, ed., Guy Daniels, trans. (Garden City: Doubleday, 1979), p. 308.

46 V. V. Yastrebtsev, *Reminiscences of Rimsky-Korsakov*, Florence Jones, ed. (New York: Columbia University Press, 1985), p. 304.

47 March 3, 1855 (Stewart Spencer and Barry Millington, trans., *Selected Letters of Richard Wagner* (New York: W. W. Norton and Company, 1987), p. 327).

48 Ibid., p. 676.

49 Mann, "Schopenhauer," p. 396; Budd, *Music and the Emotions*, p. 77.

50 Cf.: Einstein, *Music in the Romantic Era*, p. 237: "[Wagner made Schopenhauer] the fashionable philosopher of the Romantic era." For

mention of Wagner's purported corruption of Schopenhauer, see Mann, "Schopenhauer," p. 377. And note that Nietzsche tends to treat the thought of Wagner and Schopenhauer as coextensive (see esp. "The Case of Wagner: Turinese Letter of May 1888" (Walter Kaufmann, ed., *Basic Writings of Nietzsche* (New York: Modern Library, 1968), p. 620)).

51 "The Meaning of Philosophical Silence: Some Reflections on the Use of Language in Chinese Thought," *Journal of Chinese Philosophy*, 3, 1976, pp. 169–183. I have benefited greatly from this article.

52 *WWR* 1, 405.

53 Alperson also mentions philosophical quietism when he refers to Nietzsche recalling the "voice which, in a dream, told Socrates to 'practice music' [as] a caution about the limits of logic" ("Schopenhauer and Musical Revelation," p. 165, n. 25).

54 "Schopenhauer as Educator," p. 130. Cf.: Safranski, *Schopenhauer and the Wild Years in Philosophy*, p. 65: " ... the pulse of divine music has not ceased to throb throughout the centuries of barbarism"; and Dahlhaus' observation that music provides an alternative to the realities of the industrial revolution (*Between Romanticism and Modernism: Four Studies in the Music of the Later Nineteenth Century*, Mary Whittall, trans. (Berkeley: University of California Press, 1980), pp. 8–9).

55 This way of describing music is not unique to Schopenhauer. Consider E. T. A. Hoffmann's use of highly spiritual language to describe the transcendent power of instrumental music; or Eduard Hanslick's view that what is said in extra-musical terms about music is always one step removed: the language doesn't really touch music, it only links itself to music metaphorically; or even John Cage's modernist desire to protect music (or "organized sound") from human intention and intervention. We're better off, he writes in his book aptly titled *Silence*, leaving the organization of sound to chance.

56 "The Case of Wagner," p. 614.

57 *In Search of Wagner*, p. 99.

58 *On Music and Drama*, p. 179.

59 "The Relationship to the Text," *Style and Idea: Selected Writings of Arnold Schoenberg*, Leonard Stein, ed., Leo Black, trans. (New York: St. Martins Press, 1975), p. 142.

60 Ibid., p. 141.

61 Cf.: Dahlhaus: "It was the common belief of all turn of the century Wagnerian composers who adopted Schopenhauer's metaphysic – from Mahler and Strauss to Schoenberg and Pfitzner – that music, whether in music drama, symphonic poem, or Lied, articulates the meaning of the text, rather than vice versa" (*Nineteenth-Century Music*, p. 341). Cf.: also Dahlhaus, *Schoenberg and the New Music*, pp. 144–148.

62 *On Music and Drama*, pp. 186, 402.

63 Cf.: Dahlhaus on "aesthetic theology," in *Schoenberg and the New Music*, pp. 81–93.

64 *Essays on the Philosophy of Music*, pp. 219, 127.

65 Quoted in Safranski, *Schopenhauer and the Wild Years in Philosophy*, p. 343.
66 *On Music and Drama*, p. 183.
67 *Music Alone: Philosophical Reflections on the Purely Musical Experience* (Ithaca, NY: Cornell University Press, 1990), p. 47.
68 *On Music and Drama*, pp. 217–218, 187.
69 *Schoenberg and the New Music*, p. 144.
70 Ibid., p. 145.
71 *Essays on the Philosophy of Music*, pp. xxv, 195. Cf.: David Drew's comment that Schopenhauer's "pessimism was so constructed that it could serve at all times as a crucible for the base and precious metals of Bloch's optimism" (ibid., p. xxv).
72 "Criteria for the Evaluation of Music" (1946), *Style and Idea*, p. 136.
73 For Wagner's musico-political views in relation to Schopenhauer, see Josef Chytry, *The Aesthetic State: A Quest in Modern German Thought* (Berkeley: University of California Press, 1989), pp. 283–284.
74 Thanks to many friends and colleagues for their comments and advice.

11

Metaphysics and aesthetics: a case study of Schopenhauer and Thomas Hardy

T. J. DIFFEY

SCHOPENHAUER AND LITERARY AUTHORS

That Schopenhauer is among those philosophers thought to have had a considerable influence on or particular appeal to literary authors, to say nothing of his influence on Wagner, is well known. Bryan Magee names the following writers as in some way or other indebted to Schopenhauer: Tolstoy, Turgenev, Zola, Proust, Hardy, Conrad, Maupassant, Thomas Mann, T. S. Eliot, Rilke, Pirandello, Somerset Maugham, and Borges.[1]

What has interested writers in Schopenhauer, apart from his powerful literary style, is his metaphysics (and to some extent his ethics). The point as it concerns metaphysics seems too obvious to be worth making but nevertheless deserves pausing on for two reasons: first and again almost too obvious to be worth saying, speculative metaphysics is out of fashion with academic or professional philosophers. It follows therefore that if, as I am, we are concerned to understand how philosophy and literature might relate and interact, we have to face the fact that literature is likely to be concerned with those aspects of philosophy least acceptable to the professionals. This should put us on target for some ripe misunderstandings to arise between students of philosophy and students of literature.

Schopenhauer himself is not to be included in the category of the "we" who are interested in relationships between philosophy and literature. He has something to say about how the arts and philosophy might relate but, not surprisingly given his time, he evinces no interest in the category of literature. In the index to Payne's translation of the *World as Will* "literature" is not to be found; "poetry" and "poets," "authors" and "drama" and the names of many particular writers are.

However, there is something else in Schopenhauer besides his metaphysics and his ethics that we might have expected literary authors to have been interested in: namely his aesthetics. Yet, so far as I know, and this is the second reason why we should pause on the nature of the interest that Schopenhauer has held for writers, few if any of them have taken much interest in this subject. Part of the explanation for this may be that Schopenhauer's aesthetics divides predominantly into an account of the visual representational arts on the one hand and of music on the other, leaving no room for a distinctive or specific account of literature.

I place no great confidence in this explanation, however, since it makes the doubtful assumption that a literary author could only be interested in a system of aesthetics if that dealt specifically with literature; moreover, it overlooks the fact that Schopenhauer's aesthetics is embedded in his metaphysics. For, as Erich Heller has pointed out, the topic of art predominates in the *World as Will*: "The young Nietzsche's *The Birth of Tragedy* shows all the signs of his "metaphysical intoxication" with Schopenhauer's philosophy of art (and it is to art that three-quarters of *The World as Will and Idea* are devoted)".[2]

So, in as far as authors are engaged with Schopenhauer's metaphysics, are they not necessarily enmeshed in his aesthetics? This certainly seems to have been the case with Thomas Mann.

Nevertheless there is a question of emphasis here, for it remains the case that, whatever the reason, it is that aspect of Schopenhauer's metaphysics or philosophy which has to do with the Will and suffering, and not his account of our experience of representational art in disinterested perception, which has captured the imagination of writers.[3] The secondary literature on Thomas Hardy, for example, devotes a fair amount of attention to discussing the impression which Schopenhauer's ideas about Will and suffering made on Hardy[4] without ever considering whether Hardy might not also have been attracted to Schopenhauer's ideas about art and aesthetic perception.[5] But the general point that Schopenhauer's readers, including literary authors, can opt out of his aesthetics while being captivated by his metaphysics might, then, be contested by Erich Heller who sees "the separation of poetry from the condition of reality" [meaning here mundane or quotidian reality] as "most strictly prepared by Schopenhauer's metaphysics of art."[6]

However, Hardy, to stay with the case of this writer, is not in this Schopenhauerian tradition of regarding the artist as some kind of

visionary or seer; and indeed he has been quite severely criticized by
Donald Davie for this very reason, that is, for selling British poetry
short by not subscribing to grand (Schopenhauerian-type) Romantic
ideas about the role and task of the poet.

Hardy, by comparison with an ambitious poet such as Wordsworth, so Davie argues, "was very unambitious indeed." Technically
he was ambitious and highly skilled, "but disablingly modest in his
aims."[7] Some of the features of later British poetry: "an apparent
meanness of spirit, a painful modesty of intention, extremely limited
objectives – fall into place if they are seen as part of an inheritance
from Hardy" (Davie, pp. 11–12). Hardy is the scientific humanist, the
"liberal." His "engaging modesty and his decent liberalism represent
a crucial selling short of the poetic vocation" (Davie, pp. 39–40; the
scare quotation marks round "liberal" are Davie's, not mine). Hardy
is unlike Pound, Pasternak, Yeats, Hopkins, and Eliot, Donald Davie
says, for they:

> are radical in a sense that Hardy isn't. All these other poets claim, by
> implication or else explicitly, to give us entry through their poems into a
> world that is truer and more real than the world we know from statistics or
> scientific induction or common sense ... In their poems ... quotidian reality
> is transformed, displaced, supplanted; the alternative reality which their
> poems create is offered to us as a superior reality, by which the reality of
> every day is to be judged and governed. But Hardy's poems, instead of
> transforming and displacing quantifiable reality or the reality of common
> sense, are on the contrary just so many glosses on that reality, which is
> conceived of as unchallengeably "given" and final. This is what makes it
> possible to say (once again) that he sold the [poetic] vocation short, tacitly
> surrendering the proudest claims traditionally made for the act of the poetic
> imagination.   (Davie, pp. 61–62)

Hardy is taken to task by one authority then for not subscribing to
the ideal of the poet as transcendent visionary; Schopenhauer is
taken to task by another for promoting it. For Heller's charge against
Schopenhauer is precisely that he places the artist on a footing with
saints and angels, who are all united in their rejection of common
life. Schopenhauer is thus seen to be a major source of the doctrine
of aesthetic transcendence, which has been a dominant theme in
modern literature.[8]

I can scarcely pretend then that Schopenhauer's aesthetics has
been uninfluential on writers (and critics), in view of the encouragement it has given to this idea of the artist. But it is one thing to see
Schopenhauer as an influential figure in what has been a major

literary theme, and another to see writers as explicitly drawing on his aesthetics as they apparently do on his metaphysics.

SCHOPENHAUER'S AESTHETICS AND LITERATURE

What could Schopenhauer's aesthetics do for aspiring authors besides excite them with a transcendent vision of the artist? Schopenhauer himself is pretty modest and mainly negative in his answer to this question. A knowledge of aesthetics, for instance, will not teach us how to write poetry:

> For although it might be said that logic is related to rational thinking as thorough-bass is to music, and also as ethics is to virtue, if we take it less precisely, or as aesthetics is to art, it must be borne in mind that no one ever became an artist by studying aesthetics, that a noble character was never formed by a study of ethics, that men composed correctly and beautifully long before Rameau, and that we do not need to be masters of thorough-bass in order to detect discords. Just as little do we need to know logic in order to avoid being deceived by false conclusions. But it must be conceded that thorough-bass is of great use in the practice of musical composition, although not for musical criticism. Aesthetics and ethics also, though in a much less degree, may have some use in practice, though a mainly negative one, and hence they too cannot be denied all practical value ...[9]

It can scarcely be said that there is anything novel in Schopenhauer's position here; on the contrary, it is commonplace in German aesthetics since Kant. For example, Hegel (whom notoriously Schopenhauer hated) also argued that aesthetics cannot prescribe rules for artistic production.

The passage I've quoted appears early in the First Book of *The World as Will*, but Schopenhauer is a repetitive writer, although since he writes so well we easily forgive him for this; and he comes back to the point at least twice in the Fourth Book:

> Virtue is as little taught as is genius; indeed, the concept is just as unfruitful for it as it is for art, and in the case of both can be used only as an instrument. We should therefore be just as foolish to expect that our moral systems and ethics would create virtuous, noble, and holy men, as that our aesthetics would produce poets, painters, and musicians. (*WWR* 1, 271)

Schopenhauer sees common ground between philosophy and poetry (I now switch from my term "literature" to his, "poetry"): "To enrich the concept from perception is the constant endeavour of poetry and philosophy" (*WWR* 2, 74).

He makes a connected point much later:

232

Every good painting, every genuine poem, bears the stamp of the frame of mind it depicts. For only what has sprung from perception, indeed from purely objective perception, or is directly stimulated by it, contains the living germ from which genuine and original achievements can result, not only in the plastic and pictorial arts, but also in poetry, *and even in philosophy.* (*WWR* 2, 371, my italics)

From genius "all genuine works of the arts, of poetry, and even of philosophy, spring" (*WWR* 2, 376). "The work of genius may be music, philosophy, painting, or poetry; it is nothing for use or profit" (*WWR* 2, 388).

In Schopenhauer there is the Spinozistic idea that liberation from the necessity of our situation as determined by cause and effect (in Buddhistic terms liberation from the conditionality of existence) is achieved through the understanding of or intellectual insight into the causes of things.

PHILOSOPHICAL LITERATURE

The distinction I have sketched between philosophical understanding as the knowledge of causes and aesthetic insight as the perception of the forms of things is not beyond criticism. Far from it. But it does gives us a way of approaching the question: if Hardy and Wordsworth are in some sense philosophical writers, while Jane Austen and Dickens are not, how is it that Hardy's works or Wordsworth's are nevertheless *not* philosophical in the sense that, say, Kant's or Hume's works are paradigms of philosophy? In short, how is a philosophical literary author to be distinguished from a philosopher? And positively: what is philosophical about philosophical literature? There is unlikely to be any single answer to these questions, and a variety of possibilities will occur to us. For example, we are likely to approach a literary work in a different spirit from a philosophical one, in that we shall not extract or paraphrase from Hardy as we may from Hume a set of arguments which we will test for validity and which we shall seek to challenge and to refute.

An answer I suggest for consideration here, however, is that if philosophy is the understanding of causes this understanding is to be had from literature as well as from philosophy. And this gives us common ground between philosophy and literature, for there is no reason why insight into the causes of things should be confined to official philosophy writing (and no reason to suppose that it will invariably be found there).

A philosophical writer is one who seeks to suggest, by drawing to the reader's attention (with whatever degree of success or failure), the universal significance which the particulars narrated should be presumed or imagined to carry. In this sense Hardy is a philosophical writer, for not only are the sufferings of Tess *portrayed*; at the same time Hardy seeks to explain that suffering by contriving to show or suggest that suffering is inevitable in the universe which Tess (and we) are trapped in.

I say that the writer may "show" and "suggest," not "tell," "assert" or "argue" these things; but when Hardy does lapse into telling us what the world is like, that is, when he falls into making philosophical statements, he incurs artistic failure and falls into what Collingwood, criticizing the concluding lines of *Tess of the d'Urbervilles,* called "ranting."[10] What is postulated here, then, is a mode of explanation exploited by literature which "shows" without "telling." The propounding of doctrine by an author, as opposed to using it or presupposing it, is an artistic failure. In other words, literary artists fail when they become most like philosophers.

I conclude therefore that, although Hardy himself apparently showed no interest in Schopenhauer's aesthetics, that aesthetics, provided we make one adjustment to it, nevertheless does enable us to characterize an aspect of Hardy's achievement. When Schopenhauer speaks about the capacity of the artist to portray the essential forms of things, he tends, not surprisingly, since he is concerned in that part of his theory mainly with the visual arts, to speak as if the artist is depicting physical or natural objects; and in depicting a particular physical thing, such as a tree, the artist succeeds in revealing its essence or form. But when one considers a novel such as *Tess of the d'Urbervilles,* although there is much, such as the scenes at Talbothays' dairy, which through the imagination delights the senses, the essences or forms which Hardy reveals in the novel, if we are to speak in these terms, seem to be altogether more abstract than natural forms; that is to say, what is revealed, if anything, is not the essence of a tree but the injustice that attends upon and seems to be inevitable in human life.

The objection, however, that the contrast between intellectual insight into the nature of things and the aesthetic perception of real forms is open to criticism, is not avoided by its opening the way, if it does, to an answer to the question: what is philosophical about philosophical literature? Moreover, if the answer to *that* question is that the portrayal of human motivation and experience in such literature is done with an eye to its place within the universe, with how it fits into the nature of things, it is plain that *that* answer is far from clear. But if any clarification is to be had, it is unlikely to be found at this very general level. Let us now turn then to consider more closely the particular case of Schopenhauer and Thomas Hardy.

ON THE INFLUENCE OF SCHOPENHAUER ON HARDY

In 1911 an American scholar, Helen Garwood, published her doctoral thesis, completed two years earlier in 1909, on the influence of Schopenhauer on Thomas Hardy. This did not initiate but it did give some momentum to the large secondary literature on the topic of the relationship between Hardy and Schopenhauer, a literature which continues to this day but which over the years has changed somewhat in the positions taken.[11] Initially the relationship was identified, then taken for granted, that is, it was something which everybody interested in Hardy knew about, and now most recently the idea of any significant relationship is repudiated or played down. In this latest stage, principles and premises of literary criticism, which were not prominent when Garwood wrote her thesis[12] but which are influential now, are often invoked.

The answer, surely disconcerting to anyone of a realist and/or unhistoricist turn of mind, to the question what is the nature of the relationship between Hardy and Schopenhauer, depends then, so it would seem, upon the date when the question is asked. In the 1920s the predominant (though not unanimous) answer was: see how close to Schopenhauer Hardy is; in the 1950s that Schopenhauer confirmed Hardy in his own philosophical vision; but, according to some recent accounts of the matter, to use the slang now popular among literary critics in the conduct of their rhetorical wars, such remarks are "off the planet."

The literature on Schopenhauer and Hardy interests me for several reasons. For one thing, how does Schopenhauer fare when we look at him not in the context of other philosophers but of imaginative writers? Secondly, when I first encountered this literature in the 1950s (what there then was of it, for since then it has grown somewhat) I thought that contributions to it, such as *Thomas Hardy's Universe* by Ernest Brennecke, Jr.,[13] were philosophy; and indeed that Hardy himself was a philosopher (a view championed by Brennecke). Thirdly, if the influence of Schopenhauer on Hardy

235

is not what we thought it was, have we not been on a long wild-goose chase? For the secondary literature on Hardy poses in an acute form the question: what is the nature of learning in the humanities, or more bluntly, how is such learning not a waste of time?

Is it the case then that Garwood and the early writers such as Brennecke were mistaken about the relevance of Schopenhauer for Hardy and that subsequently their errors stood in need of correction by Morrell and others? If so, would it not have been better if the errors had been avoided in the first place and the public prints spared the topic altogether? What does it profit a person to become ensnared in it if it turns out that the grounds for thinking that Hardy was influenced by Schopenhauer are not good grounds? Does, say, Roy Morrell's *Thomas Hardy: The Will and the Way,* in rejecting Brennecke's position, represent a crossing out, as it were, of the statements made in *Thomas Hardy's Universe,* such that the two books taken together amount to a contradiction, the upshot of which is that nothing is successfully asserted, thereby restoring the *status ante quo,* with Thomas Hardy's works left in splendid isolation free of the contamination of commentary?[14]

The question, however, rhetorically runs away with itself. For a writer to be left in such untouched isolation, every proposition in the literature about him or her should either contradict or be contradicted by some other proposition until none is left uncontroverted; it wouldn't be sufficient for one critic to take issue with another on some particular point. And there is also the question to be considered of exactly what question is being asked. Thus, are we asking: was Thomas Hardy *influenced* in what he wrote in his novels, poems and epic drama by what he read in Schopenhauer? And here there are a number of subsidiary questions: how *extensive* as opposed to how *casual* or fleeting was the influence, and are we sure that it was Schopenhauer and not say Von Hartmann who was doing the influencing? All these questions have been considered of course in the secondary literature on Thomas Hardy. Are we saying that there are striking resemblances between a certain philosopher and a certain author? Or are we saying: no matter what books authors have read, that is irrelevant to the literary works they produce?

SCHOPENHAUER'S PHILOSOPHY AND HARDY'S

Writing in the *Westminster Review* in 1883, Havelock Ellis observed:

If it were possible to find traces of any philosophy, it would be of Schopenhauer's. "Der Mensch andert sich nie"; that is what so deeply impresses Schopenhauer, *velle non discitur;* and, as we have seen, it is that which impresses Mr. Hardy. The fragmentary ethical system of the novelist is like a pale reflection of the philosopher's, and there is the same sense of the isolation of the individual, the same feeling that there are narrow limits to what one being can be for another. In the "Parerga," there is, indeed, a short passage of which Cytherea's cry is but a paraphrase.[15]

R. G. Cox, who reprints these comments in his *Thomas Hardy: The Critical Heritage*, remarks that an affinity which Havelock Ellis notes with Schopenhauer is "probably the first time this connection was made" (Cox, p. xli).

William R. Rutland is quoted by C. H. Salter as saying that around 1880 Hardy began reading philosophy in an attempt to fill a spiritual vacuum. But as against Havelock Ellis's claim made in 1883 for a Schopenhauerian *ethical* (as much as a *metaphysical*) resemblance – Bailey is reported as having claimed that there was no influence of *Schopenhauer* on Hardy before 1886.[16] Rutland settles for "after 1884": he says although Hardy "may have taken a hint from Herbert Spencer twenty years before, there cannot be any doubt that it was Hardy's reading in Schopenhauer after 1884 which determined the final form of the poem on the Napoleonic wars ...", that is, *The Dynasts.*[17]

Hardy, so Walter F. Wright claims, never completely surrendered himself to either Schopenhauer or Hartmann (Wright, p. 53). But he concedes that Hardy's reading in Schopenhauer (and Hartmann) contributed not alone philosophical theories but food for Hardy's imagination in the creation of the mythology of *The Dynasts* (Wright, p. 91).

By 1924 Ernest Brennecke, Jr., was able to claim: "It seems to be universally recognized at the present time by everybody interested in the subject that there is the closest intellectual affinity between Arthur Schopenhauer and Thomas Hardy" (Brennecke, p. 14). Brennecke was well aware of the distinction between a resemblance and a causal influence holding between two writers. He plainly believes, in the case of Schopenhauer and Hardy, that both obtained but is mainly interested in the resemblances. This is because he is inclined to treat Hardy as a philosopher in his own right and therefore is led to compare Schopenhauer's system to Hardy's philosophical "scheme."

Brennecke immediately adds qualifications, however, to his bold statement of the "closest intellectual affinity" between the two, but with remarks which do not actually affect the truth of the main claim. He reports, then, that Hardy's friend, Edmund Gosse, denied that there was any influence by Schopenhauer on Hardy's work before 1874 – a good deal earlier incidentally than the dates in the 1880s canvassed above; moreover, so Brennecke concedes: "it is perfectly believable that the broad outlines" of Hardy's philosophy "were developed in complete independence of the writings of Schopenhauer" (Brennecke, pp. 14–15).

Indeed much later C. H. Salter was to note the following points in common between Hardy and Schopenhauer and to maintain that they were all evident in Hardy before he had read any Schopenhauer: "pessimism, dislike of Christianity, interest in art, desire for stasis and peace, ... Hellenism, a sort of spiritualism, kindness to animals" (Salter, p. 57). He holds that while a passage in *Tess* and a passage in *Jude* are indebted to Schopenhauer the result is not Schopenhauerian (Salter, p. 56).

Haldane and Kemp translated Schopenhauer's *World as Will and Idea* into English in 1883. J. O. Bailey reports that Hardy read this while composing *The Woodlanders,* which was published in 1887. "Dissertations and book-length studies have amply shown the influence of Schopenhauer upon Hardy's thought. It seems beyond question that Schopenhauer influenced Hardy to think now of the philosophers' Thing-in-Itself that he had called 'Law' as Will".[18]

SCHOPENHAUER'S INFLUENCE DISPUTED

But nothing is beyond question. Not only is the extent of Schopenhauer's influence on Hardy in dispute but where it came from is also at issue. Thus we found Havelock Ellis hinting at *Parerga and Paralipomena*: while Carl Weber plumps for *The Four-Fold Root of the Principle of Sufficient Reason,* which J. Hillis Miller reports Hardy as having read in 1889 or 1890,[19] as the source of Schopenhauer's influence on Hardy and not, as so many people have supposed, *The World as Will and Idea*.[20] Hardy's copy of *The Four-Fold Root,* Weber tells us, has survived, and the evidence from Hardy's markings in it is that he studied Schopenhauer diligently and long. But like Bailey above, Rutland reports (in effect contrary to Weber) that Hardy bought the Haldane and Kemp translation of *The World as Will,* which is [also] still in his library (Rutland, p. 93). Certainly Brennecke, who ranges widely through Schopenhauer's works in his study of Hardy, nevertheless writes as if it is *The World as Will* which is the major influence or ground of comparison with Hardy. But why can't Hardy have been influenced by all these works? And more besides; for Michael Millgate tells us that in the summer of 1891 Hardy worked his way with some care through Schopenhauer's *Studies in Pessimism*[21] and Björk points out that Hardy got many of his Schopenhauer entries for his notebooks from James Sully's *Pessimism* (Björk 1, p. 389). Those who agree that Schopenhauer's influence on Hardy was significant find it in *The Dynasts* (1904–08),[22] and *Jude the Obscure* (1896).[23] Yet Hardy claimed to be more in harmony with certain other thinkers. Carl J. Weber elucidates:

Hardy's use of the term "the Immanent Will" in *The Dynasts* had, of course, made many a reader think that Schopenhauer was its source, but Hardy was always inclined to be evasive on that point. When Helen Garwood earned a Ph.D. degree at the University of Pennsylvania with a dissertation on *Thomas Hardy: an Illustration of the Philosophy of Schopenhauer* (1911) and sent Hardy a copy of it, he replied, somewhat cryptically: "My pages show harmony of view with Darwin, Huxley, Spencer, Hume, Mill, and others, all of whom I used to read more than Schopenhauer."

(Weber, pp. 246–247)

Weber is mistaken in thinking that this was Hardy's reply to Helen Garwood. Hardy, so far as I can discover, had said nothing to her about his pages showing harmony of view with other philosophers. Rather when she published her dissertation in book form in 1911 she said in her book: "In a letter, however, which he very courteously sent me in answer to an inquiry, Mr. Hardy speaks of his philosophy being a development from Schopenhauer through later philosophers."[24] This letter appears not to have survived; at any rate it is not reprinted in Hardy's *Collected Letters*. What is to be found in the *Collected Letters*, however, is a letter which Hardy wrote to Ernest Brennecke at a much later date, that is, in 1924, in which he expresses himself in terms almost identical to those which Weber quotes as having been those in which Hardy is said by commentators to have addressed to Helen Garwood. The letter which Weber and other commentators, then, all say was written to Helen Garwood was in fact written to Ernest Brennecke. Now this is no more than a slight error in the secondary commentaries, but one which, once it was introduced into the literature by Weber, seems to have been perpetuated ever since. But more interesting, the letter (and to whom it was written does not matter in this regard) is often quoted by those writers who seek to minimize the influence of Schopenhauer on Hardy. But if one quotes the letter to Brennecke more fully than it is customary to do, in my judgment the full passage suggests a slightly less negative attitude on Hardy's part towards Schopenhauer than the short passage quoted by Weber and others on its own tends to suggest. Thus Hardy writes to Brennecke as follows:

I saw a criticism [of Brennecke's book, *Thomas Hardy's Universe: A Study of a Poet's Mind*] which remarked that it was a little too much like a treatise on Schopenhauer with notes on Hardy, and though that was a humorous exaggeration, what the critic meant, I suppose, was that Schopenhauer's was too largely dwelt upon to the exclusion of other philosophies apparent in my writings to represent me truly – that, as my pages show harmony of view with Darwin, Huxley, Spencer, Comte, Hume, Mill, and others (all of whom, as a matter of fact, I used to read more than Sch.) my kinship with them should have been mentioned as well as with him. Personally I have nothing to say on this point, though I share their opinion to some extent.[25]

There is, then, no doubting Hardy's awareness of Schopenhauer in some degree. His Apology to *Late Lyrics and Earlier*, for example, expresses respect for Schopenhauer (Salter, p. 53). Robert Gittings speaks of Hardy's "Writing to a critic who in 1911 treated the work [*The Dynasts*] as an illustration of the philosophy of Schopenhauer." Gittings goes on to speak of Hardy's disclaiming the influence of Schopenhauer, but the passage he quotes in support of this is not from the letter Helen Garwood refers to in her book in 1911 but is that which I quoted above from Hardy's letter to Brennecke. Wherever the disclaimer originates, however, Gittings is not taken in:

Yet this disclaimer is similar to his statement, over the later novels, that he had read very little Zola, and in both the motive is the same. He did not wish to acknowledge an easy tag-label, under which lazy critics or reviewers could summarize or dismiss his original work. Yet the list, to which he could well have added Fourier, illustrations of whose philosophy he copied into his earliest notebooks, does far from justice to the breadth of his philosophic reading, and its effect on *The Dynasts*. There is, it has been shown, a great deal of Schopenhauer, whom he read and noted industriously in the late 1880s and 1890s, and still more of Von Hartmann, in particular, and of Haeckel, though the latter's philosophy has been seen not so much as an influence but as a reinforcement of what were already Hardy's own views.[26]

J. Hillis Miller, for a contemporary critic, is perhaps unexpectedly respectful of the traditional view of the link between Hardy and Schopenhauer. Hardy's vision of things is one version of a world view widely present in the late nineteenth century. Its sources in his reading of Tyndall, Huxley, Darwin, Spencer, Schopenhauer, Comte, and others have been often discussed. It is impossible to demonstrate, however, that any one of these sources is uniquely important in determining Hardy's view of things. He read many of the writers who formulated the late Victorian outlook, and his notions were undoubtedly also acquired in part from newspapers, periodicals, and other such reading. What matters most is to identify the idiosyncratic emphases in his version of a current view, the personal elements in his response to this view ...   (Miller, pp. 16–17)

Indeed, I'm inclined to add that late Victorian and Edwardian England had a certain image or view of Schopenhauer, which was applied more or less indiscriminately to Hardy, much as we might say of an author that he or she is Nietzschean, Sartrean or Freudian without our necessarily having a close exegetical knowledge of those authorities. This would not mean that it was wrong to see Hardy in Schopenhauerian terms but that what those actually were would need to be spelled out in the manner we have been exploring.

Hardy's sense of man's place in the universe, Miller says later, is not too different from Nietzsche's, but Hardy's response to this vision is radically different: "As a number of critics have seen, his attitude is in some ways strikingly similar to that of Nietzsche's predecessor, Arthur Schopenhauer, the philosopher whose dissertation *On the Four-fold Root of the Principle of Sufficient Reason* Hardy read in 1889 or 1890 in Mrs. Karl Hillebrand's translation" (Miller, p. 20).

Miller might see a similarity between Nietzsche's sense and Hardy's of man's place in the universe but it is not a comparison Hardy himself would have owned to, for, so Donald Davie justifiably reminds us, "Predictably, Hardy felt for Nietzsche nothing but contempt" (Davie, footnote, p. 76). This contempt is expressed at the time of the First World War and is worth noting here since Schopenhauer emerges in Hardy's eyes in a favourable light by comparison with Nietzsche. Thus Hardy sees Kant and Schopenhauer as "close-reasoned philosophers" who were unfortunately eclipsed in Germany in 1914 by Nietzsche (Björk, 2, p. 512). To Sydney Cockerell he wrote in September 1914: "By the by it is rather rough on Kant, Schopenhauer, &C, to be swept into one net of condemnation with Nietzsche ... The truth is that in ethics Kant, Schopr &C. are nearer to Christianity than they are to Nsche" (Hardy, *Collected Letters*, vol. 5, pp. 50–51).

Dennis Taylor observes: "Hardy's attitude to Schopenhauer seems curiously ambivalent. On three widely separate occasions, in 1902, 1914, and 1922, he includes Schopenhauer in a list of philosophers he respects ..."[27] Yet when Helen Garwood sent Hardy her thesis on the subject, her delight at receiving a reply from the master himself must have been tempered by its contents: "My pages show harmony of view ... &C"; and Taylor goes on to quote the words which, whether or not they were ever written to Garwood we do not know. For there is no letter from Hardy to Garwood in his *Collected Letters* and all we have surviving it seems is Helen Garwood's paraphrase in her book of Hardy's letter to her; but the words Taylor quotes we do know were written some years later to Brennecke.

The footnote in Taylor continues: "In a letter of 1909, Gosse said that Hardy 'n'admet pas que Schopenhauer ait exerce une influence sur son oeuvre' ..."[28] What Hardy actually said in a letter to Gosse in 1909 was: "I may observe incidentally that I hope my philosophy – if my few thoughts deserve such a big name – is much more modern than Schopenhauer; as your correspondent [Frank Arthur Hedgcock who wrote a Docteur es lettres thesis on Thomas Hardy for the University of Paris, published as *Thomas Hardy, penseur et artiste* (Paris 1911)] would perceive if he were to read my latest books more carefully."[29]

The footnote in Taylor resumes: "In 1920, Gosse repeated his assertion ... 'To this day he is very slightly and superficially acquainted with the writings of Schopenhauer'. "[30]

SCHOPENHAUER'S INFLUENCE MINIMALIZED OR DISCLAIMED: HARDY'S LITERARY AESTHETICS

So begins the downgrading of the view we are asked to take of Schopenhauer's importance to Hardy. Thus Harold Orel: "Hardy's debt to Schopenhauer and Von Hartmann has been overemphasized by scholars. Hardy ... mentioned Schopenhauer only once, in passing, in his autobiography. When Helen Garwood sent him a copy of her dissertation, Hardy denied his having been influenced by the German philosopher: his own doctrine was 'a development from Schopenhauer through later philosophers.' "

Later, Orel writes: "... these attempts to emphasize the influence of Schopenhauer and Von Hartmann on Hardy have seriously distorted Hardy's achievement as a poet and dramatist. For Hardy never thought of himself as a philosopher; he troubled himself very little about theories." He read many philosophers but subscribed wholly to none – for he was depressed by their "contradictions and futilities" (Orel, pp. 23–26).

F. R. Southerington takes a not dissimilar view: Hardy's reading of philosophy influenced him. He read deeply and seriously. But his responses were conditioned by mood and subjectivity. "Hardy was a feeler first, only secondarily a thinker, and his reading was often an attempt to confirm impressions already formed."[31] In the nineteen eighties F. B. Pinion concluded that the influence of Schopenhauer on Hardy had been exaggerated.[32]

Roy Morrell is even more dismissive: "I also read some Schopenhauer; and Hardy's 'echoes' from this author seemed to me less like true echoes than like detached, slightly ironical comments."[33] In *Tess of the d'Urbervilles* Hardy disclaims any sympathy with Schopenhauer's doctrine of renunciation.[34] The assertions and counter-assertions, in a word, the contradictions, of one authority against another, are quite remarkable. Thus against Morrell consider Magee: "The book which Hardy wrote most immediately after his reading of Schopenhauer, *Tess of the D'Urbervilles,* is the one more widely regarded than any other as his masterpiece, and also the one most replete with Schopenhauerian allusions. Schopenhauer is even mentioned in it by name."[35] Magee then cites a good half-dozen heads under which passages from *Tess* may be compared with Schopenhauer.

Perry Meisel criticizes William Rutland for assuming that *Jude the Obscure* was written primarily to expound certain ideas (he might also have taken Samuel Chew similarly to task). But, says Meisel, it is wrong to write as if *Jude*'s being a novel is secondary to its being an exposition of a philosophy. Things were not always seen that way. Not only Rutland and Chew, but an early reviewer, Edward Wright, pressed Schopenhauer into the service of *Jude*: "Since writing *Tess of the D'Urbervilles*, Mr. Hardy has averted his eyes from the spectacle of the world, and devoted himself to the study of Schopenhauer and von Hartmann." Jude is "Schopenhauer's perfidious lover 'seeking to perpetuate all this misery and turmoil ....' "[36] But Meisel has allies too: "It would be difficult, to say the least, to make a case for *Jude* as optimistic or melioristic philosophy; it is equally difficult to make a case for it as philosophy at all. *Jude* is an impression, a seeming, with many fewer philosophical asides than in *Tess*" (so says F. R. Southerington, p. 143).

When a speech of a Hardy character resembles a point from Schopenhauer, Meisel continues, this is a narrative voice within the novel, not a sign that the life of Hardy's intellect is identical to the life of his imaginative creations.[37] But by a nice (Hardyan?) irony, this objection of Meisel's to Rutland was anticipated by one of the promoters of the view that Schopenhauer was a substantial influence on Hardy, namely Ernest Brennecke. Back in 1924 Brennecke wrote: "Hardy himself has warned his readers against attributing to a writer the philosophy discovered within the inverted commas of the dialogue in his imaginative work."[38] (Not that Brennecke himself seems to have been disposed to take much notice of this warning.)

Brennecke is referring to Hardy's essay, "The Profitable Reading of Fiction," which Robert Gittings calls a "collection of not very well expressed platitudes about a writer and his public" (Gittings, p. 59). On the contrary, Hardy's essay is a useful contribution to the under-developed field of the aesthetics of literature, a contribution from which in literary aesthetics at any rate, we still have something to learn.

Intrinsically interesting, *pace* Gittings, although the material is in its attempt to formulate a few general notions upon the subject of novel reading,[39] a fuller study of Hardy's essay will have to wait for another occasion. Here, and in conclusion to the present study, we can have an eye only to the relevance of Hardy's essay to the question of the relationship between Hardy and Schopenhauer; and in this regard, the answer, which by now will be of no surprise, is by no means straightforward. First, there is the warning quoted from Hardy's "Profitable Reading of Fiction" which enables Brennecke and others to say that even if Schopenhauerian thoughts appear in Hardy's texts we don't have to take them as beliefs to which Hardy himself necessarily subscribes. This point of literary criticism will be excessively familiar to us at this late date; it was often made for example by the New Critics, but in 1888 when Hardy made it it was a good deal more unusual and shows Hardy to have been somewhat modern not only in poetry but in criticism too. Hardy says, then, that if young people go to novels for their sentiments, religion and their morals:

> They should be informed that a writer whose story is not a tract in disguise has as his main object that of characterizing the people of his little world. A philosophy which appears between the inverted commas of a dialogue may, with propriety, be as full of holes as a sieve if the person or persons who advance it gain any reality of humanity thereby.
>
> (Hardy, "Profitable Reading...", p. 62)

Hardy's literary aesthetics approaches Schopenhauer's general aesthetics in the distinction Hardy draws between eternal and temporary truths: "To distinguish truths which are temporary from truths which are eternal, the accidental from the essential, accuracies as to custom and ceremony from accuracies as to the perennial procedures of humanity, is of vital importance in our attempt to read for something more than amusement" (Hardy, "Profitable Reading," p. 64). A serious concern with art will be to link it with the eternal but the manner of Hardy's doing so is not Schopenhauerian and the differences between the aesthetics of the two writers outweigh this only slight point of comparison.

First, Hardy writes much more like an analytical philosopher than he does like a speculative philosopher such as Schopenhauer. His essay, therefore, comprises a series of distinctions, for example between the various grounds on which a literary work may be judged to be good, rather than some more general synthetic claims such as are to be found in Schopenhauer about the nature of the arts. He also shows more historical awareness than Schopenhauer does, specifically about the underdeveloped nature of the branch of aesthetics he is seeking to contribute to.

Above all, Hardy makes the point, which I believe to be still valid today, that the development of the aesthetic sense through reading has been neglected as a subject of study by contrast with the volumes that have been written on the development of the aesthetic sense through the study of painting and sculpture (Hardy, "Profitable Reading," p. 66). Schopenhauer's is one of those volumes devoted to the study of painting. But there is, Hardy reminds us, beauty of shape in a story no less than in the pictorial or plastic arts. Hardy's interest in form in the arts here, then, is not focused on form in the sense in which forms as Platonic ideas in the visual arts interest Schopenhauer. In his essay on the reading of fiction Hardy is no more transcendent, so to speak, than, to the dismay of Davie, he was in his practice as a poet and in his claims for the poet.

In cast of mind Hardy was much more the rationalist and the liberal scientist than he was a post-Kantian idealist, although that does not mean that Schopenhauer's doctrines did not have a good deal of imaginative and emotional appeal for him.

Notes

1 Bryan Magee, *The Philosophy of Schopenhauer* (Oxford: The Clarendon Press, 1983), Appendix 6, "Schopenhauer and Wagner," pp. 326–378;

Appendix 7, "Schopenhauer's Influence on Creative Writers,"
pp. 379–390.

2 Erich Heller, *Thomas Mann: The Ironic German, A Study*, corrected
edition, (Mamaroneck, NY: Paul P. Appel, 1973), p. 52. Note however that
at most one-fourth of *WWR* is explicitly concerned with problems of art.

3 There are, however, exceptions to my claim that writers interested in
Schopenhauer are interested in his metaphysics. J. P. Stern cites the case
of Fontane who was apparently incurious not only about Schopenhauer's
aesthetics, which I would expect, but also about his metaphysics of the
cosmic Will. "On the other hand Schopenhauer's doctrine of the immutable 'intelligible self' corresponds by and large to the view of the
human character that informs Fontane's novels. For this, however, no
"influence" need be postulated, for both novelist and philosopher
articulate the beliefs of their age". J. P. Stern, *Idylls and Realities: Studies
in Nineteenth-Century German Literature* (London: Methuen, 1971),
p. 185.

4 Magee, pp. 382–384, draws on some of this literature: works by
Brennecke, Gittings, Bailey, Garwood and Weber. I shall be referring to
these below and to other authorities on Hardy.

5 In a trawl through the secondary literature on Hardy, the nearest I've
come to finding even a mention of Schopenhauer's aesthetics (and I
don't recall a single reference to this from my reading of Hardy himself)
is in an unsigned review of *The Dynasts* in the *Edinburgh Review* in
1908, which ends with an account of how genius, according to Schopenhauer, sees things in a kind of eternity, a sort of Platonic existence. The
man of genius is freed from bondage to the Will. Hardy, so this reviewer
speculates, must no doubt have felt this joy himself while writing *The
Dynasts.* Note this is a thought attributed to Hardy by the reviewer and
not said by Hardy himself. The anonymous review is rpt. in R. G. Cox,
ed., *Thomas Hardy: The Critical Heritage* (London: Routledge and Kegan
Paul, 1970), p. 385.

6 Heller, *Thomas Mann*, p. 79.

7 Donald Davie, *Thomas Hardy and British Poetry* (London: Routledge and
Kegan Paul, 1973), pp. 35–36.

8 Heller, *Thomas Mann*, pp. 76–85.

9 *WWR* 1, 45.

10 R. G. Collingwood, *The Principles of Art* (Oxford: The Clarendon Press,
1938), p. 123.

11 There is a concise summary of the main points of this literature in
Kristin Brady, *The Short Stories of Thomas Hardy: Tales of Past and
Present* (London: Macmillan, 1982), note 36, p. 211: "The influence of
Schopenhauer on Hardy, as he himself indicated in a letter to Helen
Garwood (quoted in Walter F. Wright, *The Shaping of the Dynasts*
(Lincoln: University of Nebraska Press, 1967), p. 38) must not be over-
emphasized, but the fact remains that Hardy was acquainted with
Schopenhauer's writings as early as 1886 (Wright, pp. 39–40), and

marked in his personal copy of *On the Fourfold Root of the Principle of Sufficient Reason* Schopenhauer's claim that the "fundamental truth" of his doctrine is "the complete separation between the will and the intellect" (Wright, p. 41), ...". Lennart A. Björk names Wright's as the most comprehensive and reliable recent discussion of the relationship between Hardy and Schopenhauer, in his edition of *The Literary Notebooks of Thomas Hardy* (London: Macmillan, 1985), vol. 1, p. 374.

12 Though ironically, as we shall see below, Hardy anticipates in one respect the sharp distinction that is drawn nowadays between authors and their works, a distinction which is the first step, not taken by Hardy himself, to excluding authors from their works, a step which leads to the demise or "death" of the author.

13 Ernest Brennecke, Jr., *Thomas Hardy's Universe: A Study of a Poet's Mind* (London: T. Fisher Unwin, 1924). This is the work which Bryan Magee conjectures brought the influence of Schopenhauer to bear on Dylan Thomas, a passionate admirer of Thomas Hardy's: Magee, Appendix 8, "A Conjecture About Dylan Thomas," pp. 391–393.

14 Compare P. F. Strawson on contradicting oneself which "is like writing something down and then erasing it, or putting a line through it. A contradiction cancels itself and leaves nothing." *Introduction to Logical Theory* (London: Methuen, University Paperbacks, 1963), p. 3.

15 Havelock Ellis, *Westminster Review*, 1883, rpt. in R. G. Cox, ed., *Hardy: Critical Heritage,* p. 131.

16 J. O. Bailey, "Evolutionary Meliorism in the Poetry of Thomas Hardy," *Studies in Philology*, 60, (1963), referred to by C. H. Salter, *Good Little Thomas Hardy* (London: Macmillan, 1981), pp. 54–55. See also p. 55 for Bailey's paraphrase of Rutland given in my text above.

17 William R. Rutland, *Thomas Hardy: A Study of his Writings and their Background* [1938] (New York: Russell and Russell, 1962), p. 96.

18 J. O. Bailey, *Thomas Hardy and the Cosmic Mind: A New Reading of* The Dynasts (Chapel Hill: University of North Carolina Press, 1956), p. 88.

19 J. Hillis Miller, *Thomas Hardy: Distance and Desire* (Cambridge, MA: The Belknap Press of Harvard University Press, 1970), p. 20. Dennis Taylor, on the other hand, in his *Hardy's Poetry 1860–1928* (Basingstoke: Macmillan, 1981, second edition, 1989), p. 173, note 77, cites Mme Karl Hillebrand's translation of *The Fourfold Root* as being published in London in 1897, too late for Hardy to have read it in 1889 or 1890. Taylor quotes a passage taken from Hardy's copy of this work, for which he cites the 1897 date. In fact, Hillebrand's translation of *FFR* appeared in 1889, with reprints in 1891, 1897, 1903, 1907, etc.

20 Carl J. Weber, *Hardy of Wessex: His Life and Literary Career* (New York: Columbia University Press, 1965), rev. ed., p. 247.

21 Michael Millgate, *Thomas Hardy: A Biography* (Oxford: Oxford University Press, 1982), p. 315.

22 Rutland, *Thomas Hardy* p. 96; Brennecke; unsigned review in the *Edinburgh Review,* 1908, rpt. in Cox.; Bailey.

23 Samuel C. Chew, *Thomas Hardy: Poet and Novelist* (New York: Alfred A. Knopf, 1928), p. 135.

24 Helen Garwood, *Thomas Hardy: an Illustration of Schopenhauer* (Philadelphia: The John C. Winston Co., 1911; Norwood Editions 1976), p. 11.

25 Thomas Hardy to Ernest Brennecke, 21 June 1924, in *The Collected Letters of Thomas Hardy*, Richard Little Purdy and Michael Millgate, ed. (Oxford: The Clarendon Press, 1987); vol. 6, 1920–1925, p. 259. What Hardy reports as a humorous exaggeration, perhaps out of politeness to the recipient of the letter, seems to me, much as I admire Brennecke's book, to be rather a good description of it. The tone of Hardy's letter to Brennecke is not unfriendly. Nevertheless, so Harold Orel reports, Hardy was concerned by Brennecke's book, "the publication of which so exercised Hardy in his final years." See Orel, *Thomas Hardy's Epic Drama: A Study of* The Dynasts (Lawrence: University of Kansas Press, 1963), p. 23.

26 Robert Gittings, *The Older Hardy* (London: Heinemann, 1978), p. 114.

27 Dennis Taylor, *Hardy's Poetry* pp. 184–185, note 70. The references Taylor gives in support of his remarks are: *Life,* p. 315; "Apology" to *Late Lyrics and Earlier; Friends of a Lifetime*, p. 280.

28 Taylor's reference for this claim is F. A. Hedgcock, *Thomas Hardy: Penseur et Artiste* (Paris: Librairie Hatchette, 1911), p. 499.

29 Thomas Hardy to Edmund Gosse, 25 July 1909, *Collected Letters,* vol. 4, p. 37 and footnote.

30 Taylor's reference for this claim is the *Literary Review* section of the *New York Evening Post,* 3 (9 September 1922), p. 18.

31 F. R. Southerington, *Hardy's Vision of Man* (London: Chatto and Windus, 1971), p. 143.

32 F. B. Pinion, *A Thomas Hardy Dictionary* (Basingstoke: Macmillan, 1989), p. 239.

33 Roy Morrell, *Thomas Hardy: The Will and the Way* (Kuala Lumpur: University of Malaya Press, 1965; Folcroft Library Edition, 1978), p. ix.

34 Morrell, p. 169. F. B. Pinion elaborates on this: Hardy's "disagreement with the unredeemed pessimism or determinism of Schopenhauer was stated about 1890 (*TD* p. xxv)," *A Hardy Companion* (London: Macmillan, 1968), p. 107.

35 Magee, p. 384. Magee gives p. 218 of the Penguin edition of *Tess* for the mention of Schopenhauer's name.

36 Edward Wright in the *Quarterly Review,* 1904, rpt. in Cox, pp. 362–363.

37 Perry Meisel, *Thomas Hardy: the Return of the Repressed: A Study of the Major Fiction* (New Haven and London: Yale University Press, 1972), pp. 29–30.

38 Brennecke, p. 22, paraphrasing Thomas Hardy's essay, "The Profitable Reading of Fiction."

39 Thomas Hardy, "The Profitable Reading of Fiction," *The Forum,* vol. V (March 1888), pp. 57–70; this point at p. 57.

12

Schopenhauer according to the Symbolists: the philosophical roots of late nineteenth-century French aesthetic theory

SHEHIRA DOSS-DAVEZAC

The future belongs to Decadism. Born of the world-weariness of a Schopenhauerian civilization, the Decadents' ... mission ... [is] to ... demolish the old order and prepare the embryonic elements of the great national literature of the twentieth century.
Le Decadent, 1890

INTRODUCTION

Almost all the painters, writers and critics of the late nineteenth century in France frequently mentioned the influence of Schopenhauer on their ideas. Every literary critic and art historian writing on the period today associates the Symbolists with Schopenhauer. Yet it is difficult to assess exactly – since no hard evidence is ever offered by either group – to what *extent* they read him, *what* they read of his work, and, in any detail, *which* ideas they borrowed. Schopenhauer's *The World as Will and Representation*, was, when it appeared in 1818 (publication date 1819), hardly read in France but became the rage among Symbolists and Decadents in the eighties and nineties after the translation of his work by among others, Theodule Ribot in his 1874 commentary *La Philosophie de Schopenhauer*, and by a later edition of fragments translated by Jean Bourdeau which came out in 1880 entitled *Pensées, Maximes et Fragments*, as well as a second edition of Ribot's work in 1885. In 1888, given the work's popularity, *WWR* was again translated into French.

Schopenhauer's philosophy found a responsive chord in a generation which had either witnessed or suffered the consequences of the stinging defeat of the Franco-Prussian war and its aftermath, and made him peculiarly satisfying to the morbid, the disillusioned, and the bohemian. His pessimism was the subject of many of the lectures given on his philosophy in the 1880s where he was either praised or condemned for it. Fear of his influence even brought warnings against his ideas by chauvinist writers who argued that his pessimism was a purely German phenomenon – the product of a beer-drinking race which was unnatural to the temperament of sippers of Burgundy and Bordeau wine.[1]

Schopenhauer's influence came, most probably, mainly from the *Pensées, Maximes et Fragments* with its easier access to his thought, just as Kant had influenced the earlier generation of Romantics principally through the popularizing of his ideas in Mme de Stael's *De l'Allemagne*. Another source came from Symbolist writers who *had* read him and who frequently quoted his work in the the little journals that proliferated at the end of the century. Among these were Albert Aurier, the brilliant and precocious art theorist and poet who had strong connections with both poets and painters, and was chief exponent of Symbolist theory through such journals as the *Mercure de France*; or the equally brilliant poet/critic Jules Laforgues, articulate defender of Neoimpressionism, who had acquired a solid education in German philosophy during the years 1881–86 spent in Berlin as reader to the Empress Augusta; or the poet Villiers de l'Isle Adam, who was reputed to be an expert on Schopenhauer; or Felix Feneon, "The Buddha" as he was called by his contemporaries, a writer and political anarchist who, together with the writer Gustav Kahn, was the principal animator of two important symbolist magazines, *La Vogue* and *La Revue Independante*.

My attempt here will be to make an educated guess as to what in Schopenhauer's writings drew the Symbolists to them, and to connect only those aspects of Schopenhauer's ideas which found resonances, if not always direct influences, in the new movements in art and literature which went under the general name of Symbolism but which, like tributaries of a river, branched out into movements variously called Symbolist, Synthetist, Decadent or Nabi. No clear-cut distinctions can safely be made between them: Symbolists at times had Decadent tendencies, Decadents infused their art with symbolic meaning, and Nabis borrowed from or contributed to Symbolist theory. The term "Synthetist" adopted by some of the painters was an attempt to clarify their position with regard to

Symbolism in general, and to the language of painting in particular: to shun overt symbolism and to elucidate meanings by the purely artistic vocabulary of line, color and form.

SCHOPENHAUER IN THE CONTEXT OF SYMBOLIST PESSIMISM

It was his pessimism above all that first attracted the generation of writers and poets of the 1880s to Schopenhauer. In *A Rebours*, an eccentric and very rapidly famous novel which appeared in 1884, and was hailed by many as the literary incarnation of Schopenhauer's metaphysics, its author, Huysmans, gives the Symbolist/ Decadent hero Des Esseintes these words: "Schopenhauer extolled to you no panacea, did not lull or distract you as a remedy for inevitable ills ... He pretended to heal nothing, offered the sufferer ... not the slightest hope; but his theory of Pessimism was ... the great consoler of ... higher souls ..."[2] Readers of the *Pensées, Maximes et Fragments* could find in Bourdeau's translation, Schopenhauer's view that "the world is hell, and men are divided into tortured souls and torturing devils."[3] The same sentiments – "I am the limbs and the wheel / the victim and the torturer" had been expressed in a well-known poem which every school boy could recite in the 1880s, written by Baudelaire, romantic poet and art theorist who quickly became a model for Symbolist/Decadent authors. Schopenhauer, like Baudelaire, seemed to them to be the mouthpiece of their own feelings: had they not themselves witnessed the irrational forces he described which drove both man and nature, dominated by a blind energy – to the edge of destruction? Had they not experienced in themselves that very Will of which he spoke which subjects man, without respite, to his needs and desires, leading one to the very precipice of the abyss? Schopenhauer wrote about their own frustrations: human desires which motivate human will far outnumber their momentary satisfactions; man is condemned to suffer, and pleasure is merely a suspension of pain; respite from the human condition can only come by the distancing of the self from worldly preoccupations. Suffering, existence itself, can be sublimated either through abnegation and asceticism or through beauty – both its creation and its enjoyment, the saint taking the first path, the artist the second. Had he not shown exactly what their aesthetic was searching for: the release from what Schopenhauer had called "the practical reason" and from the binding constraints of a body rooted in and condemned to a world governed by space, time and causality? Had he not promised loss of self, ecstasy, an intuitive vision of the absolute for which they longed, something which the science of the day could not satisfy? How like their aspirations was Schopenhauer's description of this condition: "the painless state ... of the gods; for we are for the moment set free from the miserable striving of the will; ... It is in the beauty of both nature and art that we can achieve this temporary release from the will."[4]

Schopenhauer's assessment of the human condition was poignantly confirmed in their lives, and painfully illustrated in their works. Their images reflect the despair as well as the hopes and aspirations of a generation adrift from a society they despised, hungry for a more spartan diet of the spirit. Jules Laforgue dreams of writing the history of a Parisian of the 1880s who suffers, doubts and glimpses the awful shadow of oblivion, and wants to name his book, *The Weeping of the Earth.* Alfred de Musset laments the condition of the artist in a flagrantly materialist society and evokes the image of the poet as a pelican who feeds his young from his own flesh. Gauguin represents the painter as a crucified Christ abandoned by friend and foe. Frequent representations of heads without their bodies, reflect in tangible form why it was that this period was called "Schopenhauerian." Freed from the wants and desires of the body and the blindness of physical passion, some heads are represented with eyes closed, the better to keep their inner world undisturbed; other heads are cushioned in a halo of light and flowers; or, in further reductive images, a single eye, like an enormous balloon, floats out into space towards infinity. Orpheus, in occult literature the god of music and song and the bringer of civilization to the barbarians, is a central Symbolist image. He too is represented as a severed head, symbol of the artist as musician, as creative energy, and as seer or priest. Images of bloodied heads cradled or carried by predatory women, such as Moreau's head of John the Baptist carried on a platter by a lascivious Salome, tell a different story, which, as we shall see, is also Schopenhauerian. Expressing certain fears of sex and castration, they convey a prevalent attitude towards women felt by an entire generation of young artists and poets. Symbolists often wrote of being deprived of feminine influences in childhood either because they had been sent away from their families under the threat of the Franco-Prussian war, or because, in a society bent on pleasure, they had been neglected by frivolous women who found it too onerous to look after them.[5] Consequently, ill at ease in the company of women, they either idealized or demonized them. In his preface to *Les Diaboliques* (1874), Jules Barbey d'Aurevilly explains why he has given the women in his stories the epithet "diabolical": "Why should they not be diabolical? Do they not have enough of the she-devil in them to deserve this nice name ... Like the Devil, who was an angel too but came a cropper, if they are angels, they are angels like him: head downwards, and their crupper in the air."[6] His book was a great success and spawned several images of diabolical women: Delilah, Helen of Troy, Medea, or (in the work of Gauguin), her pagan counterpart, Oviri – the cannibalistic mother-goddess who ingests her children.

It was well known how Schopenhauer felt about women, and it is significant that in the same passage quoted earlier from *A Rebours*, Des Esseintes had singled out Schopenhauer's insistence "on the innate stupidity of women" as an element that drew the Symbolists to him. Readers of Schopenhauer's "On Women," in his translated collection of essays entitled *Parerga and Paralipomena*, could find unsavory descriptions of women that were similar to and reinforced their own prejudices against them. He saw woman as "an intellectual myope," frivolous, sensual and cunning in her strategies. "Injustice is the fundamental failing of the female character." "Dissimulation is inborn in women ... From that ... arises falseness, faithlessness, treachery, ingratitude ..." He compares women to animals: cuttle-fish, bulls, lions, "who make immediate use of their weapons when attacked." In their privileged position in society, women remind him "of the sacred apes at Benares who, conscious of their sanctity and invulnerability, think that they are at liberty to do anything and everything."[7] Moreau's painting of Salome, destroyer of men, became the basic text for the generation of the 1880s. In his own description of *Salome*, one can hear the echo of Schopenhauer's views, down even to her animality: "this bored, temperamental, highly sensual woman ... so sick is she of always having her every desire satisfied. This woman walking nonchalantly, bestially, ... when I want to portray these nuances I find them ... in the real nature of woman today, ... and because she is so stupid, does not understand the horror of the most appalling situations."[8] And in his poem "Rimes dorees," Theodore de Banville, referring to the frivo-lity of women, writes: "Such is your joy, fragile dolls! / For you have taken a naive delight / in dazzling playthings and cut-off heads."

Despite their differences and the diversity of their styles, writers and painters had a bond in common – a certain mood: a disillusionment with politics, a dissatisfaction with materialism and a search for meaning, not in the natural world, but in the realm of Platonic Ideas of which the self, they believed, had intimations. As a group they had a global view of the world and of life on the one hand, and aesthetic concerns on the other. Anarchist, anti-militarist, repulsed by economic and social conditions in Europe and America, and by the Positivist ideals of Realism in painting and of Naturalism in literature, they turned their backs on traditional, academic modes of expression and went in search of a new language of the spirit in art and poetry. Positivism, they felt, called only upon parts of the total man, ignoring his spiritual needs, neglecting intuition whose intellectual resonances they argued, went far beyond the limited and limiting boundaries of reason.

In Schopenhauer's writings they could find, either explicitly or implicitly, the formulation of some of the leading ideas towards which they were groping. In his sharp demarcation between appearance and the thing-in-itself, Schopenhauer had argued the relativity of all known objects to an individual knower: "what we know is not a sun and an earth, but an eye that sees the sun and a hand that feels the earth." And he had concluded that objects have no independent being except in relation to one's ideas of them: "all that exists for knowledge is only an object in relation to a subject, the perception of a perceiver, in a word, Idea."[9] The relative existence of objects made them symbols, not independent entities. His emphasis on the interpreting subjective self, and the importance given to nature seen as symbol were to become central creeds in the symbolist aesthetic. As Remy de Gourmont, novelist, playwright and poet and an eminent contemporary critic of Symbolism had written: "our philosophical education ... had already been the product of the Schopenhauer of M. Burdeau [sic.] and that of M. Ribot. We had already discovered, and with what intoxication, at the same time that the world was evil and that it existed only relative to ourselves. 'The world is my representation' this formula had penetrated every mind that could be penetrated."[10] To the generation of young artists and writers in the 1880s, more prone to theory than the generation of their elders, their symbolist aesthetic found its deepest impulses expressed in Schopenhauer's idealistic philosophy. It seemed to them to be closer to a theory of art than to a philosophy proper: "the world is my conception"; art's "sole origin is the knowledge of Ideas; its sole purpose is the communication of these ideas ... the essence of genius is the predominant capacity for ... contemplation."[11]

254

Schopenhauer's pessimism and his misogyny, as we have seen, were important aspects of symbolist attraction to his work. His rejection of ordinary reality in favor of an art of Idea, his mysticism, his elevation of music to the highest form of art, coinciding as it did with both the great vogue of Wagner's music in the 1880s and with the Symbolists' own nascent tendencies to transform *all* the arts into a kind of music: these too were factors in the art of the late nineteenth century. I shall discuss them in turn.

SCHOPENHAUER IN THE CONTEXT OF THE PARISIAN ART SCENE

It was principally the writers – poets, novelists – who articulated the new approaches to art, followed and echoed by a coterie of artists who sat with them in Paris cafés, discussing the new art and reviling the old. Remy de Gourmont describes the artistic scene in the Paris of the 1880s in the *Mercure de France* of May 1892: "Two schools remain face to face: the Impressionists and the Symbolists: those who strive to convey on canvas, vividly and crudely, the impression pure and simple, and wholly objective ... and those who break down that same impression in order to recombine it as they see fit, intent as they are on expressing in their work ... enduring things, eternal meanings ..." By the 1880s, Impressionism was very much accepted and admired by the general public. But to the young generation of Symbolists, it was anathema. They questioned its premises and its artistic aims: it was the product, they felt, of the reigning forces of materialism and the scientific ideals of "progress" typified by France's preoccupation with bourgeois values and America's ideals based on advances in science and industry. They reiterated Baudelaire's words, written in the sixties, in protest against realistic art: "From day to day, art diminishes its self respect, prostrates itself before exterior reality, and the artist becomes more inclined to paint not what he dreams but what he sees."[12] Gauguin, speaking for the painters, criticized the Impressionists for their exclusive interest in recording the testimony of their eyes. "They ignore," he said, "the mysterious centers of thought."[13] Even among the Impressionists, Pissarro found himself attacking the very principles he had espoused a few years earlier. In a letter to his son Lucien – abroad in London in 1883 – he tells of the mood in Paris: buzzing with attacks on Naturalism and on its chief proponent Zola. He too finds Zola "too photographic" and sees the superiority of Baudelaire's *Flowers of Evil*, and the rebel-poet Verlaine's *Saturnian Poems* as more to the point, describing these as "works of art ... in a society rotten and ready to fall apart ..."[14] In other words, Schopenhauer's pessimistic view of society was finding responses in the eighties which, a decade earlier, would have been unimaginable to a generation which saw truth-to-nature as the principal and exciting goal in art. Emile Zola, the apostle of Naturalism, had given his novel of 1883 an ironical title, *The Joy of Living*, having previously considered such titles as *The Valley of Tears*, or *The Somber Death*. And in his notes for the novel, he had charted out the characteristics of his hero, Lazarus, telling himself "to make him into a pessimist, someone sick of our new science ... Flinging himself into Schopenhauer."[15]

In the spirit of Schopenhauer, if not always to the letter, there was, among the Symbolists, a concerted effort to attack the premises of Positivism. Schopenhauer's call for an art of Idea was echo'd by the Symbolists in their battles against artists such as Courbet who, in his Realist Manifesto of 1861, had proclaimed that "painting is essentially a *concrete* art and can only consist of the representation of *real* and *existing* things," to which he had added, "an object which is *abstract*, not visible, nonexistent is not within the realm of painting."[16] In addition, Schopenhauer, who had consigned science to the phenomenal world, had further confirmed the Symbolists in their belief – counter to the prevailing mood – that the arts, not science, pointed to the thing-in-itself and to ultimate truth. Broadly anti-scientific, Symbolist writers and painters argued for Schopenhauer's and later for Bergson's intuitive experience as the only true form of knowledge. The evocation of the Platonic Idea was to become for these artists the essence of art, the salvation of man's psyche, and their own redemption from a cruel, relentlessly driven world. They called for a new religion – symbolist art – an art of Idea in which they could function as high priests, distilling the eternal from the transitory, and infusing their personal representations of the world with ethical and artistic meaning. It was to be an art not of *mimesis* but of *expression*, an art akin to music, that highest of all the arts according to Schopenhauer, and they reiterated Edgar Allan Poe's statement, quoted by Baudelaire, that "it is in music perhaps that the soul most nearly attains ... the creation of supernal beauty".[17]

To stem the tide of Positivism, the Symbolists turned for inspiration to an older generation of writers and critics – to such artists, poets, and musicians as Delacroix, Baudelaire, Poe, Gautier, and

Wagner, all of whom had been responsible, earlier in the century, for articulating the movements – also escapist – that went under the name of Romanticism. Despite differences in style, Symbolists felt a kinship with them in the questions they had posed and the dilemmas they had faced in making art. In many ways, I believe Symbolism's ready and enthusiastic response to Schopenhauer's ideas came about as a result of this generation's familiarity with the writings of Baudelaire, a poet, and Delacroix, a painter, which were respectively re-edited in 1886 and 1887 after their deaths and which appeared alongside translations of Schopenhauer. The impulse that steered Delacroix's and Baudelaire's works was toward an art of spirit, with a kinship more to music than to words. Despite the fact that both Delacroix and Baudelaire had come under the influence of Kant rather than of Schopenhauer, it was perhaps in part due to Schopenhauer's own indebtedness to Kant that unconsciously, Symbolist artists linked the ideas of these Romantics to Schopenhauer and to their own. Similarities existed between the two generations: each had passed through a period of disillusionment with reality; each had sought escape from the narrow world of fact; and each was antagonistic to prevailing artistic styles. In Delacroix, leader of French Romanticism and the painter most emulated and discussed by the Symbolists, they could read passage after passage that had resonances of Schopenhauer: "The fact counts for nothing because it will pass. Nothing is left but the Idea, since the latter lends its color to it. This is what happens when the creative faculty seizes the Idea in order to animate the real world given in the transitory facts, and to derive from them pictures of the imagination."[18] "Man has in his soul innate sentiments which real objects can never satisfy and it is these sentiments that the imagination of the painter and the poet is able to give form and life. What does the first of the arts, music, imitate?[19] "Art, like music, is above thought; hence its advantage over literature ..."[20] Familiarity with Delacroix's writings on art could not help but re-enforce their interest in Schopenhauer's ideas, to whose work they were newly introduced. Familiarity with Baudelaire's poetry and art criticism also led them to Schopenhauer. Baudelaire typified the Symbolist hero, and was perhaps more than any other French writer, at the heart of Symbolist theory. Author of *The Flowers of Evil*, rebel, like them, of society, he had been scathing in his attacks on Realism and on the emerging science of photography. Above all, it was he who had taught them, in the words of Schopenhauer that "style is the physiognomy of the spirit."

SCHOPENHAUER IN THE CONTEXT OF NEOPLATONISM AND SYMBOLISM

"We made a singular mixture of Plotinus, of Edgar Poe, of Baudelaire and of Schopenhauer," wrote Maurice Denis, Nabi painter and theorist of Symbolism in 1903, looking back and summarizing the sources from which the young poets and painters of his generation in the 1880s drew their ideas.[21] What ideas, we can ask, could possibly unite such different authors? To extract and explain aspects of their shared ideas can, I believe, shed light both on Schopenhauer's own approach to art, and on why his approach was so enthusiastically adopted by the Symbolists.

The eclecticism of Maurice Denis' list is only apparent. Plotinus, Schopenhauer, Baudelaire, and Poe [through Baudelaire's translations) shared many key ideas: all were influenced by Platonism; all favored a sensual response to nature, but asked that it be sublimated through a visual contemplation of the world as Idea; all believed that, through the interpretation of nature by a system of hieroglyphs or symbols, art's mission was to open a window onto the ultimate realm of truth. The purpose of nature in the arts was not to be its faithful representation, they all agreed, but was to give the soul an opportunity to see itself, and to give the supernatural an occasion to manifest itself. All separated art from the faculty of reason, arguing that art gave a form of knowledge superior to that of science. Art was to be an "evocative magic," a sacred function, rooted in pre-logical and primitive modes of perception, following Schopenhauer's belief that "... all the arts speak only the naive and childish language of perception, not the abstract and serious language of reflection."[22] Excluding Plotinus, there was in Schopenhauer, Baudelaire and Poe a tension between an almost morbid preoccupation with evil and an otherworldly idealism. What each wanted most from art was the abolition of his state as a debased creature, and its replacement, through the medium of art, by a condition of unremitting bliss. Is it any wonder that the Symbolists saw a connection between them, and turned to them for answers? Like the Symbolists, their impulse too, had been to reject nature and physicality, endorsing Plato's view in the *Phaedo*, that "the body ... fills us full of loves, and lusts and fears ... [it] takes away from us the power of thinking at all. Whence come wars, ... and factions? Whence but from ... the lusts of the body? ... If we would have pure knowledge of anything, we must be quit of the body; the soul by herself must behold things by themselves ..."[23] Unlike them, Plotinus is more ambivalent about the evil qualities of nature, at times acceding to Plato's views but at others insisting on its links with spirit where, as in Schopenhauer, the soul "gives to the realm of sense something of its own." "The soul," Plotinus says, (in the spirit of the *Symposium*), can either "let itself be carried away by an excessive zeal and plunge deep into the body," or the soul "can rise above this condition ... and turning to account the experience of what it has seen and suffered here below, ... can know more clearly what is the better by contrast with its opposite. Knowledge of good is sharpened by experience of evil ..."[24]

"Sharpened by experience of evil," Baudelaire's whole œuvre as he writes in his preface to *The Flowers of Evil*, was to "achieve a creation by the logic of contraries, by turning evil into flowers." In accepting the doctrine of evil and the fall of man, Baudelaire sought for a doctrine of redemption through art. "To blasphemy, I shall oppose heavenward yearnings; to obscenity, Platonic flowers." Like Schopenhauer, Baudelaire was revulsed by the world of nature, seeing it as the realm of carnal instinct, of struggle, hate and ugliness. Like Schopenhauer, whose gospel could be said to be: "in the beginning was appetite, passion and the Will," nature equalled for Baudelaire man's own self interest, and, reminiscent of Plato, he writes: "We rob, kill, steal, to satisfy our needs." In his seminal article, "The Painter of Modern Life," he attacks those writers and artists who glorify the art and imitation of nature, arguing that nature "teaches us nothing or practically nothing ... it is she ... who incites man to murder his brother, to eat him, to lock him up and to torture him; ... Nature can council nothing but crime ... Nature being none other than the voice of our own self-interest ..."[25] This theme runs through all his work, and he praises those who "realize another nature, analogous to the mind and the temperament of the artist."[26] His attraction to Poe stems from shared views. In *On the Natural Wickedness of Man*, which Baudelaire had translated, Poe had written: "This mysterious force which modern philosophy refuses to take account ... this primitive, irresistable force is man's natural perversity which makes him forever and at once both homicide and suicide, murderer and hangman."[27] Schopenhauer's philosophy had indeed taken account of it, presenting men, we are reminded, as "divided into tortured souls and torturing devils." Poe had also, like Schopenhauer and Baudelaire, invested art with the power to mitigate the evil in nature. Here, then, we can find in all four authors that similarity in attitude towards nature which made the Symbolists so responsive to their writings.

Another shared aspect was their belief in the power of art to rescue nature from its materiality. It is Plotinus' view of art that they share. His faith in art's ability to redeem nature by discovering in phenomena its positive links with Idea, is claimed by all three, and it is this view that is adopted by the Symbolists. While for Plato, science and philosophy (but not art) was the road to knowledge and contemplation, for Plotinus art plays a central role in the redemption of nature, and this by intuitive rather than rational means. (It is because of its immediacy that Plotinus gives precedence to the image over the word for the very reason that words follow a logical sequence whereas the image presents itself all at once.) In defense of the arts he writes, "... the arts are not to be slighted on the ground that they create by imitation of natural objects; ... we must recognize that they give no bare reproduction of the thing seen but go back to the Ideas from which nature derives; and ... that much of their work is all their own; they are holders of beauty and add where nature is lacking."[28] In this passage, Plotinus asserts a number of principles endorsed by Schopenhauer and by the other authors associated with him. These same principles are at the heart of Symbolist theory: the soul has access to the Ideas; the artist need not be a slave to imitation for he carries the Ideas in himself; nature herself is derived from Ideas; the arts can transform nature into Idea for "the soul," as Plotinus had said, "includes a faculty peculiarly addressed to Beauty ..."[29] He argues, as Schopenhauer will later, that the essence of nature, its Ideas, can be discovered and expressed by whomever appropriates nature at its center, eschewing the outward skin for the inward symbol. This form of vision is open to the philosopher, the musician and the lover. Plotinus' philosopher achieves this vision in much the same way as Schopenhauer's saint who comes to it by "the absolute negation of the Will." The lover and the musician, on the other hand, Plotinus writes, are lovers of beauty in all its forms. But they must be taught that "what in these things quickens the pulse is their intelligible harmony – briefly, Beauty itself and not something beautiful."[30] And in the appreciation of art, he warns: "Consider even the case of pictures – those seeing by the bodily sense the production of the art of painting ... are deeply stirred by recognising in the objects depicted to the eyes ... the representation of what lies in the Idea and so are called to recollect the truth ..."[31] This is almost exactly how Schopenhauer understands the process, and, as we shall see later, is pivotal to Symbolist art. It is difficult to assess whether Schopenhauer was directly influenced by Plotinus, or indirectly through Schelling who had revived the Neoplatonic principle that both the philosopher and the artist can penetrate into the essence of the absolute. Art, Shelling had said, constitutes an active link between the soul and nature, not by the imitation of nature, but by interpreting the spirit of nature which speaks to us only in symbols.

Schopenhauer may claim that his approach is based on Plato's, yet his art theory is closer to that of Plotinus. To be sure, for Plotinus the energy that animates the world of nature is a beneficent one, and Schopenhauer's is a malignant force, yet Schopenhauer's response to nature is, in many ways, a Plotinian one. True, what he calls the Idea or Symbol is the Platonic Idea, archetype, or blueprint of phenomena, and like Plato, he argues that what is given in nature is but an approximation, a *reminiscence* of the Ideas seen *before* experience, coming to us, as in a dream, to rectify experience. But, when he speaks of the goal of art as the expression of the "Ideas," Schopenhauer parts company with Plato. Where for Plato Ideas are *conceptual standards* against which to measure the inaccuracies of the senses, Schopenhauer's meaning of the term "Idea" opposes the notion of "Concept." Like Plotinus, and unlike Plato, he distinguishes between Idea and Concept. Great art, he argues, has nothing to do with concepts, but all to do with Ideas. The Idea "is always an object of perception ...", and while the concept is useful in life and is both necessary and productive in science, it is barren and unfruitful in art. This is because "the concept is abstract, discursive ... attainable and comprehensible by him who has only reason; communicable by words without any other assistance, entirely exhausted by its definition."[32] The Idea, on the other hand, "is entirely within the sphere of intuition ... It is never the object of knowledge to the individual as such but only to the mind which has raised itself above all willing and above all individuality ... through the operation of genius."[33] (He also opposes "Idea" to "Symbol" and condemns the latter when it is used conventionally, in the medieval sense of assigning specific symbolic meanings to things, contrary to the free attachment of symbolic meaning to phenomena practiced by nineteenth-century Symbolists). Where Plato rejects art because, devoid of Ideas, it is devoid of knowledge, another word for science and mathematics, Schopenhauer accepts art *because* it is not science. The knowledge to which art aspires is very different from the knowledge that science seeks. Science aims at power over nature; it utilizes reason, logic, mathematics, and the laws of causality as its methods. Its approach is conceptual. Unlike science, art, Schopenhauer argues, is not a practical manipulation and a quantitative understanding of nature. Art manifests the Idea *visually*, rather than conceptually. "The communication of an Idea," he says, "can only take place on the path of perception which is that of art."[34] Art *means* but does not specify a specific meaning. "Just because the Idea is and remains object of perception," he argues, "the artist is not conscious in the abstract of the intention and aim of his work; not a concept but an Idea floats before his mind; therefore he can give no justification of what he does. He works ... from pure feeling, unconsciously, indeed instinctively."[35]

Schopenhauer's emphasis on the visual as opposed to the conceptual was identical to the aims of Symbolist artists. This made his arguments all the more essential to their cause. His attack on allegorical art and the reasons he gave for it, are so exactly those of the Symbolists that one can almost certainly trace their source to his door. "Allegory," he writes, "is a work of art which means something different from what it represents. But the object of perception, and consequently the Idea, expresses itself directly and completely, and does not require the medium of something else which implies or indicates it." In a work that employs allegory "the picture or statue is made to stand for what a book can more fully accomplish." Real art, he argues, is a work of discovery, not a translation of an already known concept, for "the concept is like a dead receptacle in which whatever has been put into it, actually lies side by side, but out of which no more can be taken than what was put into it." The Idea, on the other hand, "develops in him who has understood it, ideas which are new as regards the concept of the same name; it resembles a living organism, ... possessed of the power of reproduction which brings forth what was not put into it." And Schopenhauer distinguishes the work of a great artist from that of a mannerist. Where real artists work "from pure feeling, intuitively," imitators or mannerists start from the concept: "They observe what pleases and affects us, ... fix it in a concept, thus abstractly, and then imitate it ... They suck their nourishment like parasite plants from the works of others, and like polypi, they become the colour of their food."[36]

In such an art, the Idea is not an integral part of the image but a concept superimposed upon it, leading away from the contemplation of the image itself and towards the concept it illustrates. Baudelaire had said much the same thing in the Salon of 1859 when he made the distinction (similar to Schopenhauer's), between the "true artist" and the "eclectic," who consciously aims at particular effects: "The true artist, the true poet must paint according to what he sees and feels. He must avoid like the plague, from borrowing the eyes and feelings of some other man ... for his creations would be lies and not realities."[37] And in praising the work of Delacroix, he shows how it retains "the temper and stamp of its inception. It is the infinite in the finite ... the vision that comes from intense meditation."[38]

How secure one might ask, are the connections made between Schopenhauer's view of art and that of the Symbolists? It was Jean Moreas who first defined the new movement in art and poetry in his Manifesto of Symbolism, published on September 18, 1886 in *Le Figaro*: "Symbolism," he writes, "is the only word capable of adequately describing the current tendency of the creative spirit in art: to clothe the Idea in a sensitive form ... All concrete phenomena cannot manifest themselves of their own accord. They are mere perceptible appearances intended to represent their esoteric affinities with the primordial Ideas." Moreas, we are told, had just returned from Germany, and, according to the writer Morhardt, "it was he ... who was one of the first to speak of Schopenhauer to his comrades."[39] Rejecting the world of external phenomena, Symbolism sought to extract from it the essence of phenomena, and at the same time to free it from its roots in the active world, and from all practical needs and desires. For a fuller analysis of Symbolist goals and their connection with Schopenhauer's ideas, one must turn to two crucial articles on Symbolism, written by Albert Aurier, which appeared in 1890 and 1891 in the new journal, the *Mercure de France*, first launched with Aurier's close cooperation in 1889.

In "Les Peintres Symbolistes" which appeared in 1890 and which established him as a foremost critic of the arts, Aurier, basing his article on Van Gogh's art, charts out the new territory of Symbolism. He prefaces the article with an epigram from Plotinus: "Undisciplined in discernment of the inward, knowing nothing of it, we run after the outer, never understanding that it is the inner which stirs us. We are in the case of one who sees his own reflection but not realizing whence it comes, goes in pursuit of it."[40] His reference to Plotinus was not unusual. Plotinus was as much in the air in the eighties and nineties as Baudelaire and Schopenhauer had been. It will be remembered from Maurice Denis' statement quoted earlier, how his generation had made a "singular mixture of Plotinus, Poe,

Baudelaire and Schopenhauer." And in an article on Gauguin, Denis remembers how, to counter Comte's philosophy, "Serusier held forth on the doctrine of Plotinus and the School of Alexandria" to his group of Nabi painters.[41]

In "Les Peintres Symbolistes," the first article ever written on Van Gogh, Aurier praises him for his ability to go beyond realism in his depiction of an ordinary pair of working boots, a bunch of sunflowers, or a field of grain. No longer just simple, common objects, they have become transformed, under the intense vision of the artist, into their counterparts – the Ideas. Schopenhauer had himself written in a similar vein when he condemned realism which, in his words, "commends itself to the crude understanding" and "ignores or denies the first of all facts, that ... the consciousness ..of the objective existence of things is conditioned through a subject whose ideas they are ..."[42] It was Van Gogh's consciousness, in this case, which had transformed an ordinary object into its symbol. In his next article, "Le Symbolisme en Peinture: Paul Gauguin," published in February 1891, and which propelled Gauguin to fame, Aurier prefaces it with another quotation, this time from Plato's myth of the cave: "What will he reply when he is told that what he saw before was an illusion, but that now, when he is approaching nearer to being and his eye is turned towards more real existence, he has a clearer vision?"[43] Aurier here attacks the prevailing approach to art: the short-sighted copy of social anecdotes, the flat observation, "the imbecile imitation of the warts of nature," and asserts that for Symbolists, the painter of nature is a monster. His scorn is also levelled at the Idealists who think themselves superior to the Realists. Idealists are merely Realists who preach. One must, he insists, distinguish between Idealists and *Ideists* (a term difficult to translate but which involves ideas divorced from reality). Paintings done by Idealists are allegorical, illustrations of accepted concepts, not new embodiments of Ideas. Ideist art, on the other hand, is symbolic. It avoids concepts, analysis, allegory, and the faithful copy of reality.[44] One remembers how adamant Schopenhauer had been against conceptual and allegorical art. If, he had said, we see in a work of plastic art "the distinct, limited, cold, dry conception shine out ... we feel disgusted and indignant, for we see ourselves deceived and cheated out of our interest and attention ..." Real pleasure only comes when the work of art "leaves something which, with all our thinking about it, we cannot bring down to the distinctness of a conception."[45] Gauguin echos the same sentiments when he complains that the Idealist painter "Puvis de Chavane *explains* his idea but he does not *paint* it."[46] In contrast, the beauty emanating from Gauguin's work, Aurier argues, can be understood, not in terms of a concept, but as the glow or stamp of ultimate reality. Gauguin's "Vision After the Sermon," he says, aims to represent not an ordinary scene but the essence of an Idea. And, he adds, what distinguishes the Symbolist painter from the philosopher, both of whom pierce to the center of things is the artist's emotivity – not the usual sensibility before objects or people, but an emotivity capable of expanding our spiritual horizons through forms that draw us toward the vision of being and ideality. It was of course Schopenhauer who had insisted that the true artist is one who conveys an Idea of ultimate reality rather than reality itself. And this, he had argued, could be attained only by the free exercise of vision, through concentration on the perceptual object divorced from all practical contexts. His description of the process is important since I believe it to be at the core of the symbolist approach to perception. He writes: "If, raised by the power of the mind, a man relinquishes the *common way* of looking at things ... and *looks* simply and solely at *what*; if, further, he does not allow *abstract thought* ... to take possession of his consciousness ... [and] gives the *whole power of his mind to perception*," (my italics) then, he concludes, "that which is so known is no longer the particular thing as such but is the Idea ..."[47] Anything, he argues, can be experienced as Idea: nature, the past, the present, the only stipulation being that it be contemplated purely and disinterestedly [in the Kantian sense], so as to induce in the observer "the illusion that only these objects exist." In other words, the aesthetic mode of contemplation for Schopenhauer consists of two inseparable parts: knowledge of the object not as individual thing but as Platonic Idea; and the self-consciousness of the knowing subject not as individual but as pure, will-less subject of knowledge. In contemplating a tree aesthetically, "it becomes of no consequence whether it is this tree or its predecessor which flourished a thousand years ago"; and "the Idea proper is not this special form which appears before me but its expression, its pure significance, its inner being ..."[48] Schopenhauer's influence can be recognized in the words of the Irish Symbolist poet, William Butler Yeats, describing the new art that he and his fellow Symbolists on the continent were intent on forming. One must follow, he writes, not the scientist's, but the visionary's way which knows "that the mind's eye soon comes to see a capricious and variable world which the Will cannot shape or change, though it can call it up and banish it again; we must find some place upon the tree of life for the phoenix's nest, for the passion that is exhaltation and *the negation of the Will*" [my italics]. Only then can the poet "lead his soul, disentangled from unmeaning circumstances, and the ebb and flow of the world, into the presence of the gods."[49] It was Schopenhauer who had shown the Symbolists that salvation, ecstasy – "the presence of the Gods" – could be achieved only through an artist's renunciation of the ordinary world of perception. This is indeed characteristic of their paintings. In them, the Idea is divorced from time and space, very much as Schopenhauer had asked of art. Seurat's painting of a Sunday outing, his "La Grande Jatte," painted in 1884–86, is not the portrayal of bustle and activity found in earlier, Realist paintings such as Manet's "Musique Aux Tuileries." Instead, the figures stand in flattened space, still, silent and aloof, isolated from each other, each in a private dream. They have become icons suspended in a timeless eternity. Yet, contrary to the outright abstractions of Art Nouveau, in Symbolist paintings, vestiges of perspective vie with the flatness of their canvases; it is as though, new at the game, Symbolists were experiencing difficulties in quite abstracting the Idea from its physical context.

The capacity to "leave all interest, all acts of will, all intentions, completely out of account," is, for Schopenhauer, the mark of genius. It is by virtue of disinterested contemplation that the works of genius become "an unacknowledged treasure of profound wisdom, just because out of them the wisdom of the nature of things itself speaks ..." The genius anticipates nature; he "recognises the Idea in the particular thing, and thus ... understands the half-uttered speech of nature, and articulates clearly what she only stammers forth ... this anticipation is, the ideal."[50] This faculty of concentration is, according to Schopenhauer, closed to all but exceptional creatures. For the ordinary person, the Ideas remain forever hidden beneath the interposing layers of phenomena, "so that the most excellent works of every art, the noblest productions of genius must always remain sealed books to the dull majority of men, inaccessible to them, separated from them by a wide gulf."[51] Baudelaire, too, like Schopenhauer, had despaired that the common man can appropriate the Ideas in things, blinded as he is by the need to satisfy his wants and desires. Only exceptional souls, can "arrive at the truth that everything is hieroglyphic. We know that the symbols are only relatively obscure, according to the purity and inborn clearsightedness of souls."[52] The ability to "see in things only their Ideas" belongs, according to Schopenhauer, to both the genius and the madman. "The madman has a true knowledge of what is actually present, and also of certain particulars of the past, but he mistakes the connections ... and therefore falls into errors and talks non-sense." But this is exactly how the genius operates, for he too "also leaves out of sight the knowledge of relations which conform to the principles of practical reason."[53] He takes objects out of their usual context, and extracting them from associations with space, time and causality, creates a world that is both parallel to and yet more than the physical world. In the same way, great art is for Baudelaire, the result of a capacity to see in a disconnected way, as though in the context of a hieroglyphic dream, different from the usual dream, its images linked, not by ordinary associations, but by their own laws of mental gravity.

To escape the "logic of practical reason," it was both outré and fashionable to use drugs and wine. But many more Symbolists put their faith in the powers of the imagination which they believed capable of according the senses a "second vision." Without the imagination, Schopenhauer had said, the genius would be unable to "extend his horizon far beyond the limits of his actual personal experience," the imagination enabling the genius "to construct the whole out of the little that comes into his own actual apperception."[54] And in his Salon of 1859, Baudelaire had made even greater claims for the imagination: it, not reason was "Queen of the Faculties." The imagination becomes, for him, a form of mystic perception, an "immense keyboard of all correspondences," capable of penetrating the visible world and revealing its secret affinities to both the human soul and to the realm of spirit. Those possessing it, he believed, soon come to see "the earth and its show as a glimpse, a *correspondence* of heaven."[55]

Following Schopenhauer and Baudelaire, the Symbolists looked for imaginative ways to isolate the object of perception from its mundane context and make it "pass out of all relations to something outside it." They experimented with a new language of forms which would be capable of embodying rather than illustrating Ideas. This new language was to be subjective, expressive, and free from any accepted formula. Words were not to be used in the ordinary sense of factual communication, just as lines and colors were not to be used in the imitation of ordinary reality. In poetry, Symbolist poets sought to break up the logic of prose, experimenting with a mixture of various zones of vocabulary so that no definite subject-matter could be isolated. Mallarmé, the principal spokesman for Symbolist poetry, sets out, for example, "to separate on the basis of different attributes, as it were, the two-fold condition of words: crude and immediate on the one hand, essential, on the other." The immediate word, he argues, serves as a generally accessible means of exchange, as though "one were to take a coin and silently put it into another's hand." It is useful for the transmission of concepts and ideas but dies as soon as what it says is understood. It is radically different from an "essential" word; lifted out of its grammatical and connotative context, the word offers new, essential meanings, created from its music and its colors.[56] Synthetist painters sought for an "essential" language in much the same way. They found it in color and line in isolation from their function as transmitters of physical reality. Lines and colors were to become vessels of meaning in their own right. In Synthetist art, Aurier writes, "the various combinations of lines, planes, shades, and colors, constitute the vocabulary of a mysterious language which is miraculously expressive ... This language, like all languages, has its alphabet, its spelling, its grammer, its syntax, even its rhetoric which is, in other words, its style."[57] He cites Redon, Gustave Moreau, Gauguin, and Van Gogh as artists who did not represent beautiful forms for the mere sensuous pleasure in them, but instead, infused these forms and colors with what they had understood about the mysterious meanings inherent in light, color, shadow, line. They employ these elements "like an alphabet with which to write the beautiful poem of their dreams, their ideas ..."[58] Symbolists could read similar words written by the German romantic poet Heine in a passage quoted by Baudelaire in his *Curiosite Esthetique*, republished in his *Oeuvres Posthumes* in 1887, "Tones, words, colors and forms ... are merely symbols of the Idea, ... arising in the soul of the artist when he is moved by the holy spirit of the world ..."[59]

These solutions are, of course, Symbolist answers to the problem posed by Schopenhauer's distinction between the give and take of transactions in the practical world and the emergence of Ideas in works of art. We can thus summarize another important set of ideas which attracted the attention of the Symbolists towards the four authors cited by Maurice Denis as mentors of their revolution in art. For Schopenhauer as for the others, creativity involves the imagination, not reason. It acts by empowering the genius and the artist with extraordinary as opposed to ordinary perception. It takes the form of a disinterested contemplation of beauty, and beauty [and its links with reality] is perceived, not in terms of time, space and causality, but purely as Idea. What the artist achieves in the act of creation, is repeated on a lesser scale in the act of the beholder's response to art. Demands are put on him (since the meaning of the work is never explicitly stated), to recognize, as Plotinus had said, "in the objects depicted to the eyes, the representation of what lies in the Idea."

SCHOPENHAUER IN THE CONTEXT OF NINETEENTH-CENTURY MYSTICISM

"In a symbolic work of art," Aurier writes in his article on Gauguin cited earlier, "materiality barely exists ... it is mysticism that we need today, and it is mysticism alone that can save our society from brutalization, sensualism, and utilitarianism." Answering to that need, a long list of recently published works on mysticism, compiled by Teodor de Wyzewa, a Symbolist theorist and writer, was offered to readers of the *Revue Independante* in 1887, suggesting a flourishing market for such literature. While Schopenhauer's philosophy was not couched in those terms, his ideas were seen as occupying the same spiritual zone, Symbolists being prone to project what they were looking for into whatever they were searching through. A glance at some of the more popular works on that list can help to explain still another reason for their attraction to him. Resonances of his ideas could be found in the works of mystics they admired. One such was Swedenborg, a seventeenth-century mystic philosopher whose theories of correspondence had already made inroads among the Romantics. Aurier recommends him as a valuable source despite, as he says, his sometimes "cock-eyed and fuzzy" statements, and advises all contemporary writers to use as their heading Swedenborg's "profound and revelatory words": "For few is it given to understand the nature of representation and the nature of correspondences ... that there exists a spiritual world that is distinct from the natural one. And that between the spiritual and the natural exists correspondences."[60] Popular also were such works as Thomas Carlyle's *Sartor Resartus*, which claimed that "the universe is but one vast symbol of God."[61] Another, was Eliphas Levi's *Fable et Symbole* which declared that "all the universe is but one sublime temple," and which placed the power of deciphering this unity of all phenomena and culture in the hands of the artist-prophet or the artist-seer.[62] Schopenhauer's philosophy fit right in. Had he not claimed that only the artist and the saint can penetrate "the veil of Maya"? Believing that artists shared in the power of the mystic, he had called for an art of Idea capable of reproducing the profounder visions of the seer who pierces to the essence of things. Baudelaire's theory of symbols, resting as it did on an uncompromisingly mystical foundation, was seen to have direct links with Schopenhauer's ideas. His famous poem "Correspondence" had, under Sweden-borg's influence, spoken of nature as "a temple" in which "man passes through forests of symbols" whose secrets are open only to the true artist. References to Schopenhauer's mysticism were often made by prominent symbolists such as Charles Morice whose aesthetic writings, compounded out of an amalgam of Schopenhauer and Baudelaire, reflect a persistent return to mystical arguments for the supremacy of art over all other forms of human endeavor. Edouard Schure's *Grands Inities*, first published in 1889, also contributed to Schopenhauer's influence. Its immense popularity was due to its syncretic view of religion where Plato, Christ and Buddha, among others, were celebrated as prophets of one and the same single truth.

Schopenhauer too, had written that "everything that is true in Christianity is also found in Brahmanism and Buddhism," and had based this view on the life of actual ascetic Christians, Buddhists and Hindus.[63] His attitude towards non-western cultures when speaking of the "extraordinary tolerance," and the "extremely mild character" of Hinduism and Buddhism which "constantly inculcate forbearance to *all living* things,"[64] was in line with the thinking of many Symbolists. Both Schure and Schopenhauer helped to re-enforce an already existing tendency among young intellectuals to weaken the traditional rigid boundaries separating the Judeo-Christian religion from pagan, Greco-Roman and oriental philoso-phies. While some Symbolists such as Maurice Denis were ardent Catholics or, like Huysmans, eventually embraced Catholicism because, as he had said, Schopenhauer had "offered no panacea," others turned to Buddhism, or shared in Schopenhauer's and Schure's belief in the unity of all religious truths. By the end of the century, religious imagery included several images of the Buddha, at times, as in Redon's Buddha alone under a flowering tree, or placed side by side with Christ, as in Ronson's Buddha, to which he had added an Arabic inscription, symbolic of Islam, and the sacred lotus of the Hindus, so as to evoke the universality of religious truths.

Interest in Buddhism prompted interest in Schopenhauer since many of his ideas were felt to be Buddhist in temper. His interest in Buddhism was well known from biographies of his life. He shared, with the Buddha the same pessimistic view of nature. Like him, Buddha had believed that all conscious existence involves pain caused by personal striving or desire, and like him, Buddha had concluded that only through the cessation of striving and the denial of a conscious individual existence, could one accede to "nirvana" or ecstasy. A second link was their shared emphasis on the primordial importance of the self. For Buddha, this self is without limits; it is all things: Brahman and Atman are two aspects of the self, Brahman being the universal and unfathomable principle of all reality, and Atman being the principle so far as it exists in the pure self, independent of all particular cognitive, nutritive, or other functions. His view of the pure self was similar if not identical to Schopenhauer's distinction between the pure self of the saint or genius/artist and that of the common man. It was especially appealing to the Symbolists whose sole aim was, in the words of Gustav Kahn, "to objectify the subjective – the externalization of the Idea – instead of subjectifying the objective – nature seen through the eyes of a temperament. Thus we carry the analysis of the self to the extreme ..."[65]

Within this context, Schopenhauer's philosophy, with its Buddhist elements, its religious syncretism, its emphasis on the pure self of the artist, and its demand for an art of Idea, influenced the Symbolist debate on the need for mysticism in art.

SCHOPENHAUER AND MUSIC IN THE SYMBOLIST AESTHETIC

It is in Schopenhauer's approach to music that the Symbolist aesthetic perhaps found its closest resonances. "De la musique avant toute chose!" was the cry heard in this line from a poem by the Symbolist poet Verlaine. At the end of the century, that cry was adopted by all the arts. Where the traditional tendency of painting was to imitate poetry, known theoretically as the "Ut Pictura Poesis tradition" (the same in painting as in Poetry), it was to become "Ut Pictura Musica," the Symbolists having shifted the weight of *all* the arts towards music.

This move was facilitated by the great vogue of Wagner's music. Wagner, "as a symphonist, as an artist [who had used] the thousand combinations of sound to translate the tumults of the human soul"[66] had also proclaimed the unity of all the arts, expressed as he believed, in his own work. The practice of synaesthesia – a fusion of sensations by which one sense-impression conjures up another – which Wagner practiced in his operas, became a favorite game of Symbolists writers and painters. It is, for example, a central theme in Huysman's *A Rebours*. Baudelaire had already endorsed synaesthesia in his 1861 article "Richard Wagner and Tannhauser," arguing that "what would be truly surprising would be to find that sound could not suggest color, that color could not evoke the idea of a melody, and that sounds and colors were unsuitable for the translation of ideas," and defending Wagner's music after his stormy reception in Paris, he proclaims his music to be the expression of the deepest hidden secrets of the human heart.[67] In Paris in 1885, two years after Wagner's death, Villiers de L'Isle-Adam, considered the main authority on both Wagner's pantheism and Schopenhauer's philosophy, was instrumental in the founding of the *Revue Wagnerienne* which became the repository of current views on the role of music in the arts, and of Wagner's in particular. In one such article, published under the title "Richard Wagner. Reverie of a French Poet," Mallarmé denies Wagner's music the epithet "symbolic." Wagner, he argues, uses stage settings, characters, allegorical narratives. His music always tends towards the theatrical – in conflict with the nature of music itself. "Does a spiritual evocation – the preparation or development of symbols" he asks, "need to be situated in a particular place?" Music, declares Mallarmé, is none of this; music is the "vibrating prolongation of all things, of Life iself."[68]

These could have been Schopenhauer's own words. Of all the arts, music is, for Schopenhauer, the art of arts. It does not merely manifest the Ideas, nor does it objectify the will. Music is the direct expression of the Will. It is the Will become audible. The world is as much embodied music as it is embodied Will. It allows for our identification with the heart of the universe. Hearts beat at one with it, and in this fusion, individuality dissolves. Schopenhauer writes that music, unlike the other arts, appeals to pure emotion; it speaks without intermediaries directly to our souls; it is why the effect of music is so much more powerful and penetrating than that of the other arts, "for they speak only of shadows, but it speaks of the thing itself ... it never expresses the phenomenon but only ... the in-itself of all phenomena, the Will itself. It does not express this or that ... sorrow or pain ... but joy and sorrow ... in ... their extracted essence [and] to a certain extent in the *abstract*." The power and supremacy of music over the arts lies in the fact that in its "unutterable depth," it "restores to us all the emotions of our inmost nature, but entirely without reality and far removed from their pain."[69]

The identification of the arts with music rather than with words was to become the leit-motif of Symbolist, Decadent and Synthetist art. Like music, their art would henceforth exhude a semantic aura yet deliver no specific meaning. Poetry and painting would suggest and evoke, rather than state or describe. "Suggestive art," writes the Symbolist painter Redon, "is most independently and most radiantly present in the exciting sounds of music, but it is also mine through a combination of various associated elements, forms transposed and transformed, without any relation to contingencies, yet having their own logic ... My drawings *inspire* yet cannot be defined. Like music, they transport us into the ambiguous world of the undetermined."[70] To achieve musicality Symbolists insisted, words, lines and colors must be delivered from their mimetic and descriptive functions. The vocabulary of the arts must become an intuitive, experimental science of the poetic value and meaning inherent in the language of art itself, returning it to its original, primitive sense before time and culture had sullied it by reason and commerce. Poetry could then become, says Mallarmé, "the expression, by means of human lan-guage *restored to its essential rhythm*, of the mysterious aspects of existence: it endows our sojourn with authenticity, and constitutes the sole spiritual task."[71] The search for the same mystery in painting was acknowledged by Gauguin in answer to a critic who had accused him of not providing a meaning for his painting "Whence do we Come, Who are we? Where do we Go?" He writes: "... my dream is intangible, ... it comprises no allegory; it is a musical poem, it needs no libretto." And speaking of color, he adds, "think also of the musical role color will henceforth play in modern painting. Color which is vibration, just as music is, is able to attain what is most universal yet at the same time most elusive in nature: its inner force."[72]

Symbolist theories of art did not disappear with the close of the nineteenth century. These ideas were developed further by Kan-dinsky and Klee, and later by the Abstract Expressionists, who experimented with painting so as to find how best to express in Schopenhauer's words "joy and sorrow ... to a certain extent in the abstract." Their findings brought them to total abstraction which they believed to be the truest expression of reality, and which Schopenhauer had found alone of all the arts in music – the expression of the Will itself.[73]

Shehira Doss-Davezac

Notes

1 Alexandre Baillot, *Influence de la philosophie de Schopenhauer en France, 1860–1900* (Paris: Vrin, 1927), pp. 17–18.
2 J. K. Huysmans, *A Rebours* (Paris: Garnier-Flammarion, 1922), pp. 129–130.
3 Jean Bourdeau, *Pensées, Maximes et Fragments* (Paris: Germer Bailliere, 1880), p. 41.
4 *WWR* 1, Bk. III, 38 (*The World as Will and Idea*, R. B. Haldane and John Kemp, trans. (London: Routledge, 1883).
5 Ernest Raynaud, "La Generation Symboliste," in *La Melée Symboliste*, V. 2 (La Renaissance du Livre, 1920).
6 Barbey d'Aurevilly, *Les Diaboliques* [1874] (Paris: Flammarion, 1967), pp. 39–40.
7 *PP* 2, 617–622, "On Women."
8 Robert Delvoy, *Symbolists and Symbolism* (New York: Rizzoli, 1978), p. 42.
9 *WWR* 1, 3 (Haldane and Kemp).
10 Remy de Gourmont, *Promenades Litteraires* (Paris: Mercure de France, 1904–1927), p. 183.
11 *WWR* 1, Bk. III, 36 (Haldane and Kemp).
12 Baudelaire, "The Modern Public and Photography," in *Mirror of Art*, Jonathan Mayne, ed. and trans. (New York: Doubleday, 1956), p. 233.
13 Paul Gauguin, *Diverses Choses*, 1896–1897, quoted by H. Chipp in *Theories of Modern Art* (Berkeley: University of California Press, 1969), p. 65.
14 Camille Pissarro, *Lettres a son fils Lucien*, John Rewald, trans. (Santa Barbara: Peregrine Smith), pp. 40–41.
15 Sven Loevgren, in *The Genesis of Modernism: Seurat, Gauguin, Van Gogh and French Symbolism in the 1880s* (Bloomington: Indiana University Press, 1971), pp. 22–23.
16 Gustave Courbet, December 25,1861, in Linda Nochlin, *Realism and Tradition in Art 1848–1900* (Englewood Cliffs: Prentice Hall, 1966), p. 35.
17 Edgar Allan Poe, "The Poetic Principle," *Works* XIV (New York: J. A. Harrison, 1902), p. 266.
18 Eugene Delacroix, *Oeuvres Litteraires* I (Paris: J. Claye, 1865), p. 114.
19 Ibid., p. 65.
20 Delacroix, *Journal*, I (Paris: Librairie Plon, 1893), January 26, 1824.
21 Maurice Denis, in H. R. Rookmaacher, *Gauguin and 19th Century Art Theory* (Amsterdam: Swets and Zeitlinger, 1972), p. 165.
22 *WWR* 1, Supplement to Bk. III, 34 (Haldane and Kemp).
23 Plato, *The Phaedo*, 66, *Dialogues of Plato*, I, Benjamin Jowett trans. (New York: Random House, 1937).
24 Plotinus, *Enneads*, IV, 8, 7 (London: Faber and Faber, 1969).

25 Charles Baudelaire, "In Praise of Cosmetics," in *The Painter of Modern Life*, Jonathan Mayne, ed. (New York: Doubleday, 1956), pp. 31–32.
26 Baudelaire, "Eugene Delacroix," *Mirror of Art*, Mayne, ed. (New York: Doubleday, 1956), p. 59.
27 Baudelaire, "Further Notes on E. A. Poe," *The Painter of Modern Life*, p. 96.
28 Plotinus, *Enneads*, V, 8, 2.
29 Ibid., I, 6, 3.
30 Ibid., I, 3, 1.
31 Ibid., II, 9, 16.
32 *WWR* 1, Bk. III, 49 (Haldane and Kemp).
33 Ibid.
34 Schopenhauer, Supplement to Bk. III, 34 (Haldane and Kemp).
35 Ibid., Bk. III, 49.
36 Ibid.
37 Baudelaire, "Salon of 1859," *The Mirror of Art*, p. 234.
38 Ibid., "Religion, History, Fantasy," p. 252.
39 "Les Symboliques," in *Nouvelle Revue*, VLXXIV, 15, 1892, p. 768.
40 G. Albert Aurier, *Oeuvres Posthumes* (Paris: Mercure de France, 1893), p. 293.
41 Maurice Denis, *Theories 1890–1910*, 4th edition, 1920, p. 166.
42 *WWR* 1, Supplement to Bk. I, 1 (Haldane and Kemp).
43 Plato, *Republic*, Bk. VII, 515.
44 Aurier, "Le Symbolisme en Peinture: Paul Gauguin," *Oeuvres Posthumes*, 1893, p. 205.
45 *WWR* 1, Supplement to Bk. III, 34 (Haldane and Kemp).
46 Gauguin, Herschel B.Chipp, *Theories of Modern Art*, 1969, p. 66.
47 *WWR* 1, Bk. III, 34 (Haldane and Kemp).
48 Ibid., Bk. III, 41.
49 William Butler Yeats, "Magic," in *Ideas of Good and Evil* (London: Macmillan, 1903), p. 29.
50 *WWR* 1, Bk. III, 45 (Haldane and Kemp).
51 Ibid., Bk. III, 49.
52 Quoted in Guy Michaud, *Message poetique du symbolisme* (Paris: Nizet, 1966), p. 722.
53 *WWR* 1, Bk. III, 36 (Haldane and Kemp).
54 Ibid.
55 Baudelaire, "Modernity," in *Painter of Modern Life*, p. 14.
56 Stephan Mallarmé, *Divagations* [1897] in *Oeuvres Completes* (Mandor et Aubry: Gallimard, 1989).
57 Aurier, "Les Symbolistes," *Oeuvres Posthumes*, p. 302.
58 Ibid., p. 296.
59 H. Heine, Der Salon I, quoted in Rookmaaker, *Gaugin and 19th Century Art Theory* (Amsterdam: Swets and Zeitlinger), pp.192–193.
60 Aurier, "Essaie sur une nouvelle methode de critique," in *Oeuvres Posthumes*, p. 202.

61 Thomas Carlyle, *Sartor Resartus*, Charles Frederick Howard, ed. (New York: The Odyssey Press, 1937), Bk. III, ch. 3.

62 Eliphas Levi, "Sixieme Grand Symbole, le temple de l'avenir," in *Fable et Symbole* (Paris: de la Maisnie, 1862), p. 467.

63 Schopenhauer, "On Religion," *PP* 1, p. 381.

64 Ibid., p. 358.

65 Quoted by John Rewald, *Post Impressionism* (New York: Museum of Modern Art, 1978), pp. 134–135.

66 Baudelaire, "Richard Wagner and Tannhauser in Paris," *Painter of Modern Life*, p. 116.

67 Ibid.

68 Mallarmé, Letter to Leo d'Orfer, 27 June 1884, quoted in *Vogue*, April 18, 1886, pp. 70–71.

69 *WWR* 1, Bk. III, 52 (Haldane and Kemp).

70 Letter to Mellerio, August 1898, in John Rewald, *Redon, Moreau, Bresdin* (New York: Museum of Modern Art, 1961), p. 25.

71 Michaud, *Message Poetique du Symbolisme*, II (Paris: Nizet, 1966), p. 321.

72 Gauguin, in Herschel Chipp, *Theories of Modern Art*, p. 75.

73 *WWR* 2, 68 (Payne trans.).

13

Schopenhauer's philosophy of architecture

MITCHELL SCHWARZER

AGAINST THE CLASSICIST PARADIGM

Schopenhauer's *The World as Will and Representation* marks the boundary between the classical and modern paradigms of architectural knowledge. Since the Italian Renaissance, the reciprocity between structure, function, and art in architecture had always been problematic. Yet, up until the eighteenth century, architectural theorists broadly agreed on Vitruvius' dictum that architecture "must be built with due reference to durability, convenience, and beauty."[1] With classical treatises, the Vitruvian trinity portrayed architecture as an objective system. The most important element of this doctrine was the belief that all architectural forms and relations were rooted in the imitation of nature.

Economic and intellectual upheavals during the eighteenth century recast the foundations of architectural knowledge from objective nature to the subjective mind. Individual drives and behavior were increasingly studied as the key to understanding architectural form. The Vitruvian trinity, however, did not work as well as a mirror of the human mind as it did of nature. By Schopenhauer's time, in the wake of new discourses on utility and pleasure, rule and imagination, and cognition and perception, the Vitruvian trinity began to seem outdated. The modern aesthetic brought down architecture's classical edifice. In particular, Schopenhauer's aesthetic annexed architecture to the subjective Will and in turn redefined the classical notions of function, beauty, and structure.

Working from the non-instrumental framework developed within late eighteenth-century German philosophy, Schopenhauer denied artistic meaning to architecture's functional role. Kantian anti-instrumentalism prohibited the judgment of architectural beauty on the basis of utility or purpose. Therefore, even if philosophers admitted that worldly pressures inscribe specific destinies for buildings, the analysis of architectural beauty was turned inward. Built form had to be judged independent of its extension into society, politics, and economics. Praising, as did Hegel, those arts which stimulate the spirit and exhibit levels of reality unavailable to external sensual perception, Schopenhauer ranked architecture's aesthetic potential below that of painting and sculpture, literature, and music. Largely for these reasons, Schopenhauer has been read as one of the great philosophical villains of the discipline, castigating architecture as the lowest of the fine arts.

Eighteenth-century philosophical aesthetics also lie at the heart of Schopenhauer's conception of architectural beauty in association with dynamic energy and matter flows. For Schopenhauer, art is important in that it can lead the subject to an immediate apprehension of underlying cosmic reality, the world as Will in its states of striving. The rationale for the dynamic aesthetic was that artistic perception takes into account the real interaction of forces within nature, and not a representation of a mental-physical interaction. For this reason, Schopenhauer devalued the traditional understanding of architectural beauty, assigning supplemental value to ornament and secondary importance to relations such as proportion and symmetry. Ornament, while important to the beauty of buildings, belonged to the domain of painting or sculpture. Qualities of proportion and symmetry could certainly be pleasing, but remained representation; inessential to the real source of architectural beauty in structural dynamics.

In examining the problem of the perceiving subject's relationship to building, Schopenhauer proposed basing architectural aesthetics primarily upon considerations of loads and supports within a structural framework. Yet, he never advocated a description of the causal relations between building materials and forces. Considered as a fine art, independent of purpose, architecture considered aesthetically does not contribute to knowledge of efficient causes. Instead, aesthetics must look to final causes. For its part, the aesthetic apprehension of architecture must provide an immediate intuition of the lower levels of the objectifications of Will: qualities of hardness, rigidity, weight, mass, and light. In the aesthetic perception of these qualities, Schopenhauer felt, the observer could lose his individuality and transgress the barrier erected by representational knowledge between the subject and the thing-in-itself.

Critical to Schopenhauer's aesthetic of architecture was his desire to establish the primacy of the Will over the intellect. His strategy therefore had to destabilize traditional conceptions of architecture, undoing its recognizability within representational modes of thinking such as the trinity encompassing function, structure, and beauty. Nonetheless, instead of promoting a new unity for architecture through the release from representation gained by the perception of structural relations, his aesthetics actually inserted a destabilizing language of perceptual and formal initiatives.

Schopenhauer made a major contribution to two of modern architecture's pivotal identities, those of psychological/physiological perception and structural formalism. It will be the purpose of this article to discuss in detail his transmutation of the three Vitruvian categories and this stimulus it gave to these new architectural initiatives. In approaching his philosophy, I will be interested in how Schopenhauer interpreted the long series of attempts in Germany to understand the artistic relationship between the mechanical processes of nature and the inner sensations and imagination. It will be important to ask: how did Schopenhauer's theory of architecture relate to his specific vision of the qualities of the Will?; and what was the conflict between Schopenhauer's drive to Platonic essence and his equation of architecture with earthly matter and force?

FUNCTIONAL INSTRUMENTALITY

In the wake of aesthetic discourse since the late eighteenth century, Schopenhauer accepted the notion that artistic judgment constituted the sole means for determining the real nature of the world. Prior to Schopenhauer, German aesthetic philosophers had gradually come to regard art as an alternative source of ascertaining the truth of natural reality to science. From the time of Alexander Baumgarten's *Aesthetica* (1755), the central thrust of aesthetics had been that art offered a standard of truth different from that of scientific reason. Although rationalists like Baumgarten subordinated art to reason, toward the third quarter of the eighteenth century, the relevance of reason for art came under increasing skepticism. Inspired by English philosophers of the sensations – and their evocation of the powers of imagination, genius, and originality – German philosophers increasingly studied artistic reality at the level of immediate and individual perception.

This impulse was grounded most forcefully by Immanuel Kant's formulation of a central artistic sense in his *Critique of Judgment* (1790). Kant's call for artistic centrality resulted from his desire to surmount the Enlightenment fragmentation of pure perception from mediated conception and its challenge by monistic counter-Enlightenment thinkers like Johann Georg Herder. For Kant, seeking to unite the realms of phenomena and noumena he had divided in his *Critique of Reason* (1781; 1787), the aim of art was that of apprehending reality as it really is, and not as it is mediated by concepts of the understanding. For Kant, aesthetic judgment inquiries directly after the problem of existence. Unlike science or philosophy which take their task as the causal explication of reality, aesthetic judgment works toward truth in implicit fashion. Artistic judgment is private, occurring between the sensual and mental faculties of the observer and the morphology of a particular object.

Most important for architecture, Kant's formulation of aesthetic contemplation required that the judgment of a work of art occur without interest in the object as to its use or need. Aesthetic judgment means, as Kant wrote, that: "we do not want to know whether anything depends or can depend on the existence of the thing either for myself or for any one else, but how we judge it by mere observation."[2] Because aesthetic judgment is disinterested, Kant took it for granted that the pleasure derived from a work of art is independent of that work's practical function. Artistic judgments, unlike those of understanding or reason, are produced independently of both concept and desire.

To repeat, Kant arrived at this bold vision for aesthetic perception by differentiating art from the principle of sufficient reason that governs cognition. As an independent perception linked to the imagination, aesthetic judgments are instantaneous, and establish an essential connection between subject and object. What the viewer gains through art is a sudden association with the world of objects. But, because of the immediacy of the aesthetic relationship, judgments of taste must be disinterested. As Kant states the matter: "The judgment is called aesthetical just because its determining ground is not a concept, but the feeling (the internal sense) of that harmony in the play of the mental powers, so far as it can be felt in sensation."[3] The judgment of taste is not created within the properties of the object, but within the harmony of the mind's faculties. The key to Kant's aesthetic is its location within human consciousness, in the operations of the mind, in the free play of the mind's representational powers.[4] Although Kant understood aesthetic judgment as universal and purposive, he believed that its governing operations occur solely within a given subject's mind; this is understood by the famous condition of purpose without purposiveness: *Zweck ohne Zweckmäßigkeit*. Here we find a great difference from Schopenhauer's Platonic aesthetic. As T. J. Diffey writes, Kant's concept of the beautiful consists not in "the perception of some essential form or idea but the intimation of purpose, finality or design in the thing judged to be beautiful": by contrast, for Schopenhauer "the aesthetic lies not in something that is felt, but in the perception of an a-temporal object such as the Platonic form of tree."[5]

Kant's formulation of the aesthetic had tremendous consequences for the judgment of architecture. Clearly, the architectural embodiment of function was ruled out by the mandate of disinterested viewing within the aesthetic. Following Kant, the aesthetic idea of architecture became that of apprehending built forms without any regard to their purpose, a standpoint which contradicted the forceful utilitarian aspects of post-Vitruvian theorizing. Architecture, Kant himself wrote, is "the art of presenting concepts of things that are possible only through art, and whose form has for its determining ground not nature but an arbitrary purpose, with the view of presenting them with aesthetical purposiveness."[6] Despite these thoughts, Kant never formulated a clear theory of the limitations on architectural beauty. For Kant, in fact, art comprised all manner of natural objects. He made no clear distinction between natural beauty and that beauty which results from intentional art objects.

It is worthwhile pointing out that Kant's exclusion of functional considerations in architecture was not his own invention. It had been heralded within the writings of Johann Georg Sulzer, Karl Philip Moritz, and even his arch-rival, Herder. In the "Viertes Wäldchen" ["Fourth Critical Forests"] (1779), Herder portrayed architecture's preoccupation with mechanical connections as an elementary aesthetic expression. For Herder, as for Kant, the perfection of architecture cannot be its orientation to purpose, but only that excellence which occurs within the lines, surfaces, and bodies of buildings: what can be seen as a preparatory stage for the more truthful development of art in sculpture.[7] Presaging a series of condemnations of architecture's status as a fine art, Herder described that the art which expresses "unity and variety in the simplest and most apparent way is architecture."[8]

After Kant and Herder, it was readily apparent that due to

architecture's overtly functional nature, its aesthetic potential might be limited. For instance, the aesthetic treatment of art as disinterested and idealized form was further transformed by Georg Friedrich Wilhelm Hegel's dialectic into a teleological process by which human expression gradually moves from concrete to spiritual expression: from sensuous knowledge in art, to pictorial thinking in religion, and finally, to free thinking in philosophy. Hegel considered the gradual appearance of the immaterial spirit (from its first appearance in architecture to its final culmination in philosophy) to be the moving force of history. Hegel proposed knowledge of both the phenomenal and noumenal worlds; a historical process by which the Kantian "thing-in-itself" (*Ding an sich*) is achieved through a series of creative revelations that begin with the architectural art.

As related in his *Aesthetics, Lectures on Fine Art* (1826), Hegel, like other philosophers, was all too aware that architecture is driven by needs. As the most functional of the arts, architecture was relegated to the lowest level of aesthetic expression. Architecture, in Hegel's thinking, is the stage of the indeterminate idea, the unrefined expression of the idea in corporeal form. In fact, the trajectory of the unfolding of the idea to humanity begins with architecture's fulfillment of primordial demands: "need introduces into architecture forms which are wholly and entirely purposeful and belong to the (mathematical) intellect ... the straight line, right angle, level surfaces."[9] Since the teleological path of human history involves the progressive release from external appearance, we also view architecture's combinations of forms with a desire for the revelation of inner essence. Yet, because architecture is eminently functional, buildings are able to imprint the internal meaning of their external shape only symbolically. Despite architecture's status as a fine art, Hegel relegated architectural beauty to the lawful organization of its masses.

In an analogous vein, Schopenhauer also described the revelation of the thing-in-itself as the goal of all art and philosophy. More in common with Hegel than Kant, Schopenhauer described artistic judgment in terms of specific artistic works. And what is also common to both Schopenhauer and Hegel was architecture's lowly status as a fine art. Inasmuch as the common perception of a building scientifically reveals a network of causes and effects that constitute its form, it is not art.

Still, for Hegel, artistic revelation occurred within a historical, dialectical process. The arts ascended over the course of history from an initial architectural encounter with symbolism of the Will to a final philosophical union with the world spirit. Schopenhauer's aesthetics attained its heights, by contrast, in an ahistorical schema. He described the arts ascending within the definite grades of the objectification of Will. For architecture to be art, in Schopenhauer's system, it must reveal the inner conflict of the Will.

Schopenhauer also differed from Hegel in that he did not find the possibility for apprehending immediate reality within a development out of cognitive understanding. Instead, Schopenhauer contended that all intellectual activity is rational knowledge (*Wissen*), a second-order revelation of the true existence of reality.

Echoing Kant in this respect, Schopenhauer drew a distinction between the phenomenal world as representation and the thing-in-itself or true state of reality imperceivable through concepts, writing: "Everything that exists for knowledge, and hence the whole of this world, is only object in relation to the subject, perception of the perceiver, in a word, representation."[10] What can be known are the objectifications of the Will. The acts of cognition and knowledge, as such, relate to cause and effect. Yet, only feeling (*Gefühl*) and intuition (*Anschauung*), something present and not conceptualized within the consciousness, can reveal first-order existence.[11] Feeling as such is coincident with existence, or the Will. After all, the Will, and not its representations in concepts, is the underlying motive for production, creativity, and all matters of existence. As the inner nature of reality, the strivings of Will – expressed through feelings and emotions within one's body – cannot be explained by time, space, or causality. The Will is groundless.[12] Moreover, the Will is also a state of endless striving: "Eternal becoming, eternal flux, belong to the revelation of the essential nature of the Will."[13] The Will constitutes existence as a state of suffering.

Art, in Schopenhauer's philosophy, embodies a temporary release from the general condition of suffering that is life. Through art, we come to escape our volition – and hence our individuality and subjectivity – in order to rejoin the undifferentiated reality of the universe. Artistic judgment constitutes both an intimacy and release from the Will. Art is an escape, an interlude of peace, a flight from objects in their concrete sense.[14] Art, furthermore, promises pure knowledge. As Jacques Taminiaux writes of Schopenhauer's disinterestedness in the essential qualities of art: "we have art in order to learn to die, once we have overcome the deceptive order of representation, and contemplated the absurdity of the Will."[15]

Nonetheless, how are we to know of our death from our position in life? Can we rejoin an external reality seemingly only cognizable through the deceits of representation? How, given our closed subjectivity, are we to know any reality outside of ourselves? For Schopenhauer, the answer lies in an artistic intuition of the body's states of willing.

Engaged in a physiological investigation going beyond either Kant or Hegel, Schopenhauer contended that artistic intuition must begin in the subject's consciousness of his own body. Unique to the world, our bodies are both immediate expressions of our will and representations of this Will. As Brian Magee writes of Schopenhauer's notion of body actions: "They are the sole example of empirically observed movements of physical objects in space and time which are also, of their nature, known simultaneously and directly from within in a way which is not mediated through the senses."[16] Since we are our body's desires, a heightened sensitivity to the feeling of our desires leads us to feel the desires of other objects. Schopenhauer's plan to know the thing-in-itself, or Idea, emerges here, in the artistic and phenomenal appreciation of the body as extended to other objects.

This totalizing perceptual gaze into the thing-in-itself afforded through art requires a state of pure perception. As Schopenhauer described this state of artistic perception, he wrote:

it plucks the object of its contemplation from the stream of the world's course, and holds it isolated before it. This particular thing, which in that stream was an infinitesimal point, becomes for art a representation of the whole, an equivalent of the infinitely many in space and time.[17]

Artistic representation, unlike other forms of representation, is oriented to an intimate relationship with the inner states of the Will. What art aims at is a copy of the Will's states of striving which then releases the subject from the Will. Contact of artistic representation with the inner nature of the Will brings forth a pleasing elucidation of the unity of the world, freeing the subject from endless striving, if only for a moment. Given these considerations, Schopenhauer considered music to be the highest art form since it is an immediate objectification of the entire Will, and hence the world as it really is.[18]

Schopenhauer's aesthetic reflections on architecture were conditioned by stressing subjectivism and a systematic spectrum of artistic symbolism reaching from direct images of the internal Will (music) to images portraying external phenomena (architecture).

Architecture, although it is as non-representational as music, was not able to objectify as wide a spectrum of the Will's desires as music, or for that matter, the other fine arts. After all, in order to act as art, the aesthetic appreciation of architecture must be independent of use or purpose. Considerations of plan or function cannot enter into artistic perception since they constitute representations and a sort of phenomenal knowledge which would bring no pleasurable release from the Will's striving. Since buildings were rarely executed for purely aesthetic purposes, and were generally oriented to practical ends, architecture was foreign to the higher notions of art.[19]

Schopenhauer ranked architecture as one of the lesser fine arts. As was the case in Kant's and Hegel's aesthetics, architecture was condemned by Schopenhauer for its concreteness; the fact that it abstracts the human Idea or spirit only in rudimentary fashion. In its higher forms, art must be pure and close to the essence of the human desire. Architecture, for the most part, gives us the thing-in-itself in its useful countenance and expresses the Will only in the most abstract terms. As Schopenhauer wrote regarding the highest aesthetic pleasure:

the beholder is emancipated from the kind of knowledge possessed by an individual, which arouses the Will and follows the principle of sufficient reason, and is raised to that of the pure, Will-free subject of knowing. Thus it will consist in pure contemplation itself, freed from all the suffering of Will and of individuality.[20]

THE REGULARITY OF DESIRE

In addition to challenging the relationship of architectural beauty to function, Schopenhauer's aesthetic required that building ornament be categorized as painting or sculpture and not architecture. Schopenhauer's argument for associating ornament with the former arts was based on his belief that architecture is unable to represent the organic world as Idea. In the representational visual arts, including painting and sculpture, artists are able to depict higher grades of the Will's objectification: its representation of plant and animal life, and more significantly, human form and feelings.

As we have discussed above, the importance of artistic representation of the Will's stages of objectification was crucial to Schopenhauer's project to seek release from the Will's domination through non-rational means. Thus, for architecture, the separation of aesthetics from practical matters closed in artistic representation around itself, secluding ornament from utility and its structural aspects. But, it is important to point out at this point that the increasing autonomy of ornament from other aspects of the building art was also the result of an inconclusive attempt by architectural theorists themselves to rationalize the connection of classical ornament to contemporary architecture. Insofar as Schopenhauer's equation of ornament with the higher representational arts reflects aesthetic anti-rationalism, it also calls to mind the disarray that architectural rationalizations of ornament presented by the early nineteenth century.

The discourse on philosophical aesthetics in which Schopenhauer participated promised an escape from the *Querelle des Ancienes et Modernes* which had dominated architecture since the late seventeenth century. The central polemic of the Quarrel revolved around how contemporary architects should account for the artistic authority of the ancients. The philosophical advance of the Quarrel consisted in its conversion of architectural theory from faith to reason. All through the Early Modern Era – consisting of the Renaissance and Baroque Ages – questions of structure and function in architecture were determined principally by contemporary methods and interests. Only in the case of beauty, as understood through issues of symmetry and proportion within the ornamental vocabulary of the classical orders, did architects accept subservience to the ancients. All through this time, however, architects harbored the nagging suspicion that what was at stake in regard to architectural beauty was modern, individualistic reason and creativity.

By the end of the seventeenth century, in the wake of the ascendent rational discourse of Enlightenment science, this doubt took on central importance within theoretical debate. Specifically, architectural theorists began to question critically the equation of classical ornament and proportions with the concept of architectural beauty. Neither side within the Quarrel proposed dropping the centuries-old affiliation to the classical ornamental language of antiquity. Both ancients and moderns affirmed a belief that classical ornament and proportion must be the conclusive factors for determining architectural beauty. Instead, taking a metaphysical turn, the debate centered around how to derive rules from antique architecture and then apply them to modern buildings.

The ancients were represented by the Royal Academy of Architecture (1671) in Paris and its instructional text, François Blondel's *Cours d'architecture* (1675). Corresponding to the accelerating academicization of classical tradition since the Italian Renaissance, The French Academy mandated that architects study ancient principles of design as manifest in the famous buildings of Rome and their explication in architectural treatises. Following Aristotle's theory of beauty, Blondel cast the architectural art as a mimesis of reality: an imitation of the symmetrical, proportional, and eurhythmic relations of classical forms.[21] Architectural proportions, Blondel also believed, were a rational analogue of the more obvious concords of musical harmony. Blondel's theory ran into trouble, however, when its induction of universal rules from the increasingly large set of Roman classical buildings was put to the test of empirical measurement. As revealed in the drawings of Antoine Desgodets, published in 1682, the actual variety of antique proportions contradicted Blondel's belief in uniformity.[22] On the basis of this empirical discord, Claude Perrault soon afterwards established the position of the moderns.

In his *Ordonnance for the Five Kinds of Columns after the Method of the Ancients* (1683), Perrault exploited the divergence of proportional variation within antiquity and modernity for its anti-dogmatic lessons. On the basis of Desgodets' measurements, Perrault stated that neither ancient nor modern architecture gives evidence of absolute or universal rules for architectural proportions.[23] Although Perrault still believed that modern architects must work from a mean of the most worthy examples of classical proportions, his theory shook the foundations of classical architecture in the theory of antique correspondence as well as its more recent rationalizations with reference to human anatomy and musical or mathematical ratios. Most importantly, Perrault's uncovering of an inductive/ deductive circularity underlying classical architecture broke the connection of faith which had long bonded classical ornament (proportion and symmetry) and modern building methods.

During the eighteenth century, a series of theories attempted to re-solidify this bond, basing architectural beauty upon a new set of supposedly rational foundations. These efforts included Marc-Antoine Laugier's axiomatic deduction from the primitive hut and Etienne-Louis Boullée's turn to Platonic solids. What is striking about these theories, however, is that their embodiment of rationality led to a decisive abandonment of the classical ornamental language and proportional traditions of Roman antiquity. When one takes into account the contemporaneous attempts to locate a new universal center for architecture in the recently illustrated buildings of ancient

Greece, it becomes clear that by 1800 Enlightenment architectural theory had deserted the association of beauty with ancient Roman proportions and ornament.

Theories of rationalism never produced a lasting bond between classical ornament and proportions and architectural beauty. The aftermath of Perrault's subversion of faith in antiquity through modern empirical science was an unintentional and substantive subversion of the importance of ancient laws for ornament, proportion, and symmetry within architectural beauty. What was especially significant for Schopenhauer was the realization that the pursuit to explain rationally the connection of ornament and proportions to architecture increasingly led to divisiveness and relativism.

Indeed, the discursive trajectory of the Quarrel between the Ancients and Moderns embodied the most dire consequences of the famous philosophical controversy between Moses Mendelssohn and Friedrich Jacobi in the 1780s. Demonstrating how the path of speculative reason can lead not to truth but toward disunity and the abandonment of a classical tradition which for architects had been the equivalent of a religion, rational architectural theorizing seemed to buttress Jacobi's claim that reason inevitably results in conditions of nihilism and fatalism. It is no wonder, then, that Schopenhauer was eager to deny any rational connection between architectural beauty and its ornament and relations of proportion, symmetry, and eurythmy. Schopenhauer and other philosophers were eager to redefine ornament from its earlier status as analogue of architectural function and structure to a new capacity as an independent activity within the expression of the artistic imagination.

Ornament's representational qualities account for its importance to philosophical aesthetics and its detachment from other concerns of building. Understood as representation, ornament could promise an escape from the need to demonstrate reason within architecture. Ornament, considered apart from considerations of sufficient reason, allowed at least a part of architecture to enter into the ideal realm of the mind and spirit. Given Schopenhauer's preoccupation with the structure of matter as regards architectural essence, and his desire to neatly hierarchize the various art forms, it is no surprise that he considered ornament apart from the central realm of architecture.

Ornament, as an imitative art, could not possibly embody the artistic essence of architecture. Hence, Schopenhauer wrote that all ornamental work on buildings belongs to the plastic arts and not architecture: "Ornamental work on capitals, etc., belongs to sculpture and not to architecture, and is merely tolerated as an additional embellishment, which might be dispensed with."[24] This latter phrase, in and of itself, establishes the importance of Schopenhauer's contribution on architecture to the later development of anti-ornamentalism in the theories of Adolf Loos and other modern architects. In referring to ornament, however, it is unclear if Schopenhauer meant the complete decorative program of a building or merely its clearly sculptural embellishments. Did Schopenhauer, in other words, refer to plant motifs as well as human sculptures? Whereas representations of fauna in Greek architecture are generally distinguishable from structural elements, such is not the case with flora. Plant motifs adorn all aspects of columns and entablatures. If Schopenhauer called for their elimination, which seems doubtful given his overall praise for the exact appearance of Greek architecture, his theory of anti-ornamentalism would be truly radical for its time.

In further discussing Schopenhauer's theory of architecture and beauty, it is crucial to point out that he, like most aesthetic philosophers, held an ambiguous relationship to classical architecture. For one thing, his affiliation to Greek architecture contradicts his embrace of an ideal aesthetic predicated more on the Will than representation. Schopenhauer's transcendental concept of beauty argued for absolute freedom from the dictates of both reason and customary practice. The aesthetic goal to realize a non-applied and non-rational theory of architecture fundamentally transformed both metaphysical and empirical conceptions of architecture. Unlike the metaphysics of Blondel or the empiricism of Perrault, Schopenhauer's aesthetics framed the architectural art as a release from both faith and reason. Furthermore, whereas his architectural predecessors had relied upon a theory of beauty as imitation, Schopenhauer understood architectural beauty as inorganic creation. Thus, his rejection of the theory of imitative beauty for architecture indicates that he would discourage precise reproduction of ancient design.

Nevertheless, Schopenhauer's concept of beauty does not bring to mind perfection. Instead, it advocates a release from the pain of conceptualization.

And so, it is here – in his vision of art's release from both concepts and willing – that Schopenhauer departed from most eighteenth-century theories of taste, and was able to advocate the secondary nature of proportions and symmetry within architecture. For example, in Francis Hutcheson's *An Inquiry into our Ideas of Beauty and Virtue* (1738), the British writer described architectural beauty as emerging from "some kind of uniformity, or unity of proportion among the parts, and of each part to the whole."[25] For Hutcheson, absolute beauty consisted of a comparative anatomy of inert objects. His aesthetics of architecture, therefore, emphasized regularity, resemblance, and coincidence in proportions and symmetry. In the wake of Kant's emphasis on the active faculties of the mind, Schopenhauer's concept of beauty stressed a dynamic interaction between observer and object within the act of perception. Going beyond Kant, Schopenhauer also underscored the dynamic nature of the matter under perception. His aesthetic substituted the perception of active forces – gravity, rigidity, and cohesion which prevail between structural members of a building – for the earlier reliance upon a comparison of qualities of regularity, symmetry, and proportions within immobile objects. For Schopenhauer, the latter type of comparative aesthetics is overtly conceptual, stressing geometrical (hence mathematical) relations which cannot represent the Idea. Thus, within Schopenhauer's aesthetics, these formerly operative elements of beauty assume secondary status.

Despite these thoughts, Schopenhauer's frequent confusion of architecture's roles as utilitarian and artistic never led him to advocate an architectural language devoid of the classical orders and their relations of visual correspondence. Alongside his rejection of architecture as a passive, imitative art was his glowing praise for the Greek Temple.

Was Schopenhauer's prognosis for modern architecture conservative because of his reluctance to fully cast off architecture's classical heritage? After all, using dubious and cautious logic, he stated that since the essence of the art was the expression of load and support, and because this condition had been best expressed during the Greek period, architecture could not progress beyond that point. In fact, Schopenhauer went as far as to recommend Greece as the paragon of design perfection, writing that, since architecture was perfected there, it has:

no longer been capable of any important enrichment. On the other hand, the modern architect cannot noticeably depart from the rules and models of the ancients without being on the path of degeneration. Therefore there is nothing left for him to do but to apply the art handed down by the ancients, and to carry out its rules in so far as this is possible under the limitations inevitably imposed on him by want, need, climate, age, and his country.[26]

Paradoxically, through a transformation of the architectural aesthetic from issues of regularity and symmetry to those of matter and force, Schopenhauer arrived at the paragon of architectural regularity: the Greek Temple. One possible answer to this ambiguous vision lies in Schopenhauer's overall hopes for art. Although he characterized the true nature of reality as endless striving and suffering, he always hoped that art could subvert the despotism of desire. His advocacy of the Greek Temple and acceptance of the classical language of forms was, then, not as reactionary as it would first seem. As we will discuss below, Schopenhauer's vision of Greece was completely modern. His primary interest in Greece was its power to create a language of forms which, although guided by the faculty of desire and dynamism, was also capable of postulating spontaneous harmony.

SUPPORT AND LOAD

Schopenhauer regarded the objectification of mechanical forces to be the principal aesthetic matter of the architectural art. In specific, the equilibrium represented through the static lines of the Greek Temple was for him the paramount expression of artistic contemplation possible to the architectural art. In architecture, the tension of natural forces with matter ironically constitutes the basis for the artistic repression of desire in structural statics. This formulation was a great advance from prior aesthetic ruminations on architecture. For instance, John Dewey described Kant's subordination of function to contemplation in architecture as anaemic: "Carried to its logical conclusion, it would exclude from aesthetic perception most of the subject matter that is enjoyed in the case of architectural structures."[27] As is obvious, such comments cannot be made for Schopenhauer's philosophy of architecture. Here, through the devaluation of function, the separation of ornament, a new aesthetic of structural regularity emerges.

Schopenhauer held the experience of the structure of matter to be the pristine aesthetic encounter that people have with architecture. Because structural forces in building are non-representational, the building gives us not a copy, but the thing itself. Therefore, since the building as thing-in-itself is to be perceived in its dynamic conditions of existence, Schopenhauer concentrated upon the structural tensions coincident with architectural matter. He characterized architecture's essence as a conflict between elemental forces, an expression of the Will within mechanical nature.

291

In the aesthetic contemplation of architecture the Ideas apprehended are low grades of the Will's objectivity, and are not works of deep significance or suggestive content:

> Such Ideas are gravity, cohesion, rigidity, hardness, those universal qualities of stone, those first, simplest, and dullest visibilities of the Will, the fundamental base-notes of nature; and along with these, light, which is in many respects their opposite.[28]

In attributing to aesthetic contemplation a unified existence transcendent of these forms of experience, Schopenhauer's aesthetics required a transformation of the divided configurations of matter and mechanics into a transcendent whole. What art uncovers through this release is the Idea. Thus, both the variety and complexity of material existence and the imperatives of individuality were to be transformed within the aesthetic.[29]

Oddly enough, the strategy of Schopenhauer's structural aesthetic consists in a form of Platonic idealism based on realism, a movement from these low representations of matter and extension to pure Ideas. In other words, Schopenhauer encouraged a vision of the artwork as a Platonic Idea based not on eternal ideas but on the aesthetic perception of phenomena. As Ronald Bradbury described Schopenhauer's viewpoint:

> He believes that aesthetic pleasure depends entirely on the comprehension of some Platonic essence or ideas but we have seen that these Platonic essences in his architectural aesthetic are merely the qualities or properties of matter and therefore, by consequence, that they have nothing in common with his aesthetic. They belong simply to the domain of the static or the physical.[30]

In attributing this principle to Schopenhauer, it is fair to ask whether it is a contradiction in terms. Can the transcendental aims of aesthetic idealism be exhibited in the phenomenal experience of mechanical forces?

Schopenhauer was certainly not the first philosopher to recognize architecture as an art of structural connections. Nor was he the first thinker to become bogged down in the relationship of form (and matter) to content (and the spirit). Already in Herder's writings and the sensual aesthetics of Romanticism, architecture was described in conjunction with active forces and expressive materiality. As Schopenhauer wrote from this tradition a generation later, the task of architecture is to "unfold the Ideas of rigid matter,"[31] to release the sensual intuition inherent in all desire. Schopenhauer's basic proposition for architecture's structural calculus is dynamic movement toward stasis, an interaction of loads with supports that is inseparable from the encounter between the human Will and the world. For Schopenhauer, the fundamental law of architecture is that no load may be carried without sufficient support, and no support sustained without adequate load. These actions, given Schopenhauer's Greek orientation, were expressed by him through the example of the actions between column and entablature:

> Thus everything in the column, its quite definite form, the proportion of its height to its thickness, of both to the intervals between the columns, and that of the whole row to the entablature and the load resting on it, all are the accurately calculated result from the ratio of the necessary support to the given load.[32]

Still, because the demonstration of structural statics is more important than the revelation of structural powers to conquer distance or height, Schopenhauer had less praise for arcuation than trabeation. The aesthetics of structural equilibrium are most evident within the clear separation of column from support. In trabeated systems, the precise forms of a column result from a ratio of the necessary support to the given load, the entablature. Although arcuation also demonstrates structural equilibrium, the static actions of vaults are not nearly as easily comprehendible.

Therefore, despite their structural feats, Schopenhauer described Gothic works as barbarous. Unlike Greek design, where the divisions between load and support are conspicuous, he commented that the complex arcuated forms of the Gothic did not display the division of parts.[33] Harkening back to the rationalist aesthetic of the eighteenth century, where the clarity of part to whole was the basis for the presumed universality of regularity, Schopenhauer condemned the so-called Gothic irregularity. Like Hutcheson, who linked the principle of uniformity in variety with a preference for simple, and rationally explainable forms, Schopenhauer cast his lot with the orthogonality of Greece.

Because his celebration of Greek architecture depended foremost on structural statics, Schopenhauer rejected the prevailing architectural belief held since Vitruvius – and continued within early nineteenth-century Germany by the Prussian architectural theorist Alois Hirt – that the stone columns of the Greek were translations from earlier wooden buildings. Schopenhauer found the theory of wooden mimesis contrary to his belief that the demands of support and load create the principal forms of column and entablature.[34] Modelling forms upon wooden (or human) prototypes would contradict the preeminent importance of structural actions in architecture. Schopenhauer never elaborated how structural actions could be carried over from the principal elements of the Temple to ornament. Still, his rejection of wooden mimesis may have prepared the way for precisely these investigations in the writings – between 1820 and 1850 – of the architectural theorists Heinrich Hübsch, Johann Georg Wolff, and Karl Bötticher.

Despite these seemingly clear directives regarding structural balance, it is worth questioning whether Schopenhauer's aesthetics of loads and supports amounts to a theory of structural rationalism. Or, did the frequent call of the twentieth-century Modern Movement to over-express structure have part of its origins in Schopenhauer's theory of structural tension?

As we have seen, Schopenhauer frequently alternated his stances regarding architecture between the poles of disinterested artistic contemplation and purposive structural actions. In this regard, the theory of loads and supports led Schopenhauer to proclaim that architecture must produce the simplest and most honest forms it can. He stated, after all, that architects must avoid double-columns, broken entablatures, and other decorative redundancies. Still, at the same time, Schopenhauer also advocated structural actions which speak to the psychology of aesthetic perception. His vision of revealing the Idea precluded the direct pursuit of clear, ordered, and measurable structural relations. Since Schopenhauer regarded architecture's ability to excite the Idea as dependent upon the existence of a tension preceding resolution, he felt it essential that great architecture transcend worldly limitations and lead the mind to more complex visions of material appearance. In this scheme, structure had to be made more complex than was necessary. Architecture, accordingly, must extend beyond the demands of structural necessity and simplicity.

For Schopenhauer, if the principal artistic effort of architecture is the conflict between gravity and the rigidity of stone, the great artistic works of architecture must make this conflict all the more prolonged and dramatic. Insofar as this conflict is the principal aesthetic feature of architecture, architects seek to exemplify static struggle. They prolong its tension, and demonstrate its results distinctly and in many different ways. Architecture keeps its forms in suspense:

The whole mass of the building, if left to its original tendency, would exhibit a mere heap or lump, bound to the earth as firmly as possible, to which gravity, the form in which the Will here appears, presses incessantly, whereas rigidity, also objectivity of the Will, resists. But this very tendency, this effort, is thwarted in its immediate satisfaction by architecture, and only an indirect satisfaction by roundabout ways is granted to it. The joists and beams, for example, can press the earth only by means of the column; the arch must support itself, and only through the medium of the pillars can it satisfy its tendency towards the earth, and so on. By just these enforced digressions, by these very hindrances, those forces inherent in the crude mass of stone unfold themselves in most distinct and varied manner; and the purely aesthetic purpose of architecture can go no further.[35]

In this manner, going beyond simple structural logic, architects manifest the desire of the Will to a primal struggle between the qualities of stone and statics and the forces of gravity. All elements of building reveal their form through this elemental struggle, whose resolution in balance produces the feeling of beauty and pleasure we derive from buildings.[36] Structural objectivity is but a momentary diversion within the engulfing process of desire.

AESTHETIC REFLECTION

Schopenhauer's philosophy of architecture contributed to later modern discourses equating architectural beauty with perceptual immediacy and structural overstatement. First, the artistic nature of architecture emerges not in an appeal to instrumental reason or cognitive resemblance; rather, within the subjective perception of the struggle of structural forces and their resolution into harmonious form and space. Hence, aesthetic reflection is immediate, and embedded within the realm of perceptual sensuousness. Despite the ambiguity of the Will's physicality in his text, Schopenhauer's steps toward a psychology of perception based upon an awareness of one's body and the relationship of the Will to the forces of physical nature were important steps toward the development of physiological and psychological aesthetics and theories of empathy during the latter third of the nineteenth century.

Second, Schopenhauer's merger of the domain of physical science with that of ideal aesthetics was significant for the direction that the paradigm of structural realism was to take in later modern architecture. According to his principle, architecture appeals not merely to the objective resolution of loads by supports, but more to the pleasure derived by the Will from the tension created by the perception of structural statics. This ideal helped establish the explanatory value of structure to architecture as an art form, and in the same vein encouraged later architects to exaggerate their structural feats for perceptual purposes.

Overall, Schopenhauer's influence on later architectural thought is most traceable to his attempt to surmount the philosophical divide between objectivity and subjectivity created by the Enlightenment and its supposed hegemony of reason. Schopenhauer classified objective perception as representation, a second-order knowledge predicated on an irresolvable drive to demonstrate sufficient reason. As with other philosophers, he did not believe in the artistic potential of objectively described real building forces. The artistic aspect of architecture is the opposite: a release from both the restless strivings of gravity and rigidity in building matter and their complement within the subjective ego's desires for worldly domination. Moreover, in arguing for an aesthetic liberated from purpose as well as desire, Schopenhauer attempted to surmount both rational individualism and religious expressionism. At odds with modern impulses toward individualism, Schopenhauer envisioned aesthetic perception as a reconciliation of humanity with its embracing world, the submergence of the individual within the whole. His theory of art is expressly oriented to freeing the subject from his reliance on causal knowledge and his cravings for individuality. Architecture as art promises both a release from the Will's subjectivity and representation's objectivity.

Notes

1 Marcus Vitruvius Pollio, *The Ten Books on Architecture*, Morris Hicky Morgan, trans. (New York: Dover Publications, Inc., 1960), p. 17.
2 Immanuel Kant, *Critique of Judgment* [1790], J. H. Bernhard, trans. (London: Macmillan, 1931), p. 47.
3 Ibid., p. 80.
4 John Zammito, *The Genesis of Kant's Critique of Judgment* (Chicago: University of Chicago Press, 1992), pp. 94–95.
5 T. J. Diffey, "Schopenhauer's Account of Aesthetic Experience," *The British Journal of Aesthetics*, 30, 1990, p. 140.
6 Kant, *Critique of Judgment*, p. 209.
7 Johann Gottfried Herder, "Viertes Wäldchen," in Bernhard Ludwig Suphan, ed., *Herders sämmtliche Werke* (Berlin: Weidmann, 1878), 4, p. 156.

8 Ibid., p. 155.
9 Georg Wilhelm Friedrich Hegel, *Aesthetics: Lectures on Fine Art*, T. M. Knox, trans. (Oxford: The Clarendon Press, 1975), p. 655.
10 *WWR* 1, 4.
11 *WWR* 1, 51.
12 *WWR* 1, 106.
13 *WWR* 1, 163.
14 Israel Knox, *The Aesthetic Theories of Kant, Hegel, and Schopenhauer* (New York: The Humanities Press, 1958), p. 137.
15 Jacques Taminiaux, "Art and Truth in Schopenhauer and Nietzsche," *Man and World*, 20, 1987, p. 93.
16 Bryan Magee, *The Philosophy of Schopenhauer* (Oxford: The Clarendon Press, 1983), p. 125.
17 *WWR* 1, 185.
18 *WWR* 1, 257.
19 *WWR* 1, 217.
20 *WWR* 1, 216.
21 François Blondel, "Extraits du Cour's d'architecture," in *La Theorie Architecturale a L'Age Classique*, Françoise Fichet, ed. (Brussels: Pierre Mardaga, 1979), pp. 142–143.
22 See Antoine Babuty Desgodets, *Les edifices antiques de Rome dessinés et mesurés trés exactement* [1682] (Paris: Claude-Antoine Jombert, 1779).
23 Claude Perrault, *Ordonnance for the Five Kinds of Columns After the Method of the Ancients*, Indra Kagis McEwen, trans. (Santa Monica: Getty Center, 1993), p. 51.
24 *WWR* 1, 215.
25 Francis Hutcheson, *An Inquiry into our Ideas of Beauty and Virtue* [1738] (Charlottesville: IBIS, 1980), p. 24.
26 *WWR* 2, 416.
27 John Dewey, *Art as Experience* (New York: G. P. Putnam's, 1934), pp. 253–254.
28 *WWR* 1, 214.
29 See the discussion of the Idea in Jörg Engelmann, "Schönheit und Zweckmäßigkeit in der Architektur," *Schopenhauer-Jahrbuch*, 1984, pp. 157–169.
30 Ronald Bradbury, *The Romantic Theories of Architecture of the 19th Century* (New York: AMS, 1934), p. 52.
31 *WWR* 1, 218.
32 *WWR* 2, 413.
33 Interestingly, Schopenhauer's condemnation of the Gothic occurs during the same time at which research into Gothic structural logic was most robust. For a discussion of investigations between 1815 and 1840, see Georg Germann, *Gothic Revival in Europe and Britain: Sources, Influences, and Ideas*, trans. Gerald Onn (Cambridge, MA: MIT Press, 1972).
34 *WWR* 2, 414.
35 *WWR* 1, 214.

36 In the pursuit of these structural actions on matter and force, Schopenhauer also found a role for light in architecture. Light increases the
beauty of an architectural work in that it heightens the visual sharpness
of the stone masses and their connections. Light thus augments that
pleasure which we find in the apprehension of pattern and form in a
building. *WWR* 1, 216.

Bibliography
Selected sources on Schopenhauer's aesthetics

ARTHUR SCHOPENHAUER (1788–1860)

Schopenhauers sämtliche Schriften, Arthur Hübscher, ed. (Wiesbaden: Eberhard Brockhaus Verlag, 1946–1958), 7 vols.

1 *Schriften zur Erkenntnislehre*
2,3 *Die Welt als Wille und Vorstellung I,II*
4 *Schriften zur Naturphilosophie und zur Ethik; Über den Willen in der Natur; Die beiden Grundprobleme der Ethik*
5,6 *Parerga und Paralipomena I,II*
7 *Über die vierfache Würzel des Satzes vom zureichenden Grunde; Gestrichene Stellen; Zitate und fremdsprachige Stellen; Namen- und Sachregister*

English translations of Schopenhauer's works used in this book are given in the List of abbreviations.

SECONDARY PHILOSOPHICAL LITERATURE

Alperson, Philip, "Schopenhauer and Musical Revelation," *The Journal of Aesthetics and Art Criticism*, 40, 1982.

Atwell, John E., *Schopenhauer: The Human Character* (Philadelphia: Temple University Press, 1990).

Baillot, Alexandre, *Influence de la philosophie de Schopenhauer en France, 1860–1900* (Paris: Vrin, 1927).

Budd, Malcolm, *Music and the Emotions: The Philosophical Theories* (London: Routledge and Kegan Paul, 1985).

Chansky, James D., "Schopenhauer and Platonic Ideas: A Groundwork for an Aesthetic Metaphysics," in von der Luft, ed., *Schopenhauer: New Essays in Honor of his 200th Birthday*.

Copleston, Frederick, *Schopenhauer: Philosopher of Pessimism* (London: Burns, Oates, and Washburne, Ltd., 1946).

Bibliography

Desmond, William, "Schopenhauer, Art, and the Dark Origin," in Eric van der Luft, ed., *Schopenhauer: New Essays in Honor of his 200th Birthday* (Lewiston, NY: Edwin Mellen Press, 1988).

Diffey, T. J., "Schopenhauer's Account of Aesthetic Experience," *The British Journal of Aesthetics*, 30, 1990.

Durer, Christopher S., "Moby-Dick's Ishmael, Burke, and Schopenhauer," *The Midwest Quarterly*, 30, 1989.

Engelmann, Jörg, "Schönheit und Zweckmäßigkeit in der Architektur," *Schopenhauer-Jahrbuch*, 1984.

Foster, Cheryl, "Schopenhauer's Subtext on Natural Beauty," *The British Journal of Aesthetics*, 32, 1992.

Gardiner, Patrick, *Schopenhauer* (Harmondsworth: Penguin Books Ltd., 1967).

Goehr, Lydia, *The Imaginary Museum of Musical Works: An Essay in the Philosophy of Music* (Oxford: The Clarendon Press, 1992).

Hamlyn, D. W., *Schopenhauer* (London: Routledge and Kegan Paul, 1980).

Hein, Hilde, "Schopenhauer and Platonic Ideas," *Journal of the History of Philosophy*, 4, 1966.

Hübscher, Arthur, *Schopenhauer-Bibliographie* (Stuttgart: Fromann-Holzboog, 1981).

Jacquette, Dale, "Schopenhauer's Circle and the Principle of Sufficient Reason," *Metaphilosophy*, 23, 1992.

"Schopenhauer on the Antipathy of Aesthetic Genius and the Charming," *History of European Ideas*, 18, 1994.

Janaway, Christopher, "Plato's Analogy Between Painter and Poet," *The British Journal of Aesthetics*, 31, 1991.

Self and World in Schopenhauer's Philosophy (Oxford: The Clarendon Press, 1989).

Images of Excellence: Plato's Critique of the Arts (Oxford: The Clarendon Press, 1995).

Kanovitch, Abraham, *The Will to Beauty: Being a Continuation of the Philosophies of Arthur Schopenhauer and Friedrich Nietzsche* (New York: Henry Bee Company, 1923).

Keller, Hans, "Schopenhauer's 'Palestrina,'" *The Listener*, 23, May 1968.

Knox, Israel, "Schopenhauer's Aesthetic Theory," in *Schopenhauer: His Philosophical Achievement*, edited by Michael Fox (Sussex: The Harvester Press Ltd., 1980).

The Aesthetic Theories of Kant, Hegel, and Schopenhauer (New York: The Humanities Press, 1958).

Krukowski, Lucian, *Aesthetic Legacies* (Philadelphia: Temple University Press, 1992).

Magee, Bryan, *The Philosophy of Schopenhauer* (Oxford: The Clarendon Press, 1983).

Misunderstanding Schopenhauer (London: University of London Germanic Studies, 1990).

Bibliography

Malter, Rudolf, *Der eine Gedanke: Hinführung zur Philosophie Arthur Schopenhauers* (Darmstadt: Wissenschaftliche Buchgesellschaft, 1988).

Mann, Thomas, "Schopenhauer," *Essays of Three Decades*, H. T. Lowe-Porter, trans. (New York: A. A. Knopf, 1947).

McLaughlin, Sigrid, *Schopenhauer in Russland: zur literarischen Rezeption bei Turgenev* (Wiesbaden: Harrassowitz Verlag, 1984).

Nelson, Byron, "Wagner, Schopenhauer, and Nietzsche: On the Value of Human Action," *The Opera Quarterly*, 6, 1989.

Nietzsche, Friedrich, *The Complete Works of Friedrich Nietzsche*, edited by Oscar Levy (New York: Gordon Press, 1974).

"Schopenhauer as Educator," in *Untimely Meditations*, R. J. Hollingdale, trans. (Cambridge: Cambridge University Press, 1983).

Nussbaum, Martha C., "The Transfigurations of Intoxication: Nietzsche, Schopenhauer, and Dionysus," *Arion*, 3rd series, 1, 1991.

Paulsen, Friedrich, *Schopenhauer, Hamlet, Mephistopheles: drei Aufsätze zur Naturgeschichte des Pessimismus* (Berlin: Cotta Verlag, 1901).

Pfeiffer, Konrad, *Zum höchsten Dasein: Goethes Faust im Lichte der Schopenhauerschen Philosophie* (Berlin: Walter de Gruyter, 1949).

Podro, Michael, *The Manifold in Perception: Theories of Art from Kant to Hildebrand* (Oxford: The Clarendon Press, 1972).

Poggeler, Otto, "Schopenhauer und das Wesen der Kunst," *Zeitschrift für Philosophische Forschung*, 14, 1960.

Pothast, Ulrich, *Die eigentlich metaphysische Tätigkeit: über Schopenhauers Ästhetik und ihre Anwendung durch Samuel Beckett* (Frankfurt: Surkamp, 1982).

Safranski, Rudiger, *Schopenhauer and the Wild Years of Philosophy*, Ewald Osers, trans. (Cambridge, MA: Harvard University Press, 1990).

Simmel, Georg, *Schopenhauer and Nietzsche*, Helmut Loiskandl, Deena Weinstein and Michael Weinstein, trans. (Amherst: University of Massachusetts Press, 1986).

Snow, James, "Schopenhauer's Style," *International Philosophical Quarterly*, 33, 1993.

Sorg, Bernhard, *Zur literarischen Schopenhauer-Rezeption im 19. Jahrhundert* (Heidelberg: Winter Verlag, 1975).

Taminiaux, Jacques, "Art and Truth in Schopenhauer and Nietzsche," *Man and World*, 20, 1987.

Taylor, T. G., "Platonic Ideas, Aesthetic Experience, and the Resolution of Schopenhauer's Great Contradiction," *International Studies in Philosophy*, 19, 1987.

von der Luft, Eric, ed., *Schopenhauer: New Essays in Honor of his 200th Birthday* (Lewiston, NY: The Edwin Mellen Press, 1988).

Walker, Alan, "Schopenhauer and Music: A Philosopher Dear to the Hearts of Every Creative Person," *The Piano Quarterly*, 144, 1988.

Young, Julian, "The Standpoint of Eternity: Schopenhauer on Art," *Kant-Studien*, 78, 1987.

Bibliography

Willing and Unwilling: A Study in the Philosophy of Arthur Schopenhauer (Dordrecht: Martinus Nijhoff, 1987).

Zimmern, Helen, *Schopenhauer: His Life and His Philosophy* (London: G. Allen and Unwin Ltd., 1876; rev. 1932).

302

Index

Index

Index

Index